**If you think you've heard it all, you probably
haven't heard this ...**

MOST ORGANS TRANSPLANTED IN A SINGLE OPERA-
TION: Dr. Andreas Tzakis (USA) transplanted seven organs—a
liver, pancreas, stomach, large and small intestines, and two kidneys—into a 10-month-old Italian girl during 16 hours of surgery at
Jackson Children's Hospital in Miami, Florida, on March 23, 1997.
The girl suffered from megacystis microcolon syndrome, a rare
congenital defect that interferes with the body's ability to absorb
nutrients.

LARGEST FAI-APPROVED PARACHUTING FREEFALL FOR-
MATION: A freefall formation consisting of 300 skydivers was
held for 7.02 seconds over Eloy, Arizona, on December 12, 2002, at
the World Record 300-Way event.

WORLD CHAMPIONSHIP WITH THE HEAVIEST PARTICI-
PANTS: Founded in 1982, the World Elephant Polo Association
(WEPA) hosts a championship tournament every year. Elephant polo
is played by riders on elephants, four to a team. An adult male Asian
elephant can weigh over 11,000 lbs. but the contest has no weight restrictions. Rules state that participants cannot lie down in front of
the goal. The invitational tournament is held every December in
Megaluly, on the edge of Nepal's Royal Chitwan National Park.

FASTEST KANGAROO: A speed of 40 mph was recorded for a
female eastern gray kangaroo (*Macropus giganteus*). The highest
sustained speed is 35 mph recorded for a large male red kangaroo,
which died from its exertions after being paced for one mile.

LARGEST DIAMOND: A 3,106-carat diamond was found on Jan-
uary 26, 1905, at the Premier Diamond Mine, near Pretoria, South
Africa, and presented to the reigning British monarch, Edward VII.
Named "The Cullinan," it was cut into 106 polished diamonds.

## Accreditation

Guinness World Records Limited has a very thorough accreditation system for records verification. However, whilst every effort is made to ensure accuracy, Guinness World Records Limited cannot be held responsible for any errors contained in this work. Feedback from our readers on any point of accuracy is always welcomed.

## Abbreviations & measurements

**GUINNESS WORLD RECORDS LIMITED** uses both metric and imperial measurements (US imperial in brackets). The only exception is for some scientific data, where metric measurements only are universally accepted, and for some sports data. Where a specific date is given the exchange rate is calculated according to the currency values that were in operation at the time. Where only a year date is given the exchange rate is calculated from December of that year. "One billion" is taken to mean one thousand million.

"GDF" (the German Democratic Republic) refers to the East German state which unified with West Germany in 1990. The abbreviation is used for sports records broken before 1990.

The Union of Soviet Socialist Republics split into a number of parts in 1991, the largest of these being Russia. The Commonwealth of Independent States replaced it and the abbreviation "CIS" is used mainly for sporting records broken at the 1992 Olympic Games.

Guinness World Records Limited does not claim to own any right, title or interest in the trademarks of others reproduced in this book.

## General Warning

Attempting to break records or set new records can be dangerous. Appropriate advice should be taken first and all record attempts are undertaken entirely at the participant's risk. In no circumstances will Guinness World Records Limited have any liability for death or injury suffered in any record attempts. Guinness World Records Limited has complete discretion over whether or not to include any particular records in the book.

# GUINNESS
# W🏛️RLD
# RECORDS™
# 2004

BANTAM BOOKS
NEW YORK • TORONTO • LONDON • SYDNEY • AUCKLAND

GUINNESS WORLD RECORDS™ 2004
Copyright © 2003 Guinness World Records Ltd.,
a HIT Entertainment Company. All rights reserved.
Published under license.

Bantam edtion / May 2004

GUINNESS WORLD RECORDS™ is a trademark of
Guinness World Records Ltd. and is reproduced under license by
Bantam Dell, a Division of Random House, Inc.
New York, New York

Revised American editions copyright © 2004, 2003, 2002, 2001,
2000, 1999, 1998, 1997, 1996, 1995, 1994, 1993, 1992, 1991, 1990, 1989,
1988, 1987, 1986, 1985, 1984, 1983, 1982, 1981, 1980, 1979, 1978, 1977,
1976, 1975, 1974, 1973, 1972, 1971, 1970, 1969, 1968, 1966, 1965, 1964,
1963, 1962, 1960 by Guinness World Records Ltd.

ISBN 0-553-58712-9

Manufactured in the United States of America
Published simultaneously in Canada

OPM   10 9 8 7 6 5 4 3 2 1

# GUINNESS WORLD RECORDS

# 2004

MANAGING EDITOR
Claire Folkard

# Table of contents

# INTRODUCTION

Welcome to Guinness World Records 2004!

The last twelve months have been a particularly eventful and exciting time for Guinness World Records, with many impressive new achievements. We've packed this year's edition with brand new pictures and you'll find hundreds of new and broken records. We've also added some new subject areas as well as some special feature pages on all your favorite topics.

There have been a number of big events this past year. On May 29, 2003, there were celebrations to mark the 50th anniversary of the first ascent of Mount Everest by Sherpa Tensing Norgay and Sir Edmund Hillary. Their achievement has since inspired many hundreds of other people to climb the world's highest

Seb Clover

mountain, bringing about a range of new records—including the youngest and oldest people yet to climb the famous peak.

Another record-breaking epic journey was made this year by 15-year-old Seb Clover. In January 2003 he became the youngest person to cross the Atlantic singlehandedly, in a race across the ocean against his father, a sailing instructor. Encouraged by his father since he was a very young boy, Seb sailed from Tenerife in the Canary Islands, to Antigua in the Caribbean in 25 days, braving whales as big as his yacht and fierce Atlantic storms.

The athlete Paula Radcliffe also displayed great stamina and mental strength this year. Having set an incredible record time for the fastest marathon last year in London, she actually broke her own record this year, with an awe-inspiring time of 2 hours, 15 minutes and 25 seconds.

In the world of entertainment, the release of the 20th James Bond movie, *Die Another Day,* at the end of 2002 created yet more records for the movie series about the world's most famous

**Pierce Brosnan as James Bond**

**Eminem**

**Concorde**

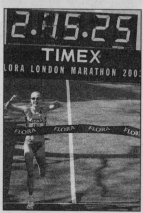

**Paula Radcliffe**

secret agent. And in the music world, Eminem continues to be the most successful rap artist ever—his album *The Marshall Mathers LP* sold a record 1.76 million copies in its first week in June 2000—and with the release of his debut movie *8 Mile* this year, the star continues to rule the world of rap.

Finally, December 17, 2003 marks the 100th anniversary of powered flight, since the Wright brothers made their first ground-breaking journey in the Wright Flyer. The end of 2003 also sees the last of commercial supersonic travel, with Concorde sadly being retired after 34 years of record-breaking transatlantic flights. But let's just imagine what another 100 years of air travel might bring!

So dive in and be inspired by the greatest the world has to offer. You don't have to be an athlete, a pop star or an explorer to hold a World Record—you could organize a group event or have a unique talent of your own. Next year we celebrate 50 years of Guinness World Records, so get thinking, and just maybe you too could be the proud owner of a Guinness World Record!

Editor, Guinness World Records

**Mount Everest**

# GUINNESS WORLD RECORDS 2004

# HUMANS

# BODY EXTREMES

**Heaviest man** The heaviest person in medical history was Jon Brower Minnoch (USA). He suffered from obesity as a child and, by 1963, when he was 22 years old and 6 ft. 1 in. (1.85 m) tall, he weighed 392 lb. (178 kg). Four years later, he weighed 700 lb. (317 kg), and by September, 1976, he weighed 975 lb. (442 kg). He was rushed to the hospital in 1978 with heart and respiratory failure, weighing an estimated 1400 lb. (635 kg). When he died in 1983 he was down to 798 lb. (362 kg).

**Heaviest woman** Rosalie Bradford (USA) is claimed to have registered a peak weight of 1,190 lb. (540 kg) in January, 1987. In August of that year, she developed congestive heart failure and was rushed to the hospital. She was consequently put on a carefully controlled diet and by February, 1994 weighed 283 lb. (128 kg).

**Greatest weight differential between a married couple** Weighing 1,400 lb. (635 kg), Jon Brower Minnoch (USA) married his 110 lb. (50-kg) wife Jeannette (USA) in March, 1978. Their weight difference was 1,290 lb. (585 kg)—the greatest for a married couple.

**Most variable stature** At the age of 21 in 1920, Adam Rainer (Austria) measured 3 ft. 10.5 in. (1.18 m). He then had a rapid growth spurt and by

**LARGEST WAIST** The largest waist was that of Walter Hudson (USA, 1944–91). It measured 119 in. (3.02 m) when he was at his peak weight of 1,197 lb. (543 kg).

Humans

**TALLEST LIVING MAN** Radhouane Charbib (Tunisia) measured 7 ft. 8.9 in. (2.359 m) as a result of measurements taken on April 22–23, 1999 at Tunis, Tunisia.

1931 had reached 7 ft. 1.75 in. (2.18 m). As a result, he became so weak that he was bedridden for the rest of his life. When he died in 1950, he measured 7 ft. 8 in. (2.34 m). He remains the only person to have been both a dwarf and a giant.

**Shortest man ever** The shortest mature human of whom there is independent evidence was Gul Mohammed (India). On July 19, 1990, he was examined at Ram Manohar Hospital, New Delhi, India, and found to be 22.5 in. (57 cm) tall.

**Shortest woman**  The shortest ever female was Pauline Musters (Netherlands). Born on February 26, 1876, she measured 12 in. (30 cm) at birth. At nine years of age she was 21.5 in. (55 cm) tall and weighed only 3 lb. 5 oz. (1.5 kg). She died of pneumonia with meningitis on March 1, 1895 in New York City, USA, at the age of 19. A post-mortem examination showed her to be exactly 24 in. (61 cm)—there was some elongation after death.

The shortest living woman is Madge Bester (South Africa), who is only 25.5 in. (65 cm) tall. She suffers from *osteogenesis imperfecta* (characterized by brittle bones and other deformities of the skeleton) and is confined to a wheelchair. Her mother Winnie is not much taller, measuring 27.5 in. (70 cm), and is also confined to a wheelchair.

**Tallest woman**  Zeng Jinlian (China) of Yujiang village in the Bright Moon Commune, Hunan Province, was 8 ft. 1.75 in. (2.48 m) when she died aged 17 years 232 days on February 13, 1982.

The tallest living woman is Sandy Allen (USA, b. June 18, 1955), who

**GREATEST HEIGHT DIFFERENTIAL BETWEEN A MARRIED COUPLE**
Fabien Pretou (France, far right) measuring 6 ft. 2 in. (1.88 m) tall, and Natalie Lucius (France, far left), who is 3 ft. 1 in. (94 cm) tall, were married at Seyssinet-Pariset, France, on April 14, 1990. The difference in height between the couple is 3 ft. 1 in. (94 cm).

when last measured was 7 ft. 7.25 in. (2.317 m) tall. She stood 6 ft. 3 in. (1.905 m) by the age of 10 and was 7 ft. 1 in. (2.16 m) tall by 16.

**Tallest man** The tallest man in history for whom there is evidence is Robert Pershing Wadlow (USA, 1918–40) who, when last measured on June 27, 1940, was found to be 8 ft. 11.1 in. (2.72 m) tall. His amazing height was the result of an overactive pituitary gland, which oversupplied his body with growth hormone.

**Longest fingernails** The combined measurement of the five nails on the left hand of Shridhar Chillal (India) was 20 ft. 2.25 in. (6.15 m) on July 8, 1998, when they were measured on the set of *Guinness World Records: Primetime,* Los Angeles, California, USA. His thumbnail was the longest, measuring 56 in. (1.42 m). The longest fingernails on a woman belong to Lee Redmond (USA). They measure a total length of 29 ft. 9 in. (6 m 62.94 cm). The longest nail is on her left thumb and measures 2 ft. 3 in. (68.58 cm).

**Largest ever feet** Robert Wadlow (USA), the tallest man ever, wore US size 37AA shoes (UK size 36), equivalent to 18.5 in. (47 cm) long. He died after attending a promotional march for Peter Shoes Company, the suppliers of his shoes. An infected blister on his left foot led to infection, and he died in his sleep on July 15, 1940.

**Longest moustache** Kalyan Ramji Sain (India) has been growing his moustache since 1976, and by July 1993, it had reached a span of 11 ft. 1 in. (3.39 m). The right side measured 5 ft. 7 in. (1.72 m) and the left side 5 ft. 6 in. (1.67 m).

**Largest hands** Robert Wadlow (USA), famously the tallest man ever, had hands that measured 12.75 in. (32.3 cm) from the wrist to the tip of his middle finger.

**Largest natural breasts** Annie Hawkins-Turner (USA) has an underbreast measurement of 43 in. (109.22 cm) and an around-chest-over-nipple measurement of 70 in. (177.8 cm). She currently wears a US size 52I bra, the largest available to buy, but by American bra estimation, her measurements would put her in a 48V bra, which is not a manufactured size.

**Longest hair** The world's longest documented hair belonged to Hoo Sateow (Thailand), a tribal medicine man from the village of Muang Nga, Chang Mai, Thailand. On November 21, 1997, his hair was unraveled and officially measured at 16 ft. 11 in. (5.15 m) long. He stopped cutting his hair in 1929, believing that his long locks held the key to his healing powers.

**Longest tongue** Stephen Taylor's (UK) tongue measures 3.7 in. (9.4 cm) from the tip to the center of his closed top lip. It was measured at Westwood Medical Centre, Coventry, Warwickshire, UK, on May 29, 2002.

# AMAZING BODY

**MOST ACTIVE MUSCLE** It has been estimated that the muscles of the eye move more than 100,000 times a day. Many of these rapid eye movements take place during the dreaming phase of sleep.

**LARGEST MUSCLE** The bulkiest of the 639 named muscles in the human body is usually the *gluteus maximus* or buttock muscle, which extends the thigh. However, in pregnancy, the uterus can increase from about 1 oz. (30 g) to over 2 lb. 3 oz. (1 kg) in weight.

**LARGEST SESAMOID BONE** The largest sesamoid bone in the body is the patella or knee cap (outlined here). Most other sesamoids are only a few millimeters in diameter and are shaped like a sesame seed, hence the name. They are usually formed in tendons close to joints or where the tendons angle sharply around bone. Their function is to take compression when a tendon is going around a joint, as when kneeling.

**MOST ABUNDANT CELL** The body contains around 30 billion red blood cells (erythrocytes, shown) with approximately $8.75 \times 10^{12}$ in every pint of blood ($5 \times 10^{12}$ in every liter). Red blood cells are produced in bone marrow, and their function is to carry oxygen and carbon dioxide around the body.

**LONGEST MEMORY OF A CELL**
Lymphocytes are a type of white blood cell produced by the immune system. The largest of the lymphatic tissues is the spleen. Each successive generation of lymphocytes produced contains the "memory" of previous illnesses that the body has fought throughout its lifetime.

**LARGEST ARTERY** The aorta is 1.18 in. (3 cm) in diameter where it leaves the heart (outlined here). By the time this artery divides at the level of the fourth lumbar vertebra, it is about 0.68 in. (1.75 cm) in diameter.

**LONGEST CELL** Motor neurons are some 4 ft. 3 in. (1.3 m) long; they have cell bodies (gray matter) in the lower spinal cord with axons (white matter) that carry nerve impulses from the spinal cord down to the big toe. The cell systems that carry certain sensations (vibration and positional sense) back from the big toe to the brain are even longer—about equal to the height of the body.

## FACT

**SMALLEST BONE**
The stapes, or stirrup bone, one of the three auditory ossicles in the middle ear, measures a tiny 0.1–0.13 in. (2.6–3.4 mm) in length and weighs from 0.03–0.066 grains (2 to 4.3 mg). The *stapedius,* the muscle that controls the stapes, is less than 0.05 in. (0.127 cm) long and is the smallest muscle in the human body.

# MEDICAL PHENOMENA

**Most common cause of sudden death** Coronary heart disease is the most common cause of sudden death. The main factors that put an individual at risk of the disease are cigarette smoking, high blood pressure, and high levels of cholesterol.

**Most common infectious disease** The common cold, caused by a group of rhinoviruses, of which there are at least 180 types, affects almost everyone on Earth, except for those living in small isolated communities or in the frozen wastes of Antarctica. There are at least 40 different viruses, either airborne or transmitted by direct contact, which cause symptoms such as sneezing, coughing, sore throat, running eyes and nose, headache, and mild fever.

**Most teeth at birth** The first deciduous or milk teeth—the upper and lower jaw first incisors—normally appear in infants at 5–8 months. There are many recorded examples of children born with teeth. Sean Keaney (UK) was born on April 10, 1990 with 12 teeth. They were extracted to prevent possible feeding problems, and he grew his second full set of teeth at 18 months. Molars usually appear at 24 months, but in a case recorded in Denmark in 1970, a six-week premature baby was documented with eight teeth at birth, with four in the molar region.

**Largest tumor at birth** The largest tumor ever recorded at birth weighed 11 oz. (311 g) and was pressing against the windpipe of Ryan James Shannon (USA). He was born seven weeks early by Caesarean section on January 2, 1996 and weighed 6 lb. 2 oz. (2.8 kg). The tumor weighed 10% of his body weight. An operation to remove the growth was carried out nine days after the birth. The procedure lasted four hours and was a complete success.

**Largest tumor ever operated** An ovarian cyst estimated to weigh

**OLDEST DISEASE Leprosy is the oldest disease, with cases described in ancient Egypt as early as 1350 BC. (The disfigured hands of a leprosy victim are pictured here.) *Tuberculosis schistosomiasi,* an infectious disease of the lungs, has also been seen in Egyptian mummies dating from the 20th dynasty (1250 to 1000 BC).**

**MOST COMMON SKIN INFECTION** *Tinea pedis,* commonly known as "Athlete's foot" (seen here under a microscope), is the most common skin infection in humans. The fungus afflicts up to 70% of the worldwide population and almost everyone will get it at least once in a lifetime. It affects the skin between the toes, which becomes dry, itchy, and sore.

328 lb. (148.7 kg) was drained during the week prior to surgical removal of the cyst shell, in Texas, USA, in 1905 by Dr. Arthur Spohn (USA). The patient recovered fully.

**Most sarcomas excised from a patient** From 1977 to 2001 a total of 1,674 sarcomas were excised under local anesthetic from the skin of a British male patient by Dr. Cecil Weintraub (South Africa). Sarcomas are malign tumors of the supporting tissues of the body. They can occur in blood vessels, muscle, fat, or in any of the other tissues that support, surround, and protect the organs of the body.

**Longest cardiac arrest** The longest cardiac arrest lasted four hours in the case of fisherman Jan Egil Refsdahl (Norway), who fell overboard off Bergen, Norway, on December 7, 1987. He was rushed to Haukeland Hospital after his body temperature fell to 75°F (24°C), and his heart stopped. He made a full recovery after being connected to a heart-lung machine.

**Longest heart stoppage** The longest recorded heart stoppage is a minimum of 3 hr. 40 min. in the case of Jean Jawbone (Canada) who, at the age of 20, was revived by a team of 26 medical staff using peritoneal dialysis in the Health Sciences Centre, Winnipeg, Manitoba, Canada, on January 8, 1977.

**Longest survival with the heart outside the body** Christopher Wall (USA, b. August 19, 1975) is the longest known survivor of the condition *ectopia cordis,* where the heart lies outside the body. The mortality rate is high, with most patients not living beyond 48 hours. He currently works for a construction tubing company in Philadelphia, USA.

**Longest coma** Elaine Esposito (USA) never regained consciousness after undergoing an appendectomy on August 6, 1941, at age six. She died on November 25, 1978, at the age of 43 years 357 days. She had been in a coma for 37 years 111 days.

**Longest time survived without a pulse** The longest time a human has survived without a pulse in their vascular system is three days. Julie Mills (UK) was at the point of death due to severe heart failure and viral myocarditus when, on August 14, 1998, cardiac surgeons at The John Radcliffe Hospital, Oxford, UK, used a non-pulsatile blood pump (AB180) to support her for one week, during which time her heart recovered, and the pump was removed.

**Lowest heart rate** The lowest resting heart beat on record is 28 bpm (beats per minute) and belongs to the cyclist Miguel Induráin (Spain) who

**LARGEST TUMOR REMOVED INTACT** The largest tumor ever removed intact was a multicystic mass of the right ovary (shown here) weighing 303 lb. (137.6 kg). The operation, which took over six hours, was performed by Professor Katherine O'Hanlan of Stanford University Medical Center, California, USA. The growth had a diameter of 3 ft. (1 m) and was removed in its entirety in October 1991 from the abdomen of an unnamed 34-year-old woman. The patient made a full recovery. She left the operating room on one stretcher, with the tumor on another.

was tested at the University of Navarra, Pamplona, Spain, in 1995. The average resting heart rate is 66–72 bpm, with most athletes having 40 bpm. Induráin also has a lung capacity of 14 pints (8 liters) and a heart capable of pumping 88 pints (50 liters) of blood per minute—double that of a normal healthy man.

**Lowest body temperature** The lowest authenticated body temperature is 57.5°F (14.2°C) (rectal temperature) for Karlee Kosolofski (Canada) then age two, on February 23, 1994. She had accidentally been locked outside her home for six hours in a temperature of -8°F (-22°C). Despite severe frostbite, which meant the amputation of her left leg above the knee, she made a full recovery.

**Highest body temperature** Willie Jones (USA) was admitted to Grady Memorial Hospital, Atlanta, Georgia, USA, with heatstroke on July 10, 1980, a day when the temperature reached 90°F (32.2°C) with 44% humidity. Jones's temperature was found to be 115.7°F (46.5°C); he was discharged after 24 days.

**Highest blood alcohol level** The University of California Medical School, Los Angeles, USA, reported in December, 1982 the case of a confused but conscious 24-year-old female who was shown to have a blood alcohol level of 1,510 mg per 100 ml of blood. This is triple the normal lethal limit. The US driving limit is 0.08% of alcohol per 100 ml of blood.

**Highest blood sugar level** Twelve-year-old Michael Dougherty (USA) had a blood sugar level 19 times above average at 2,350 while still conscious on November 21, 1995. The normal blood sugar range is between 80 and 120.

**Most artificial joints** Anne Davison (UK) had 12 major joints (both shoulders, elbows, wrists, hips, knees, and ankles) and three knuckles replaced by the age of 47. Diagnosed with arthritis at the age of 13, the first joint that Anne had replaced was her right knee, at the age of 27. The record is shared with Charles N. Wedde (USA), who has rheumatoid arthritis, and also had 12 major joints replaced, between 1979 and 1995.

**Longest attack of hiccups** Charles Osborne (USA) began hiccuping in 1922 while attempting to weigh a hog before slaughtering it. He was unable to find a cure but led a normal life in which he had two wives and fathered eight children. He continued hiccuping until one morning in February, 1990, 68 years later.

**Longest sneezing fit** The longest recorded sneezing fit is that of Donna Griffiths (UK). She began sneezing on January 13, 1981 and sneezed an estimated one million times in the first 365 days. Her first sneeze-free day came 978 days later on September 16, 1983.

**Fastest sneeze** The highest speed at which expelled particles from a sneeze have been measured to travel is 103.6 mph (167 km/h).

**Loudest snoring** Kåre Walkert (Sweden), who suffers from the breathing disorder apnea, recorded peak snoring levels of 93 decibels on May 24, 1993.

# BIRTH & LIFE

**Most prolific mother ever** The greatest recorded number of children born to one mother is 69, to the first wife of Feodor Vassilyev (Russia). In 27 pregnancies between 1725 and 1765 she gave birth to 16 pairs of twins, 7 sets of triplets, and 4 sets of quadruplets. Only two of the children failed to survive their infancy. The mother also holds the records for giving birth to the most sets of twins and the most sets of quadruplets.

**Longest family tree** The lineage of K'ung Ch'iu or Confucius (China, 551–479 BC) can be traced back farther than that of any other family. His great-great-great-great-grandfather Kung Chia is known from the 8th century BC. Kung Chia has 86 lineal descendants.

**Greatest number of descendants** In polygamous countries, the number of a person's descendants can be incalculable. Moulay Ismail, the last Sharifian Emperor of Morocco, was reputed to have fathered a total of 525 sons and 342 daughters by 1703, and achieved a 700th son by 1721. The most recorded living descendants of a monogamous person, however, is 824, by Samuel S. Mast (USA). At the time of his death on October 15, 1992 at age 96, he had 11 children, 97 grandchildren, 634 great-grandchildren, and 82 great-great-grandchildren.

**Most children delivered at a single birth** The highest medically recorded number of children born at a single birth is nine to Geraldine Brodrick (Australia) at the Royal Hospital for Women, Sydney, NSW, Australia, on June 13, 1971. None of the children (five boys [two stillborn] and four girls) lived for more than six days.

**Longest interval between births** The longest interval between the birth of two children to the same mother is 41 years for Elizabeth Ann Buttle (UK), who had a daughter, Belinda, in 1956 and a son, Joseph, on November 20, 1997.

**Most premature baby to survive** James Elgin Gill was born to Brenda and James Gill (both Canada) on May 20, 1987 in Ottawa, Ontario, Canada, 128 days premature and weighing 1 lb. 6 oz. (624 g). The normal human gestation period is 280 days (40 weeks). Much of James's body was still developing, including his skin, hands, ears, and feet, with his eyes still fused shut. James survived and is now a healthy teenager.

**Oldest mother** It was reported that Rosanna Dalla Corte (Italy, b. February 1931) gave birth to a baby boy on July 18, 1994 at the age of 63 years.

**OLDEST LIVING TRIPLETS** Douglas Haig Wilkins, Winnie Elsa Le Notre, and Elsa Winnie Luxon (all UK, pictured here as babies and adults) were verified on March 4, 2002 to be the oldest living triplets, at age 84 years 349 days. They were born in Guernsey, UK, on March 21, 1917 to Mary and Frederick Wilkins.

This record is also attributed to Arceli Keh (USA, b. February 1933) who was thought to be age 63 when, after IVF treatment, she gave birth to a daughter at Loma Linda University Medical Center, California, USA, on November 7, 1996.

**Oldest living man** Yukichi Chuganji (b. March 23, 1889) of Ogori, Fukuoka Prefecture, Japan, became the oldest man in the world on January 4, 2002 at the age of 112 years 288 days.

**Oldest man ever** The greatest age to which any man has ever lived is 120 years 237 days in the case of Shigechiyo Izumi of Isen, Tokunoshima—an island 820 miles (1,320 km) southwest of Tokyo, Japan. He was born on June 29, 1865 and was recorded as a six-year-old in Japan's first census of 1871. He died at 12:15 GMT on February 21, 1986 after developing pneumonia.

**MOST CHILDREN DELIVERED AT A SINGLE BIRTH TO SURVIVE** A set of septuplets (four boys, and three girls, above) was born to Bobbie McCaughey (USA) on November 19 at the University Hospital, Iowa, USA. Conceived by in vitro fertilization, the babies were all delivered after 31 weeks by caesarean in the space of 16 minutes. They weighed between 2 lb. 5 oz. and 3 lb. 4 oz. (1.048 kg and 1.474 kg).

Another set of surviving septuplets was born eight weeks prematurely on January 14, 1998 to 40-year-old Hasna Mohammed Humair (Saudi Arabia). The four boys and three girls, the smallest of which weighed just under 2 lb. (907 g), were born at the Abha Obstetric Hospital, Aseer, Saudi Arabia. The unplanned pregnancy was the result of a fertility drug prescribed to regulate the mother's menstrual cycle.

**Oldest living woman** The oldest living woman in the world whose date of birth can be fully authenticated is Kamato Hongo (Japan, b. September 16, 1887). She took the title at age 114 years 183 days on the death of Maude Farris-Luse (USA, b. January 21, 1887), who died on March 18, 2002.

**Oldest woman ever** The greatest fully authenticated age to which any human has ever lived is 122 years 164 days by Jeanne Louise Calment (France). Born on February 21, 1875, she died at a nursing home in Arles, southern France, on August 4, 1997.

**Oldest living male twins** William and Fred Barrett (UK, b. May 5, 1904) have lived in the southwest of the UK all of their lives, and became the oldest male twins living in the world on April 16, 2001, at age 96 years 346 days.

**Oldest living male conjoined twins** Ronnie and Donnie Galyon (USA, b. October 25, 1951) are the oldest living conjoined male twins. For 36 years, they traveled in side shows, carnivals, and circuses, but they retired in 1991 and now live in Ohio, USA.

**Oldest female conjoined twins** Masha and Dasha Krivoshlyapova (Russia, b. January 3, 1950) were rare conjoined twins with the condition known as *dicephales tetrabrachius dipus*. Between them they had two heads, four arms, and two legs. They died at age 53 in April 2003, within 17 hours of each other.

**Oldest living mixed twins** Louisa Dunn (*nee* Adams) and Fred Adams were born on March 9, 1907 in Wood Green, London, UK. They became the oldest living mixed twins on November 3, 1999, aged 92 years 199 days.

**Oldest ever quadruplets** The quadruplet siblings Adolf, Anne-Marie, Emma, and Elisabeth Ottman (Germany) were born on May 5, 1912. All four quads lived to the age of 79.

**Heaviest quadruplets at birth** The heaviest quadruplets weighed a total of 22 lb. 15.75 oz. (10.426 kg) at birth. The two girls and two boys were born to Tina Saunders (UK) at St. Peters Hospital, Chertsey, Surrey, UK, on February 7, 1989.

**Most single siblings sharing the same birthday** There is one verified example of a family producing five single children with coincident birthdays. Carolyn and Ralph Cummins' (USA) children Catherine (1952), Carol (1953), Charles (1956), Claudia (1961) and Cecilia (1966), amazingly, were all born on February 20. The odds against five single siblings sharing a birthdate are one in 17,797,577,730—almost four times the world's population.

**Longest separated twins** On April 27, 1989, through the New Zealand television program *Missing,* twins Iris Johns and Aro Campbell (New Zealand, b. January 13, 1914) were reunited after 75 years of separation.

**OLDEST FEMALE TWINS EVER** Kin Narita and Gin Kanie (Japan, b. August 1, 1892), whose names mean gold and silver, were the oldest authenticated female twins. Kin died of heart failure on January 23, 2000 at the age of 107 years 175 days. They lived in Nagoya, Japan, the town of their birth.

# ASTONISHING OLDIES

**Oldest Olympic gold medalist**  Oscar Swahn (Sweden) was in the winning Running Deer shooting team at the 1912 Olympic Games in Sweden, aged 64 years 258 days. In the same event at the 1920 Olympics in Belgium he won silver, becoming the oldest winner of any Olympic medal at 72 years 280 days.

**Oldest competitor at a Winter Olympic Games**  The oldest ever competitor at the Winter Olympic Games is James Coates (GB) who competed in the skeleton at St. Moritz, Switzerland, in 1948 at age 53 years 328 days.

The oldest female competitor at a Winter Olympic Games is Anne Abernathy (US Virgin Islands) who took part in the luge at Salt Lake City, USA, on February 13, 2002 at age 48 years 307 days.

**Oldest snowboarder**  George Blair (aka Banana George, USA, b. January 22, 1915) of Winter Haven, Florida, USA, is the world's oldest active snowboarder, snowboarding for between 45 and 60 days a year.

**Oldest man to reach the summit of Mt. Everest**  Yuichiro Miura (Japan, b. October 12, 1932) reached the summit of Everest aged 70 years 222 days on May 22, 2003, becoming the oldest person ever to have accomplished this feat.

**Oldest woman to reach the summit of Mt. Everest**  Tamae Watanabe (Japan, b. November 21, 1938) was 63 years 177 days old when she reached the summit of Mt. Everest at 9:55 am on May 16, 2002, becoming the oldest woman ever to do so.

Watanabe reached the summit on its busiest day ever, when 54 other climbers reached the top of the 29,028-ft. (8,848-m) peak.

**Oldest person to fly solo around the world**  Fred Lasby (USA, b. May

**OLDEST BADMINTON PLAYER** As of February 2003, 96-year-old Henry Paynter (Canada, b. UK, February 27, 1907) was still a regular player at the Kelowna Badminton Club, Kelowna, British Columbia, Canada.

28, 1912) completed a solo round-the-world flight at the age of 82 years 84 days in his single-engined Piper Comanche. Leaving Fort Myers, Florida, USA, on June 30, 1994, he flew west for 23,218 miles (37,366 km), making 21 stops and arriving back at Fort Myers on August 20, 1994.

**Oldest aeronautical record breaker** The oldest pilot to have set a world record as recognized by the world governing body, the Fédération Aéronautique Internationale (FAI), is retired Wing Commander Kenneth Wallis (UK). Wallis was 85 years 213 days old when, on November 16, 2002, he set a speed record of 129 mph (207.7 km/h) over a distance of 1.8 miles (3 km) in a piston-engine-powered autogyro over Norfolk, UK.

**Oldest BASE jumper** BASE jumpers parachute from high man-made structures and natural formations. On August 2, 2002 James Talbot Guyer (USA, b. June 16, 1928) parachuted from the 486-ft.-high (148-m) Perrine Bridge near Twin Falls, Idaho, USA, at the age of 74 years 47 days.

**Oldest woman to make a solo parachute jump** Sylvia Brett (UK) was 80 years 166 days old when she parachuted over Cranfield, Bedfordshire, UK, on August 23, 1986.

**Oldest football player** Enrique Alcocer (Mexico, b. August 28, 1924) is currently the world's oldest regular football player. He plays for the Reforma Athletic Club in Mexico City, Mexico. Alcocer began playing regularly in 1936 for Grosso junior and high school in Mexico City. He then played professionally for the Marte Football Club in Mexico's first division in 1944 before joining his current club in 1952.

**Oldest ball boy in a major tennis championship** The oldest ball boy to participate in a major tennis championships is Manny Hershkowitz (USA) who worked on court at the US Open at Flushing Meadow, New York, USA, in September 1999 at age 82.

**Oldest English Channel swimmer** The oldest person to swim the English Channel was Bertram Batt (Australia, b. December 22, 1919), who was aged 67 years 241 days when he swam from Cap Gris-Nez, France, to Dover, UK, in 18 hr. 37 min. from August 19–20, 1987. The oldest woman to achieve the feat was Susan Fraenkel (South Africa, b. April 22, 1948), who was 46 years 103 days old when she did the swim in 12 hr. 5 min. on July 24, 1994.

**Oldest windsurfer** Otto Comanos (Australia, b. Greece, November 16, 1913) took up the sport of windsurfing shortly after his retirement in 1986 and regularly windsurfs two to three times a week in the lakes in and around Sydney, New South Wales, Australia.

**Oldest drag boat race champion** Paul Showman (USA) is recognized by the International Hot Boat Association (IHBA) as being the oldest person

**OLDEST FEMALE SINGER TO REACH NO. 1 IN THE UK CHART** Deborah Harry (USA, b. 1 July 1945), the lead singer of Blondie, became the oldest female vocalist to top the UK charts when she went to No. 1 with "Maria" on February 13, 1999 at the age of 53 years 227 days.

to compete in an officially sanctioned drag boat race and the oldest ever IHBA Champion in the 12-second class, when he won in 1998 at the age of 83 in his boat *The Legend*.

**Oldest boxing champion** Archie Moore (USA) was recognized as a light heavyweight champion up until February 10, 1962 when his title was removed. His date of birth is uncertain, but he was believed to be between 45 and 48 years old. During his career (1936–63) he won a record 145 fights by knockout.

**Oldest competing female bareback bronc rider** Jan Youren (USA, b. October 2, 1943) has ridden bulls and broncs for over 35 years and is a former world champion in the sport.

**Oldest tightrope walker** The oldest known tightrope walker is "Professor" William Ivy Baldwin (USA, 1866–1953), who crossed a portion of the Eldorado Canyon, Colorado, USA, on his 82nd birthday. He walked a 320-ft.-long (97.5-m) wire spanning a 125-ft. (38.1-m) drop.

**Oldest clown** The record for world's oldest professional clown is held jointly by Josep Andreu I. Lasserre (aka Charlie Rivel, Spain) and Arnold Schmidt (aka Guggele, Denmark). Both clowns were entertaining circus crowds up until the age of 87.

**Oldest Formula One Grand Prix winner** The oldest Grand Prix winner (in pre-World Championship days) was Tazio Giorgio Nuvolari (Italy, 1892–1953), who won the Albi Grand Prix at Albi, France, in his Maserati 4CL on July 14, 1946 at the age of 53 years 240 days.

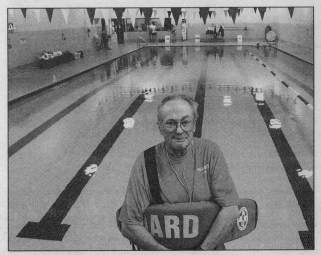

**OLDEST LIFEGUARD The oldest lifeguard in the world is Haywood Leroy Stewart (USA, b. May 22, 1916) of Wheat Ridge, Colorado, USA, who has been a lifeguard since 1938.**

**Oldest drivers**  There are three drivers who were issued with new driving licenses at age 104: Maude Tull (USA) of Inglewood, California—who took to driving at age 91 after her husband died—was issued a renewal to her license on February 5, 1976 when at 104; Layne Hall (USA), whose date of birth is uncertain (b. 1884 or 1880), was issued with a New York State license on June 15, 1989 when he was either 104 or 109; and most recently, Fred Hale Sr. (USA, b. December 1, 1890) was issued with a driving license on February 29, 1995 at age 104. The license was valid until his 108th birthday in 1998.

**Oldest bell ringer**  As of March 10, 2003 Reginald Bray (UK, b. October 28, 1902) was still an active member of the bell ringing team of St. Cyr and St. Julitta, Newton St. Cyres, Devon, UK, ringing bells regularly at age 100 years 133 days.

**Oldest female chorister**  Clarissa Lee (UK, b. October 20, 1892) was a chorister at St. Mary and St. Andrew Church, Pitminster, Somerset, UK, from 1914 to the end of 1996, when she was 104. She sang with the choir every week.

**Oldest male stripper**  Bernie Barker (USA, b. July 31, 1940), a regular performer at Club LeBare, Miami Beach, Florida, USA, began his career in 2000 at the age of 60 as a way to get in shape after recovering from prostate cancer. Since leaving his previous job of selling real estate, he has won over 30 male stripping contests.

# FOOD FEATS

**Fastest time to drink a pint of beer upside-down**  Peter G. Dowdeswell (UK) of Earls Barton, Northamptonshire, UK, drank a pint of beer in 3 seconds while standing on his head at BBC Radio Leicester studios, UK, on February 16, 1988. He also holds the record for drinking the fastest yard of ale (2.5 pints or 1.42 liters), which he achieved in 5 seconds at RAF Upper Heyford, Oxfordshire, UK, on May 5, 1975.

**Fastest tomato ketchup drinker**  Dustin Phillips (USA) consumed 91% of a standard 14-oz. (397-g) bottle of Heinz tomato ketchup through a 0.25-in.-diameter (0.63-cm) drinking straw in just 33 seconds at the studios of *Guinness World Records: Primetime,* Los Angeles, California, USA, on September 23, 1999.

**Most cream cookies eaten**  Ambrose Mendy (UK) ate three cream cookies in a record time of 49.15 seconds at the offices of Guinness World Records, London, UK, on October 29, 2002.

**Most meatballs eaten in one minute**  Nick Marshall (UK) consumed 27 meatballs in one minute using a toothpick, during a national meatball

**MOST HOT DOGS EATEN IN THREE MINUTES** Peter Dowdeswell (UK)
ate four hot dogs (sausages and buns) in three minutes as part of the
Wimpy National Hotdog Championships at the Trocadero Centre,
London, UK, on July 27, 2001.

eating competition held at IKEA, Leeds, West Yorkshire, UK, on November
18, 2002.

**Fastest sausage swallower** Jimmy Sköld (Sweden) swallowed whole
seven cooked sausages—each measuring a minimum of 6.29 in. (16 cm)
long and 0.68 in. (1.75 cm) in diameter—in one minute on the set of *Guinness World Records: Primetime,* Los Angeles, USA, on March 11, 2001.

**Most baked beans eaten with a cocktail stick in five minutes** The
greatest number of baked beans eaten with a cocktail stick in five minutes is
226 by Andy Szerbini (UK) at London Zoo, London, UK, on November 18,
1996.

**Most worms eaten in 30 seconds** Mark Hogg (USA) swallowed a total of 94 night crawler worms in 30 seconds on the set of the *Regis Philbin Show* in October 2000. Although Hogg can swallow handfuls of live
worms—which have been thoroughly washed—without hesitation, he
doesn't care for eating sushi.

**Most Big Macs consumed** Donald Gorske (USA) has eaten Big Macs
daily since 1972. He consumed his 18,250th on March 7, 2002.

**Most jam doughnuts eaten in three minutes** The record for most
jam doughnuts eaten in three minutes without licking the lips is six and is
held by Steve McHugh (UK) who achieved this at the offices of Guinness
World Records, London, on June 28, 2002.

**Most ice cream eaten in 30 seconds** The world record for the most ice cream eaten in 30 seconds with a teaspoon is 5.8 oz. (167 g) and belongs to Jaime André Sargento da Silva (Portugal) who achieved his feat in Lisbon, Portugal, on November 11, 2002.

**Most Smarties eaten with chopsticks in three minutes** The record for the most Smarties eaten with chopsticks in three minutes is 108 by Kathryn Ratcliffe (UK) at WH Smith's store in Gateshead, Tyne & Wear, UK, on September 28, 2002.

**Largest bubblegum bubble blown with the mouth** Susan Montgomery Williams (USA) blew the world's largest bubblegum bubble in New York, USA, on July 19, 1994. Measured under the strict rules of this competitive activity, it had a 23 in. (58.4 cm) diameter.

**Farthest marshmallow nose-blow** The farthest a marshmallow has been blown out of one person's nostril and caught in the mouth of another person is 16 ft. 3.5 in. (4.96 m), by blower Scott Jeckel (USA) and catcher Ray Perisin (USA) on the set of *Guinness World Records: Primetime* in Los Angeles, California, USA, on August 13, 1999.

**Farthest spaghetti nasal ejection** Kevin Cole (USA) holds the record for the longest spaghetti strand blown out of a nostril in a single blow. On December 16, 1998, Cole successfully achieved a record distance of 7.5 in. (19 cm) on the set of *Guinness World Records: Primetime* in Los Angeles, California, USA.

**Most M&MS flipped and caught in one minute** The record for flipping peanut M&Ms from the back of one person's ear into another person's mouth is 16 in one minute by Mark Needle (USA) who flipped the sweets

to his brother, Ben, on the set of *Guinness World Records: Primetime,* Los Angeles, USA, on August 18, 1998.

**MOST HAMBURGERS STUFFED IN THE MOUTH** The record for stuffing the most regulation size hamburgers (including buns and condiments) in the mouth at one time is three. Johnny Reitz (USA) performed this feat on the set of *Guinness World Records: Primetime* on June 17, 1998. The rules of the event require the participant not to swallow any of the hamburgers.

Humans

**LARGEST GINGERBREAD HOUSE** Roger A. Pelcher (USA) built a gingerbread house with an internal volume of 33,196 ft.³ (940 m³) at Wolfchase Galleria, Memphis, Tennessee, USA, in December 2001. The house was 57.5 ft. (17.5 m) tall at its highest point, and approximately 29.5 ft.² (9 m²) at the base.

**Largest pizza order** On August 19, 1998, Little Caesar's took an order from the VF Corporation of Greensboro, North Carolina, USA, for 13,386 pizzas for 40,160 employees at 180 locations across the United States. The average cost of each pizza was $7.99 (then £4.94), which resulted in a total cost of $106,959.41 (then £66,077.40).

**Longest pizza delivery** On March 22, 2001 Bernard Jordaan of Butlers Pizza, Cape Town, South Africa, hand delivered a pizza to Corne Krige, the captain of the Fedsure Stormers rugby team, in Sydney, Australia—a distance of 6,861 miles (11,042 km) as the crow flies.

**Longest curry delivery** MadAboutCurry.co.uk arranged for a vegetable biryani curry and a peshwari naan to be delivered from the Rupali restaurant, Newcastle-Upon-Tyne, Tyne and Wear, UK, to Rachael Kerr (UK) in Sydney, Australia, a distance of 10,811 miles (17,398 km) as the crow flies. The delivery arrived at its destination on February 26, 2001.

**Most grapes trodden in two minutes** Angel Amigo and Juan Manuel Fuertes (both Spain) trod 110.2 lb. (50 kg) of grapes in two minutes, resulting in 26.4 pints (15 liters) of juice, at the International Grape Treading Championships, Villa Franca del Bierzo, Castilla-León, Spain, on August 30, 1998.

**Fastest sandwich made using feet** Using just his feet, Rob Williams (USA) made a Bologna smoked sausage, cheese, lettuce, sliced tomato, mustard, mayonnaise, and sliced pickle sandwich—complete with olives on cocktail sticks—in 1 min. 57 sec. on the set of *Guinness World Records: Primetime* on November 10, 2000.

**Most pancakes made in eight hours by a team** The most pancakes made in eight hours is 30,724 by members of the Lubbock Lions Club, Lubbock, Texas, USA, at the 50th Annual Pancake Festival, Lubbock Memorial Civic Center, on February 23, 2002.

**Fastest chicken pluck** On January 19, 1939 Ernest Hausen of Fort Atkinson, Wisconsin, USA, was timed at 4.4 seconds for completely plucking a chicken.

**Highest formal meal eaten** The highest altitude at which a formal meal has been eaten is 22,205 ft. (6,768 m), at the top of Mt. Huascarán, Peru. On June 28, 1989 nine members of the Ansett Social Climbers from Sydney, Australia, scaled the mountain with a Louis XIV dining table, chairs, silverware, a candelabra, wine, and a three-course meal.

# ODD TALENTS

**Most clothes pins clipped on a face** Garry Turner (UK), known for his unusually stretchy skin, managed to clip 133 ordinary wooden clothes pins on his face, at the offices of Guinness World Records, London, UK, on August 3, 2001.

**Greatest vertical height walked on stilts** On June 9, 2002, Colin Tschida and Ryan Hamilton (both USA) hiked 3 miles (4.82 km) on

**MOST SPOONS BALANCED ON THE FACE** Jonathan Friedman (USA) balanced seven stainless steel spoons on his face for five seconds at Lake Oswego, Oregon, USA, on February 24, 2002. The spoons weighed 0.69–1.4 oz. (19.8–42.5g). He placed one on each ear and cheek, one on his nose, and two on his chin.

wooden stilts to reach the top of Harney Peak, which has an elevation of 7,242 ft. (2,207 m), in the Black Hills of South Dakota, USA. The climb took 2 hr. 25 min. 21 sec. Walking on stilts with footholds 2 ft. (60 cm) above the ground, they rested on four occasions, remaining on their stilts by leaning against trees. They fell off their stilts a total of nine times between them.

**Fastest human crab over 65 ft.** Agnès Brun (France) traveled a distance of 65 ft. (20 m) in a crab position in 33.3 seconds at the studios of *L'Émission des Records* in Paris, France, on November 30, 2001.

**Most cartwheels in one minute without hands** Mohammed Elachi (France) completed 32 cartwheels in one minute without using his hands

**MOST BASKETBALLS SPUN SIMULTANEOUSLY** The most basketballs spun simultaneously is 28 by Michael Kettman (USA, pictured here spinning 20 basketballs) on May 25, 1999 in London, UK.

and without straying out of a 2-ft. diameter (60-cm) circle in Paris, France, on May 28, 2002.

**Fastest frog jump** Bastien Lecomte (France) covered 32 ft. 6 in. (10 m) while frog jumping (holding on to his toes) in a time of 11.58 seconds at the studios of *L'Émission des Records* in Paris, France, on May 23, 2002.

**Most soap bubble domes** Soap bubble artist Fan Yang (Canada) set the world record for the most soap bubble domes created inside one another at the studios of *Guinness World Records* in Helsinki, Finland, on October 20, 2001. He blew a total of 12 soap bubble domes within each other in the manner of a Russian matriska doll.

**Longest card throwing distance** The record for the longest throw of a single playing card is 216 ft. 4 in. (65.96 m) by Rick Smith, Jr. (USA). The record was set at the Cleveland State Convocation Center, Ohio, USA, on March 21, 2002.

**Most packs of cards memorized** Dominic O'Brien (UK) memorized, on a single sighting, a random sequence of 54 separate packs of cards all shuffled together (2,808 cards in total) at Simpson's-In-The-Strand, London, UK, on May 1, 2002. He memorized the cards in 11 hr. 42 min. then recited them in the exact sequence in a time of 3 hr. 30 min. With only a 0.5% margin of error allowed (no more than 14 errors), he broke the record with just eight errors.

**Farthest eyeball popper** Kim Goodman (USA) can pop her eyeballs to a protrusion of 0.43 in. (11 mm) beyond her eye sockets. Her eyes were measured achieving this feat on the set of the US television show *Guinness World Records: Primetime* on June 13, 1998.

**Largest simultaneous one-handed hat spin** Francois "Jester Coco" Chotard (France) spun with one hand a total of 23 hats simultaneously, balanced on the tops of individual poles measuring between 67–87 in. long (170 cm and 220 cm) at Bolton, Greater Manchester, UK, on September 14, 2001.

**Most bowling balls stacked in three minutes by a team** Jäni Yli-Länttä and Niko Korkeakangas (both Finland) managed to stack nine standard bowling balls vertically without the use of adhesives in three minutes on the set of *Guinness World Records* in Helsinki, Finland, on October 23, 2001.

**Most layered bed of nails sandwich** The most layered bed of nails sandwich was made up of four people lying between three double-sided beds of nails in Deal, Kent, UK, on August 27, 2001.

**Heaviest bed of nails concrete block break** Ciro Gallo (UK) had 37 concrete blocks with a total weight of 519.8 lb. (235.8 kg) placed on his

**MOST CHAINSAW JUGGLING THROWS** Tom Comet (Canada) juggled three gas-driven chainsaws for 44 throws (14 complete rotations and two catches) on August 5, 2002 at Princess Street Gardens, Edinburgh, UK.

chest and broken with a 14-lb. (6.35-kg) sledgehammer while he lay on a bed of nails at Hemel Hempstead, Herts, UK, on August 24, 2002.

**Most balloon sculptures in one hour** John Cassidy (USA) made 494 balloon shapes in one hour in New York, USA, on August 29, 2002. He broke his own record of 468 balloons.

**Most tightrope skipping jumps** Juan Pedro Carrillo (USA) achieved 780 consecutive turns skipping with a rope on a high-wire in San Antonio, Texas, USA, on June 30, 2000. The tightrope was 26 ft. (7.9 m) high.

**Longest full-body ice contact endurance** Wearing only his swimming trunks, Wim Hof (Netherlands) endured standing in a tube filled with ice cubes for 1 hr. 6 min. 4 sec. in London, UK, on March 13, 2002.

**Highest flame by a fire breather** Henrik Segelström (Sweden) blew a flame to a height of 9.8 ft. (3 m) in Stockholm, Sweden, on November 28, 2001.

**Most bras unhooked in one minute with one hand** Jason Dahmer (Canada) unhooked one-handed 16 bras worn under t-shirts at Columbus, Ohio, USA, on August 17, 2001.

**Longest time spinning a frying pan on a finger** Anders Björklund (Sweden) was able to spin a frying pan on his finger for 14 minutes on the set of *Guinness Rekord TV,* Stockholm, Sweden, on November 29, 2001.

# MASS PARTICIPATION

**Largest dog walk** On April 20, 2002, 3,117 dogs took part in the world's largest dog walk. The dogs were taken on the 3.4-mile (5.5-km) Mighty Texas Dog Walk, starting from Austin High School, Austin, Texas, USA. The event was organized by Texas Hearing & Service Dogs.

**Largest group hug** A total of 4,703 people hugged each other for at least 10 seconds at the Scout 2001 event at Rinkaby Skjutfält, Kristianstad, Sweden, on August 3, 2001. The record-breaking hug was televised for the *Guinness Rekord TV* show.

**Largest human centipede** A total of 2,026 people—Nagoya Otani High School students, their parents, and teachers—succeeded in creating the world's largest human centipede at Tsuruma Track and Field Stadium, Nagoya, Japan, on June 13, 2001. The ankles of all participants were firmly tied to the ankles of the next person. The human centipede successfully moved a distance of 98 ft. 6 in. (30 m) without any mishaps.

**Largest Mexican wave** The world's longest Mexican wave consisted of 5,805 participants and occurred on Aberavon beach, Neath Port Talbot, UK, on April 14, 2002, in support of the British Heart Foundation.

**Largest gathering of Santas** The world's largest gathering of Santas took place on December 7, 2002, when 2,685 costumed Santas paraded down the streets of Bralanda, Sweden. All participants wore red Santa cos-

**MOST PEOPLE MAKING SNOW ANGELS SIMULTANEOUSLY**
A record 1,791 people made snow angels on the grounds of the Capitol Mall at Bismark, North Dakota, USA, on March 23, 2002. The event was organized by the State Historical Society of North Dakota.

tumes with matching hats and fake white beards.

**Most people on a single pair of skis** A total of 80 people skied a distance of 394 ft. (120 m) on a 250-ft. long (76-m) pair of skis at the Norway/Keskinada Giant Ski Event at Ottawa, Ontario, Canada, on February 2, 2002. The participants were led by the Governor General of Canada, Adrienne Clarkson, and the Norwegian Ambassador to Canada, Ingvard Havnen. The event was organized by the Norwegian Embassy and the executive committee of the Keskinada Loppet cross-country ski race. It took place at Rideau Hall, the Canadian Governor General's residence.

**Longest paperclip chain by a team** A 20-mile-long (32.2-km) paperclip chain was made in 24 hours by 60 people as part of an art exhibition at the SKOL Contemporary Art Centre, Montreal, Canada, on April 1, 2001.

**Largest human image** On July 24, 1999 a total of 34,309 people, organized by Realizar Eventos Especials of Portugal, gathered at the National Stadium of Jamor, Lisbon, Portugal, to create the Portuguese logo for Euro 2004. The event was part of the successful Portuguese bid to UEFA to hold the European soccer championship in 2004. The kicking leg of the player in the logo was composed of 651 gymnasts wearing black and white capes, which, when turned over, created the illusion of the player kicking the ball. Once the ball was kicked, it released 10,000 red and green helium balloons—the colors of the Portuguese flag.

**Largest group drum roll** A total of 1,434 drummers, led by Micky Dolenz (USA), Davy Jones (UK) and Peter Tork (USA)—former members of The

Monkees—played a drum roll for 3 min. 22 sec. to mark the opening of the Hard Rock Hotel at Universal Orlando, Florida, USA, on February 27, 2001.

**Largest simultaneous yodel** The world's largest simultaneous yodel involved 937 people, yodeling the popular Swiss song "Von Luzern uf Wäggis zue" for more than one minute at the Ravensburger Spielland, Meckenbeuren, Germany, on October 5, 2002.

**Largest bell ringing ensemble** At an event held in the city of Gdańsk, Poland, 10,000 people gathered in Dlugi Targ Street and rang their bells simultaneously on December 31, 2000 to celebrate the turn of the century.

**Largest simultaneous yo-yo** On June 13, 2002 the world's largest yo-yo took place at the Royal Dublin Society, Dublin, Republic of Ireland, with 426 people yo-yoing for two minutes.

**Most people juggling at the same time** At the European Juggling Convention held in Edinburgh, UK, on August 7, 1998, a total of 1,508 people juggled a minimum of three balls each for ten seconds.

**Most people fire breathing** A total of 50 people, organized by Frankenberg Entertainment (Sweden), gathered in Stockholm, Sweden, to blow fire from torches on October 3, 2001.

**LARGEST MASCOT GATHERING** On September 29, 2002, a record total of 90 costumed mascots gathered to compete in the British Mascot Grand National at Huntingdon Racecourse, Huntingdon, UK.

**LARGEST TIRE-ROLLING GROUP** On October 13, 2001, 81 people rolled a tire down a 328-ft. (100-m) course in the "Running of the Tires," in Toronto, Ontario, Canada. The event was sponsored by Dunlop Tires and Big Brothers of Toronto.

**Largest simultaneous whoopee cushion sit** The record for the most people to sit on whoopee cushions at the same time was broken by 982 people, all employees of Walkers Ltd. (UK), at the International Convention Centre in Birmingham, UK, on January 15, 2002.

**Most trees planted in a day** The most trees planted in 24 hours is 80,244 by a team comprising 300 citizens of Nagapattinam District, Tamil Nadu, India, on December 4, 2002.

**Most couples on simultaneous blind dates** A total of 123 couples (246 people) participated in blind dates as part of the "Desperate and Dateless Ball" organized in aid of The British Red Cross on February 16, 2002. Couples met at a bar before attending the party at Planit Arches, London, UK. Before the event, singles completed a questionnaire stating their likes and dislikes and were computer matched by internet dating agency loveandfriends.com.

**Largest aerobics demonstration** The largest number of participants in an aerobics display is 38,633. They took part in the University of Guadalajara's Capital Aeróbica event held in Guadalajara, Mexico, on June 6, 1998.

**Largest tap dance** The greatest ever number of tap dancers in a single routine was 6,951, gathered at the City Square, Stuttgart, Germany, on May 24, 1998. The routine, choreographed by Ray Lynch (USA), lasted 2 min. 15 sec. and was danced to the tune "Klicke-di-Klack" that Lynch composed for the event.

**Largest motorcycle pyramid** The Dare Devil's Team of the Indian Army Signal Corps (India) achieved a motorcycle pyramid consisting of 210 men balanced on a total of 10 motorcycles on July 5, 2001, at Gowri Shankar Parade Ground, Jabalpur, India. The pyramid traveled a distance of 424 ft. (129 m).

**Longest scarf knitted by a team** The longest scarf ever knitted measured 20 miles (32.2 km). It was created by the able hands of the residents of Abbeyfield Houses for the Abbeyfield Society of Potters Bar, Hertfordshire, UK, and was completed on May 29, 1988.

**Largest multiple-venue simultaneous tap dance** Organized by the North London Performing Arts Centre, London, UK, a total of 7,596 children from 40 schools across north London tap danced simultaneously to the tune "To the Show" for five minutes beginning 10:00 am on March 22, 2002.

**Largest simultaneous balloon pop** A total of 368 people popped balloons simultaneously at the Mid States Camping Conference in the Pheasant Run Resort and Conference Center, Charles, Illinois, USA, on April 4, 2002.

**Largest simultaneous jump** The largest ever simultaneous jump occurred on September 7, 2001 to celebrate the launch of Science Year in the UK. At precisely 11:00 am, 559,493 people began jumping up and down for one minute. The total number of participants was 569,069. The extra numbers represent disabled pupils who contributed to the seismic activity by dropping objects on the ground or hitting the ground with their fists.

**LARGEST SIMULTANEOUS PERCUSSION PERFORMANCE** The world's largest percussion performance was held at the Hong Kong Coliseum, Hong Kong, China, on July 2, 2002. A record 10,102 people played a percussive rhythm for over six minutes as part of "The Music of the Dragons" concert.

**LARGEST SIMULTANEOUS CHEERLEADING** The largest simultaneous cheerleading event occurred when 328 past and present cheerleaders between the ages of 4 and 60 performeed a cheer in full uniform on the field of Cardinal Stadium, Louisville, Kentucky, USA, on October 20, 2001. The event was organized by the Power Cheer Training Center.

**Most people hula-hooping simultaneously** The record for the most people hula-hooping simultaneously is 2,290 and was set during an event organized by the China Food GMP Development Association and the Bureau of Health, Kaohsiung City Government, at Chung Cheng Stadium, Kaohsiung City, Taiwan, on October 28, 2000.

**Most people brushing teeth simultaneously** A total of 2,883 individuals simultaneously brushed their teeth for one minute on February 3, 2001 at Yuba City High School, California, USA.

**Largest line dance** A record total of 11,967 people took part in a line dance organized by NTUC Income Insurance Cooperative Ltd., Singapore, at the Singapore Expo Centre, Singapore, on May 1, 2002, dancing to "Rasa Sayang" for 7 min. 9 sec.

**Largest multiple-venue simultaneous dance** A total of 196,569 people from 681 schools across Canada danced simultaneously for eight minutes from 11:15 am CST (10:15 am PDT/2:15 pm ADT) during "activ8 the Nation's Schools Hokey Pokey Challenge" on April 9, 2002.

**Most people to parachute from a balloon simultaneously** A total of 16 members of the Velvet Toilet Tissue Team simultaneously jumped from a hot-air balloon at an altitude of 10,500 ft. (3,200 m) over Peterborough, Cambridgeshire, UK, on May 31, 2002. They all jumped from a single large basket suspended beneath the balloon. The balloon was captained by David Fish (UK) and the skydiving team was led by Ian Ashpole (UK).

**Largest simultaneous BASE jump** The largest simultaneous BASE jump involved 15 participants from five countries who skydived from the Petronas Towers, Kuala Lumpur, Malaysia, seconds before midnight on December 31, 1999 as part of the new millennium celebrations.

**Most trees planted simultaneously** On October 15, 2000, 10,000 people at 152 locations throughout Malaysia planted 110,461 trees simultaneously. The event was organized by the Government of Malaysia through the National Landscape Department of the Ministry of Housing and Local Government, Kuala Lumpur City Hall, The Tree Planting Group of the Malaysia Nature Society and all state governments.

**Largest simultaneous multiple-venue sing-along** The largest simultaneous sing-along was staged by Young Voices, Sargent Cancer Care for Children and EMI (all UK). There were 83,121 participants from hundreds of schools across the UK who simultaneously sang a specially written song, "Tell Me Why," at different venues on December 9, 2002.

**Largest "YMCA" dance** A total of 13,588 people danced to the song "YMCA" for five minutes prior to the baseball game between the Spikes and the Salt Lake Stingers at Johnny Rosenblatt Stadium, Omaha, Nebraska, USA, on July 4, 2001.

**Most people skipping with the same rope** The record for the most people skipping with the same rope is 220. The record was set by a team of skippers at the International Rope Skipping Competition, Greeley, Colorado, USA, on June 28, 1990.

**Largest salsa dance** A total of 3,868 people danced to Pérez Prado's "Mambo No. 5" for five minutes to create the largest salsa dance on October 19, 2000, at Palau Sant Jordi, Barcelona, Spain.

The record for most salsa-dancing couples was set by a total of 173 couples, who danced a rueda at Bayfront Park, Florida, USA, on June 24, 2001.

**LARGEST MULTIPLE-VENUE SIMULTANEOUS QUADRILLE A total of 7,518 dancers danced a quadrille in nine towns across Slovenia on May 24, 2002. A quadrille is a French square dance originating from the 18th century and is executed by four couples.**

**Most people doing the twist** To raise money for Breakthrough Breast Cancer (UK), a total of 1,150 people "twisted away" on the beach at Burnham-on-Sea, Somerset, UK, for five minutes on August 11, 2002.

**Longest conga line** The Miami Super Conga consisted of 119,986 people who gathered to conga in Miami, Florida, USA, on March 13, 1988.

**Largest Christmas cracker pull** On December 2, 2001, 971 people participated in a simultaneous Christmas cracker pull at a party to celebrate the 25th birthday of the Museum of London, London, UK.

# STRENGTH

**Heaviest combined weight balanced on the head in one hour** The heaviest combined weight balanced on the head in one hour is 11,420 lb. (5,180 kg) by John Evans (UK) at the Lowestoft Motorcycle Show, Lowestoft, Suffolk, UK, on July 23, 2000. This record load was the combined weight of 92 people Evans balanced individually on his head for at least ten seconds.

**Most weight on the body** Eduardo Armallo Lasaga (Spain) lay on a wooden board beneath 3,086 lb. (1,399.8 kg) of concrete blocks, in Madrid, Spain, on October 18, 2001.

**Heaviest boat pulled** On November 19, 1988 in Rostock, Germany, David Huxley (Australia) pulled the *Delphin,* weighing 2,217,847 lb. (1,006 tonnes) with a cargo of 175 cars plus passengers, over a distance of 23 ft. (7 m).

**Heaviest weight lifted with the ear** The heaviest weight lifted using only the ear is 110 lb. (50 kg) by Li Jian Hua (China), who lifted a column of bricks hanging from a clamp attached to one of his ears and held the weight for 9.3 seconds on December 17, 1998 at the studios of *Guinness World Records: Primetime* in Los Angeles, USA. The column of bricks was stacked in a metal casing and suspended from the ear clamp by a chain.

**Heaviest train pulled** Juraj Barbaric (Slovakia) single-handedly pulled a 20-car freight train weighing 2.2 million lb. (1,000 tonnes) a distance of 14 ft. 9 in. (4.5 m) along a railroad track in Kosice, Slovakia, on June 1, 1999. He trained for eight months prior to the record attempt, with weekly train-pulling practice sessions.

**Heaviest truck pulled over 100 feet** The heaviest truck pulled over 100 ft. (30.5 m) weighed 54,320 lb. (24.64 tonnes) and was pulled by Kevin Fast (Canada) at Cobourg, Ontario, Canada, on June 30, 2001.

**MOST TELEPHONE DIRECTORIES TORN IN THREE MINUTES** Rick Belden (USA) ripped 19 telephone directories, each with 1,494 pages, in a record time of 3 minutes in Charlotte, North Carolina, USA, on November 2, 2002.

**Highest beer keg toss** Juha Rasanen (Finland) threw a 27-lb. (12.3-kg) beer keg over a bar at a height of 22 ft. 9 in. (6.93 m) on the set of *El Show de los Récords* in Madrid, Spain, on September 21, 2001.

**Most consecutive one arm chin-ups** On December 3, 1982 Robert Chisholm (Canada) completed 22 consecutive one-arm chin-ups using a ring at Queen's University, Kingston, Ontario, Canada.

**Heaviest hod carried on the flat and up a ladder** Russell Bradley (UK) carried bricks weighing 582 lb. (264 kg) in a hod weighing 105 lb. 13

oz. (48 kg) a distance of 16 ft. 5 in. (5 m) on the flat, before ascending a ladder to a height of 8 ft. 2 in. (2.49 m) at Worcester, Worcestershire, UK, on November 20, 1993.

**Fastest piano smashing** The record time for demolishing an upright piano with a sledgehammer and passing the entire wreckage through a circle 9 in. (22.8 cm) in diameter is 1 min. 37 sec. by six members of the Tinwald Rugby Football Club, Ashburton, New Zealand, on November 6, 1977.

**Fastest concrete block break on body** On September 28, 2002 Frederick Burton (UK) piled 16 concrete building blocks on his chest and had them systematically broken with a sledgehammer by Peter Johnson (UK) in 12.7 seconds, in Cheadle, Staffordshire, UK.

**Most trucks pulled simultaneously** The most trucks pulled simultaneously at several locations is 21 for the Motability and National Freight Consortium (now Exel plc) Truck Pull held in the UK on September 11, 1999. A total of ten trucks were pulled a distance of at least 100 ft. (30 m) by teams of differing sizes.

### Most decks of cards torn in half in 30 seconds Scott Fraze (USA)

**MOST MILK CRATES BALANCED ON THE HEAD** John Evans (UK) balanced 96 milk crates on his head in Hyde Park, London, UK, on April 6, 2001. John has several other outstanding strength records, including balancing the heaviest car on his head, when he sustained a gutted Mini car weighing a total of 352 lb. (159.6 kg) on his head for 33 seconds at The London Studios, London, UK, on May 24, 1999.

**HEAVIEST WEIGHT LIFTED WITH A BEARD** The heaviest weight lifted with a human beard is 135 lb. (61.3 kg) when Antanas Kontrimas (Lithuania) lifted Ruta Cekyte (Lithuania) off the ground for 15 seconds on August 18, 2001 at the VIII International Country Festival 2001 in Visaginas, Lithuania.

ripped 13 decks of cards (with 52 cards and two jokers in each) in a time of 30 seconds on the set of *Guinness World Records: Primetime* in Los Angeles, California, USA, on December 21, 2000.

**Heaviest weight pulled with the teeth** Walter Arfeuille (Belgium) used his teeth to pull eight railway carriages, with a total weight of 493,570 lb. (223.8 tonnes), a distance of 10 ft. 5 in. (3.2 m) along rails at Diksmuide, Belgium, on June 9, 1996.

**Most weight lifted with the ears, tongue, and nipples** The most weight simultaneously lifted using the ears, tongue, and nipples is 29 lb. 1.6 oz. (13.19 kg) by Joe Hermann (USA), a member of the Jim Rose Circus (USA). He successfully lifted two standard 2-lb. 4.8-oz. (1.04-kg) steam irons with his earlobes, picked up a 5-lb. (2.26-kg) car battery with his tongue, and supported the weight of a 15-lb. oz. (7.12-kg) cinderblock from his nipples on the set of *Guinness World Records: Primetime* in Los Angeles, California, USA, on September 25, 1998.

**Heaviest single plane pulled** David Huxley (Australia) pulled a Boeing 747-400 airplane weighing 412,264 lb. (187 tonnes) a distance of 298 ft. 6 in. (91 m) in 1 min. 27.7 sec. on October 15, 1997 at Sydney, Australia.

# MARATHON FEATS

**Longest singing marathon by an individual**  The longest continuous singing marathon by an individual is 24 hr. 4 min. by Cliff Lath (UK) at Barton Rovers Football Club, Luton, Bedfordshire, UK, on August 10–11, 2002. For each music marathon record, the attempt requires the player to perform a playlist of recognized pieces with a combined length of at least four hours, which can then be repeated.

**LONGEST ELVIS SINGING MARATHON**  The longest Elvis Presley singing marathon is 25 hr. 33 min. 30 sec. performed by Gary Jay (UK, pictured) at Planet Hollywood, London, UK, on October 8–9, 2002. A total of 408 Elvis numbers were sung, from a rolling playlist of 35 songs.

**Longest roller coaster marathon** Deguchi Manami and Ikegami Hiroto (both Japan) rode a roller coaster continuously for 35 hr. 30 min. from August 25 to 27, 2001 at Washuzan Highland theme park in Kurashiki, Japan. They completed 1,050 rounds of the 2,130-ft. (650-m) coaster. The hair-raising stunt was part of a competition to win a car, with the person remaining on the coaster the longest the winner. Eventually, because neither of the participants had eaten during their marathon, the organizers decided to end the event for health reasons and declared them both winners.

**Longest drumming marathon** Michael MacPherson (South Africa) played the drums for 50 hr. 30 min. from November 28 to 30, 2002 at the Shelly Centre, Shelly Beach, KwaZulu-Natal, South Africa.

**Longest keyboard marathon** On December 24–26, 2002 John Conte (USA) played the piano for 52 hr. 20 min. in Greenwich Village, New York, USA.

**Longest organ-playing marathon** On June 13–14, 2002 Matthew Penn (UK) played a church organ for 24 hr. 17 min. at the Holy Trinity Church, Stratford-upon-Avon, Warwickshire, UK.

**Longest tuba-playing marathon** The longest tuba marathon by an individual lasted for 24 hr. 8 min. and was achieved by Rodney Kenny (UK) on August 16–17, 2002 at The Salvation Army, Gosport, Hampshire, UK.

**Longest skiing marathon** The longest time spent skiing non-stop is 150 hr. 12 min. 44 sec. by Franz Frank (Austria) at Wagrain, Austria, between January 27 and February 2, 2002. During that time, Frank skied a combined distance of a staggering 1,031.2 miles (1,659.7 km) and a combined altitude of 1,318,034 ft. (401,737 m).

**Fastest marathon skipping** The fastest marathon run while skipping is 5 hr. 19 min. 14 sec. by Carlos Argüeta López (Guatemala) at the Los Angeles Marathon, California, USA, on March 5, 1995.

**Longest club DJ mixing session** The longest

**FASTEST ORANGE NOSE PUSH** Myles Anderson (UK) pushed an orange with his nose for 1 mile (1.6 km) in 1 hr. 14 min. from London Bridge to Bishopsgate, London, UK, on March 22, 2002.

club DJ mixing session is 74 hours by Martin Boss (USA) at Vinyl Frontier in Orlando, Florida, USA, on February 1–4, 2002.

**Longest TV-watching marathon** The record for the longest time spent watching television is 47 hr. 16 sec. and belongs to Steven Hayes, Adam King, Nick Tungatt and Sam Beatson (all UK), who continually watched TV on December 4–6, 2002 at Covent Garden, London, UK, and at The Printworks, Manchester, UK.

**Longest lecture** Dustin Buehler's (USA) lecture on "The History and Evolution of the American Presidency" at Willamette University, Salem, Oregon, USA, on April 25–27, 2003 lasted for a record 51 hrs. 44 min. 17 sec.

**Fastest coal bag carrying marathon** Brian Newton (UK) covered a distance of 26 miles 385 yd. (42.195 km) while carrying 112 lb. (50.8 kg) of household coal in an open bag in a time of 8 hr. 26 min. on May 27, 1983.

**Longest netball marathon** The longest endurance marathon for a game of netball is 54 hr. 15 min. by members of Castle View School, Canvey Island, Essex, UK, from March 22–24, 2002.

**Longest pool marathon** The longest pool marathon lasted 103 hr. 5 min. and was set by a team at the Prince of Wales pub, Bracknell, Berkshire, UK, from January 27 to 31, 2002. Team members were Dean Howell, Gary Lynn, Jon Moss, and Anthony McDonagh (all UK).

**Longest hula-hooping marathon** The longest recorded marathon for a single hoop is 72 hours by Kym Coberly (USA) in Denton, Texas, USA, on October 17–20, 1984.

**Longest reading aloud marathon** The longest reading aloud marathon is 53 hr. 2 min. and was set by a team of six people—Carlo Marzani, Ivana Albergo, Lorenzo Cantori, Graziano Ferrari, Giovanni Garau, and Paola Giovanazzi (all Italy) at the cultural center of Rovereto, Tento, Italy, from November 29 to December 2, 2002.

**Longest tattoo session** The longest tattoo session lasted for 33 hours and was completed by Chris Goodwill (UK), who tattooed Kevin Budden (UK) at the Electric Pencil Tattoo Studio, Plumstead, Greater London, UK, on April 12–13, 2003. Eight designs were tattooed onto Budden's body during the attempt.

**Longest softball marathon** The longest game of softball lasted 30 hr. 5 min. at Shelbyville softball complex, Indiana, USA, on September 14–15, 2002. The first pitch was thrown at 8:08 am on September 14, 2002, and the game ended at 2:13 pm the next day. Played between Bat-a-Ball-a-Harda and United Players, Bat-a-Ball-a-Harda won, with a score of 322 runs to 292.

**LONGEST MOVIE WATCHING MARATHON** An audience of 23 people (all South Africa) watched 32 films for 59 hr. 27 min. at an event at Northgate SterKinekor cinema, Johannesburg, South Africa, from August 26 to 28, 2002.

**Longest time spent living with scorpions** Kanchana Ketkaew (Thailand) lived in a glass room measuring 130 ft.$^2$ (12 m$^2$) that contained 3,000 scorpions for 32 days, from September 21 to October 23, 2002 at Royal Garden Plaza, Pattaya, Thailand. Over the course of the 32 days over 400 scorpions were born and 200 died, replaced by 400 more on the 19th day. Ketkaew was stung a total of nine times.

**Longest kiss** Louisa Almedovar and Rich Langley (both USA) kissed for a record 30 hr. 59 min. 27 sec. on December 5, 2001 at the television studios of *Ricki Lake,* New York City, USA.

**Longest water-skiing marathon** Ralph Hildebrand and Dave Phillips (both Canada) water-skied for 56 hr. 35 min. 3 sec. around Indian Arm at Rocky Point, BC, Canada, from June 9 to 12, 1994. They covered a distance of 1,337.46 miles (2,152.3 km) at an average speed of 30 mph (48 km/h).

# INSPIRING PEOPLE

**Longest period of incarceration for a country's future head of state** The former President of the Republic of South Africa, Nelson Rolihlahla Mandela, spent almost 27 years in prison in South Africa from 1964 until his release on February 11, 1990. He had been found guilty of sabotage and treason during the years of the government's apartheid system. Four years later, on May 10, 1994, he was elected State President of the Republic of South Africa—the first democratically elected President in South Africa's history.

**Longest serving 20th century British Prime Minister** Margaret Thatcher, now Baroness Thatcher (UK), was the longest-serving British Prime Minister of the 20th century. She was in office for 11 years 208 days from May 4, 1979 to November 28, 1990.

**Longest biography** The longest biography in publishing history is the ongoing biography of Winston Churchill (UK), begun by his son Randolph and continued by biographer Martin Gilbert (both UK). The book currently comprises eight volumes plus a total of 16 companion volumes, all containing around 10 million words.

**MOST PROLIFIC PAINTER** In a career that lasted 75 years, Pablo Diego José Francisco de Paula Juan Nepomuceno de los Remedios Crispin Cipriano de la Santisima Trinidad Ruiz y Picasso (Spain) was the most prolific of all professional painters. It has been estimated that he produced about 13,500 paintings and designs, 100,000 prints and engravings, 34,000 book illustrations, and 300 sculptures and ceramics. His oeuvre has been valued at $788 million (£500 million) and by May 1997, his works had been sold at auction 3,579 times.

**Most fire personnel lost in one incident** According to the International Association of Fire Fighters, the unprecedented tragedy of September 11, 2001 claimed the lives of 344 New York City fire personnel in just one incident. Their rescue efforts saved thousands of civilian lives. This was the largest single-event loss of life sustained by modern-day fire service personnel in war or peace times. In contrast, a total of 102 US fire fighters died nationwide in 2000. The most US fire fighters lost at once prior to September 11 was 24, during an incident that occurred over 100 years ago.

**Most money raised by an individual marathon runner** Retired advertising executive John Spurling (UK) raised a record £1.13 million ($1.87 million) for charity by running the London Marathon in London, UK, on April 18, 1999.

**Largest fundraising charity** For 10 consecutive years the Salvation Army, USA, has raised more funds annually than any other charity. In 2001 alone, the charity raised $1.39 billion (£889 million), down from $1.44 billion (£921 million) the previous year.

**Most artists saved** Varian Fry (USA), known as "The Artists' Schindler," journeyed from the USA to France in 1940 with a list of 200 prominent artists and intellectuals known to be in parts of Nazi-occupied Europe. He subsequently helped to save around 4,000 people from the Gestapo, among them some of the most famous cultural figures of our age, including Max Ernst (Germany), Marc Chagall (France), André Breton (France), and Nobel Prize-winning chemist Otto Meyerhof (Germany).

**Largest racial equality rally** On August 28, 1963 civil rights leader Martin Luther King, Jr. (USA) led more than 250,000 demonstrators in a march down the Mall in Washington, DC, USA. They gathered in front of the Lincoln Memorial to call for equal civil rights for all Americans, irrespective of race or color.

**Largest volunteer ambulance organization** Abdul Sattar Edhi (Pakistan) began his ambulance service in 1948, ferrying injured people to hospital in Karachi. Today, his radio-linked ambulance fleet is 500 vehicles strong and operates all over Pakistan, through $5 million (£3,050,000) funding raised annually. Edhi has also established 300 relief centers, three air ambulances, 24 hospitals, three drug rehabilitation centers, women's centers, free dispensaries, adoption programs, and soup kitchens that feed 100,000 people a month. He has paid for and supervised the training of 17,000 nurses. The ambulance service even picks up corpses, and the organization arranges Muslim burials. Edhi has not taken a holiday in 45 years.

**Most cash raised for charity by a sports event** The London Marathon, run annually since 1981 through the streets of London, UK, raises more money for charity than any other single sports event in the world. A record total of £31 million ($48.7 million) was raised in April 2002, the last year for which figures were calculated.

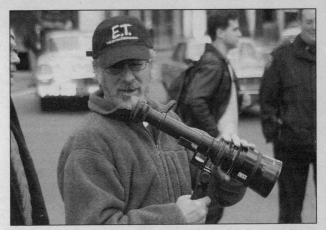

**MOST COMMERCIALLY SUCCESSFUL FILMMAKER** Three of Steven Spielberg's (USA) films are in the top 10 grossing movies of all time and have grossed $2.23 billion (£1.39 billion) in total. The films are: No. 3, *Jurassic Park* (USA, 1993) $920.1 million (£570 million; No. 7, *ET the Extra Terrestrial* (USA, 1982) $700.8 million (£434.1 million); No. 10, *Jurassic Park: The Lost World* (USA, 1997) $614.1 million (£380.4 million).

**Royal patron to the most charities** As of December 2000 Princess Anne, the Princess Royal (UK) was patron of a record 233 charity organizations. She is best known for her charity work with Save the Children UK, of which she has been president since 1970. She also heads her own Princess Royal Trust for Carers, which raises awareness of the UK's estimated six million caregivers.

**First power-driven flight** The first controlled and sustained power-driven flight occurred near the Kill Devil Hill, Kitty Hawk, North Carolina, USA, at 10:35 am on December 17, 1903. Orville Wright (USA) flew the 9-kW 12-hp chain-driven *Flyer I* for a distance of 120 ft. (36.5 m) at an airspeed of 30 mph (48 km/h), a ground speed of 6.8 mph (10.9 km/h), and an altitude of 8–12 ft. (2.5–3.5 m) for about 12 seconds. He was watched by his brother Wilbur and four other men. The *Flyer I* is now exhibited in the National Air and Space Museum at the Smithsonian Institution, Washington DC, USA.

**Most heavyweight world title recaptures** Three boxers have regained the heavyweight championship twice: Muhammad Ali (USA), Evander Holyfield (USA), and Lennox Lewis (UK). Ali first won the title on February 25, 1964, defeating Sonny Liston (USA). He defeated George Foreman (USA) on October 30, 1974, having been stripped of the title by the world boxing authorities on April 28, 1967, and won the WBA title from

**EARLIEST PERFUME LAUNCHED BY A COUTURIER** Fashion designer Gabrielle (Coco) Chanel (France), whose name became synonymous with elegance and chic, launched her Chanel No. 5 perfume in 1921. A designer ahead of her time, Chanel was always sharp and elegant. The clothes she designed transformed the way women looked and how they looked at themselves.

Leon Spinks (USA) on September 15, 1978, having previously lost to him on February 15, 1978.

**Most Oscars won in a lifetime** Walt Disney (USA) won more Oscars than any other person, with a record 26 awards from 64 nominations between 1932 and 1969. He won his first Oscar for a short cartoon entitled *Flowers and Trees* (USA, 1932).

**Most charts topped around the world with the same album** Since its release on November 13, 2000, the album entitled *1,* by the Beatles—a compilation of every No. 1 hit they ever had in the UK and the US—has topped the charts in 35 countries from Australia to Venezuela.

**Most Grammy awards won by a female artist** Aretha Franklin (USA) is the female recording artist to have won the most Grammys. She has won a total of 15 since receiving her first in 1967 for Best Female R&B Vocal Performance with "Respect." She won her 15th Grammy in 1988, for Best Female Soul Gospel Performance, with "One Lord, One Faith, One Baptism."

# COURAGE & ENDURANCE

**Deepest seawater dive** The deepest scuba dive was one of 1,010 ft. (307.8 m) made by John Bennett (UK) on November 6, 2001 off Escarcia Point, Puerto Galera, The Philippines. The descent, aided by a weighted sled, took just over 12 minutes. The ascent, however, took 9 hr. 36 min. to allow for decompression, and Bennett needed 60 oxygen tanks. At the bottom of the dive he lost his vision and experienced muscle spasms. The highest pressure on his body was 480 lb./in.$^2$ (3,309 kPa).

**Longest underwater scuba submergence in a controlled environment** The continuous duration record—with no rest breaks—for remaining underwater using breathing apparatus is 212 hr. 30 min. by Michael Stevens (UK) in a Royal Navy tank at the National Exhibition Centre, Birmingham, UK, on February 14–23, 1986.

**Longest open freshwater scuba dive** Jerry Hall (USA) spent 71 hr. 39 min. 40 sec. underwater on August 6–9, 2002 in South Holston Lake, Bristol, Tennessee, USA. Using scuba gear for his dive, Hall spent most of the time reclining on a wooden platform suspended by cables underwater.

**Deepest freshwater cave dive** On August 23, 1996, Nuno Gomes (South Africa) scuba-dived to a depth of 927 ft. 2 in. (282.6 m) at the Boesmansgat Cave, Northern Cape, South Africa.

**Longest distance by kite surfer** Neil Hutchinson, Kent Marincovik and Fabrice Collard (all USA) traveled a distance of 88 nautical miles (101.3 miles or 163 km) between Key West, Florida, USA, and Varadero, Cuba, on boards pulled by kites, on December 21, 2001. Their journey, during which they were not per-

**FASTEST ATLANTIC CROSSING BY AQUABIKE** Alvaro de Marichalar (Spain) crossed the Atlantic on an aquabike in 17 days 1 hr. 11 min., departing from Hierro, Canary Islands, Spain, on May 4 and reaching English Harbour Town, Antigua, on May 21, 2002.

mitted to touch any other vessel, lasted 8 hr. 38 min., and was completed at an average speed of 12 knots (14 mph or 22 km/h).

**Fastest solo row across the Atlantic** The fastest solo trans-Atlantic row, as recognized by the Ocean Rowing Society, is 46 days 4 hr. by Fyodor Konyukhov (Russia), who rowed from San Sebastian, Gomera, Canary Islands, Spain, to Port St. Charles, Barbados, from October 16 to December 1, 2002. The journey was made in the 22-ft. 7.2-in. (6.9-m) fiberglass *Uralaz,* which weighed 771 lb. (350 kg) empty and 1,433 lb. (650 kg) fully loaded. It had solar panels, a gas cooker, and navigation equipment.

**Fastest transatlantic row** In 1997, Phil Stubbs and Rob Hamill (both New Zealand) rowed across the Atlantic, from the Canary Islands to Barbados, in 41 days. Despite having to anchor for two days to ride out a 60-mph (96-km/h) storm, they beat the previous record, set in 1971 by Don and Geoff Allum (UK), by 32 days.

**Greatest distance by pedal boat** Kenichi Horie (Japan) crossed the Pacific Ocean by pedal boat, from Honolulu, Hawaii, USA, to Naha, Okinawa, Japan, from October 30, 1992 to February 17, 1993. He covered a record distance of 4,660 miles (7,500 km).

**Longest time adrift at sea** The longest known time that anyone has survived adrift at sea is approximately 484 days, by Japanese captain Oguri Jukichi and one of his sailors Otokichi. They were shipwrecked in a storm off the Japanese coast in October 1813 and drifted in the Pacific Ocean before being rescued by a US ship off California on March 24, 1815.

**Greatest distance covered in 24 hours by wheelchair** Rafael Emilio de León Lebrón (Dominican Republic) wheeled himself a distance of 112.5 miles (181.147 km) in 24 hours on December 13–14, 2001 at the Juan Pablo Duarte Centro Olímpico, Santo Domingo de Guzmá, Dominican Republic.

**Longest wheelie in a wheelchair** Robert Hensel (USA) traveled 6.178 miles (9.943 km) nonstop on the rear wheels of his wheelchair at Scriba, New York, USA, on October 3, 2002.

**Longest journey by wheelchair** Rick Hansen (Canada), who was paralyzed from the waist down in 1973 as a result of a car accident, wheeled his wheelchair 24,901.55 miles (40,075.16 km) through four continents and 34 countries. He started his journey from Vancouver, British Columbia, Canada, on March 21, 1985 and arrived back there on May 22, 1987.

**Fastest seven summit ascent** Andrew Salter (UK) climbed the highest peak on each continent in a record 288 days between May 16, 2000, when he reached the summit of Mt. Everest in Nepal (Asia), and February 27, 2001, when he climbed Aconcagua in Argentina (South America). He also scaled the Vinson Massif in Antarctica, Mt. McKinley in Alaska (North America),

Mt. Kilimanjaro in Tanzania (Africa), Puncak Jaya in Indonesia (Australasia), and Elbrus in Russia (Europe).

**Earliest ascent of Mt. Everest** The summit of the world's highest mountain Mt. Everest (29,029 ft. or 8,848 m) was first reached at 11:30 am on May 29, 1953 by Edmund Hillary (New Zealand), and Sherpa Tenzing Norgay (Nepal). The successful expedition was led by Col. (later Hon. Brigadier) Henry Cecil John Hunt (UK).

**Most conquests of Mt. Everest** Apa Sherpa (Nepal) completed his 13th successful climb of Mt. Everest on May 26, 2002.

**First solo ascent of Mt. Everest** Reinhold Messner (Italy) was the first person to successfully climb Mt. Everest solo, reaching the summit on August 20, 1980. It took him three days to make the ascent from his base camp at 21,325 ft. (6,500 m), and the climb was made all the more difficult by the fact that he did not use bottled oxygen.

**Fastest ascent of Mt. Everest** Lakpa Gelu Sherpa (Nepal) made a successful ascent of Mt. Everest in 10 hr. 56 min. 46 sec. on May 26, 2003, the fastest ever climb from base camp to the summit of the world's tallest mountain.

**Youngest person to climb Mt. Everest** Temba Tsheri Sherpa (Nepal) reached the summit of Mt. Everest on May 23, 2001, aged 16 years 7 days. He had attempted to climb Mt. Everest in 2000 at the age of 14, but had to turn back just 72 ft. (22 m) from the summit. He lost parts of several fingers to frostbite.

**Longest journey by skateboard** Jack Smith (USA) traveled just under 3,000 miles (4,830 km) on a skateboard from Lebanon, Oregon, to Williamsburg, Virginia, USA, in July 1976 and July 1984. The same journeys also broke the record for the fastest trans-America skateboard trip. The first trip took him 32 days, with two companions, and the second trip, made with three team members, took 26 days.

**FASTEST MOTORCYCLE CIRCUMNAVIGATION** Kevin Sanders, with his wife Julia (both UK) as a passenger, circumnavigated the world on a motorcycle in 19 days 8 hr. and 25 min. between May 11 and June 22, 2002. Guinness World Records no longer endorses such attempts.

**Fastest trans-USA journey on inline skates** Russell "Rusty" Moncrief (USA) crossed the USA on inline skates in 69 days 8 hr. 45 min. from January 5 to March 15, 2002. He skated from Crescent Beach, near Jacksonville, Florida, to Soltana Beach, near San Diego, California, covering 2,595 miles (4,175 km).

**Most crash tests** By February 2003 WR "Rusty" Haight (USA) had endured 718 collisions in cars as a "human crash test dummy," thanks to his work as a traffic collision reconstructionist.

**Fastest circumnavigation by car** The fastest circumnavigation of the world by car, under the rules applicable in 1989 and 1991, embracing more than an equator's length of driving (24,901 road miles or 40,075 km), is held by Mohammed Salahuddin Choudhury and his wife Neena (both India). The journey took 69 days 19 hrs. 5 min. from September 9 to November 17, 1989, starting and finishing in Delhi, India. Guinness World Records no longer endorses car circumnavigation attempts.

**Longest taxi ride** The longest taxi ride is a 21,691-mile (34,908-km) journey costing $63,500 (£40,210), when Jeremy Levine, Mark Aylett (both UK), and Carlos Arrese (Spain) went from London, UK, to Cape Town, South Africa, and back, from June 3 to October 17, 1994.

**Longest bicycle wheelie journey** Kurt Osburn (USA) traveled 2,839.6 miles (4,569 km) on his bicycle, doing a wheelie the whole way, from the Guinness World of Records Museum in Hollywood, California, to the Guinness World of Records Museum in Orlando, Florida, USA, between April 13, and June 25, 1999.

**Fastest trans-USA unicycle ride** Akira Matsushima (Japan) crossed America, from Newport, Oregon, to Washington, DC, by unicycle in a record 23 days, from July 10 to August 22, 1992.

**Highest altitude cycling** Siegfried Verheijke, Luc Belet (both Belgium) and Martin Adserballe (Denmark) rode mountain bikes at an altitude of 22,992 ft. (7,008 m) on the slopes of the Muztagata peak in China on August 11, 2000.

**Longest wind-powered land journey** Robert Torline (USA) traveled from Brownsville, Texas (on the Mexican border), to Maida, North Dakota (on the Canadian border), USA, covering 2,119 miles (3,410 km) on his wind-powered street sailer from April 29 to June 16, 2001.

# EPIC JOURNEYS

**FASTEST SOLO CROSSING OF ANTARCTICA** The fastest and first ever unaided solo crossing of the Antarctic continent was achieved by Borge Ousland (Norway), who completed the 1,671-mile (2,690-km) trek on January 18, 1997, 64 days after setting out on November 15, 1996. He dragged his 408-lb. (185-kg) supply sled from Berkner Island in the Weddell Sea to Scott Base in McMurdo Sound.

**LONGEST SOLO TREK ACROSS ANTARCTICA** Japanese adventurer Mitsuro Ohba (center) walked, skied, and parasailed a total of 2,376 miles (3,824 km) across the Antarctic continent in 99 days from November 9, 1998. Ohba began his trek on the South African side of continent and was aiming to reach Walgreen Coast, facing Chile, but he was picked up by plane when bad weather forced him to abandon his attempt 124 miles (200 km) short of his intended target.

**FASTEST SOLO TRANS-PACIFIC ROW** Jim Shekhdar (UK) rowed unaided across the Pacific Ocean in 273 days 13 hr. 12 min., beginning from Ilo in Peru on June 29, 2000, and ending near Brisbane, Australia, on March 30, 2001.

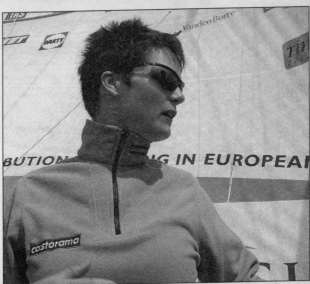

**FASTEST SOLO SAILING CIRCUMNAVIGATION BY A WOMAN** Ellen MacArthur (UK) circumnavigated the globe in 94 days 4 hr. 25 min. 40 sec., starting and finishing at Les Sables d'Olonne, France, from November 5, 2000 to February 11, 2001.

**LONGEST SUCCESSFUL SOLO BALLOON FLIGHT** On July 4, 2002, on completion of his 20,627-mile (33,195-km) solo circumnavigation of the Earth by balloon, Steve Fossett (USA) set the record for the longest successful solo balloon flight.

**YOUNGEST SOLO TRANS-ATLANTIC SAILOR** Sebastian Clover (UK) sailed across the Atlantic Ocean singlehandedly from Santa Cruz de Tenerife, Canary Islands, Spain, to English Harbour, Antigua & Barbuda, at the age of 15 years 362 days, from December 19, 2002 to January 12, 2003.

**YOUNGEST PERSON TO CYCLE THE PAN-AM HIGHWAY** Emmanuel Gentinetta (USA), was 18 years 266 days old when he completed his solo cycle journey of the Pan-American Highway from Prudhoe Bay, Alaska, to Bahia Lapataia, Tierra del Fuego, Argentina, from June 23, 1999 to March 9, 2000. The trip took 261 days and covered some 15,234 miles (24,516 km).

**FIRST SUCCESSFUL MT. EVEREST ASCENT** At 11:30 am on May 29, 1953 Edmund Hillary (New Zealand, left) and Sherpa Tenzing Norgay (Nepal, right) became the first people to reach the summit of Mt. Everest.

# FACT

**DID YOU KNOW . . . ?**
That the Earth is not perfectly round? It is actually slightly flatter at the poles and bulges at the Equator, the result of the planet spinning on its own axis. So if it were possible to walk around the Earth in a straight line, circumnavigators would be better off walking pole-to-pole rather than following the Equator, because the Earth's equatorial circumference is 82.6 miles (1.33 km) greater than its polar circumference.

# NATURAL
# WORLD

# THE EARTH

**Oldest volcanic rocks on earth** Volcanic rocks dated at 3,825 billion years have been discovered in the Inukjuak area in the northern reaches of Quebec, Canada. The precise dating of the rocks was performed by the University of Quebec, Montreal, Canada, and the Simon Fraser University in British Columbia, Canada, in 2002.

**Earliest evidence for plate tectonics** On July 8, 2002 a team of Chinese and US scientists announced their discovery of rocks indicating that plate tectonics were active on Earth some 2.5 billion years ago. This is 500 million years earlier than previously thought. The evidence comes from a belt of rock not far from the Great Wall of China at Dongwanzi, Hebei. The 2.5-billion-year-old rock contains chromite (iron chromium oxide), which is normally found only in rocks deep on the ocean floor.

**Largest continent ever** Over 250 million years ago all of today's continents were joined together as one "supercontinent," named Pangea (meaning "all lands" in Greek). However, around 180 million years ago, plate tectonics caused Pangea to slowly break apart, eventually resulting in the continents we know today. Evidence of Pangea can be seen by observing the way existing coastlines from different continents, such as Africa and South America, seem to fit together.

**LARGEST STEAM RINGS** The active volcano Mount Etna, in Sicily, Italy, is the tallest and most active in Europe. A complex physical process, thought to involve the unusual geometry of the shape of one of the volcano's vents, is causing the volcano to produce huge steam rings (pictured). The steam rings are around 650 ft. (200 m) across and can last for up to 10 minutes as they slowly drift upward to a height of 3,300 ft. (1,000 m) above the volcano.

**LARGEST GEOLOGICAL FEATURE DISCOVERED FROM SPACE** The
Richat Structure in the Sahara Desert of Mauritania is a multi-ringed
sedimentary basin around 30 miles (50 km) in diameter. Originally
thought to be an impact crater, it is now believed to be the eroded
remains of an uplifted sedimentary dome. This "bullseye" was
discovered from orbit by US astronauts Jim McDivitt and Ed White
during the *Gemini IV* mission in June 1965.

**Oldest confirmed impact on earth** On August 23, 2002 a team of US
scientists led by Gary Byerly and Donald Lowe announced their discovery of
a 3.47-billion-year-old asteroid impact on Earth. They had studied ancient
rock samples from Australia and South Africa and analyzed the spherules
contained within. These tiny particles are a common by-product of meteoritic
impact and were used to date the impact, along with local zircon crystals. The
8–12-in.-thick (20–30-cm) spherule beds in the rock indicate that the impact-
ing body had a rough diameter of 12 miles (20 km). However, no crater has
been found, as Earth's geological processes have had time to erase it.

**Fastest melting glacier** A volcanic eruption under Vatnajokul glacier in
Iceland (Europe's largest) in October 1996 topped Lake Grimsvotn with
meltwater. The meltwater flowed from the lake at an estimated 1.6 million
ft.²/sec. (45,000 m²/sec.), making it the greatest melting of a glacier in
recorded history.

**Largest single crystal on earth** The Earth's mostly iron spherical inner core is around 1,500 miles (2,400 km) across. At 9,000–11,000°F
(5,000–6,000°C) it is solid rather than liquid, due to the immense pressures
in the Earth's interior. Many geologists now believe that this gigantic ball of
iron is actually a single crystal. The core is about three-quarters the size of
the Moon and has a mass of around one hundred million million million
tons.

**Highest mountain** Mount Everest in the eastern Himalayas on the Tibet–Nepal border has a height of 29,028 ft. (8,848 m). It was officially recognized as the world's highest mountain in 1856, following surveys carried out by the Indian government. The mountain was named after Col. Sir George Everest (UK), Surveyor-General of India from 1830 to 1843.

**Largest doline** A doline is typically a funnel-shaped basin formed when limestone caves subside. Xio Zhai Tien (The Great Doline) is the largest doline in the world. Situated in the Sichuan region of central southern China, this huge depression measures 1,600 ft. (500 m) across and 2,100 ft. (660 m) deep.

**Largest active volcano** Mauna Loa, Hawaii, USA, which last erupted in 1984, rises 13,680 ft. (4,170 m) above sea level, has the shape of a broad, gentle dome, and is 75 miles (120 km) long and 31 miles (50 km) wide. It has a volume of 10,200 miles² (42,500 km²) of which 84.2% is below sea level. Its caldera (crater), Mokuaweoweo, measures 4 miles² (10.5 km²) and is 500–600 ft. (150–180 m) deep.

**Most active volcano** The world's most active volcano is Kilauea, in Hawaii, USA, which has erupted on a continuous basis since 1983 and is discharging lava at a rate of 176 ft.³ (5 m³) per second.

**LONGEST RIFT SYSTEM** The East African Rift System is approximately 4,000 miles (6,400 km) long with an average width of 30–40 miles (50–65 km). The escarpments around the edge of the valley have an average height of 2,000–3,000 ft. (600–900 m). The rift system begins in Jordan and extends southward to Mozambique in southern Africa. This extensive rift system has been gradually forming for around 30 million years, as the Arabian peninsula has separated from Africa.

**Greatest eruption volume** The total volume of matter discharged in the eruption of Tambora, a volcano on the Indonesian island of Sumbawa, between April 5 and 10, 1815, was estimated to be 36–43 miles$^2$ (150–180 km$^2$). This is the greatest known eruption volume from any volcano, comparing with a probable 14–16 miles$^3$ (60–65 km$^3$) ejected by Santorini (Greece) in 1628 B.C. and 5 miles$^3$ (20 km$^3$) ejected by Krakatoa (Indonesia) in 1883.

**Deepest lava cave** The deepest lava cave—an open tube down the inside of a solidified lava flow—is Kazumura Cave, on Hawaii, USA. It is 36.9 miles (59.3 km) long and descends 3,605 ft. (1,099 m) down the eastern flank of Kilauea volcano.

**Highest temperature in a fumerole** The highest temperature in a fumerole or smoke vent was 1,726°F (941°C) and was recorded in the hot dome (central section) of the Kudryavy volcano, Iturup, Kurile Islands, Russia, in 1996–97.

**Tallest granite monolith** El Capitan, in Yosemite National Park, California, USA, is 3,593 ft. (1,095 m) tall.

**Deepest valley** The Yarlung Zangbo valley in Tibet is 16,400 ft. (5,000 m) deep on average. Its deepest point has been measured at 17,657 ft. (5,382 m).

# WATER WORLD

**Deepest point in the ocean** The Marianas Trench in the Pacific Ocean was first pinpointed as the deepest part of the ocean in 1951 by HM Survey Ship *Challenger*. On January 23, 1960 the US Navy bathyscaphe *Trieste* descended to the bottom, and on March 24, 1995 the unmanned Japanese probe *Kaiko* also reached the bottom and recorded a depth of 35,797 ft. (10,911 m). This is the most accurate measurement to date.

**Fastest ocean current** During the monsoon season, the Somali current in the northern Indian Ocean flows at 9 mph (12.8 km/h).

**Largest continuous ocean current system** The thermohaline conveyor belt is a vast global system of ocean circulation, driven by differences in sea water density and salinity. It transports cold and salty deep water from the north Atlantic down to the Southern Ocean, where it travels east and north to the Indian and Pacific Oceans. Here it rises and becomes warm, traveling back westward where it sinks again in the north Atlantic. The entire cycle can last for a thousand years.

**Most southerly ocean** The most southerly part of the oceans is located at 87°S, 151°W, at the snout of the Scott Glacier, 200 miles (320 km) from the South Pole.

**LARGEST OCEAN** The Pacific Ocean is the largest ocean in the world. (Bora Bora Island, located in the Pacific, is pictured here). Excluding adjacent seas, the Pacific represents 45.9% of the world's oceans and covers an area of 64,186,000 miles$^2$ (166,241,700 km$^2$). The average depth is 12,925 ft. (3,940 m).

**Highest wave** The highest officially recorded ocean wave was calculated at 112 ft. (34 m) from trough to crest. It was measured by Lt. Frederic Margraff (USA) from the USS *Ramapo,* proceeding from Manila, Philippines, to San Diego, California, USA, on the night of February 6–7, 1933 during a hurricane that reached a speed of 68 knots (78 mph or 126 km/h).

**Largest bay** The world's largest bay by shoreline length is Hudson Bay in Canada, with 7,623 miles (12,268 km) of shoreline and an area of 476,000 miles$^2$ (1,233,000 km$^2$). Measured by area, the Bay of Bengal, in the Indian Ocean, is larger, at 839,000 miles$^2$ (2,172,000 km$^2$).

**Tallest hydrothermal vent** The tallest known hydrothermal vents on the ocean floor measure around 180 ft. (55 m) high. They were discovered by researchers from the Woods Hole Oceanographic Institution (USA) in December 2000. These vents, dubbed "The Lost City," are part of a system of hydrothermal vents on the mid-Atlantic Ridge, itself the largest system of vents discovered.

**Largest aquifer** The Great Artesian Basin underlies around one fifth of Australia. This huge underground water resource extends over 660,000 miles$^2$ (1,711,000 km$^2$) and has an estimated water storage volume of 64,900 million million liters (17,145 million million gal.). The basin, consisting of alternating layers of water-bearing sandstone and non-water-bearing siltstones and mudstones, was formed between 100 and 250 million years ago.

**Deepest brine pool** The Orca Basin in the Gulf of Mexico lies 7,200 ft. (2,200 m) below sea level. This 4-×13-mile (7-×21-km) depression is filled with water that has a salt content of 300 g per liter—around eight times saltier than the Gulf itself. Effectively a hypersaline lake at the bottom of the sea, its salinity is caused by salt leaching out of the salt deposits under the sediment on the ocean floor.

**Greatest submarine mountain range** The greatest of all mountain ranges is the submarine Mid-Ocean Ridge, which extends 40,000 miles (65,000 km) from the Arctic Ocean to the Atlantic Ocean, around Africa, Asia, and Australia, and under the Pacific Ocean to the west coast of North America. It has a maximum height of 13,800 ft. (4,200 m) above the base ocean depth.

**Largest sea cave** The Sea Lion Caves close to Florence on the Oregon coast, USA, have a chamber 310 ft. (95 m) long, 165 ft. (50 m) wide, and around 50 ft. (15 m) high, in a wave-cut passage 1,315 ft. (400 m) long.

**Largest lagoon** Lagoa dos Patos, located near the seashore in Rio Grande do Sul, southernmost Brazil, is 174 miles (280 km) long and extends over 3,803 miles$^2$ (9,850 km$^2$), separated from the Atlantic Ocean by long sand strips. It has a maximum width of 44 miles (70 km).

**Largest iceberg** The largest known tabular iceberg was over 12,000 miles$^2$ (31,000 km$^2$) in area. It was 208 miles (335 km) long and 60 miles (97 km) wide (larger than Belgium), and was sighted 150 miles (240 km) west of Scott Island, in the Southern Ocean, Antarctica, by the USS *Glacier* in November 1956.

**Largest subglacial lake** Lake Vostok in Antarctica was discovered in 1994 by

**HIGHEST OCEAN TEMPERATURE** The highest temperature ever recorded in an ocean is 759°F (404°C), measured above a hydrothermal vent some 300 miles (480 km) off the American west coast in 1985 (an example of a hydrothermal vent is pictured here). The record temperature was measured by an American research submarine examining these largely unexplored ocean features.

**LARGEST ATOLL** The atoll with the largest land area is Christmas Atoll (pictured), in the Line Islands in the central Pacific Ocean. It has an area of 251 miles$^2$ (649 km$^2$), of which 124 miles$^2$ (321 km$^2$) is land.

The world's largest atoll is Kwajalein in the Marshall Islands, in the central Pacific Ocean. Its slender 176-mile (283-km) long coral reef encloses a lagoon of 1,100 miles$^2$ (2,850 km$^2$).

analyzing radar imagery of the icy continent. Buried under 2.5 miles (4 km) of the East Antarctic Ice Sheet, it is the most pristine lake on Earth, having been completely isolated from the rest of the world for at least 500,000 years and perhaps much longer. With an area of some 5,400 miles$^2$ (14,000 km$^2$), it is the world's 18th-largest lake and has a depth of at least 330 ft. (100 m).

**Largest freshwater lake by volume** The freshwater lake with the greatest volume is Lake Baikal in Siberia, Russia, with an estimated volume of 5,500 miles$^3$ (23,000 km$^3$). With a maximum depth of 5,371 ft. (1,637 m), Lake Baikal is also the world's deepest lake. It contains one-fifth of all the world's fresh surface water.

**Largest lake** The largest inland sea or lake is the Caspian Sea in Azerbaijan, Russia, Kazakhstan, Turkmenistan and Iran. It is 760 miles (1,225 km) long and has a total area of 143,550 miles$^2$ (371,800 km$^2$). Of its total area, 38.5% (55,280 miles$^2$ or 143,200 km$^2$) is in Iran. Its maximum depth is 3,360 ft. (1,025 m), and the surface is 93 ft. (28.5 m) below sea level.

**Largest underground lake** The largest underground lake is that in the Drachenhauchloch (Dragon's Breath) cave near Grootfontein, Namibia, discovered in 1986. When surveyed in April 1991 the surface area was found to be 6.45 acres (2.61 ha). The surface is some 217 ft. (66 m) underground, and the lake has a depth of 276 ft. (84 m).

**Saltiest lake**  Don Juan Pond in Wright Valley, Antarctica, is so salty that it remains liquid even at temperatures as low as -63.4°F (-53°C). The percentage of salt by weight is 40.2%, compared to 23.1% and 3.38% for the Dead Sea and the world's oceans respectively.

**Largest lake in a lake**  The largest lake in a lake is Manitou Lake, with an area of 41 miles² (106 km²). It is found on the world's largest lake island, Manitoulin Island (with an area of 1,068 miles² or 2,766 km²), in the Canadian part of Lake Huron.

**Greatest river flow**  The Amazon in South America discharges an average of 7,100,000 ft.³/sec. (200,000 m³/sec.) into the Atlantic Ocean, increasing to more than 12,000,000 ft.³/sec. (340,000 m³/sec.) in full flood. The lower 900 miles (1,450 km) averages 55 ft. (17 m) in depth, but the river has a maximum depth of 407 ft. (124 m). Although it is shorter than the Nile, its flow is 60 times greater.

**Longest river**  The Nile is credited as the world's longest river. Its main source is Lake Victoria in East Africa. From its farthest stream in Burundi, it extends 4,160 miles (6,695 km) in length.

# WEIRD PLANTS

**Tallest living tree**  The world's tallest living tree is the "Stratosphere Giant," which measured 369 ft. 4.8 in. (112.6 m) in 2002. This coast redwood (*Sequoia sempervirens*) was discovered by Chris Atkins (USA) in August 2000 in the Rockefeller Forest of the Humboldt Redwoods State Park, California, USA.

**Largest living tree**  The world's largest living tree is "General Sherman," a giant sequoia (*Sequoiadendron giganteum*) growing in the Sequoia National Park, California, USA. It stands 271 ft. (82.6 m) tall, has a diameter of 27 ft. 2 in. (8.2 m), and a circumference of 85 ft. (25.9 m). The trunk had a volume of 52,508 ft.³ (1,487 m³) in 1980 when it was last measured accurately, but it is now thought to be almost 53,000 ft.³ (1,500 m³). The tree is estimated to contain the equivalent of 630,096 board feet of lumber—enough to make over five billion matches—and its red-brown bark is up to 24 in. (61 cm) thick in parts. The tree's weight, including its vast root system, is estimated to be 4,000,000 lb. (2,000 tonnes). "General Sherman" is thought to be 2,100 years old.

**Largest tree ever**  The world's largest ever tree was the "Lindsey Creek Tree," a coast redwood (*Sequoia sempervirens*) that grew in California, USA, until it was blown over in a storm in 1905. The tree had a total mass of 6,000,000 lb. (2,720 tonnes).

**LARGEST SEED** The largest seed in the world is that of the giant fan palm, (*Lodoicea maldivica*)—commonly known as the double coconut or coco de mer—found wild only on the Seychelle islands in the Indian Ocean. The single-seeded fruit weighs up to 44 lb. (20 kg), can be larger than a basketball, and take 10 years to develop. The seeds grow on the palm until they are too heavy, when they fall to the ground.

**Living tree with the greatest girth** The living tree with the greatest circumference (girth) is "El Arbol del Tule," in Oaxaca state, Mexico. This Montezuma cypress (*Taxodium mucronatum*) was last measured in 1998, and was 137 ft. (42 m) tall, had a diameter of 38 ft. (11.5 m), and a girth of 119 ft. (36 m), taken at 5 ft. (1.5 m) above the ground.

**Most massive plant** The world's most massive plant was reported in December 1992 to be a network of quaking aspen trees (*Populus tremuloides*) growing in the Wasatch Mountains, Utah, USA, from a single root system covering 106 acres (43 ha) and weighing an estimated 13,227,720 lb. (6,000 tonnes). This network of trees (belonging to the willow family) is a genetically uniform clonal system and acts as a single organism, with all the component trees changing color or shedding leaves in unison.

**Heaviest pine cone** The heaviest pine cones belong to the Coulter pine (*Pinus coulteri*) of North America. The average weight of the cones, when green, is 1–5 lb. (0.4–2.2 kg). However, the heaviest recorded weighed 9 lb. (4 kg).

**Largest leaf** The largest leaves of any plant are those of the raffia palm (*Raphia farinifera*) of the Mascarene Islands in the Indian Ocean, and the Amazonian bamboo palm (*Raphia taedigera*) of South America and Africa. The leaf blades on each of these plants can measure 65 ft. 7 in. (20 m) long, with petioles (the stalk by which a leaf is attached to a plant) measuring up to 13 ft. (4 m).

**Fastest growing plant** The world record for the fastest growing plant belongs to certain species of the 45 genera of bamboo, which can grow at up to 35 in. (91 cm) per day.

**Fastest growing flowering plant** The world's fastest growing flowering plant is a *Hesperoyucca whipplei* of the Liliaceae family, which had grown 11 ft. 11 in. (3.65 m) in 14 days or about 10 in. (25.4 cm) per day. This was reported by people from Tresco Abbey, Isles of Scilly, Cornwall, UK, in July 1978.

**Slowest flowering plant** The slowest flowering plant is the rare *Puya raimondii,* the largest of all herbs, discovered at a height of 12,992 ft. (3,960 m) in Bolivia in 1870. The flowering parts of the plant emerge after about 80–150 years of the plant's life; the plant then dies. One specimen planted near sea level at the University of California's Botanical Garden, Berkeley, USA, in 1958 grew to 24 ft. 11 in. (7.6 m) and bloomed in 1986, after only 28 years.

**Longest distance traveled by a drift seed** The record for the longest distance traveled by a drift seed belongs to Mary's bean (*Merremia discoidesperma*). It has the widest documented drift range for any seed or tropical fruit, traveling over 15,000 miles (24,140 km) from the Marshall Islands in the north Pacific Ocean to the beaches of Norway on the northern Atlantic Ocean. The bean can be traced along this distance as it comes only from a few locations in the Pacific.

**Deepest living plant** The greatest depth at which plant life has been found is 882 ft. (269 m) for algae found by Mark and Diane Littler (both USA) off San Salvador Island, Bahamas, in October 1984. The maroon-colored plants survived even though 99.9995% of sunlight was filtered out.

**Oldest plant clone** Clonal plants flower but do not produce any seeds. They spread by dropping parts of their branches, which take root and form new plants that are genetically identical to the parent plant. The oldest known colony of genetically identical plants is one of King's holly (*Lomatia tasmanica*) which was found in Tasmania's (Australia) southwestern wilderness region and is believed to be over 43,000 years old.

**LARGEST PREY CONSUMED BY A CARNIVOROUS PLANT** Of all the carnivorous plants, the ones that consume the largest prey are the pitcher plants of the Nepenthaceae family (genus *Nepenthes,* shown here). Both the *Nepenthes rajah* and *Nepenthes rafflesiana* have been known to digest frogs, birds, and rats. These species are commonly found in the rainforests of Asia, particularly in Borneo, Indonesia, and Malaysia.

**Oldest tree clone** The world's oldest colony of genetically identical trees is the stand of Huon pines (*Lagarostrobus franklinii*) on the west coast of Tasmania, Australia. The stand is believed to have developed from an original tree 10,500 years old, but no individual tree is that age.

**Oldest living individual tree** The oldest living individual tree is the ancient bristlecone pine (*Pinus longaeva*) "Methuselah," which is 4,767 years

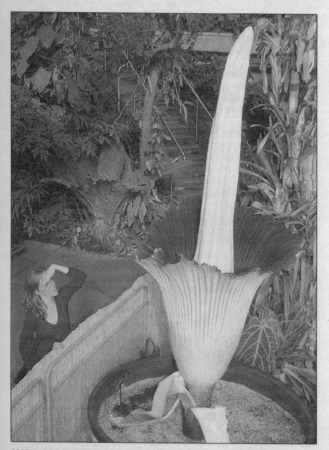

**SMELLIEST FLOWER** Commonly known as the corpse flower, *Amorphophallus titanum* (pictured) is the smelliest flower on Earth. When it blooms it releases a foul odor similar to that of rotten flesh and can be smelled half a mile away.

old. It was found by Edmund Schulman (USA) in the White Mountains, California, USA, and dated in 1957.

**Highest tree ring count** The highest actual ring count made on any tree is held by "Eon Tree," a redwood that fell in a storm in the USA in late 1977. Ron Hildebrant (USA) counted 7,223 annual rings at 140 ft. (42.6 m) above the base. The age of the tree is estimated to be over 9,000 years old.

**Earliest surviving tree species** The oldest surviving species of tree is the maidenhair (*Ginkgo biloba*) of Zhejiang, China, which first appeared about 160 million years ago. It was rediscovered by Engelbert Kaempfer (Germany) in 1690, but has been grown in Japan since c. 1100, where it is known as *ichou*.

**Most poisonous common plant** Based on the amount it takes to kill a human, the most poisonous common plant in the world is the castor bean (*Ricinus communis*). According to the *Merck Index: An Encyclopedia of Chemicals, Drugs, and Biologicals* (1997) a dose of 2 millionths of an ounce (70 micrograms) is enough to kill a person weighing 160 lb. (72 kg or 11 st. 4 lb.). The plant's poison is called ricin and is a protein found in the seeds of the castor bean.

**Most poisonous fungi** The world's most poisonous fungi is the death cap (*Amanita phalloides*), which can be found worldwide, including North America and the UK. It is responsible for 90% of all fatal poisonings caused by fungi. Cooking does nothing to neutralize the poisonous chemicals in this fungus. If eaten, it destroys the liver and kidneys. Symptoms begin to occur between six and 15 hours after eating. The effects are vomiting, delirium, collapse, and death.

# GARDEN WONDERS

**Longest beetroot** The world's longest beetroot measured 18 ft. 0.6 in. (5.504 m). Peter Glazebrook (UK) presented his winning beetroot at the UK National Giant Vegetables Championship 2002, Shepton Mallet, Somerset, UK, on September 6, 2002.

**Largest bunch of bananas** The largest bunch of bananas, containing 473 individual bananas, was grown by Kabana SA and Tecorone SL (Spain) on the island of El Hierro, Canary Islands, Spain, and weighed 287 lb. (130 kg) on July 11, 2001.

**Largest cantaloupe** A cantaloupe weighing 63 lb. 8 oz. (28.8 kg) with a circumference of 45 in. (114 cm) and a length of 21 in. (53 cm) was grown by Bill Rogerson (USA) of Robersonville, North Carolina, USA, in 1997.

**LARGEST PUMPKIN** The largest pumpkin weighed 1,337 lb. 9 oz. (606.7 kg) at the pumpkin weigh-off at Topsfield Fair, Massachusetts, USA, on October 5, 2002. It was grown by Charles Houghton (USA, pictured) and later carved into this Halloween image by Scott Cully (USA).

**Tallest umbrella plant** The world's tallest umbrella plant (*Schefflera arboricola*) measured 27 ft. (8.22 m) on January 4, 2002. It is currently growing inside Konsta's Restaurant, Richmond, Virginia, USA, which is owned and managed by Konstantinos Xytakis and Sara Guterbock (both USA).

**Most heads on one sunflower plant** The world record for most heads on one sunflower plant (*Helianthus*) is 837. The sunflower plant was grown by Melvin Hemker (USA) on his farm in St. Charles, Michigan, USA, and the heads were counted on September 18, 2001.

**Largest sunflower head** A sunflower (*Helianthus*) with a diameter of 32 in. (82 cm) was grown by Emily Martin of Maple Ridge, British Columbia, Canada, in 1983.

**Tallest sunflower** In 1986 M. Heijms (Netherlands) grew a sunflower (*Helianthus*) that reached a record height of 25 ft. 5.4 in. (7.76 m).

**Largest rose bush** A specimen of the rose bush Lady Banks (*Rosa banksiae*), at Tombstone, Arizona, USA, has a trunk circumference of 13 ft. 6 in. (4.09 m), stands around 9 ft. (2.75 m) high, and covers an area of 8,000 ft² (743 m²).

**Longest carrot** Bernard Lavery (UK) grew a 132-in. (335-cm) carrot in 1987. Internationally famous, Dr. Lavery has held 26 world records for his out-sized plants and vegetables.

**Longest corncob** A corncob grown by Bernard Lavery of Llanharry, Rhondda Cynon Taff, UK, in 1994 measured 36.25 in. (92 cm) in length.

**Tallest runner bean plant** In 1992 Bernard Lavery (UK) grew a 35-ft. (10.7-m) bean plant (*Phaseolus vulgaris*).

**Largest kohlrabi** The largest kohlrabi was grown by Scott Robb (USA) and weighed 43 lb. 11 oz. (19.8 kg) at the Alaska State Fair, Palmer, Alaska, USA, on August 29, 2001. The kohlrabi was a giant winter kohlrabi (*Brassica oleracea*). Robb has also broken the world record for the heaviest rutabaga (swede).

**Longest cucumber** The world's longest cucumber measured 43.5 in. (1.1 m) and was grown by A.C. Rayment of Chelmsford, Essex, UK, in 1986.

**Longest parsnip** A 16-ft. 4.5-in.-long (5-m) parsnip was grown by Peter Glazebrook (UK). He presented the parsnip at the UK National Amateur Gardening Show Giant Vegetable Championship, held on September 1, 2000.

**Largest gourd** Robert Weber (Australia) grew a gourd 70 in. (177 cm) in circumference and presented it at the Australisian Giant Pumpkin and Vegetable Competition in Victoria, Australia, on April 7, 2001.

**HEAVIEST LEEK The world's heaviest leek weighed 17 lb. 13 oz. (8.1 kg). Grown by Fred Charlton (UK), it was entered in the UK National Giant Vegetable Championship 2002, in Shepton Mallet, Somerset, UK, on September 6, 2002.**

**Tree bearing the most different fruit** The greatest number of different fruits produced from the same tree is five: apricot, cherry, nectarine, plum, and peach. The fruit species were grafted onto a prune tree in 2000 by Luis H. Carrasco E of Lo Barnechea, Santiago, Chile.

**Tallest fuchsia** A fuchsia (*Begonia fuchsioides*) grown by Bernard Lavery (UK) in 1995 grew to a height of 13 ft. 9 in. (4.2 m).

**Rose with the most blooms** A "Cecile Brunner" rose (family *Rosaceae*) with 5,470 blooms was grown by Clifton Martin of Merrylands, New South Wales, Australia, in 1982.

**Tallest hollyhock** A hollyhock (*Alcea rosea*) 19 ft. 7 in. (5.97 m) in height was grown by George Palmer (UK) in 1978.

**Tallest daffodil** A daffodil (*Narcissus*) grown by M. Lowe of Chessell (UK) in 1979 reached a height of 5 ft. 1 in. (1.55 m).

**Tallest home-grown cactus** The tallest home-grown cactus (*Cereus uruguayanus*) measured 60 ft. (18.2 m) on December 10, 2002 and was grown by Pandit Munji in Dharwad, Karnataka, India.

**Tallest orchid** A height of 49 ft. (15 m) has been recorded for the orchid *Galeola foliata*, a saprophyte of the vanilla family that grows in the decaying rain forests of Queensland, Australia. It is not free-standing but is supported by other trees in the rain forest.

**Tallest geranium** A geranium (*Pelargonium x hortorum*) grown by B. Tournebize of Puy-de-Dôme, France, grew to a height of 20 ft. (6.1 m).

**Tallest rose bush** The world's tallest rose bush (family *Rosaceae*) measured 11 ft. 1 in. (3.38 m) on January 29, 2003 and grows in the garden of Kathleen Mielke-Villalobos (USA), who lives in San Diego, California, USA.

**LONGEST ZUCCHINI** The world's longest zucchini measured 53 in. (1.34 m) on October 1, 2002. It was grown by Sher Singh Kanwal (USA) at his home in Niagara Falls, New York, USA.

**Most leaves on a clover** A red clover *(Trifolium pratense)* with a record 14 leaves was reported by Paul Haizlip (USA) at Bellevue, Washington, USA, on June 22, 1987. Another record-breaking 14-leafed clover, this time a white one *(Trifolium repens),* was found by Randy Farland (USA) near Sioux Falls, South Dakota, USA, on June 16, 1975.

**Largest grape vine** As of December 2002 the "Great Vine" at Hampton Court Palace, Greater London, UK, had a record circumference of 9 ft. 10 in. (3 m) and branches up to 108 ft. 3 in. (33 m) long. Planted in 1768, the "Great Vine" produces an average yield of 703 lb. (318.8 kg) of grapes every year.

## ★ HEAVIEST FRUITS & VEGETABLES ★

| FRUIT/ VEGETABLE | WEIGHT | NAME AND VENUE | DATE |
|---|---|---|---|
| Apple | 3 lb. 8 oz. (1.67 kg) | Alan Smith, Laddington Farm, Linton, Kent, UK | 1997 |
| Beetroot | 51 lb. 9.4 oz. (23.4 kg) | Ian Neale, National Giant Vegetable Championship, Shepton Mallet, Somerset, UK | 2001 |
| Broccoli | 35 lb. (15.87 kg) | John and Mary Evans, Palmer, Alaska, USA | 1993 |
| Brussels sprout | 18 lb. 3 oz. (8.3 kg) | Bernard Lavery, Llanharry, UK | 1992 |
| Cabbage | 124 lb. (56.24 kg) | Bernard Lavery, Llanharry, UK | 1989 |
| Celery | 52 lb. 7.5 oz. (23.8 kg) | Ian Neale, Abertysswg, Mid Glamorgan, UK | 2001 |
| Garlic | 2 lb. 10 oz. (1.19 kg) | Robert Kirkpatrick, Eureka, California, USA | 1985 |
| Grapefruit | 6 lb. 12 oz. (3.065 kg) | Debbie Hazelton, Queensland, Australia | 1995 |
| Lemon | 8 lb. 8 oz. (3.88 kg) | Donald and Charlotte Knutzen, California, USA | 1983 |
| Mango | 4 lb. 4 oz. (1.94 kg) | John Painter, Bokeelia, Florida, USA | 1999 |
| Marrow (squash) | 135 lb. (61.23 kg) | John Handbury, Temple Normanton, Chesterfield, UK | 1998 |
| Onion | 15 lb. 7.9 oz. (7.03 kg) | M. Ednie, Anstruther, Fife, UK | 1997 |
| Parsnip | 5 lb. 13.5 oz. (2.56 kg) | Barry Micklethwaite, Barnsley, South Yorkshire, UK | 2000 |
| Peach | 25.6 oz. (725 g) | Paul Friday, Michigan, USA | 2002 |
| Pineapple | 17 lb. 12 oz. (8.06 kg) | E. Kamuk, Ais Village, Papua New Guinea | 1994 |
| Potato | 7 lb. 13 oz. (3.5 kg) | K. Sloane, Patrick, Isle of Man, UK | 1994 |

*cont. next page*

| Quince | 5 lb. 2 oz. (2.34 kg) | Edward Harold McKinney, Alabama, USA | 2002 |
| Radish | 68 lb. 9 oz. (31.1 kg) | Manabu Oono, Kagoshima, Japan | 2003 |
| Rhubarb | 5 lb. 14 oz. (2.67 kg) | E. Stone, East Woodyates, Wiltshire, UK | 1985 |
| Squash | 962 lb. (436 kg) | Steve Hoult, Ontario, Canada | 1997 |
| Strawberry | 8.17 oz. (231 g) | G. Andersen, Folkestone, Kent, UK | 1983 |
| Swede (rutabaga) | 75 lb. 12 oz. (34.35 kg) | Scott Robb, Palmer, Alaska, USA | 1999 |
| Sweet potato | 49 lb. 9 oz. (22.5 kg) | Belinda Love, Gingin, Western Australia | 1998 |
| Tomato | 7 lb. 12 oz. (3.51 kg) | G. Graham, Edmond, Oklahoma, USA | 1986 |
| Watermelon | 262 lb. (118.84 kg) | B. Carson Arrington, Tennessee, USA | 1990 |

# MAMMALS

**LARGEST HERD** The largest herds on record are those of the springbok (*Antidorcas marsupialis*) during migration across the plains of the western parts of southern Africa in the 19th century. A mass migration of the springbok was observed in 1849. It was said to have taken three days for the animals to pass through the settlement of Beaufort West, Western Cape, South Africa.

**ONLY TRANSIENT MASCULINIZATION** The only female mammal that temporarily changes sex is the juvenile female fossa (*Cryptoprocta ferox*) of Madagascar. Research from Aberdeen University (UK) discovered that young female fossas have a protrusion resembling male genitalia but outgrow this state as adults, when ready to mate and raise young.

**LARGEST CARNIVORE ON LAND** The largest of all the carnivores is the polar bear (*Ursus maritimus*). Adult males typically weigh 880–1,320 lb. (400–600 kg), and have a nose-to-tail length of 7 ft. 10 in.–8 ft. 6 in. (2.4–2.6 m).

**LONGEST TONGUE** South America's giant anteater (*Myrmecophaga tridactyla*) has the longest tongue on a mammal relative to its body size. With an average body length of 3–6 ft. (1–2 m), its tongue typically measures 23 in. (60 cm) long.

**MOST EFFICIENT SCAVENGER**
The spotted hyena (*Crocuta crocuta*) utilizes the carcasses of its prey more efficiently than any other carnivore. It is the only animal with a digestive system that can break down bones, hooves, horns, and hides.

**LONGEST GESTATION** The Asiatic or Indian elephant (*Elephas maximus*) has an average gestation period of one year nine months and a maximum of two years one month—over twice that of a human pregnancy.

**Mammals**

**LARGEST MAMMAL TO BUILD A NEST** The 385-lb. (175-kg) European wild boar (*Sus scrofa*) has such small piglets that the mother builds a nest to protect them from predators.

**FASTEST HEARTBEAT** The shrew (family Soricidae pictured) has the fastest heartbeat of any mammal, with a rate of 1,200 beats per minute, which is similar to that of a hummingbird when hovering.

**HIGHEST FREQUENCY HEARING** Bats (family Vespertilionidae shown here) have the most acute hearing of any land animal, using frequencies in the 20–80 kHz range, compared with 20 kHz for humans.

**LARGEST COLONY OF MAMMALS** A colony of black-tailed prairie dogs (*Cynomys ludovicianus*) discovered in 1901 contained around 400 million individuals and was estimated to cover 23,700 miles² (61,400 km²).

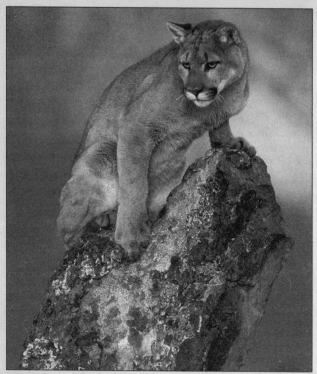

**MOST NAMES** Because of its wide distribution across North and South America, the mammal with the highest number of different names is the puma (*Puma concolor*). In the English language alone, it has over 40, including cougar, mountain lion, red tiger, catamount, and Florida panther.

# PETS & DOMESTIC ANIMALS

**Tallest dog** Harvey, a Great Dane born in 1993 and owned by Charles Dodman of Marford, Clwyd, UK, stands at 41.5 in. (105.4 cm) tall, as measured from ground to the top of the shoulder. The Great Dane is one of the tallest of the working dog breeds, yet the average Great Dane stands around 29.5 in. (75 cm) tall. Harvey is also the longest dog alive, measuring 7 ft. 5 in. (231.14 cm) from nose to tail tip. He weighs 197 lb. (88.45 kg) and eats 7 lb. 14 oz. (3.6 kg) of food daily.

Harvey shares the tallest dog record with Shamgret Danzas, a Great Dane owned by Wendy and Keith Comley of Milton Keynes, Buckinghamshire, UK. Their dog also stood 41.5 in. (105.4 cm) tall. Shamgret Danzas died on October 16, 1984.

**Oldest dog** The world's oldest living dog is Butch, a 27-year-old beagle. Butch was bought in 1975 as a puppy and is owned by Gregory Duncan of Keswick, Virginia, USA.

Most dogs live for 8–15 years but the greatest reliable age recorded for a dog is 29 years 5 months for an Australian cattle dog named Bluey, owned by Les Hall of Rochester, Victoria, Australia. Bluey was bought as a puppy in 1910 and worked among cattle and sheep for nearly 20 years before retiring. He finally passed away on November 14, 1939.

**Smallest dog** The world's smallest living dog is Whitney, a Yorkshire terrier who measured 3 in. (7.6 cm) to the shoulder and 9.5 in. (24.1 cm) from nose to tail-tip on November 26, 2002. Whitney is owned by Christopher and Patricia Sheridan of Shoeburyness, Essex, UK. The smallest dog ever on record is a fist-sized, dwarf Yorkshire terrier owned by Arthur Marples of Blackburn, Lancashire, UK. When fully grown, this tiny dog stood 2.8 in. (7.11 cm) at the shoulder and measured 3.75 in. (9.5 cm) from the tip of its nose to the tip of its tail. The dog died in 1945, just before its second birthday.

**Oldest dog breed** The world's oldest known breed of domesticated dog is the saluki, believed to have emerged in 329 B.C. Saluki dogs were revered in ancient Egypt, and they were kept as royal pets.

**LONGEST GOAT HORNS** The world's longest goat horns were measured tip-to-tip at 3 ft. 6 in. (1.09 m) on April 9, 2002. They belong to a goat owned by Amilcar Reis Mendes (Portugal), who lives in Casal Branco, Ourém, Portugal.

**Longest eyelashes on a dog** The longest eyelashes ever measured on a dog were 3.5 in. (9 cm) long on April 27, 2002, and belong to Borders, a Lhasa apso owned by Angela Barrett of Belleville, Ontario, Canada.

**Longest dog swim** On September 2, 1995, two black Labradors named Kai and Gypsy swam the "Maui Channel Swim" from Lanai to Maui Island, in Hawaii, USA—a distance of 9.5 miles (15.2 km). The swim took 6 hr. 3 min. 42 sec., and owner Steve Fisher (USA) swam along aside them.

**Deepest scuba dive by a dog** Dwane Folsom (USA) regularly takes his dog, Shadow, a black mongrel (half retriever, half Labrador) scuba diving off the coast of Grand Cayman Island. The deepest the pair usually go is approximately 13 ft. (4 m). When diving, Shadow wears a specially adapted diving suit made up of a helmet, weighted dog jacket, and breathing tube, which is connected to his owner's air tank.

**Highest jump by a guinea pig** The world record for the guinea pig high-jump belongs to Puckel Martin, who jumped 7.8 in. (20 cm) on March 16, 2003. Puckel Martin is owned by Madde Herrman (Sweden) of Vargön, Sweden.

**Highest jump by a rabbit** The world record for the highest rabbit jump is 18 in. (46 cm) and was achieved by Golden Flame on August 29, 2002. Golden Flame is a three-year-old castor satin rabbit belonging to Sam Lawrie of Lavant, West Sussex, UK.

**Rabbit with the longest ears** The longest ears on a rabbit belong to Toby III, a black male English lop rabbit whose ears measured 30.25 in. (76.8 cm) long and 7.75 in. (19.7 cm) wide on June 3, 2002, when he was two years old. Toby III is owned by Phil Wheeler of Barnsley, South Yorkshire, UK.

**Longest goldfish** The longest goldfish (*Carassius auratus*) in the world measures 14.6 in. (37.2 cm) from its snout to the end of its tail fin. Bruce, as the goldfish is called, is two years old and owned by Chan Chun Ping Louis and Jackie Chan (both China), who run the Tung Hoi Aquarium Company Ltd. in China.

**DOG WITH THE LONGEST EARS** The dog with the longest ears is Mr. Jeffries, a bassett hound whose ears measured 11.5 in. (29.2 cm) on November 3, 2002. Mr. Jeffries lives with his owner, Phil Jeffries (UK), in Southwick, West Sussex, UK.

**TALLEST LIVING HORSE** The world's tallest living horse is Lyrical Bend (pictured), a dark bay Percheron/Thoroughbred cross gelding (male) born on May 6, 1994. He measures 19.37 hands (76.375 in. or 193.99 cm). Lyrical Bend is owned by Lucinda W. Fayrer-Hosken (USA) and lives on her farm in Monroe, Georgia, USA. The tallest horse ever was the shire gelding Sampson (UK). Foaled in 1846, he measured 21.2½ hands (7 ft. 2.5 in. or 2.19 m).

**Oldest pet parrot** The longest lived pet parrot was one called Prudle, who was reared by Iris Frost, of East Sussex, UK, as a pet after being found in Jinja, Uganda, in 1958. Prudle learned over 800 different words and could even conduct polite conversation, before its death in 1994, at age 35.

**Cat with the longest tail** The longest tail of a domestic cat belongs to Furball, who lives with her owner, Jan Acker (USA), in Battle Creek, Michigan, USA. Furball's tail measured 16 in. (40.6 cm) on March 21, 2001.

**Cat with the most toes** The cat-toe record holder is Jake, a five-year-old male ginger tabby who has 28 toes, with 7 on each paw. Jake lives in Bonfield, Ontario, Canada, with his owners, Michelle and Paul Contant (both Canada). The toes were officially counted on September 24, 2002, with each toe having its own claw, pad, and bone structure.

**Longest cat** The world's longest cat is Verismo's Leonetti Reserve Red (aka Leo), who measured 48 in. (121.9 cm) from his nose to the tip of his tail on March 10, 2002, aged five. Leo is a male Maine Coon cat who lives with his owners, Frieda Ireland and Carroll Damron, in Chicago, Illinois, USA. Leo has a normal diet, but prefers to eat blue cheese.

**Most flights made by a cat** The world record for the most flights made by a cat is held by Smarty, who made his 64th flight on May 6, 2002. All of Smarty's flights have been trips between Cairo, Egypt, and Larnaca, Cyprus, with his owners Peter and Carole Godfrey (UK) who live in Cairo. Smarty also holds the record for most quarantined domestic animal, with 32 stays in quarantine.

**Longest cat's whiskers** The longest whisker on a cat measured 5.5 in. (13.9 cm) on February 18, 2003 and belongs to Sylvester, a black and white long-haired cat owned by Amy Heckethorn of Burlington, Iowa, USA.

# SPEED

**SLOWEST MAMMAL** The three-toed sloth (*Bradypus tridactylus*) of tropical South America has an average ground speed of 6–8 ft. (1.8–2.4 mi.) per minute (0.07–0.1 mph or 0.1–0.16 km/h). In the trees it can accelerate to 15 ft. (4.6 m) per minute (0.17 mph or 0.27 km/h).

**FASTEST MAN** The men's 100-m record is 9.78 sec. and is held by Tim Montgomery (USA). The record was set in Paris, France, on September 14, 2002. This equals 22.9 mph (36.8 km/h).

**FASTEST LAND MAMMAL OVER DISTANCE** The American antelope (*Antilocapra americana*) is the fastest land animal when measured steadily over a long distance. It has been observed to travel continuously at 35 mph (56 km/h) for as far as 4 miles (6 km). It is found in western USA, southwestern Canada, and parts of northern Mexico.

**FASTEST AIR SPEED** The highest recorded speed in an aircraft capable of taking off and landing under its own power is 2,193.17 mph (3,529.56 km/h) by Capt. Eldon W. Joersz and Maj. George T. Morgan, Jr. (both USA) in a Lockheed SR-71A "Blackbird" (shown here) at Beale Air Force Base, CA, over a 15.5-mile (25-km) course on July 28, 1976. This is about the same speed as a rifle bullet. The Blackbird has flown from New York to London in 1 hr. 55 min., compared to Concorde's average of around 3 hr. 50 min.

**FASTEST KANGAROO** A speed of 40 mph (64 km/h) was recorded for a female eastern gray kangaroo (*Macropus giganteus*). The highest sustained speed is 35 mph (56 km/h) recorded for a large male red kangaroo, which died from its exertions after being paced for 1 mile (1.6 km).

**FASTEST LAND MAMMAL OVERALL** When measured over a short distance, the cheetah (*Acinonyx jubatus*) can maintain a steady maximum speed of about 62 mph (100 km/h) on level ground. That's almost the national speed limit!

**FASTEST LAND SPEED** The official one mile land-speed record is 763.035 mph (1,227.985 km/h) or Mach 1.020, set by Andy Green (UK) on October 15, 1997 in the Black Rock Desert, Nevada, in Thrust SSC. The supersonic car is powered by two Rolls-Royce Spey 202 jet engines that generate 50,000 lb. (222 kN) of thrust.

**FASTEST BIRD IN LEVEL FLIGHT**
The red-breasted merganser (*Mergus serrator*), the eider (*Somateria mollissima*), the canvasback (*Aythya valisineria*), and the spur-winged goose (*Plectropterus gambensis*) can reach up to 56–62 mph (90–100 km/h).

## FACT

Compare the times over 100 m. . . .

9.78 sec.  6.4 sec.  5.6 sec.  3.6 sec.  0.029 sec.

# BIRDS

**Heaviest flying bird** The heaviest flying bird is the mute swan (*Cygnus olor*), which can grow to a weight of 40 lb. (18 kg). There is a record from Poland of a cob (male) weighing 49 lb. 10 oz. (22.5 kg) that had temporarily lost the power of flight.

**Largest bird ever** The largest bird that ever lived is the elephant bird or vouron patra (*Aepyornis maximus*), which became extinct about 1,000 years ago (although sightings were reported as late as 1658). This flightless bird from the island of Madagascar grew to around 10–11 ft. (3–3.3 m) tall and weighed about 1,100 lb. (500 kg).

**Bird with the largest vocabulary** A budgerigar called Puck, owned by Camille Jordan (USA), knew an estimated 1,728 words before its death in 1994.

**Most abundant bird** The most abundant bird is the red-billed quelea (*Quelea quelea*), a seed-eating weaver of the drier parts of sub-Saharan

Africa, which has an estimated adult breeding population of 1.5 billion. At least 200 million of these "feathered locusts" are slaughtered annually without having any impact on this number.

**Longest feathers** The longest feathers on a bird found in the wild and not bred for ornamental purposes are those of the male crested argus pheasant *(Rheinhartia ocellata).* The feathers reach a length of 5 ft. 8 in. (1.73 m).

**Oldest bird** The greatest irrefutable age reported for any bird is over 80 years for a male sulfur-crested cockatoo *(Cacatua galerita)* named Cocky, who died at London Zoo, UK, in 1982. An unconfirmed age of 82 years was reported for Wolf, a male Siberian white crane *(Grus leucogeranus)* at the

**RAREST BIRD OF PREY** Only 49 Californian condors *(Gymnogyps californianus),* most of which were bred in captivity, exist in the wild, with about 99 in captivity following a recent study, making it one of the rarest birds of prey.

International Crane Foundation, Baraboo, Wisconsin, USA. Wolf died in 1988 after breaking his bill while repelling a visitor near his pen.

Excluding the ostrich, which has been known to live up to 68 years, the longest lived domesticated bird is the goose (*Anser domesticus*), which has a normal lifespan of about 25 years. On December 16, 1976 a gander named George, owned by Florence Hull (UK), died at the age of 49 years 8 months.

**Longest bill** The longest bill is that of the Australian pelican (*Pelecanus conspicillatus*). It is between 13 and 18 in. (34 and 47 cm) long.

The longest beak in relation to overall body length is that of the sword-billed hummingbird (*Ensifera ensifera*) found in the Andes from Venezuela to Bolivia. The beak measures 4 in. (10.2 cm), making it longer than the bird's actual body, if the tail is excluded.

**Largest bird** The largest living bird is the north African ostrich (*Struthio camelus camelus*). Male examples of this flightless (ratite) sub-species have been recorded up to 9 ft. (2.75 m) tall and weighing 345 lb. (156.5 kg).

**Smallest flightless bird** The Inaccessible Island rail (*Atlantisia rogersi*) of Inaccessible Island, South Atlantic, weighs a

**MOST DANGEROUS BIRD** The most dangerous of all birds are all three species of cassowary (family Casuariidae), which live in New Guinea and northeastern Queensland, Australia. They are large birds (up to 6 ft. 6 in. tall or 2 m), and on each foot they have three forward-pointing toes with strong claws to provide grip while running, the inner toe having a 5-in.-long (12-cm) spike for defensive purposes, which it kicks out when cornered. A cornered or wounded bird can be extremely dangerous and will leap into the air and kick, damaging vital organs or causing massive bleeding to its victim. Its kick is powerful enough to rip open a person's stomach or even kill.

**TALLEST FLYING BIRD** The tallest of the flying birds are cranes, which are waders belonging to the family Gruidae. The largest can stand to a height of almost 6 ft. 6 in. (2 m) high.

mere 1.4 oz. (40 g). First discovered in 1870, and described as being the size of a three-day-old black chicken, the adult birds are a dark chestnut brown above and gray-brown below. The males are darker than the females, but both adult birds have fiery-red eyes.

**Largest wingspan** The largest wingspan of any living species of bird was that of a male wandering albatross (*Diomedea exulans*) of the southern oceans, with a wingspan of 11 ft. 11 in. (3.63 m). It was caught by members of the Antarctic research ship USNS *Eltanin* in the Tasman Sea on September 18, 1965.

**Smallest bird** The smallest bird is the bee hummingbird (*Mellisuga helenae*) of Cuba and the Isle of Pines (New Caledonia). Males measure 2.25 in. (57 mm) in length, half of which is taken up by the bill and tail, and weigh 0.056 oz. (1.6 g). Females are slightly larger. This is believed to be the lowest weight limit for any warm-blooded animal.

**Largest bird egg** The largest bird egg on record was an ostrich egg weighing 5 lb. 2 oz. (2.35 kg). It was laid in June 1997 at Datong Xinda ostrich farm, Datong, Shanxi, China.

**Highest flying bird** The highest altitude recorded for a bird is 37,000 ft. (11,300 m) for a Ruppell's vulture (*Gyps rueppellii*), which collided with a commercial aircraft over Abidjan, Ivory Coast, on November 29, 1973. The impact damaged one of the plane's engines, but it landed safely.

**Heaviest bird of prey** The heaviest bird of prey is the Andean condor (*Vultur gryphus*), males of which average 20–27 lb. (9–12 kg) and have a wingspan of 10 ft. (3 m).

A weight of 31 lb. (14.1 kg) has been claimed for a male Californian condor (*Gymnogyps californianus*), now preserved in the California Academy of Sciences at Los Angeles, California, USA. This species is generally much smaller than the Andean condor and rarely exceeds 23 lb. (10.4 kg).

**Most poisonous bird** The hooded pitohui (*Pitohui dichrous*) from Papua New Guinea is one of a small number of poisonous birds in the world. It was discovered in 1990 and has puzzled scientists ever since. Its feathers and skin contain the powerful poison homobatrachotoxin, the same one secreted by the dart frogs of South America. Like many other poisonous animals, this bird also emits a foul smell and advertises its toxicity with bright colors. The venom affects the nerves of the victim, but it is not known how the species acquired it.

**Strongest bird of prey** The bird of prey capable of killing and carrying away the largest animal is the female Harpy eagle (*Harpia harpyja*), which, in spite of its weight (20 lb. or 9 kg), manages to hunt animals of equal or superior size. A Harpy eagle swooping down at 20 mph (32 km/h) generates around 8,300 Newton-meters (13,500 foot-pounds) of energy. That is more than twice the muzzle energy of a bullet shot from a rifle.

# AQUATIC LIFE

**Shortest lived fish** The shortest-lived fish are probably certain species of Killifish (family Aplocheilidae), which are found distributed broadly throughout a variety of fresh and brackish water habitats in Africa. They normally live for about eight months in the wild.

**Strongest bite** Experiments carried out with a "Snodgrass gnathodynamometer" (shark-bite meter) at the Lerner Marine Laboratory in Bimini, Bahamas, revealed that a 6-ft. 6.75-in. (2-m-long) dusky shark (*Carcharhinus obscurus*) could exert a force of 132 lb. (60 kg) between its jaws. This is the same as a pressure of 42,500 lb./in.$^2$ (3 tons/cm$^2$) at the tip of its teeth. The bite of a larger shark such as a great white (*Carcharodon carchrias*) must be considerably more spectacular, but it has never been measured.

**Longest survival out of water** Six species of lung fish (Lepidosirenidae, Protopteridae and Ceratodidae) live in freshwater swamps that

**LARGEST FISH** The world's largest fish is the rare plankton-feeding whale shark (*Rhincodon typus*), which is found in the warmer areas of the Atlantic, Pacific, and Indian Oceans. The largest scientifically recorded example was caught off Baba Island, near Karachi, Pakistan, on November 11, 1949. It was 41 ft. 6 in. (12.65 m) long and measured 23 ft. (7 m) around the thickest part of the body. It weighed between 33,000 and 46,300 lb. (15 and 21 tons).

frequently dry out for months or even years at a time. Two of the four species found in Africa are considered to be the real experts. As the water recedes, they burrow deep into the ground and secrete a mucus to form a moisture-saving cocoon around their bodies. They then build a porous mud plug at the entrance of the burrow—and wait. Abandoning gill breathing in favor of their air-breathing lungs, they can live for up to four years in this dormant position.

**Largest oyster** In 1999 a common oyster (*Ostrea edulis*) at Chesapeake Bay, Virginia, USA, weighed 8 lb. 2.5 oz. (3.7 kg). It was 12 in. (30 cm) long and 5.5 in. (14 cm) wide.

**Heaviest sponge** In 1909 a wool sponge (*Hippospongia canaliculatta*) measuring 6 ft. (1.83 m) in circumference was collected off the Bahamas. It initially weighed between 80–90 lb. (36 and 41 kg). This fell to 12 lb. (5.5 kg) after it had been dried and drained of all excrescences. It is now preserved in the National Museum of Natural History in Washington, DC, USA.

**Largest invertebrate** The largest invertebrate is the Atlantic giant squid (*Architeuthis dux*). The heaviest ever recorded was stranded aground in Thimble Tickle Bay, Newfoundland, Canada, on November 2, 1878. Its body was 20 ft. (6.1 m) long, and one tentacle measured 35 ft. (10.7 m).

**Deepest fish** The 8-in.-long (20-cm) *Abyssobrotula galatheae*, a species of the cuskeel (family Ophidiidae), has been collected from the Puerto Rico Trench at a depth of 27,455 ft. (8,370 m).

**Oldest mollusc** The longest lived mollusc is the ocean quahog (*Arctica islandica*), a thick-shelled clam found on both sides of the Atlantic and in the North Sea. A specimen with 220 annual growth rings was collected in 1982. Although this implies an age of 220 years, not all biologists accept these growth rings as an accurate measure of age.

**Highest density of crabs** An estimated 120 million red crabs (*Gecarcoidea natalis*) live on the 52-mile$^2$ (135-km$^2$) Christmas Island, Pacific Ocean, a density of approximately one crab per square meter for the whole island. They occur nowhere else in the world.

**Most abundant animal** Copepods are crustaceans and are found almost everywhere where water is available. They have colonized almost every habitat—from 32,800 ft. (10,000 m) down in the deep sea to lakes 16,400 ft. (5,000 m) high in the Himalayas—and from subzero polar waters to hot springs. They include over 12,000 species and, with krill, form the most important members of zooplankton. They form groups that can reach a trillion individuals. Most are very small, less than 0.04 in. (1 mm) long, but some rare oceanic species are over 0.4 in. (1 cm).

**LARGEST CLAM** The largest of all existing bivalve shells is that of the marine giant clam (*Tridacna gigas*), found on the Indo-Pacific coral reefs. One 3-ft. 9.25-in.-long (115-cm) specimen weighing 734 lb. (333 kg) was collected off Ishigaki Island, Okinawa, Japan, in 1956.

Natural World

**LARGEST MARINE CRUSTACEAN** The largest of all crustaceans is the Japanese spider crab (*Macrocheira kaempferi*) which is found off the southeastern coast of Japan and has an average body size of 10 × 12 in. 25.4 × 30 cm) and an average leg span of 8–9 ft. 2.43–2.74 m).

**Smallest sponge** The widely distributed *Leucosolenia blanca* is just 0.11 in. (3 mm) tall when fully grown.

**Smallest marine fish** The shortest recorded marine fish—and the shortest known vertebrate—is the dwarf goby (*Trimmatom nanus*) of the Indo-Pacific. Average lengths recorded for a series of specimens collected by the 1978/79 Joint Services Chagos Research Expedition of the British Armed Forces were 0.34 in. (8.6 mm) for males and 0.35 in. (8.9 mm) for females.

**Smallest freshwater fish** The shortest and lightest freshwater fish is the dwarf pygmy goby (*Pandaka pygmaea*), a colorless and nearly transparent species found in the streams and lakes of Luzon in the Philippines. Males grow up to only 0.38 in. (9.9 mm) long and weigh 0.00014–0.00018 oz. (4–5 mg).

**Longest living marine invertebrate** The tubeworm *Lamellibrachia,* which survives by digesting seeps of oil leaking from the sea floor, can live for 170–250 years.

**Largest starfish** Out of the 1,600 known species, the largest starfish in the world is the very fragile brisingid (*Midgardia xandaros*). In 1968, a specimen was collected in the Gulf of Mexico by a Texas A&M University research vessel *The Alaminos*. The starfish measured an astonishing 4 ft. 6 in. (1.38 m) from tip to tip.

**Aquatic Life**

**Smallest starfish** The smallest known starfish is the asterinid sea star (*Patiriella parvivipara*) discovered on the west coast of the Eyre peninsula, South Australia, in 1975. It has a maximum radius of only 0.18 in. (4.7 mm) and a diameter of less than 0.35 in. (9 mm).

**Deepest dive by a mammal** The deepest authenticated dive by a mammal was made by a bull sperm whale (*Physeter macrocephalus*) off the coast of Dominica in the Caribbean in 1991. Scientists recorded the dive to be 6,500 ft. (2,000 m) deep, lasting a total of 1 hr. 13 min.

**Fastest marine mammal** On October 12, 1958 a bull killer whale (*Orcinus orca*) estimated to be 20–25 ft. (6.1–7.6 m) long was timed at 34.5 mph (55.5 km/h) in the Pacific. Similar speeds have been reported for Dall's porpoises (*Phocoenoides dalli*) in short bursts.

**Largest jellyfish** An Arctic giant jellyfish (*Cyanea capillata arctica*) of the northwestern Atlantic, that washed up in Massachusetts Bay, USA, in 1870, had a bell diameter of 7 ft. 6 in. (2.28 m) and tentacles stretching 120 ft. (36.5 m). Their stings can be fatal to humans, but they live very deep in the ocean.

# CREEPY CRAWLIES

**LARGEST MOTH** The atlas moth (*Attacus atlas*) of southeast Asia has a wingspan of 12 in. (30 cm) and is often mistaken for a bird. They have no mouths and therefore live for only about four days.

**STRANGEST INSECT DEFENSE MECHANISM** The bombardier beetle (genus *Brachinus*) stores two benign chemicals in a chamber in its abdomen. When threatened, they are released into a second chamber and mix with an enzyme causing a violent reaction and the release of considerable heat (up to 212°F or 100°C) from its anus.

**FASTEST CATERPILLAR** The larvae of the mother-of-pearl moth (*Pleuroptya ruralis*) can travel 15 in./sec. (38.1 cm/sec.)—the equivalent of 150 mph (241 km/h). It reaches this speed by forming into a "wheel" and rolling away.

**MOST VENOMOUS SCORPION** The Tunisian fat-tailed scorpion (*Androctonus australis*) is responsible for 80% of stings and 90% of deaths from scorpion stings in North Africa.

**MOST DANGEROUS BEE** The Africanized honey bee (*Apis mellifera scutellata*) will generally attack only when provoked but is persistent in pursuit. Its venom is no more potent than that of other bees, but the number of stings it inflicts, which can result in death, is greater than any other.

**MOST DESTRUCTIVE INSECT** The single most destructive insect is the desert locust (*Schistocerca gregaria*), native to the dry and semi-arid regions of Africa, the Middle East, and western Asia. Individuals are only 1.8–2.4 in. (4.5–6 cm) long but can eat their own weight in food every day. In a single day, a "small" swarm of about 50 million locusts can eat food that would sustain 500 people for a year.

**LARGEST SPIDER** The world's largest known spider is a male goliath bird-eating spider (*Theraphosa blondi*) collected by members of the Pablo San Martin Expedition at Rio Cavro, Venezuela, in April 1965. It had a record leg span of 11 in. (28 cm)—sufficient to cover a dinner plate.

Creepy Crawlies

**STRONGEST SPIDER** The Californian trap-door spider (*Bothriocyrtum californicum*) has been proved to be able to resist a force 38 times its own weight attempting to open its trap-door—a silken structure covering the entrance to its underground burrow. This is the same as a 180-lb. (82-kg) man trying to keep a door closed that was being pulled on the other side by the weight of a small jet.

**STRONGEST INSECT** In proportion to their size, the strongest animals are the larger beetles of the Scarabaeidae family. In tests they were found to support 850 times their own weight upon their back. A human can support up to 17 times his own body weight.

# FACT

**KILLER ANT!**
The most dangerous ant is the bulldog ant (*Myrmecia pyriformis,* left) found in Australia. It is so named because of its ferocity and determination during an attack. The ant stings its prey a number of times—injecting more venom each time. In an attack, the ant will hold on to its victim with long toothed mandibles, curl its body underneath, and thrust its long barbless sting into the skin. This sting has been known to kill adult humans within 15 minutes.

# REPTILES

**Largest tortoise** Goliath, a Galapagos tortoise (*Chelonoidis nigra*), resided at the Life Fellowship Bird Sanctuary in Seffner, Florida, USA, from 1960 until his death in November 2002. He was 4 ft. 5.5 in. (1.358 m) long, 3 ft. 3.6 in. (1.02 m) wide, 2 ft. 3 in. (68.5 cm) tall, and weighed 920 lb. (417 kg).

**Fastest chelonian** The highest speed claimed for any reptile in water is 22 mph (35 km/h) by a frightened Pacific leatherback turtle (*Dermochelys coriacea*).

**Oldest lizard** The greatest age recorded for a lizard is over 54 years for a male slow worm (*Anguis fragilis*) kept in the Zoological Museum in Copenhagen, Denmark, from 1892 until 1946.

**Heaviest venomous snake** The heaviest venomous snake is the eastern diamondback rattlesnake (*Crotalus adamanteus*) of southeastern USA, which weighs 12–15 lb. (5.5–6.8 kg) and is 5–6 ft. (1.52–1.83 m) in length. The heaviest on record weighed 34 lb. (15 kg) and was 7 ft. 9 in. (2.36 m) long.

**Longest snake** The reticulated python (*Python reticulatus*) of southeast Asia, Indonesia and the Philippines often exceeds 20 ft. 6 in. (6.25 m), and the record length is 32 ft. 9.5 in. (10 m) for a specimen shot in 1912 in Celebes, Indonesia.

**LARGEST LIZARD** The largest lizard is the Komodo dragon (*Varanus komodoensis*), also known as the Komodo monitor or ora, which is found on the Indonesian islands of Komodo, Rintja, Padar and Flores. Males average 7 ft. 5 in. (2.25 m) in length and weigh about 130 lb. (59 kg). The largest accurately measured specimen was a male presented to a US zoologist in 1928 by the Sultan of Bima. In 1937 it measured 10 ft. 2 in. (3.1 m) in length and weighed 365 lb. (166 kg).

**Natural World**

**MOST DANGEROUS LIZARD** The Gila monster (*Heloderma suspectum*) is a large—up to 24 in. (60 cm) long—heavily built, brightly colored lizard that lives in the arid parts of Mexico and southwestern USA. It has eight well-developed venom glands in its lower jaws and carries enough venom to kill two adult humans. The venom is not injected but seeps into the wound caused when the Gila monster bites its victim with its sharp fragile teeth. Because of this, the lizard may continue to hang on after it has bitten and chew for several minutes. In one study of 34 people bitten by the Gila, there were eight fatalities.

**Shortest venomous snake** The namaqua or spotted dwarf adder (*Bitis schneideri*) of Namibia has an average length of 8 in. (20 cm).

**Smallest lizard** The record for smallest lizard is held by both the *Sphaerodactylus parthenopion* and *Sphaerodactylus ariasae* which have been recorded as having an average snout-to-vent length of only 0.6 in. (16 mm). They both share the distinction of being the smallest of the approximately 23,000 species of amniote vertebrates.

**Longest fangs** The longest fangs of any snake are those of the highly venomous Gaboon viper (*Bitis gabonica*) of tropical Africa. In a specimen 6 ft. (1.83 m) long, the fangs measured 2 in. (50 mm). The Gaboon viper is considered to produce more venom than any other venomous snake. A single adult male may have enough venom to inject lethal doses into 30 individual men. Not only do they produce more venom than any other snake but they also inject more deeply.

**Heaviest snake** The heaviest snake is the green anaconda (*Eunectes murinus*) of South America and Trinidad. The normal length is 18–20 ft. (5.5–6.1 m). A female shot in Brazil c. 1960 was 27 ft. 7 in. (8.45 m) long with a girth of 44 in. (1.11 m), and was estimated to have weighed 500 lb. (227 kg).

**Smallest chelonian** The smallest chelonian is the speckled cape tortoise or speckled padloper (*Homopus signatus*), with a shell length of between 2.3 and 3.7 in. (6 and 9.6 cm). The smallest marine turtle in the world is the Atlantic ridley (*Lepidochelys kempii*), which has a shell length of 20–28 in. (50–70 cm) and a maximum weight of 176 lb. (80 kg).

**Longest venomous snake** The longest venomous snake is the king cobra (*Ophiophagus hannah*), also called the hamadryad, which measures 12–15 ft. (3.65–4.5 m) in length and is found in southeast Asia and India. The head of the king cobra is as big as a man's hand, and it can stand tall enough to look an adult human being in the eye. Its venom can stun the nervous system and cause asphyxiation while other toxins begin digesting the paralyzed victim. The venom in a single bite from a king cobra is enough to kill 20 people.

**Most venomous land snake** The most venomous land snake in the world is the inland taipan or small-scaled (or fierce) snake (*Oxyuranus microlepidotus*), which measures up to 5 ft. 7 in. (1.7 m) and is found mainly in the Diamantina River and Cooper Creek drainage basins in Queensland and western New South Wales, Australia. In a single strike a taipan can inject

0.002 oz. (60 mg) of venom, sufficient to quickly paralyze a small marsupial but also more than enough to kill several human adults. The average venom yield after milking is 0.00155 oz. (44 mg) but one male specimen yielded 0.00385 oz. (110 mg), enough to kill 250,000 mice. Fortunately this species only lives in the arid deserts of central eastern Australia, and no human deaths have been reported from its bite.

**LONGEST LIZARD** The Salvadori or Papuan monitor (*Varanus salvadorii*) of Papua New Guinea has been measured at up to 15 ft. 7 in. (4.75 m) in length, but nearly 70% of its total length is taken up by the tail.

**SLOWEST CHELONIAN** In a speed test carried out in the Seychelles, a male giant tortoise (*Geochelone gigantea*) could cover only 14 ft. 11 in. (4.57 m) in 43.5 sec. (0.23 mph or 0.37 km/h), despite the enticement of a female tortoise.

**Largest crocodilian** The largest reptile in the world is the estuarine or saltwater crocodile (*Crocodylus porosus*), which ranges throughout the tropical regions of Asia and the Pacific. The Bhitarkanika Wildlife Sanctuary in Orissa State, India, houses four protected estuarine crocodiles measuring more than 19 ft. 8 in. (6 m) in length, the largest being over 23 ft. (7 m) long. There are several unauthenticated reports of specimens up to 33 ft. (10 m) in length. Adult males typically measure 14–16 ft. (4.2–4.8 m) in length and weigh about 900–1,150 lb. (408–520 kg).

**Smallest crocodilian** The Cuiver's dwarf caiman (*Paleosuchus palpebrosus*) of northern South America is the smallest crocodilian in the world today. Females rarely exceed 4 ft. (1.2 m) in length, and males rarely grow to more than 4 ft. 11 in. (1.5 m).

**Shortest snake** The world's shortest snake is the very rare thread snake (*Leptotyphlops bilineata*), known only in Martinique, Barbados, and St. Lucia. The longest known specimen was 4.25 in. (10.8 cm) long, and had such a matchstick-thin body that it could have entered the hole left in a standard pencil after the lead has been removed. The Brahminy blindsnake (*Ramphotyphlops braminus*) is also under 4.25 in. (10.8 cm) long.

**Oldest chelonian** The greatest authentic age recorded for a chelonian is at least 188 years and was set by a Madagascar radiated tortoise (*Astrochelys radiata*) that was presented to the Tonga royal family by Captain Cook in either 1773 or 1777. The animal was called Tui Malila and remained in their care until its death in 1965.

**Most widely distributed venomous snake**  The saw-scaled or carpet viper (*Echis carinatus*), which is found from West Africa to India, bites and kills more people in the world than any other species.

**Oldest snake**  The greatest reliable age recorded for a snake is 40 years 3 months 14 days for Popeye, a male common boa (*Boa constrictor*) who died at Philadelphia Zoo, Pennsylvania, USA, on April 15, 1977.

# CONSERVATION

**Endangered species**  *Many animals are known only from a single or type specimen and the population size of others is unknown. This makes it very difficult to establish the identity of the world's rarest species and, conse-quently, this selection simply highlights some of the better known examples from the 2002 International Union for the Conservation of Nature's Red List of Threatened Species.*

**Rarest bird**  The blue macaw (*Cyanopsitta spixii*) is considered to be one of the rarest birds in the world. The only hope for the sur-vival of this species lies with the 66 individuals kept in captivity. In 2000, this species was judged to be critically endangered and ex-tremely close to extinction. The

**MOST ENDANGERED WILDCAT**
The Iberian lynx (*Lynx pardinus*) is restricted to Spain and Portugal, and in 2000 it was estimated that there were only 600 survivors in an extremely fragmented population. The Iberian lynx was once widespread all over Spain but through agriculture and development has lost much of its habitat. A major cause of the decline in numbers was the introduction of the disease myxomatosis in an attempt to reduce the rabbit population. As rabbits are the Iberian lynx's main food source, this had a direct impact on the population. This wildcat is now legally protected.

**RAREST AMPHIBIAN** The golden toad (*Bufo periglenes*) is found in a small area (less than 4 miles² or 10 km²) contained in the Monteverde Cloud Forest Preserve in the Cordillera de Tilaran, near Monteverde, Provincia de Puntarenas, Costa Rica. Its numbers mysteriously plummeted in little over a decade, with the last recorded sighting of one specimen dating back to between 1988 and 1989.

single known wild bird almost certainly died toward the end of 2000 and thus the species may now be extinct in the wild.

**Most endangered fish** The Devil's Hole pupfish (*Cyprinodon diabolis*), which number between 200 and 500, are restricted entirely to an unusual system of water holes in Nevada, USA. Their main threats come from the pumping of groundwater for irrigation and the introduction of exotic fish species in the area.

**Rarest land mammal** The Javan rhinoceros (*Rhinoceros sondaicus*), a solitary, single-horned species, is thought to be the world's rarest large mammal. Once widely distributed in southeast Asia, its population has declined to an estimated 60 animals (about 50 on the remote western tip of Java, Indonesia, and the rest in Vietnam).

**Rarest marine mammal** The baiji, or Yangtze River dolphin (*Lipotes vexillifer*), has an estimated population of only a few dozen. The population is still falling owing to competition with fisheries, accidental capture in nets, pollution, disturbance, and habitat destruction. The baiji is also killed for its meat and oil. The few survivors live mainly in the middle reaches of the Yangtze River, China. Despite being a national treasure in China, the baiji is expected to become extinct soon.

**Most endangered primates** Because of the difficulty in establishing definite numbers for individual primates, there are several species that are considered critically endangered.

Although the species was discovered only in 1985, there are believed to be only approximately 1,000 golden bamboo lemurs (*Hapalemur aureus*) living wild in Madagascar's eastern rainforest. The main threat to its existence is the rampant slash-and-burn agriculture around its habitat.

The total number of remaining Cross River gorillas (*Gorilla gorilla diehli*) on the Nigeria-Cameroon border in 2000 was somewhere between 150 and 200 individuals. Bushmeat trade is popular in this part of the world, and this has greatly reduced numbers.

There are only about 400 black-faced lion tamarins (*Leontopithecus caissara*) in the states of Paraná and São Paulo, Brazil. Their discovery in 1990 was considered one of the most significant primatological events of the 20th century because they had been undetected for so long in what is a very densely populated area of Brazil.

The Cat Ba Island golden-headed langur (*Trachypithecus poliocephalus*) is found only on the island of Cat Ba, the largest of more than 3,000 islands located in northeastern Vietnam's Halong Bay. There are estimated to be only approximately 100 left in the wild as they have suffered over the years from human encroachment and hunting.

**Rarest insect** Scientists believe there may be as few as ten specimens of the Lord Howe Island stick insect (*Dryococelus australis*) in existence. The giant stick insect evolved before the dinosaurs and was presumed extinct for 80 years until scientists rediscovered it on a remote island off Australia in February 2001. Several eggs were also found. This species can grow up to 6 in. (15 cm) long and their bodies are 0.5 in. (1.3 cm) thick.

**Largest tropical forest reserve** The Tumucumaque National Park in the northern Amazonian state of Amapa, Brazil, measures some 15,010 miles$^2$ (38,875 km$^2$) in area, and contains many endangered species of plant and animal. The creation of the park was announced on August 22, 2002.

**Largest afforestation project** The world's largest afforestation project is the "Green Great Wall." This 2,783-mile-long (4,480-km) forest belt is being created in northwest China in order to combat the threat of desertification and over-farming, which has ruined vast areas of cultivated land. The project was initiated in 1978 and is set to last until 2050 when a total of 87.9 million acres (35.6 million hectares) of land will be afforested. It is currently being coordinated by the State Forestry Administration of China.

**Largest landscape restoration project** The largest ecological restoration project in history is the current $8 billion (£5 billion) project that will restore the Everglades wetlands of Florida, USA.

**Rarest tree** The Wollemi pine (*Wollemia nobilis*), a member of the Araucaria family, was discovered in Wollemi National Park, 93 miles (150 km) northwest of Sydney, Australia, in 1994. Only 43 adult trees have been found, all growing in a 1.5-acre (0.5-ha) grove in the park in three small stands. The pine is unusual in being covered with brown, knobby, spongy bark. The trees grow on wet ledges in a deep, sheltered gorge. The tallest measures 131 ft. (40 m) and has a girth of some 9 ft. (3 m).

**Earliest zoo** The earliest known collection of animals was established at modern day Puzurish, Iraq, by Shulgi, a 3rd-dynasty ruler of Ur from 2097–2094 B.C.

**Largest environmental petition** Greenpeace collected 8.5 million signatures worldwide in 1995 to call upon France's President Jacques Chirac to end French nuclear testing in Mururoa in the South Pacific. Despite world-wide condemnation, France completed six nuclear tests. However, as France had initially intended to perform eight tests, Greenpeace took it as a success that they only performed six.

**Highest diversity of plants per unit area** The area of the world regarded as having the greatest diversity and endemism of plants per unit area is the small island of Juan Fernández in the Pacific Ocean off the coast of Chile, which has a total surface area of 39 miles² (100 km²). In this small area scientists have so far identified 209 species of vascular plants (126 of which are endemic), an endemic plant family (Lactoridaceae), a primitive dicotyledon and 12 fully endemic plant genera.

**Most environmentally friendly country** The country regarded as the most environmentally sustainable is Finland, which heads the Environmental Sustainability Index (ESI) compiled in 2002 by the World Economic Forum. Based on 20 core indicators covering five broad areas—environmental systems (e.g. air and water quality), reducing environmental stress (e.g. pollution levels), reducing human vulnerability to environmental degradation, social, and institutional capacity to respond to environmental threats, and contribution to global stewardship—Finland scored 73.9 out of 100. The lowest was Kuwait with 23.9. The USA was 45th with 53.2. The UK was 91st with a score of 46.1. In total, 142 countries are listed.

GREATEST BIODIVERSITY The area considered to have the greatest biodiversity is the tropical Andes region, covering 485,716 miles² (1,258,000 km²). This area runs through Venezuela, Colombia, Ecuador, Peru, Bolivia, and northern Argentina. So far, 45,000 species of vascular plant have been described (15–17% of the world's species), as well as 1,666 bird species, 414 mammal species, and 1,309 reptile and amphibian species.

**Greatest environmental management** In terms of receiving ISO 14001 certification for environmental management, Japan leads the world with 8,123 certifications as of December 2001. ISO 14000 provides guidelines for organizations that need to systematize and improve their environmental management efforts. The ISO 14000 standards came as a result of the 1992 Rio Summit on the Environment.

# PREHISTORIC LIFE

**Largest prehistoric flying bird** The largest known flying bird was the giant teratorn *Argentavis magnificens,* which lived in Argentina about 6–8 million years ago. Fossil remains discovered at a site 100 miles (160 km) west of Buenos Aires, Argentina, in 1979 indicate that this gigantic vulture-like bird had a wing span of possibly up to 25 ft. (7.6 m) and weighed about 176 lb. (80 kg).

**LARGEST EVER CARNIVORE** In 1995 a skeleton of the largest predatory dinosaur was discovered in Neuquen, Patagonia, Argentina. This new dinosaur, *Giganotosaurus carolinii,* was 40 ft. (12.5 m) long and weighed 17,000 lb. (8 tonnes). The bones suggest that it was both taller and more heavily built than *Tyrannosaurus rex.* It lived about 110 million years ago so is 30 million years older than *T. rex.*

**LARGEST DINOSAUR EGGS** The largest known dinosaur eggs are those of *Hypselosaurus priscus* ("high ridge lizard"), a 40-ft.-long (12-m) titanlosaurid which lived about 80 million years ago. Examples found in the Durance valley in France in October 1961 would have been, uncrushed, 12 in. (30 cm) long—with a diameter of 10 in. (255 mm).

**Earliest bird** The earliest fossil bird is known from two partial skeletons found in Texas, USA, in rocks dating back 220 million years. Named *Protoavis texensis* in 1991, this pheasant-sized creature has caused much controversy by pushing the age of birds back many millions of years from the previous record, that of the more familiar *Archaeopteryx lithographica* found in Jurassic sediments in Germany. It is unclear whether *Protoavis* will be widely accepted as a true bird, making *Archaeopteryx,* the 153 million-year-old crow-sized flier, the earliest unambiguous fossil bird.

**Earliest dinosaur** Fossils of the oldest known dinosaur were found in 1996 in Madagascar by international scientists led by John Flynn (USA). Believed to date from 230 million years ago during the Triassic period, they may belong to prosauropods—plant-eating dinosaurs the size of a kangaroo, with a small head and a long neck.

**Longest prehistoric snake** The longest prehistoric snake was the python-like *Gigantophis garstini,* which inhabited what is now Egypt about 38 million years ago. Parts of a spinal column and a small piece of jaw discovered at Fayum in the Western Desert indicate a length of about 36 ft. (11 m). This is 3 ft. 3 in. (1 m) longer than the reticulated python, the present-day longest snake.

**Oldest vomit** On February 12, 2002, a team of palaeontologists, led by Peter Doyle (Greenwich University, UK) announced their discovery of the fossilized vomit of a marine reptile. Discovered in a quarry in Peterborough, Cambridgeshire, UK, the 160-million-year-old vomit could provide an insight to the feeding habits of ichthyosaurs.

**Earliest animal to walk on land** The earliest animal to walk on land was *Pederpes finneyae,* which lived around 350 million years ago. This tetrapod was discovered in 1971 north of Dumbarton, UK. The identification of the legs and one complete foot was announced on July 4, 2002. The identification was made by Jenny Clack (UK), from the University Museum of Zoology, University of Cambridge, UK.

**Longest prehistoric tusks** The longest tusks of any prehistoric animal were those of the straight-tusked elephant (*Hesperoloxodon antiques germanicus*), which lived in what is now northern Germany about two million years ago. The average length in adult bulls was 16 ft. (5 m).

**Oldest flowering plant** On May 3, 2002, scientists announced the discovery of the fossilized remains of the earliest flowering plant discovered to date. At least 125 million years old and named *Archaefructus sinensis* ("ancient fruit from China"), it was found in stone in northeast China and is possibly the ancestor of all the flowering plants in the world today. Its closest living relative may be the water lily, as the ancient plant lived in clear shallow water, with its flowers and seeds extending above the surface.

**Oldest ceratopsian dinosaur** The oldest ceratopsian dinosaur discovered to date is *Liaoceratops*. It was discovered in the Yixian Formation, a fossil-rich rock bed in northeast China. The rocks date the creature at having lived 120–145 million years ago. This dog-sized herbivore was a precursor to the more famous *Triceratops*. The discovery was announced on March 21, 2002.

**Largest flying creature** The largest ever flying creature was the pterosaur *Quetzalcoatlus northropi* ("feathered serpent"). About 70 million years ago it soared over what is now Texas, Wyoming, and New Jersey in the USA, Alberta in Canada, Senegal and Jordan. Partial remains found in Big Bend National Park, Texas, USA, in 1971 indicate that it must have had a wing span of 36–39 ft. (11–12 m) and weighed about 190–250 lb. (86–113 kg).

**Largest prehistoric carnivorous bird** The largest ever carnivorous bird was the *Titanis walleri*, known to have lived until the late Pleistocene (Ice Age) in Florida. It had a to-

**OLDEST FOSSIL SPIDER TRAPPED IN AMBER** The oldest fossil spider trapped in amber has been dated to 125–135 million years old. It is from the family Linyphiidae, and was discovered in Lebanon and analyzed by David Penney and Paul Selden (both University of Manchester, UK) who announced their discovery on December 26, 2002.

**DINOSAUR WITH THE MOST TEETH** The dinosaur with the most teeth was the duck-billed hadrosaur, which, despite being a herbivore with a toothless beak, had up to 960 self-sharpening cheek teeth in the side of its strong jaws for chewing tough plants.

tal body height of 8 ft. (2.5 m), and its weight probably reached 440 lb. (200 kg).

**Largest trilobite** The largest fossil trilobite was discovered in northern Manitoba, Canada, and measures over 27.5 in. (70 cm) in length—more than 12 in. (30 cm) longer than the previous largest trilobite. The discovery of the 445-million-year-old specimen was announced on October 9, 2000.

**Largest prehistoric insect** The largest prehistoric insect was the dragonfly *Meganeura monyi*, which lived about 280 million years ago. Fossil remains found at Commentry, France, indicate a wing expanse possibly up to 27.5 in. (70 cm).

**Largest plesiosaur** The largest plesiosaur ever to swim in the oceans was *Liopleurodon*, which was up to 82 ft. (25 m) long. *Liopleurodon* was carnivorous and had a long (10 ft. or 3 m) head, a short neck, and four powerful flippers. These cousins of the dinosaurs lived in the late Jurassic period, between 165 and 150 million years ago.

**Best preserved dinosaur remains** "Leonardo," the fossilized remains of a 77-million-year-old duck-billed dinosaur, was discovered in northern Montana, USA, in the summer of 2000. The 23-ft.-long (7-m) *Brachylophosaurus* is the fourth dinosaur ever discovered to be classified as a mummy. Around 90% of its body is covered in fossilized soft tissue,

**Prehistoric Life**

including skin, muscles, scales, footpads, and even its last meal has been preserved in its stomach. The creature was between three and four years old when it died.

**Longest dinosaur** The longest vertebrate on record was a diplodocid excavated in 1980 from New Mexico, USA. Named *Seismosaurus halli,* it was estimated to be 128–170 ft. (39–52 m) long, based on comparisons of individual bones. In 1999, the bones were reconstructed at the Wyoming Dinosaur Center, to measure a total length of 134 ft. (41 m). It was disassembled in August 1999 to tour the USA.

**Largest dinosaur footprint** In 1932 the gigantic footprints of a large bipedal hadrosaurid ("duckbill") measuring 4 ft. 5.5 in. (1.36 m) in length and 32 in. (81 cm) wide were discovered in Salt Lake City, Utah, USA.

**Tallest dinosaur** Dinosaur remains found in 1994 in Oklahoma, USA, belong to what is believed to be the largest creature to have ever walked the Earth. The *Sauroposeidon* stood at 60 ft. (18 m) tall and weighed 132,000 lb. (60 tonnes). Its neck is about a third longer than that of the *Brachiosaurus,* its nearest competitor. It lived about 110 million years ago, during the mid-Cretaceous period.

# THE UNIVERSE

**Longest channel in the Solar System** The longest channel in the Solar System is Baltis Vallis on Venus. It is around 4,300 miles (7,000 km) in length and has an average width of around 1 mile (1.6 km). It was discovered by the Magellan radar mapper, which orbited Venus from May 1989 to October 1994, and is believed to have been formed by molten lava.

**Largest Kuiper Belt object** The Kuiper Belt is a vast belt of icy bodies beyond the orbit of Neptune. The largest object found there is 2002 LM60, which measures around 800 miles (1,300 km) across. It was first discovered by Chad Tru-

**BRIGHTEST REMNANT OF A SUPERNOVA The Crab Nebula (M1) in the constellation of Taurus is the brightest supernova remnant in the sky. It has a magnitude of 8.4. The picture here, captured by the Chandra X-ray space telescope in August 1999, shows the rapidly spinning pulsar at its center.**

jillo and Mike Brown (both USA) at Caltech, Pasadena, California, USA, on June 4, 2002. It is the largest object discovered in the Solar System since Pluto was found in 1930. The discoverers have proposed the name "Quaoar" for this new world, after a creation god of the Tongva tribe—the original inhabitants of the Los Angeles area. It has an orbital period of 288 years and orbits the Sun at a distance of around 4 billion miles (6 billion km).

**Faintest planet in the Solar System** The faintest of the nine planets as seen from Earth is Pluto (magnitude 15.0), which can only be viewed through a telescope.

**Planet with the greatest axial tilt** Uranus has the greatest axial tilt of all the planets in the Solar System. Its axis of spin is tilted 97.86 degrees from the plane of its orbit. The Earth's axis of tilt is 23.45 degrees.

**Largest structure in the universe** The largest structure found to date in the universe is the Great Wall. This giant sheet or filament of galaxies was discovered in 1989 by Margaret Geller and John Huchra (both USA) while analyzing data from the Harvard-Smithsonian Center for Astrophysics (CfA) Redshift survey. It has been estimated at being around $270 \times 700$ million light years in extent, and around 15 million light years thick. One light year is the distance light travels in a year, about 6 trillion miles (9.5 trillion km). Although invisible to the naked eye, the Great Wall stretches across the whole of the northern sky.

**Nearest brown dwarf** Brown dwarfs are often called "failed stars." Like other stars, they form from clouds of galactic gas and dust that collapse under their own gravity. The nearest brown dwarf to the Earth is Epsilon Indi B, a companion to the star Epsilon Indi, which is 11.8 light years away. First seen in archive photographs, its nature was confirmed by astronomers using the 11-ft. 6-in. (3.5-m) New Technology Telescope at La Silla Observatory, Chile. Its discovery was announced on January 15, 2003.

**Most luminous object** Believed to be the most luminous object in the universe, quasar APM08279+5255 was discovered in March 1998 by a team of astronomers using the 8-ft. (2.5-m) Isaac Newton Telescope (INT) at La Palma, Canary Islands, Spain. This quasar is between four and five million billion times brighter than the Sun and is estimated to be more than 10 times brighter than any other known quasar.

**Fastest meteor shower** The fastest annual meteor shower is the Leonids, which occurs between November 15 and 20. Entering the Earth's atmosphere at around 44 miles (71 km) per second, the Leonids begin to glow at an altitude of around 96 miles (155 km). The high speed of the Leonids is because the motion of the parent meteroid stream from comet P/55 Tempel-Tuttle is almost directly opposite to the orbital motion of the Earth around the Sun. This causes an almost head-on collision between the tiny particles and the Earth.

**FASTEST WINDS IN THE SOLAR SYSTEM** The planet Neptune (pictured) has the fastest winds of any world in the Solar System. Measured by NASA's Voyager 2 probe in 1989, they blow at around 1,500 mph (2,400 km/h).

**Most distant object in the universe** It was announced on March 15, 2002 that astronomers using the Keck II observatory in Hawaii, USA, had discovered a galaxy (HCM 6A) with a redshift of 6.56, corresponding to a distance of around 13 billion light years. Light from the galaxy provides a snapshot of the universe when it was just 780 million years old.

**Largest visible lunar crater** The largest wholly visible crater is the walled plain Bailly, toward the Moon's South Pole, which is 183 miles (295 km) across, with walls rising to 14,000 ft. (4,250 m).

**Planet with the most satellites** In March 2003 astronomers announced the discovery of four new tiny moons orbiting the giant planet Jupiter, bringing its total number of natural satellites to 52. A team led by Scott Sheppard and David Jewitt (both University of Hawaii, USA) made the discovery using the 11-ft. 9.6-in. (3.6-m) Canada France Hawaii Telescope in Hawaii, USA.

**Youngest lunar crater** In December 2002 US scientists announced their discovery of a fresh crater on the Moon. The 1.2-mile (2-km) wide crater is in the same location as a bright flash photographed in 1953 by amateur astronomer Leon Stuart (USA). This is the only lunar crater known to have been formed in modern times. The asteroid that caused this crater would have been around 980 ft. (300 m) across and would have detonated on impact with a force around 35 times more powerful than the Hiroshima bomb.

**Most distant planet** The most distant extrasolar planet detected to date is around 5,000 light years away. Roughly the same size as our own giant planet Jupiter, this world, known as Ogle-TR-56b, orbits its parent star once every 29 hours. It was discovered by astronomers at the Harvard-Smithsonian Center for Astrophysics, Massachusetts, USA, and announced on January 6, 2003.

**Oldest star in the Milky Way** In 2002 a team led by Norbert Christlieb (Germany) announced that they had identified the oldest star in our own Milky Way galaxy. Called HE0107-5240, it is a giant star around 36,000 light years from Earth. Its age is measured by its composition. When the universe was formed, it consisted of hydrogen with some helium. As it evolved, the rest of the chemical elements appeared, formed by nuclear synthesis in stars. HE0107-5240 has almost no metal content in it—it has only 1/200,000th of the metal content of our own Sun, meaning it must have formed from clouds

**MOST MASSIVE STAR VISIBLE TO THE NAKED EYE** Eta Carinae (seen here in an image by the Hubble Space Telescope) is a rare supergiant, some 9,000 light years from Earth. With a mass estimated at between 100 and 200 times that of the Sun, it is one of the most massive stars in the galaxy. Today, along with its surrounding gas, it is just visible to the naked eye, with a magnitude of 6.21. Around 150 years ago it became one of the brightest stars in the sky as it underwent massive explosive outbursts. It is one of the most unstable stars known to astronomers, and will almost certainly destroy itself in a supernova at some time in the future.

of gas consisting of almost pure hydrogen and helium when the universe was young. It could date back to over 13 billion years ago.

**Nearest supermassive black hole**  Unlike normal black holes, which weigh several times the mass of the Sun, supermassive black holes reside in the hearts of galaxies and can be as massive as several hundred million times that of the Sun. Many astronomers now believe that such a terrifying force exists at the center of our own galaxy, the Milky Way, only 30,000 light years away.

**Nearest planetary nebula**  At a distance of around 400 light years, the Helix Nebula (also known as NGC 7293) is the closest planetary nebula to the Earth. It formed when a dying star threw off its outer layers, which are gradually expanding into space. Planetary nebulae are so called because astronomers originally believed they were new planets. The Helix Nebula is around 100 times more distant than the nearest stars (excluding the Sun). If the Helix Nebula were bright enough to be visible to the naked eye, it would cover an area around half the size of the full Moon.

# CLIMATE & WEATHER

**Warmest year on record**  The warmest year since records began (around 1880) was 1998. It was 1.026°F (0.57°C) warmer than the average global temperature, measured between 1961 and 1990. The 1990s was the warmest decade on record: the six warmest years on record were all in the 1990s.

**Most powerful short-term natural climate change**  The El Niño Southern Oscillation occurs as a result of cyclic warming of the eastern and central Pacific Ocean. Apart from the seasonal effects of the Earth moving around the Sun, it is the most powerful short-term natural climate change on Earth. The entire cycle of El Niño and La Niña (its cooler counterpart and opposite) lasts between three and seven years. It causes unusual weather conditions all around the world, particularly notable in the 1982/83 and 1997/98 events.

**Earliest image of a sprite**  Sprites are atmospheric electrical phenomena associated with lightning. These unusual flashes shoot upward from the tops of thunderstorms to altitudes up to 62 miles (100 km) above the surface of the Earth. Historical reports of these phenomena were not taken seriously until the first image was taken, accidently, in 1989 when a low-level-light TV camera was pointed above a thunderstorm. Sprites have since been caught on video from the US space shuttle. Scientists have yet to fully understand them.

**Greatest temperature range**  The greatest recorded temperature ranges in the world are around the Siberian "cold pole" in the east of Russia. Tem-

**GREATEST DISPLAY OF SOLAR HALOS** On January 11, 1999 at least 24 types of solar halo were witnessed by scientists at the geographic South Pole. They are formed by sunlight being reflected and refracted by ice crystals in the atmosphere, causing rings around the Sun and bright colored patches in the sky. Atmospheric conditions at the South Pole are conducive to this type of phenomenon.

peratures in Verkhoyansk (67°33′N, 133°23′E) have ranged 188°F (105°C), from -90°F (-68°C) to 98°F (37°C).

The greatest temperature variation recorded in a single day is 100°F (56°C). The temperature fell from 44°F (7°C) to -56°F (-49°C) at Browning, Montana, USA, between January 23 and 24, 1916.

**Clouds with the greatest vertical range** In the tropics, cumulonimbus has been observed to reach a height of nearly 65,600 ft. (20,000 m), nearly 2.5 times the height of Mt. Everest.

**Highest atmospheric phenomena** Of all the phenomena visible in our skies, the very highest are the aurorae, also known as the northern and southern lights. Often visible at night from low and high latitudes, these colored, shimmering lights are the result of charged particles from the Sun interacting with the upper atmosphere. The lowest aurorae occur at altitudes of 62 miles (100 km) and the highest extend up to around 248 miles (400 km).

**Most strokes in a lightning flash** Most lightning flashes consist of several "strokes"—major pulses of current. It is these pulses that cause some flashes to appear to flicker. The most pulses detected in a single flash is 26, in a cloud-to-ground flash in New Mexico, USA, noted by Marx Brook (USA) in 1962.

**Wettest place** By average annual rainfall, the wettest place in the world is Mawsynram, in Meghalaya State, India, with 467 in. (11,873 mm) per annum.

**Driest place** Between 1964 and 2001 the average annual rainfall for the meterological station in Quilagua, in the Atacama Desert, Chile, was just 0.02 in. (0.5 mm). This discovery was made during the making of the documentary series *Going to Extremes,* by Keo Films in 2001. The weather station has a 2,631-ft. (802-m) elevation and is located at 21°38′S, 69°33′W.

**Largest snowflake** It is reported that on January 28, 1887 at Fort Keogh, Montana, USA, ranch owner Matt Coleman (USA) measured a snowflake

**LARGEST MIRAGE** The largest mirage on record was that sighted in 1913 in the Arctic at 83°N, 103°W by Donald B. MacMillan (USA). It appeared as the same "hills, valleys and snow-capped peaks" that Robert Peary (USA) had misidentified as Crocker Land six years earlier.

On July 17, 1939 a mirage of Snaefellsjkull (alt. 4,744 ft. or 1,446 m) on Iceland was seen from the sea from 335–350 miles (540–560 km) away.

that was 15 in. (38 cm) wide and 8 in. (20 cm) thick, which he later described as being "larger than milk pans" in *Monthly Weather Review* magazine.

**Heaviest hailstones** The heaviest hailstones on record weighed up to 2 lb. (1 kg) and are reported to have killed 92 people in the Gopalganj area of Bangladesh on April 14, 1986.

**Greatest monthly rainfall** For a calendar month, the rainfall record is 366 in. (9,300 mm) at Cherrapunji, Meghalaya, India, in July 1861. The 12-month record was also set at Cherrapunji with 1,041.75 in. (26,461 mm) between August 1, 1860 and July 31, 1861.

**Highest shade temperature** The highest shade temperature ever recorded is 136°F (58°C) at Al'Aziziyah in the Sahara Desert, Libya, on September 13, 1922.

**Greatest rainfall in 24 hours** A record 73 in. (1,870 mm) of rain fell in 24 hours in Cilaos (alt. 3,940 ft. or 1,200 m), Reunion, Indian Ocean, on March 15 and 16, 1952. This is equal to an astonishing 16,653,700 lb. (7,554 tonnes) of rain per acre.

**Fastest wind speed** Scientists using the "Doppler on Wheels" mobile weather observatory (University of Oklahoma, USA) recorded a 302 +/-20 mph (486 +/-32 km/h) wind speed associated with a large tornado near Bridge Creek, Oklahoma, USA, on May 3, 1999. The previous record was measured using a 3-mm Doppler radar, which registered a 286-mph (460-

km/h) wind speed associated with a tornado near Red Rock, Oklahoma, USA, on April 26, 1991. For both speeds, the measurement was taken 100–200 ft. (30–60 m) above the ground. The ground speed is not known.

**Most intense rainfall** Difficulties attend rainfall readings for very short periods, but the figure of 1.5 in. (38.1 mm) in one minute at Basse-Terre, Guadeloupe, in the Caribbean, on November 26, 1970, is seen as the most intense recorded by modern methods.

**Largest piece of fallen ice** On August 13, 1849 a 20-ft.-long (6-m) piece of ice was reported to have fallen from the sky in Scotland, UK, after a clap of thunder. The ice was clear but looked like it was made up of smaller pieces. One possible explanation is that hailstones were fused together by lightning.

**Coldest permanently inhabited place** The coldest permanently inhabited place is the Siberian village of Oymyakon (pop. 4,000), 63°16′N, 143°15′E (alt. 2,300 ft. or 700 m), in Russia, where the temperature reached -90°F (-68°C) in 1933, and an unofficial -98°F (-72°C) has been published more recently.

**Most tornadoes in 24 hours** The record number of tornadoes over a 24-hour period is 148. They swept through "Tornado Alley"—the southern and midwestern USA—between April 3 and 4, 1974.

**MOST TORNADOES BY AREA** The highest frequency of tornadoes by area is reported in the UK where in an average year one tornado is reported per 2,856 mile$^2$ (7,397 km$^2$). The equivalent figure for the USA is one tornado per 3,345 mile$^2$ (8,663 km$^2$).

**Largest measured tornado** The largest measured tornado occurred on May 3, 1999 near Mulhall, Oklahoma, USA. Its diameter, around 5,250 ft. (1,600 m), was measured using the University of Oklahoma's "Doppler on Wheels" mobile weather observatory operated by Joshua Wurman (USA).

**Longest ice age** Geological evidence suggests that Earth endured many severe ice ages in its early history. The longest and most severe was between 2.3 and 2.4 billion years ago, and lasted around 70 million years.

# NATURAL DISASTERS

**Worst drought famine** The worst famine caused by drought was in northern China in 1876–79, when between nine and 13 million people are estimated to have died after the rains failed for three consecutive years. At around the same time (1876–78), approximately five million Indians died when the monsoon failed in successive years.

**Greatest recorded climatic impact of a volcanic eruption** The cataclysmic 1815 eruption of the Tambora volcano in Indonesia caused global average temperatures to drop by as much as 5.4°F (3°C). It led to 1816 being known as "the year without summer," with massive crop failures and

**FASTEST AVALANCHE** The volcanic explosion of Mt. St. Helens, Washington, USA, on May 18, 1980 triggered the fastest recorded avalanche in history down its north slope. The velocity reached a staggering 250 mph (402.3 km/h).

other weather-related disruptions throughout Europe and North America. The eruption killed around 92,000 people—the highest death toll from a volcanic eruption.

**Greatest flood**   Roughly 18,000 years ago an ancient 75-mile (120-km) long lake in Siberia ruptured, causing the greatest freshwater flood in history. The discovery of this event in 1993 suggests a catastrophic flood 1,600 ft. (490 m) deep and traveling at 100 mph (160 km/h).

**Highest death toll from a flood**   When the Huang He (Yellow River), Huayan Kou, China, flooded its banks in October 1887, 900,000 people are believed to have been killed.

**Worst homeless toll from a flood disaster**   Monsoon rains caused extensive river flooding in India's Bengal state during September 1978 with 15 million out of a population of 44 million made homeless. London's population is just over seven million: this disaster would have made twice London's population homeless.

**Farthest distance from where a volcanic eruption has been heard**   On August 27, 1883, when the Krakatau volcano on the island of Rakata, Indonesia, erupted, it was heard by people on Rodriguez Island 2,908 miles (4,653 km) away. According to witnesses, it sounded like the distant roar of heavy guns and continued at intervals of three to four hours during the night. Krakatau erupted with a force nearly 10,000 times that of the atom bomb dropped on Hiroshima, Japan. It caused a tsunami wave 131 ft. (40 m) high, throwing a steamship 1.6 miles (2.5 km) off course.

**Costliest natural disaster**   The devastating Kobe earthquake of January 1995 in Japan resulted in overall losses of $100 billion (£63.04 billion), making it the costliest natural disaster to befall any one country. The quake measured 7.2 on the Richter scale, killed more than 6,400 people, and injured around 27,000.

**Highest death toll from a tsunami**   Up to 27,000 people drowned when a giant tsunami inundated the Japanese coastline on the Sea of Japan in 1896. Japan has about 1,500 seismic occurrences every year, the most recent major one being in Kobe in January 1995.

**Greatest mass extinction**   Approximately 248 million years ago, at the end of the Permian geological period, a mass extinction wiped out around 90% of all marine species and 70% of all higher land animals. Its cause is not known.

**Most people trapped in an avalanche disaster**   A total of 240 people died and over 45,000 were trapped on January 20, 1951 when a series of avalanches, caused by a combination of hurricane-force winds and wet snow (due to heavy rain) overlaying powder snow, thundered through the Swiss, Austrian, and Italian Alps.

**Worst death toll from an avalanche disaster** An estimated 40,000–80,000 men died during the First World War in the Tyrolean Alps, owing to avalanches triggered by gunfire.

**Highest tsunami wash** The highest tsunami ever reported was 1,719 ft. (524 m) high and occurred along the fjord-like Lituya Bay, Alaska, USA, on July 9, 1958. It was caused by a giant landslip and moved at a terrifying 100 mph (160 km/h). This wave was so high it would easily have swamped the Petronas Towers in Kuala Lumpur, Malaysia, which at 1,483 ft. (452 m) are the world's tallest office buildings.

**Worst homeless toll from a cyclone disaster** Hurricane Mitch, which struck Central America (Honduras and Nicaragua) between October 26 and November 4, 1998, destroyed 93,690 dwellings and left around 2.5 million people dependent on international aid.

**Worst damage toll from a landslide disaster** A total of $138 million (£57 million) worth of damage was caused in southern California, USA, by a series of mudslides brought about by nine days of torrential rain and a subtropical storm that raged between January 18 and 26, 1969.

**Deadliest lake** The lake responsible for the most deaths without drowning is Lake Nyos in Cameroon, west Africa, where toxic gases have claimed

**WORST DAMAGE TOLL FROM A CYCLONE DISASTER** Hurricane Andrew, which hit Homestead, Florida, USA, between August 23 and 26, 1992, caused an estimated $15.5 billion (£7.8 billion) worth of damage in terms of insured losses.

**MOST WATERLOGGED CITY** Venice is the most frequently flooded city on Earth. Early in the 20th century Venice flooded four or five times a year; by 1989 this number had increased to 40. By 1998 the squares and streets were flooded one day in three. In the next 50 years it is estimated that the water level in Venice will rise by 8 in. (20.3 cm).

nearly 2,000 lives in recent decades. On one night in August 1986, between 1,600 and 1,800 people and countless animals were killed by a large natural release of carbon dioxide gas. Scientists disagree on the source of Lake Nyos' deadly gas. Some believe that the decomposition of organic material near the bottom of the lake causes the gas to build up, and seasonal changes in surface temperature triggers mixing of deep and shallow water, allowing the gas to be released. Because Nyos lies in the crater of an old volcano, others believe that the gas is volcanic in origin.

**Highest tsunami landslide**  The highest tsunami triggered by a submarine landslide was one that struck the island of Lanai in Hawaii, USA, c. 105,000 years ago. It deposited sediment up to an altitude of approximately 1,230 ft. (375 m).

**Worst death toll from a lightning strike**  A total of 81 people aboard a Boeing 707 jet airliner died when the plane was struck by lightning near Elkton, Maryland, USA, on December 8, 1963.

**Highest earthquake tsunami**  The highest tsunami or giant wave caused by an offshore earthquake appeared off Ishigaki Island, Ryukyu island chain, Japan, on April 24, 1771. It was possibly as high as 279 ft. (85 m), and tossed a 1,653,000-lb. (750-tonne) block of coral more than 1.5 miles (2.5 km) inland.

**Most trees destroyed by storms**  Around 270 million trees were felled or split by storms that hit France on December 26 and 27, 1999. The storm lasted 30 hours and caused 87 deaths. The damage was estimated at FF 52.3 billion ($8 billion or £5 billion). In Paris, the Bois de Boulogne and Bois de

Vincennes lost 140,000 trees. It will take an estimated 100 to 200 years to replace some of the forests.

# MAN & ENVIRONMENT

**Highest waste generation** The USA produces the most municipal waste per capita in the world, according to figures issued by the Organization for Economic Cooperation and Development in 1999. The estimated figure stands at 1,585 lb. (720 kg) per capita.

**Worst coastal damage from an environmental disaster** On March 25, 1989 the *Exxon Valdez* oil tanker ran aground in Prince William Sound, Alaska, USA, spilling over 10.8 million gal. (41 million liters) of oil. In total 1,500 miles (2,400 km) of coastline was polluted.

**Worst oil tanker spill** The collision of the *Atlantic Empress* with the *Aegean Captain* off Tobago in the Caribbean Sea on July 19, 1979 resulted in the loss of 42.7 million gal. (161.6 million liters) of oil.

**Worst oil spill disaster** The world's worst oil spill occurred as a result of a marine blow-out beneath the drilling rig *Ixtoc I* in the Gulf of Campeche,

**MOST POLLUTED MAJOR CITY** Mexico City is the world's most polluted major city and the most polluted capital city. It is classified as having serious problems with sulfur dioxide, suspended particulate matter, carbon monoxide, and ozone—in all of which World Health Organization (WHO) guidelines are exceeded by more than a factor of two—plus moderate to heavy pollution for lead and nitrogen dioxide. The city's altitude, its climate, and its location contribute to the problem, since emissions are trapped by the surrounding mountains.

Gulf of Mexico, on June 3, 1979. The oil slick reached an incredible length of 400 miles (640 km) by August 5, 1979. It was eventually capped on March 24, 1980 after an estimated loss of up to 167.7 million gal. (635 million liters).

**Most acidic acid rain** A pH reading of 1.87 was recorded at Inverpolly Forest in the Scottish Highlands, UK, in 1983, and 2.83 was recorded over the Great Lakes, USA/Canada, in 1982. These are the lowest pH levels ever recorded in acid precipitation, making it the most acidic acid rain. pH values range from 0 to 14, with 7 being neutral. The lower the number, the higher the acid level of any given substance.

**Worst acid rain damage to forests** The Czech Republic has the greatest damage to forests caused by acid rain, with 71% of the country's forests being affected. Temperate forests are the most seriously affected by acid rain.

**Worst marine pollution** A fertilizer factory on Minamata Bay, Kyushu, Japan, deposited mercury waste into the sea between 1953 and 1967. Up to 20,000 people were affected, 4,500 seriously, and 43 people died from the poisoning.

**Greatest sulfur dioxide pollution** The Bulgarian Maritsa power complex releases 770 million lb. (350,000 tonnes) of sulfur dioxide into the Maritsa River every year. Sulfur dioxide is an acidic gas, which, when released into the atmosphere, combines with water vapor in the clouds to form sulfuric acid. This is one of the major causes of acid rain.

**Worst nuclear waste accident** The overheating of a nuclear waste container caused the December 1957 explosion at a complex at Kyshtym in Russia, which released radioactive compounds that dispersed over a vast area. More than 30 small communities within a 460-mile$^2$ (1,200-km$^2$) area were eliminated from maps of the USSR in the three years following the accident, and about 17,000 people were evacuated.

**Most devastating air pollution** More than 6,300 people have died from the effects of a poisonous cloud of methyl isocyanate that escaped on December 3, 1984 from a Union Carbide pesticide plant near Bhopal, Madhya Pradesh, India. The gas was released into the air when a valve in the underground storage tank failed. Survivors still suffer from damage to their brains, lungs, livers, and kidneys, as well as being blinded.

**Largest deforestation** Between 1990 and 2000 Brazil cleared an average area of forest of 8,596 miles$^2$ (22,264 km$^2$) every year (an area almost equivalent to El Salvador). Between 1994 and 1995, deforestation rates in Brazil nearly doubled to 11,200 miles$^2$ (29,000 km$^2$) annually. This is the greatest increase in the rate of deforestation ever recorded. Since then, rates have returned to the levels of the early 1990s—about 5,000 miles² (13,000 km²) per year.

**Most devastating animal introduction** In 1859 a farmer introduced 24 wild rabbits to Australia. With few natural predators, the rabbit population exploded. They eat crops, chew the bark of young trees, and their burrows damage the soil. There are now over 300 million rabbits in Australia.

**Worst destruction of the natural environment by fire** Deliberately lit forest fires made 1997 the worst year in recorded history for the destruction of the natural environment. The largest and most numerous were in Brazil, where they ranged along a 1,000-mile (1,600-km) front.

**Worst river pollution** On November 1, 1986 firemen fighting a blaze at the Sandoz chemical works in Basel, Switzerland, flushed 66,150 lb. (30 tonnes) of agricultural chemicals into the river Rhine. Half a million fish died as a result.

**Lowest recorded ozone layer levels** Ozone levels reached a record low on September 28, 1994 over the South Pole in Antarctica, when a figure of 88 Dobson units (DU) was recorded. A figure of 300 DU is considered adequate to shield the Earth from solar ultraviolet radiation and sustain our biological systems.

**Largest hole in the ozone layer** In September 2000, scientists at NASA's Goddard Space Flight Center, Maryland, USA, detected the largest hole so far in the ozone layer. With an area of around 11 million miles² (28.3 million km²), the hole above Antarctica is three times the area of the USA.

**Lowest carbon dioxide emissions** Of the major industrialized nations, France has the lowest emissions of carbon dioxide ($CO_2$). France's commitment to nuclear power has helped cut her fossil fuel-related $CO_2$

**WORST MARINE OIL POLLUTION** In the 1991 Gulf War, Saddam Hussein (Iraq) ordered oil refineries in Kuwait to release a total of 240 million gal. (908 million liters) of oil into the Persian Gulf. This was over 20 times larger than the oil spill from the *Exxon Valdez*. Iraqi forces set fire to 600 oil wells, which created clouds of black smoke that deposited soot as far away as the Himalayas in India.

**WORST NUCLEAR REACTOR DISASTER** A nuclear reactor disaster at Chernobyl No. 4 in the former USSR (now Ukraine) on April 26, 1986 at 1:23 A.M. local time resulted in an official Soviet death toll of 31 people. No proper records were kept of subsequent deaths, but over 1.7 million people were exposed to radiation.

emissions. In 1999 France released around 880 billion lb. (400 million tonnes) of $CO_2$ into the atmosphere.

**Highest carbon dioxide emissions per capita** The United Arab Emirates (UAE) has the highest carbon dioxide ($CO_2$) emissions per capita. In 1995 the emissions level reached 68,100 lb. (30.9 tonnes) of $CO_2$ per capita. The total amount of $CO_2$ emissions for the UAE in 1995 was 150.5 billion lb. (68.3 million tonnes).

**Highest carbon dioxide emissions** The USA has the highest emissions of $CO_2$, one of the key gases responsible for the "greenhouse effect." The country emitted some 11,600 billion lb. (5,800 million tonnes) of $CO_2$ in 2000, a 3.1% increase on 1999. The burning of fossil fuels is a primary cause.

**Most lethal smog** Between 3,500 and 4,000 people, mainly the elderly and children, died in London, UK, from acute bronchitis caused by thick smog between December 4 and 9, 1952. It was caused by the burning of fossil fuels combined with a weather inversion that trapped smoke particles near the ground. Visibility in the streets was only 12 in. (30 cm), and movies had to close because it was impossible to see the screens.

**Longest running environmental campaign** Greenpeace has been campaigning against nuclear testing since it was founded in 1971, with the first campaign directed against nuclear testing off the Alaskan coast. The environmental organization is still campaigning on the nuclear issue worldwide.

# MAN & EARTH

**Deepest underground nuclear explosion** A 2.5-kiloton nuclear device was detonated at the bottom of a shaft 9,350 ft. (2,850 m) deep at a location 37 miles (60 km) south of Nefte-yugamsk, Siberia, Russia, on June 18, 1985. The detonation was carried out in an attempt to stimulate oil production. For a comparison, the Hiroshima bomb had a yield of 20 kilotons.

**Largest diamond** A 3,106-carat diamond was found on January 26, 1905 at the Premier Diamond Mine, near Pretoria, South Africa, and presented to the reigning British monarch, Edward VII. Named "The Cullinan," it was cut into 106 polished diamonds.

**Largest manmade excavation** The Bingham Canyon copper mine near Salt Lake City, Utah, USA, is the world's largest manmade excavation. Since it began operations in 1906, more than 6 billion tons of rock have been excavated from it. It measures 2.5 miles (4 km) across and 0.5 miles (0.8 km) deep and is visible from space.

**Greatest oil gusher** The greatest "wildcat" ever recorded blew at Alborz No. 5 well, near Qum, Iran, on August 26, 1956. An incredible 62,100 kPa (9,000 lb./in.$^2$) of pressure blasted the uncontrolled oil to a height of 170 ft. (52 m), producing 120,000 barrels per day. It was closed after 90 days' work by B. Mostofi and Myron Kinley of Texas, USA.

**Oldest mine** The oldest mine in the world is the chert (silica) mine at Nazlet Sabaha, Garb, Egypt. It is thought to have first been in use around 100,000 years ago.

**Largest producer of natural diamonds** The world's largest producer of natural diamonds is Australia, which provides around 34% of the world's annual production of 110 million carats.

**LARGEST PRODUCER OF COMMERCIAL ENERGY** In 1995 the USA produced 75,387 petajoules (joules x 10$^{15}$) of commercial energy. USA resources include solid (e.g. coal), liquid (oil), and gaseous fuels as well as primary electricity.

**LARGEST HYDROGEN BOMB CRATER** On March 1, 1954, the US government performed its largest ever nuclear weapons test on Bikini Atoll, Marshall Islands (Pacific Ocean). The 13.6-megaton hydrogen bomb explosion, code-named "Bravo," vaporized two and a half islands and millions of tons of sand, coral, and sea and plant life. It left behind a crater (pictured here) with a diameter of around 6,000 ft. (1,800 m) and a depth of around 240 ft. (70 m).

Owing to their relatively low quality, they only account for 5% of the annual value. Botswana diamonds are much higher quality and account for 21% of the world's annual production in terms of value.

**Largest crater from an underground nuclear explosion** On January 15, 1965, a 104-kiloton nuclear device was detonated at the Semipalatinsk Test Site, Kazakhstan, 583 ft. (178 m) beneath the dry bed of the Chagan river, leaving a crater 1,338 ft. (408 m) wide with a maximum depth of 328 ft. (100 m). A major lake later formed behind the 65–114 ft. (20–35 m) upraised lip of the crater, which was then cut through with earthmoving equipment to allow it to be used as a reservoir.

**Highest oil consumption** The largest oil consumer in the world is the USA with 19.6 million barrels per day in 2001, 25% of the world's total.

**Largest oil field** The Ghawar field in Saudi Arabia, developed by Saudi company Aramco, stretches over 150 × 22 miles (240 × 35 km) and has an EUR (estimated ultimate recovery) of 82 billion barrels of oil.

**Largest oil producing company** The world's largest oil producing company is the Saudi Arabian Oil Co. (Saudi Aramco) supplying 11% of the world's oil demand and controlling oil reserves of approximately 259 billion barrels (roughly 25% of the world's total and 12 times the US reserves).

**Fastest time to sink a mine shaft** The one-month (31-day) world record for sinking a standard shaft, 26 ft. (7.9 m) in diameter, is 1,251 ft. (381.3 m) at Buffelsfontein Mine, Northern Province, South Africa, in March 1962.

**Largest source of world energy by fuel type** In 1996 the largest source of world energy by fuel was oil, which generated 41% of the world's total energy. Coal was second, with 24% of the total.

**Heaviest oil platform** The world's heaviest oil platform is the *Pampo* platform in the Campos Basin off Rio de Janeiro, Brazil, built and operated by the Petrobros company. Opened in the 1970s, the platform weighs 52.9 million lb. (24,000 tonnes), covers 42,000 ft.$^2$ (3,900 m$^2$) and produces 33,000 barrels per day.

**Largest piece of amber** The largest piece of amber was unearthed in Sarawak, Malaysia, in 1991. The original size of the piece was several square meters, but it was impossible to excavate in one piece. It was broken up into smaller fragments, the largest of which weighs 50 lb. (23 kg) and is now in the Staatliches Museum für Naturkunde in Stuttgart, Germany. This largest fragment of the original piece still breaks the previous record.

**Longest ice core** The longest ice core in the world measures 11,886 ft. (3,623 m) in length and was drilled from the ice above Lake Vostok, Antarctica, in 1998. The drilling stopped at around 492 ft. (150 m) above the surface of the lake in order to avoid possible contamination of the lake's pristine environment.

**Largest natural gas production** The world's largest producer of natural gas in 2001 was the USA, with 24,641 billion ft.$^3$ (697 billion m$^3$).

**Largest natural gas field** The Urengoy gas condensate field in Siberia, Russia, is the world's largest, with estimated reserves of 282 trillion ft.$^3$ (8 trillion m$^3$). Discovered in 1966, it provides one third of the total annual Russian gas production.

**Deepest penetration into the Earth's crust** A geological exploratory borehole near Zapolyarny on the Kola peninsula of Arctic Russia was begun on May 24, 1970. It reached a depth of 40,236 ft. (12,261 m) by 1983, when work stopped due to lack of funds. The temperature of the rocks at the bottom of the hole is about 410°F (210°C). The object of the Kola hole was not oil or gas extraction but firsthand knowledge of the nature of the Earth's interior, particularly the "zone of discontinuity."

**Longest oil pipeline** The world's longest crude oil pipeline is the Interprovincial Pipe Line Inc. installation. It spans the North American continent from Edmonton, Alberta, Canada, through Chicago to Montreal—a distance of 2,353 miles (3,787.2 km). Along the pipe, 82 pumping stations maintain a flow of 1.6 million barrels (254,000 m$^3$) a day.

**DEEPEST MINE** The Western Deep Levels gold mine in Carletonville, Gauteng, South Africa, is the world's deepest mine. A depth of 11,749 ft. (3,581 m) was attained on July 12, 1977. The shaft is 6,800 ft. (2,072 m) deep with an elevator that winds at a maximum speed of 3,595 ft. (1,095 m) per minute.

**Deepest water bore** The world's deepest water bore is the 7,320-ft. (2,231-m) Stensvad Water Well 11-W1 drilled by the Great Northern Drilling Co., Inc. in Rosebud County, Montana, USA, from October to November 1961. The Thermal Power Co. geothermal steam well, begun in Sonoma County, California, USA, in 1955 is down to 9,029 ft. (2,752 m).

**Greatest geothermal power capacity** The USA has the capacity to generate 2,700 megawatts of electricity directly from the Earth. The Geysers Power Plant, California, USA, is the largest geothermal plant in the world, and it can generate 1,700 megawatts of electricity.

# MODERN
# WORLD

# NATIONS

**Most remote city from the sea** The city most remote from the sea is Urumqi, the capital of China's Xinjiang Uygur autonomous region, which lies at a distance of about 1,500 miles (2,500 km) from the nearest coastline.

**Most crossed border** The border crossed most often is that between the USA and Mexico. In 2000, over 290 million people crossed from Mexico into the USA, and a similar number passed in the opposite direction. This is equivalent to the entire population of the USA crossing the border twice in one year. Of the travelers crossing into the USA, 47 million were on foot, while the rest were carried in approximately 91 million personal vehicles and 270,000 buses. The border extends for 1,933 miles (3,110 km), with numerous border-crossing points.

**Longest boundary** The world's longest boundary lies between Canada and the USA. Including the Great Lakes boundaries but excluding the 1,582-mile (2,547-km) border with Alaska, the boundary extends for 3,986 miles (6,416 km). If the Alaskan border is added, the US-Canada boundary is 5,569 miles (8,963 km) long.

**Longest coastline** Canada has the longest coastline of any country in the world, with 151,489 miles (243,798 km) including islands.

**Most maritime boundaries** The country with the largest number of maritime boundaries is Indonesia, with 19 (including boundaries with disputed territorial claims).

**LARGEST ADVERTISING EXPENDITURE** The USA (Times Square, New York, USA, shown here has the largest advertising expenditure, with $236.3 billion (£155.9 billion) spent in 2000. The estimated expenditure for 2001 was $233.7 billion (£161.2 billion), and the forecast for 2006 is $285 billion (£177 billion).

**Highest GNI per capita** According to the World Bank Atlas, the country with the highest gross national income (GNI) for 2001 was Luxembourg, with a GNI of $41,777 (£28,826). GNI is the total value of goods and services produced by a country in one year, divided by its population. GNI per capita shows what part of a country's GNI each person would have if GNI were divided equally. The 2001 World Bank figures (of 205 countries) reveal that the USA ranks seventh with $34,870 (£24,060), and the UK is 16th with $24,230 (£16,718).

**Lowest road fatality rate** Malta has the lowest fatality rate in road accidents with 1.6 per 100,000 population.

**Lowest and highest life expectancy** The country with the lowest life expectancy at birth, as of 2000, is Zambia with 38 years. Japan is the country with the highest life expectancy at birth, in 2000. The average for the total population is 80.7 years.

**Most common surname** The most common surname in the world is Li. China alone has 87 million people with this surname—accounting for 7.9% of the total population.

**Largest shortage of men** The country with the largest recorded shortage of males is Latvia, where 54% of the population is female.

**Largest shortage of women** The country with the largest recorded shortage of women is the United Arab Emirates, where the male population numbers 66.6%.

**Oldest capital city** The oldest capital city in the world is Damascus (Dimashq), Syria. It has been continuously inhabited since c. 2500 B.C. In 1998 it had an estimated population of 1,431,821.

**Most populous city** The largest conurbation in Asia, and the most populous urban agglomeration in the world, is Tokyo, Japan, with an estimated population of 26.4 million in March 2000 according to the United Nations.

**Most populous country** China is the world's most populated country. It had an estimated population of 1,274,915,000 in 2001.

**Least populous country** Vatican City, or the Holy See, has the world's smallest population with just 890 inhabitants in 2001. With an area of only 108.7 acres (44 ha) Vatican City is also the world's smallest country.

**Most sparsely populated country** The most sparsely populated sovereign country is Mongolia, with a population of 2,435,000 (2001) in an area of 603,930 miles$^2$ (1,564,160 km$^2$), giving a density of 4 people to every 1 mile$^2$ (1.6 people to every 1 km$^2$).

**Most populous island** The world's most populous island is Java, Indonesia, which, in 1999, had an estimated population, of 121,193,000, all living in an area of 49,227 miles$^2$ (127,499 km$^2$).

**Most densely populated island** The world's most densely populated island is Ap Lei Chau, off the southwest coast of Hong Kong Island. Ap Lei Chau has a population of 80,000 living in an area measuring 0.5 miles$^2$ (1.3 km$^2$). The actual population density, therefore, is 160,000 per 1 mile$^2$ (60,000 per 1 km$^2$).

**Most densely populated country** Monaco is the most densely populated country. It had a population density of 42,400 per mile$^2$ (16,307 per km$^2$) in 2001.

**Country with most official languages** The Republic of South Africa has 11 official languages. These are: English, Afrikaans, isiZulu, isiXhosa, Sesotho, Setswana, Sepedi, Xitsonga, siSwati, isiNdebele and Tshivenda. The population of South Africa was 43,792,000 in 2001.

**Most private housing** The greatest percentage of private housing is in Mongolia where, in 1997, 100% of homes were owner-occupied.

**Least private housing** The smallest percentage of private housing is in Estonia where, in 1995, only 18.3% of property was owner-occupied.

**LOWEST GNI PER CAPITA According to the World Bank Atlas, Ethiopia (members of Ethiopia's Karo tribe shown here) had the lowest GNI per capita in 2001, with a GNI of only $100 (£69).**

**MOST BOUNDARIES BY CONTINENT** There are 306 national land boundaries in the world. The continent with the greatest number is Africa, with 112. Part of the border between Zambia and Zimbabwe is formed by the mighty Victoria Falls.

**Lowest suicide rate** Antigua and Barbuda (1995), the Dominican Republic (1994), Saint Kitts and Nevis (1995), and St. Vincent and The Grenadines (1986) all recorded the lowest suicide rates with no cases reported in the years shown.

**Highest suicide rate** The country with the highest suicide rate is Lithuania with 87 per 100,000 people in 1998.

# POLITICS & GOVERNMENT

**Largest gathering of world leaders** The United Nation's 55th session of the General Assembly began with the Millennium Summit held in New York, USA, held September 6–8, 2000. It brought together 144 kings, presidents, prime ministers, and heads of state.

**Most descendants to become Prime Minister** Since 1947 a total of three descendants of the Nehru-Gandhi family have become Prime Minister of India. Jawaharlal Nehru became India's Prime Minister when the country attained independence in August 1947 and remained in power until his death in 1964. His daughter Indira Gandhi served as Prime Minister from 1966 to 1977 and from 1980 until she was assassinated on October 31, 1984. Rajiv Gandhi, Indira's eldest son, became Prime Minister following

**YOUNGEST ELECTED AS US PRESIDENT** John F. Kennedy (USA), the Democratic victor in the 1960 US presidential election, was, at the age of 43, the youngest man ever to win the American presidency. Winning by a narrow margin in the popular vote, Kennedy became the first Roman Catholic president. He was also the youngest to die in office.

his mother's death and won the 1984 elections by a landslide. He served until 1989 and was assassinated while campaigning for the premiership on May 21, 1991.

**Longest reigning living queen** Currently, the longest reigning, living queen is Her Majesty Queen Elizabeth II (b. 1926), who succeeded to the throne on February 6, 1952 on the death of her father. Elizabeth II is Queen of the UK and Head of the Commonwealth. The year 2002 saw the Queen's Golden Jubilee, marking the 50th anniversary of her accession.

The longest reigning queen ever was Victoria, Queen of Great Britain (1837–1901) and, from 1876, Empress of India, who reigned for 63 years 216 days.

**Most handshakes by a head of state** President Theodore Roosevelt (USA) set a record for a head of state by shaking hands with 8,513 people at an official White House function in Washington, D.C., USA, on January 1, 1907.

**Youngest mayor** Shane Mack (USA, b. November 15, 1969) was elected mayor of Castlewood, South Dakota, USA, at the age of 18 years 169 days on May 3, 1988. He held office for eight years.

**Most spent per vote in an election** Michael R. Bloomberg (USA), the Republican candidate for the November 6, 2001 New York City mayoral election, spent $92.60 (£56.65) for each of the 744,757 votes he won against Democrat Mark Green (USA), a total campaign spend of $68,968,185 (£44,446,855). His opponent spent roughly $16.5 million (£11.2 million) on his campaign.

**Heaviest monarch** The world's heaviest monarch is King Taufa'ahau Tupou IV of Tonga, who, in September 1976, was weighed on the only adequate scales in the country—at the airport—recording a weight of 462 lb.

(209.5 kg or 33 st). By 1985 he was reported to have slimmed down to 308 lb. (139.7 kg), in early 1993 he was 280 lb. (127 kg), and by 1998 he had lost more weight as a result of a fitness program.

**Most presidents in three weeks**  In December 2001, amid intense rioting due to an economic crisis, Argentina had five presidents within a three-week period.

**Earliest country to pass women's suffrage**  The 1893 Women's Suffrage Petition led to New Zealand becoming the earliest self-governing nation to grant women the right to vote. Governor Glasgow signed the Electoral Bill on September 19, 1893.

**Most candidates on a ballot**  For the November 1994 municipal elections in Prague, Czech Republic, there were 1,187 candidates on the ballot for the single city constituency.

**Most votes for a chimpanzee in a political campaign**  In the 1988 mayoral election campaign in Rio de Janeiro, Brazil, the anti-establishment "Brazilian Banana Party" presented a chimpanzee called Tião as their candidate. The chimp came third out of 12 candidates, taking just over 400,000 votes. Known for his moody temper, Tião's campaign slogan was "Vote monkey—get monkey." Tião passed away in December 1996 at the age of 33.

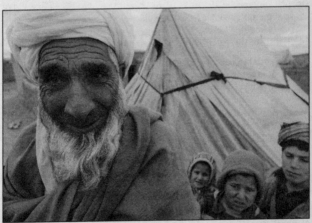

**COUNTRY OF ORIGIN FOR MOST REFUGEES**  The country with the most people seeking asylum elsewhere is Afghanistan. According to the 2001 figures from the United Nations High Commission for Refugees, Afghans (pictured) account for approximately 3.8 million, or one-third, of the 12-million global refugee population.

**Oldest ever royal** Prussian Princess Leonilla Bariatinskaya of Sayn-Wittgenstein-Sayn (1816–1918) is the oldest known royal in history, with a lifespan of 101 years 268 days. Princess Leonilla lived 30 days longer than HM Queen Elizabeth, the Queen Mother (UK), who died in March 2002, and held the record for the oldest king's consort.

**Most failed assassinations** The target for the most failed assassination attempts on an individual head of state in modern times was Charles de Gaulle (France), President of France from 1958 to 1969. He was reputed to have survived no fewer than 31 plots against his life between 1944 and 1966.

**Country receiving most applications for political asylum** According to the United Nations High Commission for Refugees (UNHCR) 2001 statistical report, a total of 915,000 asylum applications were submitted to 144 countries during 2001. The country that receives the highest number of applications for political asylum is the UK. According to figures from the UNHCR, the UK received 92,000 applications in the year 2001. Germany was the second most popular with 88,300 applications, followed by the USA with 83,200. Afghanistan was the main country of origin for political asylum seekers in 2001 (66,800 people), followed by Iraq (60,800) and Turkey (41,300).

**Oldest president** Joaquin Balaguer (1907–2002) was president of the Dominican Republic 1960–62, 1966–78, and 1986–96. He ultimately left office at the age of 89. He held the presidency for no fewer than 22 years.

**Most immigrants** The USA regularly receives the most legal immigrants. The Immigration and Naturalization Service (USA) website shows that between 1820 and 1996 the USA received 63,140,227 official immigrants. In 1996 the illegal alien population was 5 million, of which 2.7 million were Mexican.

**Most presidential palaces** As of February 2003, Saddam Hussein (Iraq), President of Iraq since 1979, had eight principal palaces plus other minor residences throughout Iraq, which contain a total of 1,058 buildings. In Babylon, Saddam had a palace built alongside the remains of the palace of Nebuchadnezzar II (620–562 B.C.); every brick is stamped with the legend "The Leader, Saddam Hussein, Victor of Allah."

**Largest parliament** The largest legislative assembly in the world is the National People's Congress of the People's Republic of China. The Eighth National People's Congress, the first session of which was convened in March 1993, is composed of 2,978 deputies indirectly elected from 22 provinces, five autonomous regions, and four municipalities directly under the Central Government, and from the Chinese People's Liberation Army; it represents the Communist Party of China, eight allied "democratic" parties,

**YOUNGEST CURRENT QUEEN** HM Queen Rania Al-Abdullah of Jordan (b. August 31, 1970), wife of King Abdullah Bin Al-Hussein, is currently the youngest queen in the world. Married on June 10, 1993, her husband was crowned on February 7, 1999 when she was just 28 years 160 days.

and "people without any political affiliations." The Congress is elected for a term of five years.

**Longest embassy siege**  In September 1979 a crowd of about 500 people seized the US embassy in Tehran, Iran. Of the approximately 90 people inside the embassy, 52 remained in captivity until the end of the crisis 444 days later, on January 20, 1981.

**Longest serving US senator**  The longest serving senator in US history is Republican Strom J. Thurmond (1902–2003) who served the state of South Carolina, USA, a total of 48 years in the Senate between 1954 and 2002, seeing the terms of 18 US presidents.

**Most women ministers**  Worldwide, the greatest representation of women in a government cabinet is in Sweden where, following a general election in March 1996, a new cabinet containing 11 women out of 22 ministers was formed.

# WAR & PEACE

**Youngest guerrilla leaders**  On January 24, 2000, a renegade ethnic group from Myanmar (Burma) led by two 12-year-old twins Luther and Johnny Htoo said to possess "mystical powers," took 700 people hostage for 24 hours at a hospital in Ratchaburi, Thailand. The hostage-takers, known as "God's Army," demanded that doctors treat wounded colleagues at their mountain base. All hostages were later freed during a military operation carried out by Thai commandos on the morning of January 25, 2000.

**Youngest nobel Peace Prize winner**  In 1992 Rigoberta Menchú Tum (Guatemala, b. 1959), was awarded the Nobel Peace Prize "in recognition of her work for social justice and ethnocultural reconciliation based on respect for the rights of indigenous people." At age 33, she was the youngest person ever to receive this honor.

**Largest armed forces**  The strength of China's People's Liberation Army in 1997 was estimated to be 2.84 million (comprising land, sea, and air forces). The reserves that can be mobilized number around 1.2 million, plus many more for local militia duty.

**Largest contributors to peacekeeping**  Canada and the island nation of Fiji have taken part in virtually every one of the 55 United Nations (UN) peacekeeping operations to date.

**Peacekeeping mission with most contributing nations**  The United Nations Mission in Bosnia and Herzegovina (UNMIBH) drew troops from 44 nations. UNMIBH was an umbrella organization overseeing

**LARGEST MILITARY EVACUATION** The greatest military evacuation was that carried out by 1,200 Allied naval and civil craft from the beachhead at Dunkerque (Dunkirk), France, between May 26 and June 4, 1940 (evacuees shown here). A total of 338,226 British and French troops were taken off the beaches in the face of advancing German troops. The expression "Dunkirk spirit" is still used to describe a refusal to concede in a crisis.

the activities of the International Police Task Force (IPTF) set up in Bosnia and Herzegovina after the United Nations Protection Force (UNPROFOR) mission came to an end in 1995.

**Longest running peacekeeping operation** The United Nations Truce Supervision Organization (UNTSO) has been in place since June 1948. UNTSO's headquarters are in Jerusalem, but it maintains military observation posts throughout the Middle East. This was also the first UN peacekeeping operation.

**Largest peacekeeping deployment** The UN peacekeeping mission with the largest deployment was UNPROFOR, which took place in the former Yugoslavia from February 1992 to March 1995. The mission reached a strength of 39,922 personnel in September 1994, including a "Rapid Reaction Force."

**Most expensive peacekeeping operation** The most expensive UN peacekeeping mission to date is UNPROFOR, which cost a massive $4.6 billion (£2.96 billion). This included all the missions deployed in the former Yugoslavia during this period.

**MOST NATIONALITIES IN A SINGLE MILITARY FORCE** As of February 2003 the French Foreign Legion (in training here) had 7,700 men serving in its ranks with a diverse range of nationalities from 136 countries. Most new recruits hail from former Eastern Bloc nations.

**Bloodiest UN peacekeeping operation** The conflict in the Balkans during the 1990s led to more fatalities than any other UN peacekeeping mission. The total number of fatalities for all missions in the region is 268, including 210 fatalities in UNPROFOR alone.

**Oldest army** The oldest established military unit is the 80–90-strong Pontifical Swiss Guard in Vatican City, with a regular foundation dating back to 1506. Its origins, however, predate 1400.

**Bloodiest wars** By far the most costly war in terms of human life was World War II (1939–45), in which the total number of fatalities, including battle deaths and civilians of all countries, is estimated to have been 56.4 million, assuming 26.6 million Soviet and 7.8 million Chinese fatalities. The country that suffered most in proportion to its population was Poland, with 6.028 million or 17.2% of its population of 35.1 million killed.

**Bloodiest siege** The worst siege in history was the 880-day seige of Leningrad, USSR (now St. Petersburg, Russia), by the Germany Army from August 30, 1941 until January 27, 1944. The best estimate is that between 1.3 and 1.5 million defenders and citizens died. This included 641,000 people who died of hunger in the city and 17,000 civilians killed by shelling. More than 150,000 shells and 100,000 bombs were dropped on the city. The longest recorded siege was that of Azotus (now Ashdod), Israel, which according to Herodotus was besieged by Psamtik I of Egypt for 29 years in the period 664–610 B.C.

**Bloodiest modern battle**  The greatest death toll in a battle has been estimated at 1.109 million in the Battle of Stalingrad, USSR (now Volgograd, Russia), which started in the summer of 1942 and ended with the German surrender on January 31, 1943. Approximately 650,800 Soviet soldiers were wounded but survived.

**Largest civilian evacuation**  An estimated two million Germans were evacuated from East Prussia in 1945 when the region was ceded to the Soviet Union under the Potsdam Agreement. The German population of East Prussia was replaced by Russians, Belorussians, Ukrainians, and other Soviet citizens.

**Largest anti-war rally**  On February 15, 2003, anti-war rallies took place across the globe, the largest occurring in Rome, Italy, where a crowd of three million gathered to protest against the USA's threat to invade Iraq. On the same day, 1.3 million people attended a peace rally in Barcelona, Spain, and one million people participated in a peace march through the streets of London, UK. Police figures from around the world reported that millions more demonstrated in nearly 600 cities worldwide.

**Greatest air and sea battle**  The greatest battle involving both ships and aircraft was the World War II Battle of Leyte Gulf, in the Philippines, in which 218 Allied warships battled 64 of their Japanese counterparts over six days from October 22 to 27, 1944. In the skies above, 1,280 US and 716 Japanese aircraft were engaged in combat. In the end, 26 Japanese and six US vessels were sunk.

**Greatest ancient naval battle**  The greatest of ancient naval battles was the Battle of Salamis, Greece, in September 480 B.C. There were an estimated 800 vessels in the defeated Persian fleet and 380 in

**MOST NOBEL PEACE PRIZES BY NATIONALITY**  The majority of Nobel Peace Prize winners have been from the USA. Between 1907 and 2002, 270 Americans received the award including former US president Jimmy Carter, who was awarded the Peace Prize in 2002 for his decades of untiring efforts to find peaceful solutions to international conflicts.

the victorious fleet of the Athenians and their allies, with a possible involvement of 200,000 men.

**Greatest modern naval battle** The greatest purely naval battle of modern times was the World War I Battle of Jutland on May 31, 1916, in which 151 British Royal Navy warships squared up against 101 German warships. The Royal Navy lost 14 ships and 6,097 men, and the German fleet 11 ships and 2,545 men.

# CRIME & PUNISHMENT

**Largest compensation for wrongful imprisonment** Robert McLaughlin (USA) was awarded $1,935,000 (£1,225,000) in October 1989 for wrongful imprisonment after a murder in New York City, USA, in 1979, which he did not commit. The 29-year-old had been sentenced to 15 years in prison and actually served six years, from 1980 to 1986, before his foster father proved to the authorities that he had nothing to do with the crime, resulting in Robert's release.

**Largest prison capacity** The largest prison recorded in modern times (from countries in which figures are kept) was the State Prison of Southern Michigan, USA, which had a maximum capacity of 6,500 inmates. It no longer houses such a large number.

The largest prison currently in existence, in terms of inmates, is San Quentin State Prison, California, USA, with 5,967 prisoners as of January 2003.

**Most prolific murder partnership** Sisters Delfina and María de Jesús Gonzáles (Mexico) abducted girls to work in bordellos and are known to have murdered at least 90 of

**LARGEST JEWEL ROBBERY** At the Antwerp Diamond Center, Belgium, over the weekend of February 15/16, 2003, 123 of the 160 vaults were emptied, with an estimated loss of at least $100-million (£62-million) worth of jewels. There was no sign of a break-in, alarms did not go off, and the bomb-proof vault doors were not tampered with.

**MOST PROLIFIC SERIAL KILLER** The Shipman Inquiry concluded that family doctor Harold Shipman (UK) murdered 215 of his patients between 1975 and 1998. He killed his elderly (mainly female) victims with the administration of drugs. Found guilty in January 2000, he will spend the rest of his life in prison.

them and their clients. The sisters were sentenced to 40 years imprisonment in 1964.

### Largest sex discrimination payout for an individual

The largest payout ever awarded to an individual in a sex discrimination case was £1,412,823 ($2.2 million) to Julie Bower (UK) in April 2001. She was awarded compensation after a British tribunal ruled that she had been forced out of her job as a result of sex discrimination by her former employer, Schroder Securities. The Equal Opportunities Commission supported her case.

### Most people killed in a terrorist act

The most individuals killed in a terrorist act, according to the official count from the authorities, is 2,823, as a result of the attack on the World Trade Center, New York City, USA, on September 11, 2001. The total number of people killed aboard the two aircraft that crashed into the twin towers was 157. On the same day, a hijacked aircraft was crashed into the Pentagon, Washington, D.C., USA, with the loss of 189 lives, and a fourth plane crashed in a field in Pennsylvania, killing 44 people.

### Most hangings survived

The survivor of the most legal hanging attempts is Joseph Samuel, a 22-year-old who was sentenced to death for murder in Sydney, Australia. On September 26, 1803 the first attempt at execution failed when the rope broke. The second attempt failed when the rope stretched so much that the victim's feet touched the ground. At the third attempt, the second replacement rope broke. Samuel was then reprieved.

John Lee (UK) also survived three attempted hangings in Exeter, Devon, UK, in 1885, when each time the trap door failed to open.

### Most viewed trial

A daily average of 5.5 million Americans watched live coverage of the OJ Simpson (USA) trial on three major cable television networks between January 24 and October 3, 1995. Simpson, an American football player and actor, was on trial for the murder of his ex-wife, Nicole, and a waiter, Ronald Goldman (both USA) on June 12, 1994. He was acquitted of the charges when the jury reached a verdict of not guilty on October 3, 1995.

### Most common method of execution

The most common method of execution in the world is by firing squad, which is practiced in 73 countries.

Hanging is the second most common method, practiced in 58 countries worldwide. Beheading is still practiced in three countries, while electrocution is carried out only in the USA.

**Largest robbery by a mugger**  Treasury bills and certificates of deposit worth £292 million ($435 million) were stolen when a mugger attacked a money-broker's messenger in the City of London, UK, on May 2, 1990. As details of the documents stolen were quickly flashed on the City's market dealing screens and given to central banks worldwide, the chances of the thief benefiting from the theft were considered to be very remote.

**Shortest jury deliberation**  On June 2, 1998, in the case of *Eastwood v. Capriotti* in the 234th Judicial District Court of Harris County, Texas, USA, the jury of 12 people ruled in favor of the defendant after only two minutes of deliberation. Shannon Eastwood (USA) had brought the suit against Robert Capriotti (USA) and the Capriotti Cosmetic and Laser Surgery for negligence and carelessness.

**Largest seizure of narcotics assets**  In December 1998 illicit drugs profits of nearly $280 million (120.7 million) were seized by the US government, making it the largest narcotics bust in history.

**Last legal execution for witchcraft**  The last legal execution of a witch was that of Anna Göldi at Glarus, Switzerland, on June 18, 1782. It is estimated that at least 200,000 witches were executed during the European

**LONGEST SERVING PRISONER ON ALCATRAZ** Killer, thief and kidnapper Alvin Karpis, known as "Public Enemy No. 1," spent 26 years as an inmate of Alcatraz prison, San Francisco, California, USA, from August 1936 to April 1962 when he was transferred to USP McNeil Island.

witch hunts of the 16th and 17th centuries. At the village of Quedlingburg, near Leipzig, Germany, 133 witches were burned in one day in 1589.

**Longest serving executioner** The longest period of office for a public executioner is 45 years (1829–74), served by William Calcraft (UK) who officiated at Newgate Prison, London, UK.

**Most prolific "hanging" judge** In 1685 George Jeffreys (UK), the Chief Justice who presided over the trials known as the "Bloody Assizes," sentenced approximately 320 alleged rebels to death in Somerset, Dorset, and Devon, UK. Most were hung, drawn, and quartered.

**Largest race discrimination settlement** The Coca-Cola company (USA) agreed to pay out $192.5 million (£121.3 million) in November 2000 after four African-Americans, representing 2,000 other employees, accused the company of race discrimination. Every employee involved in the case was ordered to receive in the region of $40,000 (£27,900) in compensation and back pay, while the four who took the case to court could receive up to $300,000 (£209,000) each.

**Largest drug seizures** On September 29, 1989 in Sylmar, California, USA, officers from the Drug Enforcement Administration based in Alexandria, Virginia, USA, seized 47,554 lb. (21,570 kg) of cocaine. The largest heroin seizure took place in Bangkok, Thailand, on February 11, 1988 when officers seized 2,816 lb. (1,277 kg) of heroin.

**Most criminals positively identified from the composites of one artist** Since 1982 more than 135 criminals have been positively identified and brought to justice in Texas, USA, thanks to the detailed composites drawn by forensic artist Lois Gibson (USA). Police officials claim these criminal cases dealing with murder, rape, and robbery would have gone unsolved without Lois's drawings.

**Highest modern kidnap ransom** Two Hong Kong businessmen, Walter Kwok and Victor Li, paid off gangster Cheung Tze-keung (aka "Big Spender") a record total of $206 million (£127.3 million) in return for their freedom after they were kidnapped in 1996 and 1997, respectively. Cheung Tze-keung, who originally planned to kidnap the top 10 tycoons in Hong Kong, was executed in China on December 5, 1998.

**Largest payout in compensation by a tobacco company** The most compensation paid to and received by an individual is $1.1 million (£668,000), awarded to a 70-year-old ex-smoker in 1995 by Brown & Williamson Tobacco (USA).

**Most civil damages awarded to a company** The most damages awarded in legal history were the $11.12 billion (£7.69 billion) damages due to Pennzoil Co. against Texaco, Inc. concerning the latter's allegedly unethical tactics to break up a merger between Pennzoil and Getty Oil Co. in January 1984. An out-of-court settlement of $5.5 billion (£3 billion) was reached on December 19, 1987 after a 48-hour negotiation period.

# BUSINESS & WEALTH

**Largest currency introduction** The largest currency introduction took place on January 1, 2002 when 15 billion euro banknotes and 50 billion euro coins—with a value of over c664 billion ($592 billion or £407 billion)—were put into circulation in Austria, Italy, Belgium, Finland, France, Germany, Greece, Ireland, Luxembourg, The Netherlands, Portugal, and Spain.

**Largest airline corporation** The largest airline corporation is AMR, based in Fort Worth, Texas, USA, which had a total revenue of $17,299 million (£11,709 million) and profits of around $3,511 million (£2,376 million) in 2002 with a workforce of over 125,000 employees. As well as a fleet of over 800 jetliners and hubs in Chicago, Dallas/Fort Worth, Miami, and San Juan, Puerto Rico, it also heads Oneworld, a global marketing alliance with British Airways and others.

**Greatest rise of the Dow Jones Industrial Average** On March 16, 2000 the Dow Jones Industrial Average gained 499.19 points (4.93%), the greatest rise in history, closing at 10,630.6 points.

**LARGEST SINGLE TRADING FLOOR** The largest single trading floor belongs to the financial service firm UBS (formerly known as UBS Warburg) in Stamford, Connecticut, USA, and covers an area of 93,070 ft.² (8,625 m²). There are 1,400 traders occupying the space sitting alongside 5,000 computers. The trading floor is the size of 20.5 basketball courts or 44 singles tennis courts.

**Greatest fall of the Dow Jones Industrial Average** On September 17, 2001 the Dow Jones Industrial Average fell by 684.81 points (7.13%) to 8,920.70, the biggest points loss in history. This occurred when the New York Stock Exchange reopened after the attack on the World Trade Center on September 11, 2001.

**Greatest annual profit ever** In the year 2000 the integrated oil company Exxon Mobil based in Irving, Texas, USA, had profits of $17 billion (£12 billion), equivalent to a net increase in growth in one year of 124%.

**Greatest percentage rise of the FTSE 100** The greatest percentage rise in a day of the Financial Times Stock Exchange (FTSE) 100 share index was 7.89% to 1943.8 points on October 21, 1987, a rise of 142.2 points.

**Greatest percentage fall of the FTSE 100** The greatest percentage fall in a day's trading of the FTSE 100 share index was 12.22% to 1801.6 points on October 20, 1987, a fall of 250.7 points.

**Largest gold reserves** The United States Treasury had approximately 262 million fine ounces of gold during 1996, equivalent to $100 billion (£65 billion) at the June 1996 price of $382 (£249) per fine ounce.

**Most corporate debt failures** In 2001 a record 211 companies defaulted on $115.4 billion (£79.5 billion) of debt, setting the record in both number of defaults and total amount. This is an increase of more than 120% from 2000 when 132 companies defaulted on $42.3 billion (£39.1 billion) of debt.

**Largest corporation** Based on revenues, the largest corporation in the world as of April 2002 was Wal-Mart Stores (USA), which had revenues of $219,812 million (£154,264 million), almost $30 billion (£21 billion) more than Exxon Mobil, which held the top spot the previous year.

**Largest stock market flotation** The stock market launch of ENEL, Italy's state-owned electricity generator and distributor, on October 31, 1999 became the world's largest ever initial public offering after the Italian government sold c18-billion-worth ($19.26-billion or £11.8-billion) of shares.

**Largest annual trading volume by shares** The largest annual trading volume at the New York Stock Exchange, New York City, USA, was achieved in 2002, when 363,135,930,000 shares were traded.

**Largest corporate bankruptcy** The largest corporate bankruptcy in terms of assets amounted to $103.9 billion (£65.8 billion) filed by the telecommunications company WorldCom, Inc. (USA) on July 21, 2002.

**Largest check by value** The greatest amount paid by a single check in the history of banking was £2,474,655,000 ($3,971,821,324). Issued on

March 30, 1995 and signed by Nicholas Morris (UK), Company Secretary of Glaxo plc, the check represented a payment by Glaxo plc to Wellcome Trust Nominees Limited in respect of the Trust's share in Wellcome plc. The Lloyds Bank Registrars computer system could not generate a check this large, and so it was completed by a Lloyds employee using a typewriter. The typist was so overawed by the responsibility that it took three attempts to produce the check.

**Largest hostile takeover bid** British cell phone company Vodafone AirTouch Plc launched a hostile £85-billion ($137.7-billion) takeover bid for German telecommunications and engineering rival Mannesmann in November 1999. The bid ultimately resulted in a £103.4-billion ($171.1-billion) merger completed after EU Phase 1 clearance on April 12, 2000. The company's name changed to Vodafone Group Plc on August 11, 2000.

**Largest commercial and savings bank** The world's largest commercial and savings bank is Mizuho Holdings, Inc. (Japan), with revenues of $40,074 million (£28,110 million), profits of $7,358 million (£5,161 million) and a workforce of 30,262. Mizuho Holdings, Inc. was created in September 2000 by the consolidation of the Dai-Ichi Kangyo Bank, the Fuji

**LARGEST DOLLAR VOLUME STOCK EXCHANGE** The largest stock exchange in terms of the total value of share trading in one year is the New York Stock Exchange, which in 2002 reached $10.3 trillion (£6.2 trillion). In comparison, the National Association of Securities Dealers Automated Quotation System (NASDAQ, a dealer shown here) was second with $7.2 trillion (£4.3 trillion), and the London Stock Exchange was third with $3.9 trillion (£2.3 trillion).

**MONARCH ON THE MOST CURRENCIES** The image of Her Majesty Queen Elizabeth II (b. 1926) appears on the coinage of at least 35 countries—more than any other living monarch. Elizabeth II is Queen of the United Kingdom and Head of the Commonwealth.

Bank Ltd. and the Industrial Bank of Japan. It is the first bank to have over $1 trillion in assets (£600 billion).

**Largest company merger** America Online (USA), the world's largest internet company, announced a $350,000-million (£213,000-million) merger with media corporation Time Warner on January 10, 2000. The completed merger created the world's largest media company.

**Greatest annual loss** The greatest annual net loss by a company is the $98.7-billion (£60-billion) loss reported by AOL Time Warner (USA) on January 30, 2003. This figure is about the same size as the gross domestic product of Israel. It works out at a loss of $10.10 (£6.10) per share, much higher than the company's 2001 losses of $4.9 billion (£2.9 billion) or $1.10 (£1.70) a share.

**Earliest cash dispenser** The world's first cash dispenser was installed at Barclays Bank, Enfield, Middlesex, UK, on June 27, 1967. Customers were issued paper vouchers that they fed into the machine, which retained the voucher and dispensed a single £10 ($28) note. Within a year there were machines in France, Sweden, and Switzerland. In 1969 both the USA and Japan installed their first machines.

**Largest fine imposed on an individual** The record for an individual fine is $200 million (£122 million), which Michael Milken (USA) agreed to pay on April 24, 1990 in settlement of a criminal racketeering and securities fraud suit brought by the US government. In addition, he agreed to settle civil charges filed by the Securities and Exchange Commission. He was released from a 10-year prison sentence in 1993.

**Longest continuous issuer of banknotes** The Bank of England (UK) has been issuing banknotes without interruption since 1694 when it was first established to raise money for King William III's war against the French.

**Lowest inflation** Hong Kong had the lowest inflation at -3.6% according to the Economist Intelligence Unit in 2000. Hong Kong experienced what is known as "deflation"—that is, a fall in the general price level or a contraction of credit and available money. A freeze in government fees and the ongoing stagnating property market and existing excess capacities have been blamed.

**Largest bank by branches** The bank with most branches is the State Bank of India, which had 13,542 outlets on March 31, 2002 and assets of $92 billion (£64 billion).

# MODERN SOCIETY

**Country with most higher education institutions** Mexico has the greatest number of tertiary-level institutions (universities, colleges, and other comparable institutions), with a total of 10,341.

**Oldest doctorate** At the age of 90 years 58 days, Elizabeth Eichelbaum (USA) became the oldest person to receive a doctorate (Ph.D.). She received her doctorate in Education on May 12, 2000 from the University of Tennessee, USA.

**Largest employment agency** The world's largest employment agency is Adecco SA (Switzerland) with 250,000 clients in more than 5,800 offices in 63 countries. Adecco found employment for nearly four million people around the world in 2002.

**Most employers** The greatest number of different paid jobs recorded in a working life is the 110 accumulated by D. H. "Nobby" Clarke (UK).

The female record is held by Anna Petty (USA), who worked for 67 companies during her working career.

**BIGGEST ELECTRICITY CONSUMPTION** The world's greatest consumer of electricity is the USA, which used 3,235.9 billion kilowatts per hour in 1999—almost a quarter of the total net electricity consumption of the whole world, which came to 12,832.7 billion kilowatts per hour.

**LARGEST COMPANY BY EMPLOYEES** The largest federal company employer in the world is the US Postal Service, based in Washington, D.C., USA, which had 750,000 employees as of the end of 2001.

**Highest cost of living** According to the Economist Intelligence Unit's twice-yearly report, Tokyo and Osaka/Kobe in Japan are the most expensive cities in the world, jointly holding the top spot. Five of the world's most expensive locations are in Asia: Tokyo, Osaka/Kobe, Hong Kong, Singapore, and Taipei.

**Lowest cost of living** According to the Economist Intelligence Unit's twice-yearly report, Tehran in Iran became the least expensive city in the world in June 2001. It displaced New Delhi and Mumbai (Bombay), which had jointly held the top spot the previous year.

**Highest defense budget** The USA has the world's highest government defense budget with $362 billion (£220 billion) approved for the financial year of 2002.

**Largest school by pupils** In September 2002 the City Montessori School, Lucknow, India, had a record enrollment of 26,312.

**Highest consumption of calories** The country with the highest daily consumption of calories is the Republic of Ireland, where the average intake is 3,952 calories per day.

**Country with the largest energy consumption** The USA is the world's largest consumer of both fossil fuels (coal, oil, and natural gas) and of commercial energy (fossil fuels plus nuclear and hydro power). In 1998 the USA consumed a total of 1,937 million metric tons of oil equivalent (Mtoe) of fossil fuels and 2,147 Mtoe of commercial energy.

**Frozen food consumption** According to studies conducted in 1999, Norway annually consumes 78 lb. (35.6 kg) of frozen food per person. This is followed by Denmark with 71 lb. 9.6 oz. (32.5 kg) per person and the UK with 68 lb. (30.9 kg). In comparison, the USA consumes only 35 lb. (16.3 kg) of frozen food per person.

**Largest donation to education**  The greatest single gift in the history of education was the $365 million (£256 million) donated by philanthropist, publisher, and diplomat Walter H. Annenberg (USA) in December 1993.

**Highest consumption of cigarettes**  South Korea has the highest per capita consumption of cigarettes anywhere in the world, at 4,153 units per annum. Japan comes second with 2,739 and Hungary third with 2,689. US consumption for 1999 was 1,836 per capita. An estimated 4.6 trillion cigarettes were smoked in the world in 1999.

**Largest simultaneous lesson**  The world's largest simultaneous lesson involved 28,101 people each learning phrases in a new language. It was part of the "Learning Day" organized by Birmingham City Council, Birmingham, UK, on March 21, 2002.

**Greatest fast food expenditure**  In 2000, Americans spent over $110 billion (£67.1 billion) on fast food, more than on higher education, personal computers, or new cars. On any one day approximately 25% of US adults visit a fast food outlet. A typical American eats roughly three burgers and four orders of fries a week.

**Most chewing gum consumed per capita**  In Andorra each person consumed an average of 2 lb. (900 g) of chewing gum in the year 2000.

**Highest breakfast cereal consumption**  The country with the largest per capita breakfast cereal consumption is Sweden with 22 lb. (10.4 kg) per person according to studies done in 2000. This is followed by Canada with 17 lb. (7.8 kg) per person.

**Highest ice cream consumption**  The country that consumes the most ice cream per capita is Australia where, on average, 35 pints (16.6 liters) of ice cream were consumed per person in 2000.

**Highest alcohol consumption**  The country with the largest per capita consumption of alcohol is the Republic of Ireland with 26 pints (12.3 liters) of pure alcohol per person according to surveys done in 2000. This intake is based on the amount of pure alcohol consumed (wine, beer, and spirits). Luxembourg comes in at second place with 25.6 pints (12.1 liters) per person, followed by Romania with 24.7 pints (11.7 liters).

**Highest chocolate consumption**  In Switzerland the average person consumed 25 lb. 6 oz. (11.5 kg) of chocolate during 2000.

**Highest education budget percent**  New Caledonia in the South Pacific Ocean has the largest expenditure for education as a percentage, spending 13.5% of its GNP on primary, secondary and tertiary education according to the latest figures recorded in *Britannica Book of the Year 2002*. St. Lucia is second with 9.8% (1998) of GNP. The UK spends 5.3% (1997) and the USA 5.4% (1998).

**LOWEST EDUCATION BUDGET PERCENT** As of 2002, Somalia spends least on education, allocating just 0.4% of its GNP to primary, secondary and tertiary education. This is followed by Nigeria (0.7%) and Sierra Leone (0.9%, students pictured).

**Highest paper recycling rate** Germany recycles between 70 and 80% of its consumption of paper and cardboard per year.

**Longest teaching career** Medarda de Jesus Leon de Uzcategui (Venezuela) taught in Caracas, Venezuela, for over 80 years from 1911.

# RELIGION & BELIEFS

**Largest religion** Christianity is the world's predominant religion, with approximately 1,999,560,000 adherents in 2000, or 33% of the world's population.

**Fastest growing religion** Islam is the fastest growing religion in the world. In 1990, 935 million of the world's population were Muslim. This grew to 1,188,242,000 in 2000, which means that approximately 20% of the world's population follows Islam.

**Most threatened denomination** Only six members of the United Society of Believers in Christ's Second Appearance (Shakers) remain. They live in a small community near New Gloucester, Maine, USA. The sect was founded in Manchester, UK, by Ann Lee (UK) in 1772. At its peak of popularity (c. 1830–40) there were around 6,000 members scattered over 19 communities. The drop in numbers is partly due to their belief in celibacy.

**Largest annual gathering of women** In February or March each year, over one million women gather at the Attukal Bhagavathy Temple,

**LARGEST GATHERING OF RELIGIOUS LEADERS** The Millennium World Peace Summit of Religious and Spiritual Leaders involved 1,000 people. It was held at the United Nations headquarters in New York, USA, between August 28 and 31, 2000. Among the attendees were: Pope John Paul II, The Dalai Lama (shown here with an admirer) and Dr. Abdullah Salehal-Obaid, the Secretary of the World Muslim League. The aim of the meeting was to create a commitment to achieving world peace.

Thiruvananthapram, Kerala, India, for the "Pongala" offering. The women, who come from all religions and communities in Kerala, gather with their cooking pots to perform a ritual for the health and prosperity of their families. The highest attendance recorded was on February 23, 1997, when 1.5 million women took part in the festival. The ceremonial duties, which involve cooking rice as an offering to the deity, last six hours.

**Earliest places of worship** Many archaeologists think that the decorated Upper Paleolithic caves of Europe (dating from c. 30,000–10,000 B.C.) were used as places of worship or religious ritual.

**Largest papal crowd** On January 15, 1995 Pope John Paul II offered Mass to a crowd of between four and five million people at Luneta Park, Manila, during his visit to the Philippines.

**Youngest elected pope** Pope Benedict IX was just 11 years old when he became Pope in 1032.

**Longest lived pope** Of all the popes whose ages can be proved, the longest-lived was Leo XIII (Gioacchino Pecci, Italy, 1810–1903), who died at the age of 93 years 140 days.

**Longest papal reign** The longest papal reign was that of Pius IX (Giovanni Maria Mastai-Ferretti, Italy), who was pope for 31 years 236 days between 1846 and 1878. St. Peter, the first pope (c. 33–67), is said to have been head of the Church for 34 years although this cannot be dated accurately.

**Pope to create most saints** By 1998 Pope John Paul II (Poland), who ascended the papal throne in 1978, had canonized (declared to be a saint) and beatified (declared worthy of public religious veneration) just over 1,000 people—ten times as many people as all his 20th-century predecessors put together and the largest number of any pontiff. On October 6, 2002 Josemaria Escriva de Balaguer (Spain) became the 468th person to be canonized by Pope John Paul II. A crowd of over 300,000 gathered at St. Peter's Square to witness the founder of Opus Dei (a personal prelature of the Catholic Church) become a saint.

**Longest period of stigmatism** Father Pio (Francesco Forgione, Italy), a devout Italian Capuchin friar, bore the stigmata (the wounds received by Christ on the Cross) from 1918 until his death in 1968. The wounds were seen by thousands of pilgrims. He was canonized on June 16, 2002.

**Largest wooden church** The world's largest wooden Christian church is the Kerimäki church in Kerimäki, Finland. It measures 147 × 137 × 88 ft. (45 × 42 × 27 m), and its dome is 121 ft. (37 m) high. It seats 3,000 people and standing capacity is 5,000.

**MOST INACCESSIBLE RELIC** The relic believed by the Ethiopian Orthodox Church to be the Ark of the Covenant is kept in a chapel in Axum, Ethiopia, where it is guarded by a single priest, and he alone is allowed to see it or enter its presence. A representation of the relic, rather than the relic itself, is carried in procession.

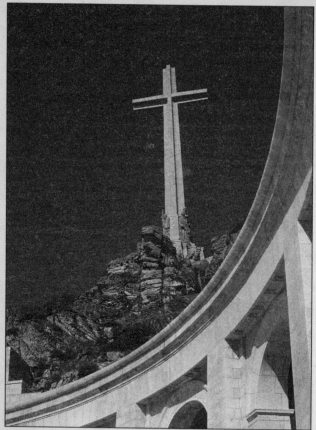

**LARGEST FREE-STANDING CROSS** The largest free-standing cross
measures 500 ft. (152.4 m) high and is made of stone. It stands above an
underground church in the Valley of the Fallen, Madrid, Spain. The
cross can be seen from a distance of 30 miles (48.2 km). It was designed
by Juan de Avalos (Spain) and was built as a memorial to all those who
died in the Spanish Civil War.

**Largest religious theme park** The world's largest religious theme park
is The Holy Land Experience. The 15-acre (6.07-ha) site in Orlando,
Florida, USA, opened on February 5, 2001. It is a re-creation of Jerusalem,
Israel, from 1450 B.C. to A.D. 66. Created and funded by Reverend Marvin
Rosenthal (USA) and Zion's Hope, Inc., a Christian organization, the $16-

million (£9.8-million) project averages 900 visitors per day. Among the attractions are the Jerusalem Street Market, The Wilderness Tabernacle, Cavalry's Garden Tomb, authentically costumed people, music, and even a library for research and biblical study.

**Longest church** The crypt of the underground Civil War Memorial Church in the Guadarrama Mountains, in the Valley of the Fallen 28 miles (45 km) from Madrid, Spain, is 853 ft. (260 m) in length, making it the longest church in the world. It took 21 years (1937–58) to build, at a reported cost of $229 million (£140 million or £211 million).

**Most Muslim pilgrims** The annual pilgrimage (hajj) to Mecca, Saudi Arabia, attracts greater numbers than any other Islamic mission, with an average of two million people a year.

**Longest law enforcement standoff with a cult** The longest standoff between members of law enforcement agencies and a cult was for 51 days at the Mount Carmel Compound in Waco, Texas, USA, in 1993. The cult involved was the Branch Davidians, led by the failed rock star David Koresh (USA). The standoff began on February 28, 1993 when federal agents tried to enter the compound, and ended on April 19 when police stormed the building and fire broke out. Over 80 people died inside, including 17 children and the leader himself. Federal agents were also killed in the standoff.

**Largest underground temple** The world's largest underground temple has been excavated over 16 years by members of the 800-strong Damanhur religious community living in Baldissero near Turin, Italy. Dug into the side of a hill, it takes up a total volume of 211,888 ft.$^3$ (6,000 m$^3$). The Damanhur or "City of Light" was founded by Oberto Airaudi, the son of a Turin policeman, in 1978. They have dug out their temple, known as the Temple of Humankind, using only pick-axes and buckets.

**Longest irregular religious war** The Reconquista—the series of campaigns in the Iberian Peninsula to recover the region from the Islamic Moors—began in 718 and continued intermittently for 774 years until 1492, when Granada, the last Moorish stronghold, was finally conquered.

**Most prolific "crying" statue** On 14 days between February 2 and March 17, 1995, a 15.75-in. (40-cm) plaster statue of the Virgin Mary, standing at the Marian shrine at Medjugorje, Bosnia and Herzegovina, apparently wept tears of blood. One such manifestation was witnessed by the diocesan bishop. Unlike this occasion, most reports of weeping statues do not receive any form of recognition from the Roman Catholic Church.

**Most recent apparition of Mary** The most recent apparition of the Virgin Mary recognized by the Roman Catholic Church was at the cave of Betania, Cau, in Venezuela. This has been seen at intervals since March 1976 by

Maria Esperanza Medrano Bianchini (Spain), and later by hundreds of other people. The apparitions were officially recognized by the Roman Catholic Church in 1987.

**Most witnesses to an apparition** On the occasion of the sixth, and last, apparition of the Virgin Mary to three children at Fatima, Portugal, on October 13, 1915, some 70,000 people witnessed the Sun appear to "dance" in the sky immediately after the children received the vision. The Fatima apparitions were officially recognized by the Roman Catholic Church in 1930.

# WEDDINGS

**Longest engagement** The longest engagement on record is between Octavio Guillan and Adriana Martinez (both Mexico). They finally took the plunge after 67 years in June 1969 in Mexico City. Both were age 82.

**Bride with the most bridesmaids** There is a tie for the record of bride with the most bridesmaids. Accompanied by 28 bridesmaids age 2 to 40, bride Jane Williams married Julian Davis (both UK) at Priory Church in Depping St. James, Lincolnshire, UK, in 2001.

Debbie-Jane "DJ" Hunt (UK) had 28 bridesmaids when she married Jason Clark (UK) at St. Mary's Church, Southampton, Hampshire, UK, in summer 2000.

**City with the most weddings** Regarded as the wedding capital of the world, Las Vegas, Nevada, USA, has over 100 chapels performing approximately 8,400 marriage ceremonies per month—280 per day or one wedding every 5 min. 17 sec. Of these, 12% are between couples from outside the USA. The appeal of a Vegas wedding may be that there is no blood test (a legal requirement in some US states) and a waiting period of only 15–30 minutes to obtain a marriage license at a cost of $50 (£30) from the Clark County Courthouse.

**Longest marriage** The longest marriages on record were both for 86 years. Sir Temulji Bhicaji Nariman and Lady Nariman (both India), who were married from 1853 to 1940, were cousins, and the marriage took place when both were age five. Sir Temulji died at 91 years 11 months of age in August 1940.

Lazarus Rowe and Molly Webber (both USA), both born in 1725, were recorded as marrying in 1743. Molly died first, in June 1829, also after 86 years of marriage.

The longest-married living couple are Yung-Yang Liu (b. October 7, 1900) who married Yang-Wan Yang (b. February 18, 1901) in Kweishan Hsiang, Taoyan County, Taiwan, on March 10, 1917. Aged 102 and 101 respectively, they have been married over 85 years.

**Most couples married simultaneously** Some 35,000 couples officiated over by Sun Myung Moon (South Korea) of the Holy Spirit Association
for the Unification of World Christianity were married in the Olympic Stadium in Seoul, South Korea, on August 25, 1995. A further 325,000 couples
around the world took part in the ceremony through a satellite link.

**Country with the highest marriage rate** Antigua and Barbuda was
the sovereign country with the highest marriage rate in the world with 22.1
per 1,000 population in 1998.

**Country with the highest divorce rate** As of September 2002 the
country with the highest divorce rate in the world is the Maldives with 10.97
divorces per 1,000 inhabitants per year. The Maldives is followed by Belarus with 4.63 and the USA with 4.34 per 1,000.

**MOST COUPLES MARRIED UNDERWATER** On February 14, 2001
(Valentine's Day) 34 couples from 22 countries simultaneously
exchanged wedding vows 32 ft. 9.6 in. (10 m) underwater off Kradan
Island, southern Thailand. Couples received waterproof certificates
before removing their mouthpieces for a watery kiss.

**LARGEST WEDDING BOUQUET**
The world's largest wedding bouquet measured 137 ft. 8.4 in. (42 m) long, weighed 132 lb. (60 kg) and was made up of roses, orchids, asparagus stems, and beargrass. It was created by Fatima Fernandes (Portugal) for the wedding of Mal Carlos and Tânia Santos (both Portugal) on September 29, 2002 at the church of Almargem do Bispo, Lisbon, Portugal.

**Most expensive wedding dress** A wedding outfit created by Hélène Gainville with jewels by Alexander Reza (both France) was estimated to be worth $7,301,587 (£4,269,934) when the dress, embroidered with diamonds mounted on platinum, was unveiled in Paris, France, on March 23, 1989.

**Longest wedding veil** Katsura Yumi Bridal House of Tokyo, Japan, created the world's longest bridal veil measuring 6,639 ft. 11.5 in. (2,023.86 m). It was used in a civil wedding ceremony at the Takarazuka Hotel, Takarazuka, Hyogo, Japan, on December 31, 2000. Around 10,000 people helped the bride with her veil.

**Longest wedding dress train** On February 16, 2002, newlyweds Ernst Boekhorst and Jorien Schuit (both Netherlands) walked hand-in-hand through Haastrecht, Netherlands, with a wedding train measuring 2,545 ft. (776 m) trailing behind Jorien's gown. The 250 guests helped carry the train through the village.

**Best man at the most weddings** The world champion best man is Ting Ming Siong (Malaysia) who served as best man at a record 1,247 weddings between September 1975 and April 1, 2001.

**Oldest best man** On August 14, 1999, Philip Hicks (UK, b. March 26, 1906) served as best man at his daughter's wedding at the age of 93. At the civil ceremony in St. Michel de Vax, France, Philip proudly gave his daughter away before promptly moving to the right to become the best man of his future son-in-law.

**Largest motorcycle wedding procession** Motorcycle enthusiasts Peter Schmidl and Anna Turceková (both Slovakia) had a wedding procession of 597 motorcycles when they tied the knot in Bratislava, Slovakia, on May 6, 2000.

**Largest mass prison wedding** On June 14, 2000, 120 inmates of Carandiru prison, São Paulo, Brazil, married their fiancées in a mass ceremony.

**Most marriages** The greatest number of monogamous marriages by a woman is 23, by Linda Essex (USA).

The greatest number of marriages contracted by one man in the monogamous world is 29, by former Baptist minister Glynn "Scotty" Wolfe (USA) who first married in 1927 and believed he had a total of 41 children. In June

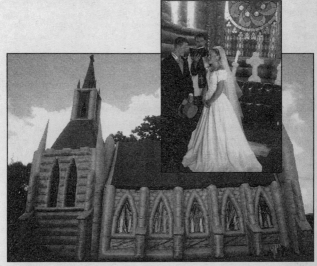

**LARGEST INFLATABLE CHURCH** The world's largest inflatable church is owned by InnovationsUK.com Ltd (UK). It is 47 ft. (14.3 m) long, 25 ft. (7.6 m) wide, and has a 47-ft. (14.3-m) high spire, plus stained glass windows, an altar, and a pulpit. The church can be rented for any occasion.

1996, Wolfe and Essex married—for a publicity stunt, some have said—but Wolfe died 10 days before their first anniversary.

**Most marriage vows reaffirmed by the same couple**  Lauren Lubeck Blair and David E Hough Blair (both USA) married each other for the 66th time on April 26, 2002 in Loxwood, Westfield, Woking, Surrey, UK. The Blairs have married each other a total of 66 times since they first got hitched in 1984; all the wedding ceremonies have been in separate locations.

**Fastest wedding video production**  Videotapes of the royal wedding of HRH Prince Andrew and Sarah Ferguson (both UK) on July 23, 1986 were produced in record time by Thames Video Collection (UK). Live filming ended with the departure of the honeymoon couple from Chelsea Hospital by helicopter at 4:42 pm, and the first fully edited and packaged VHS tapes were bought at 10:23 pm, 5 hr. 41 min. later, from the Virgin Megastore in Oxford Street, London, UK.

**Oldest couple to marry**  On February 1, 2002 French couple François Frenandez (b. April 17, 1906) and Madeleine Francineau (b. July 15, 1907) exchanged vows at the rest home Le Foyer du Romarin, Clapiers, France, at the age of 96 and 94 respectively. The total aggregate years between them at the time of wedding ceremony was a record 190.

The oldest recorded bride is Minnie Munro (Australia), age 102, who married fellow Australian Dudley Reid, age 83, at Point Clare, New South Wales, Australia on May 31, 1991.

# FOLLOWERS & FANS

**Longest running rock group fan club**  The Official Queen Fan Club was set up by EMI after the 1973 launch of the band's first album, *Queen,* in 1973, because of the unprecedented amount of fan mail the group was receiving. At its peak, the club had more than 20,000 members, although this number has now dropped to 9,500.

**Longest running solo artist fan club**  The Club Crosby, celebrating the work of singer/actor Bing Crosby (USA), was founded in 1936 and currently has 450 members worldwide. Its official magazine, *Bingang,* is published twice a year.

**Most fan mail**  Although fan mail is traditionally associated with film stars, no actor or actress has received in the course of a career the number of letters delivered to Charles Lindbergh following his solo nonstop transatlantic flight in May 1927—a total of 3.5 million. He took off in *Spirit of St. Louis* from Roosevelt Field, Long Island, USA, on May 20, 1927 and landed on May 21 at Le Bourget, near Paris, France, after flying 3,600 miles (5,793 km) in 33 hr. 30 min.

**Most fan mail received in one year**  According to the US Postal Service, the highest confirmed volume of mail received by any private citizen in one year is 900,000 letters sent to the baseball star Hank Aaron (USA) in June 1974.

**Most fan clubs for a singer**  There are more than 613 active Elvis Presley fan clubs worldwide, with a total membership of 510,489 as of March 2000. The longest running of these is the French *La Voix d'Elvis* (The Voice of Elvis), founded in January 1956 by Evelyne Bellemin (France).

**Most Hollywood fan mail**  Cartoon character Mickey Mouse was reported to have received 800,000 fan letters in 1933, an average of 66,000 a month.

In 1936 seven-year-old actress Shirley Temple (USA) was receiving just over 60,000 letters a month.

Charlie Chaplin (UK) created a fan-mail record when he received 73,000 letters in the first three days of his return home to London, UK, in 1921.

Clara Bow (USA) received 33,727 items of mail during the month of April 1928. Three full-time secretaries were employed to reply, costing the modern equivalent of $26,763 (£16,975).

In 1926, 32,250,000 fan letters were sent to various Hollywood studios, with Paramount receiving the most, according to a report by *Variety* in April 1927.

**Largest same-name gathering**  The world's largest same-name gathering occurred on September 22, 2001 at the Australasian Shirley Club's inaugural "Shirley Conference" in the Rydges Plaza Resort, Alice Springs, Northern Territory, Australia. There were 122 Shirleys in attendance, all of whom produced birth certificates to prove their authenticity.

**Most popular political cat**  Socks, a stray cat rescued by a neighbor of Bill and Hillary Clinton (both USA) when they lived at the governor's mansion in Little Rock, Arkansas, USA, was adopted by the future First Family in 1991. At the height of his fame, Socks is

**MOST WIDELY SUPPORTED SOCCER CLUB** The Official Supporters Club of Manchester United (UK, a fan shown here) has 152,000 paid-up members in addition to 45,000 season ticket holders. There are 108 UK branches, 78 Irish, and 24 worldwide including countries as far afield as Mauritius and Australia.

said to have received 75,000 letters and parcels a week. The popular tabby answered every piece of fan mail with help from his personal correspondence staff.

**Most condolences on the net** Messages were left by 580,000 people on the memorial page of the official website of the British monarchy in September 1997, following the death of Diana, Princess of Wales (UK).

**Largest free rock concert attendance** Rod Stewart's (UK) free concert at Copacabana Beach, Rio de Janeiro, Brazil, on New Year's Eve 1994, reportedly attracted an audience of 3.5 million.

**Largest internet pop concert** On November 28, 2000, Madonna (USA) performed a concert at the Brixton Academy, London, UK, which was also broadcast live on the internet by Microsoft Network and watched by 11 million people online. MSN emailed their 75 million Hotmail users to advertise the event in addition to homepage promotions in 17 different languages on more than 30 internet sites worldwide.

**Largest magic society** Founded in 1968 in New York, USA, The International Magicians' Society boasts 23,000 members worldwide. These include David Copperfield (USA), the world's highest paid magician.

**Largest stamp collecting organization** With over 55,000 members in more than 110 countries, the American Philatelic Society is the largest non-profit society in the world for stamp collectors and postal historians. It is supported entirely by membership dues, gifts, and the sale of its publications and services. The APS was founded in 1886.

**Largest soccer match attendance** The greatest recorded crowd at any soccer match was 199,854 for the Brazil v. Uruguay World Cup match in the Maracanã Municipal Stadium, Rio de Janeiro, Brazil on July 16, 1950.

**LARGEST BEER FESTIVAL** Munich's (Germany) Oktoberfest 99 (September 18 to October 5) stood on a site as large as 50 soccer fields and was visited by seven million people who consumed a record 1,275,820 gal (5.8 million liters) of beer in 11 beer tents.

**LARGEST STAR TREK FAN CLUB** Starfleet: the International *Star Trek* Fan Association, founded in 1974 and based in Maryland, USA, boasts over 4,100 annual members dedicated to the ideals of the *Star Trek* television series. Two "Trekkies" are pictured.

**Most rodeos attended** James Newland (USA) has annually attended every performance of the Black Hills Roundup Rodeo since it was founded in 1918 when he was seven years old. This represents 82 years of uninterrupted rodeo attendance.

**Oldest Rotary Club** Paul Harris (USA), together with three friends, started the first Rotary Club on February 23, 1905. The club had a total of 30 members by the end of the year. Rotary International now consists of 29,500 clubs in 162 countries. The USA has the most rotary clubs with 7,485, followed by Japan with 2,280.

**Longest career as an Elvis impersonator** Victor Beasley (Belgium) has been appearing and performing as "The King" since 1955, a total of 47 years. On July 6, 2002, Beasley gave his 48th annual show. During the course of his distinguished career, Beasley has also been made Honorary Citizen of Tupelo, Mississippi, USA, birthplace of the legendary Elvis Presley.

**Most viewers for a simultaneous charity rock concert** Live Aid, the world's largest simultaneous charity rock concert in terms of viewers, was organized by Bob Geldof (Ireland). Held in London, UK, and Philadelphia, USA, on July 13, 1985, over 60 of rock music's biggest acts played for free to an estimated 1.5 billion TV viewers watching via satellite throughout the world to raise money for African famine relief.

**Most successful tour** The Rolling Stones' 1989 "Steel Wheels" North American tour earned an estimated $310 million (£185 million) and was attended by 3.2 million people in 30 cities.

**Largest tamale festival** A tamale is a popular Mexican dish that usually consists of spiced meat wrapped in a layer of cornmeal dough. The annual Indio International Tamale Festival that takes place in Indio, California, USA, had an attendance of over 154,000 people at its eleventh event in December 2000.

**Largest trucking company fan club** The Eddie Stobart Ltd. (UK) haulage company has a fan club with over 25,000 members, including some in Australia and the USA. Founded in 1970, the green, red, and gold trucks (each given a girl's name) driven by polite, tie-wearing, uniformed drivers soon attracted the attention of other road users. Club members, or "Eddie Spotters," as they are known, receive a "fleet manual" detailing the name, number, and type of each of the 800 trucks that members can spot.

**Largest gnome and pixie collection** Since 1978 Ann Atkin (UK) has collected a total of 2,010 gnomes and pixies, all of which live in her 4-acre (1.6-ha) Gnome Reserve. The reserve enjoys an average of 25,000 visitors per year, who are encouraged to don hats and temporarily turn into gnomes for their magical journey through the woodland.

**Most peripatetic soccer fan** Ken Ferris (UK) watched a League match at all 92 League grounds in England and Wales (including Berwick Rangers) in just 237 days—from September 10, 1994, until May 6, 1995. He began at Brunton Park (Carlisle Utd) and finished at Goodison Park (Everton).

# TRAVEL & TOURISM

**Fastest circumnavigation by scheduled flights, visiting six continents** Michael Bartlett and David J. Springbett (both UK) circumnavigated the globe on scheduled flights from October 18 to 21, 1999, setting foot on all six continents in 68 hr. 5 min. Their journey began in London and took them via Cairo, Singapore, Sydney, San Francisco, Dallas, and Caracas back to their starting point.

**Most popular tourist destination** According to the World Tourism Organization (WTO), France attracted 76.5 million international visitors in 2001—11% of all international travelers that year—making it the world's most popular tourist destination. Spain was second, with 49.5 million visitors, and the USA third, with 45.5 million.

**Largest export industry** Tourism is widely regarded as the largest export industry in the world, with a massive $555 billion (£343 billion) flow-

**LARGEST CARNIVAL** Rio de Janeiro's (Brazil) annual carnival, held during the first week of March, attracts an approximate daily crowd of two million people, 300,000 of whom are tourists. In 1998 the four-day event generated £100 million ($165 million).

ing into countries through the selling of services to visiting foreign tourists in 1999. The automotive industry (cars and car parts) is the second largest, accounting for $549 billion (£340 billion) of exports in that year.

**Most scheduled flights in 24 hours** Michael Bartlett (UK) made 42 scheduled passenger flights with Heli Transport of Nice, southern France, between Nice, Sophia-Antipolis, Monaco, and Cannes in 13 hr. 33 min. on June 13, 1990.

**Most scheduled flights in a week** Tae Oka (Japan) completed 70 scheduled flights in seven days on Thai Airways International between February 14 and 20, 2001. The flights were all internal flights between the Thai cities of Chiang Mai, Chiang Rai and Mae Hong Son, and all lasted 70 minutes. All flights were on Boeing 747-400s, and the total value of the flights was THB69,960 ($1,642 or £1,135 at 2001 rates).

**Shortest time to visit 15 EU countries** David Beaumont (UK) visited all (then) 15 European Union countries as a passenger on scheduled flights in a time of 35 hr. 8 min. between May 2 and 3, 1995.

**Biggest tourist spenders** The biggest overseas travel spenders are US citizens, who in 2001 spent a massive $58.9 billion (£40.87 billion) while on vacation in foreign countries (excluding airfares) according to the WTO. Germany and the UK were second and third respectively, spending $45.9 billion (£31.85 billion) and $36.9 billion (£25.6 billion).

**Busiest airport for domestic and international passengers** Hartsfield International Airport, serving Atlanta, Georgia, USA, was the world's busiest in terms of passengers in 2001, with 75.8 million people using it that year. The 2001 statistics reveal a fall of 5.4% on the previous year, the result of the September 11 attacks in New York and economic slowdown.

**Busiest airport for international passengers** According to the Airports Council International (ACI), London's Heathrow Airport handled

53.79 million passengers arriving from, or departing to, destinations outside of the UK during 2001, making it the world's busiest airport for international passengers. However, it is only the fourth busiest airport overall.

**Busiest airport for cargo** Memphis International Airport, Tennessee, USA, is the world's busiest airport in terms of the amount of cargo passing through it, according to the ACI. In 2001, 5.8 billion lb. (2.631 million tonnes) of freight was handled, with around 95% belonging to international express transport company FedEx, which has its main overnight sorting facility at the airport.

**Busiest international airline** According to IATA, the German carrier Lufthansa is the biggest carrier of international passengers. In 2001 the airline carried 29.1 million passengers to and from destinations outside of Germany on regular scheduled flights. British Airways (UK), the former champion, took the number two spot with 28.1 million passengers.

**Largest airport by acreage** The $3.17-billion (£2.1-billion) King Khalid international airport outside Riyadh, Saudi Arabia, covers an area of 55,040 acres (22,273 ha). It was opened on November 14, 1983.

**MOST VISITED TOURISM REGION** According to the WTO, the region that received the most international tourists in 2001 was Europe (the popular destination of Florence, Italy, shown here), with 400.3 million arrivals. Although its market share is gradually shrinking, the continent still attracts 57.8% of all international travelers.

**Longest hiking trail** The world's longest complete designated hiking trail is the Pacific Crest Trail, which runs for 2,650 miles (4,260 km) along the West Coast of the USA between the Mexican and Canadian borders.

**Longest wilderness horse trail** The Australian Bicentennial National Trail is the longest marked horse-trekking trail in the world at 3,312 miles (5,330 km). It winds through wilderness areas from Cooktown in North Queensland to Healesville in Victoria, following historic coach and stock routes, packhorse trails, and country roads.

**Longest single air ticket** A 39-ft. 4.4-in. (12-m) single air ticket was issued to Bruno Leunen (Belgium) in December 1984 for a 53,203-mile (85,623-km) round trip on 80 airlines, with 109 stopovers.

**Most expensive trip by a tourist** American businessman Dennis Tito and South African internet millionaire Mark Shuttleworth each paid Russia a reported $20 million (£14 million) for their trips to the International Space Station (ISS). Tito's trip lasted from April 28 to May 6, 2001, and Shuttleworth's from April 25 to May 5, 2002.

**Fastest trans-atlantic flight** A British Airways (UK) Concorde took 2 hr. 52 min. 59 sec. to travel the 3,750 miles (6,035 km) between JFK airport, New York, USA, and Luton Airport, Bedfordshire, UK, on February 7, 1996, breaking its own record (set in April 1990) by 1 min. 30 sec. The plane, piloted by Captain Leslie Scott (UK), flew at an average speed of over 1,250 mph (2,011 km/h).

**Youngest person to have traveled to all seven continents** The youngest person ever to have traveled to all seven continents is Tanya Daniella Donkin (South Africa, b. January 2, 1997) who, on November 16, 2000, landed in Dubai, United Arab Emirates (Asia) at the age of 3 years 319 days, thereby visiting her seventh continent. All her travels were with her parents Dave and Irene Donkin.

**Safest air travel year on record** Despite the attacks on the World Trade Center in New York, USA, which are regarded as acts of terrorism and not accidents, 2001 was the safest year in modern times for travel on scheduled air services, according to International Civil Aviation Organization data. In this year there was, on average, one fatal accident for every 1.2 billion miles (2 billion km) flown by passenger aircraft, and one fatality for every 3.1 billion miles (5 billion km) flown.

**Youngest person to visit both poles** Jonathan Silverman (USA, b. June 13, 1990) reached the North Pole on July 25, 1999 and the South Pole on January 10, 2002, age 11 years 211 days. He traveled as part of tourist expeditions.

**Busiest scheduled airline overall** According to the International Air Transport Association (IATA), Delta Air Lines (USA) carried 93.4 million

**BUSIEST AIRPORT FOR NUMBER OF AIRCRAFT** A total of 909,535 takeoffs and landings by aircraft were made during 2001 at O'Hare International Airport (pictured), Chicago, Illinois, USA, making it the world's busiest in terms of the number of aircraft using it. However, O'Hare is still in second place behind Atlanta's Hartsfield International in terms of the number of passengers being served.

passengers on scheduled services during 2001, making it the world's largest airline. Delta operates a fleet of around 820 aircraft and carries most of its passengers within the USA. American Airlines (USA) was in second place, with 78.1 million passengers.

**Highest earnings from tourism** Despite a fall of nearly 12% in 2001, the USA remains the world leader in terms of earnings from international tourism, taking $72.3 billion (£50.1 billion) in that year. This is equivalent to a world market share of 15.6%. The nearest rivals, Spain and France, have 7.1% and 6.4% of market share respectively.

**Longest ring-road** Work on the 121.8-mile-long (195.5-km) M25 London Orbital Motorway (mostly six lanes), UK, commenced in 1972 and was completed on October 29, 1986 at an estimated cost of $1,333 million (£909 million), or $7 million (£4.6 million) per km.

**Longest motorable road** The Pan-American Highway, from Fairbanks, Alaska, USA, to Santiago, Chile, and eastward via Buenos Aires, Argentina, to Brasilia, Brazil, is over 15,000 miles (24,140 km) long. However, there is an incomplete section in Panama and Colombia known as the Darién Gap. This 70-mile (110-km) stretch of rainforest is the subject of debate between those who want the road completed and those who oppose it for environmental reasons.

# MATERIAL
# WORLD

# SPENDING POWER

**Most valuable baseball** A baseball was sold at Guernsey's auction house, New York, USA, for $3,054,000 (£1,874,655) including commission to Todd McFarlane (USA) on January 12, 1999. The ball had been hit by Mark McGwire (USA) of the St. Louis Cardinals for his 70th and final home run in his record-setting season in 1998.

**Most valuable baseball glove** Former New York Yankee Lou Gehrig's (USA) glove from his final baseball game on April 30, 1939 was sold for $389,500 (£236,778) at Sotheby's, New York, USA, on September 29, 1999.

**Most valuable cigars** On November 16, 1997 at Christie's, London, UK, a record $16,877 (£9,980) was paid for 25 Trinidad cigars made by the Cuban National Factory.

**Most expensive meal per head** On July 5, 2001 six diners at Pétrus, London, UK, spent $61,941 (£44,007) on one meal. The bill consisted mainly of five bottles of wine as, once the bill had been added up, the $422 (£300) charge for food was taken off. The most expensive bottle was a 1947 Chateau Pétrus vintage claret worth $17,312 (£12,300), followed by the slightly cheaper 1945 Chateau Pétrus at $16,327 (£11,600). A 1946 Chateau Pétrus cost $13,230 (£9,400) apparently due to this being a poor year. A 1900 Château d'Yquem dessert wine cost $12,949 (£9,200), and 1982 bottle of Montrachet was a bargain at $1,970 (£1,400). The remaining $150 (£107) consisted of water, a fruit juice, cigarettes, and six glasses of champagne.

**Largest auction of comic books** The world's largest auction of comic books, comic art, movie posters, and related memorabilia took place on October 13, 2002. The four-day auction, conducted by Heritage Comic Auctions of Dallas, Texas, USA, realized $5,207,430.65 (£3,335,958).

**Most valuable coin** The most valuable coin in the world is the 1933 "Double Eagle," a $20 gold coin that was auctioned at Sotheby's, New York, USA, on July 30, 2002 and brought in a massive $7,590,020 (£4,856,370) including buyer's premium.

**Most valuable camera** The prototype Phantom Camera Unit, designed by the eccentric British inventor and MP Noel Pemberton Billing, was sold for $216,826 (£146,750) at auction by Christie's, London, UK, on January 16, 2001. The buyer was a private photographic museum. The final bid for the Phantom was more than 12 times its original estimated value (£8,000–£12,000), an incredible amount considering it was never fully finished.

**MOST VALUABLE GUITAR** Jerry Garcia's "Tiger" guitar sold for $957,500 (£657,850) to an anonymous bidder at a Guernsey's auction in New York, USA, on May 9, 2002. Garcia died in 1995 and left his guitars to guitar maker Doug Irwin, who settled a lawsuit against The Grateful Dead in November 2001 and put the instruments up for sale.

**Most valuable manuscript** On December 6, 1983 Hans Kraus (Germany), acting for the Hermann Abs consortium, paid $11.7 million (£8.14

million) for the 226-leaf manuscript *The Gospel Book of Henry the Lion, Duke of Saxony* at Sotheby's, London, UK. The book which measures 13.5 × 10 in. (34.3 × 25.4 cm), was illuminated with 41 full-page illustrations, c. 1170 by Herimann, a monk at Helmarshausen Abbey, Germany.

**Most valuable cello** The highest ever auction price for a violoncello is $1,217,711 (£682,000) paid at Sotheby's, London, UK, on June 22, 1988 for a Stradivarius known as "The Cholmondeley," which was made in Cremona, Italy, around 1698.

**Most valuable hair** The most valuable hair clippings sold at auction are a mass of dark black cuttings from the hair of Elvis Presley (USA), which were sold by his personal barber for $115,120 (£72,791) to an anonymous buyer during an online auction held by MastroNet Inc. on November 15, 2002.

**Most valuable beer can** A Rosalie Pilsner and a Tiger beer can each sold for $6,000 (£2,760) in the USA in April 1981. The beer was brewed in the 1930s by the Manhattan Brewing Company of Chicago, and the cans have become collectors' items. Vintage beer can collecting is very popular with the Beer Can Collectors of America: there are over 5,000 members, who make beer cans their passion.

**Most valuable cigarette card** The most valuable cigarette card is one of the six known baseball series cards of Honus Wagner (USA), who was a

**MOST VALUABLE ATLAS** A version of ancient Greek astronomer Ptolemy's *Cosmographia* dating from 1492 was sold for $1,144,947 (£1,666,666) at Sotheby's, New York City, USA, on January 31, 1990.

**MOST VALUABLE POP MEMORABILIA** John Lennon's (UK) 1965 Phantom V Rolls Royce was bought for $2,229,000 (£1,702,827) by Jim Pattison, Chairman of the Expo 86 World Fair in Vancouver, Canada, at Sotheby's, New York, USA, on June 29, 1985.

non-smoker, which was sold during an online eBay auction for $1,263,000 (£842,781) to an anonymous buyer on July 15, 2000.

**Most valuable flag** The Royal Standard rescued by Sir Ernest Shackleton (UK) from his doomed ship *Endurance* in 1915 went to an anonymous buyer in September 2002 for $180,635 (£116,000) at Christie's in London, UK.

**Most valuable jacket** The most valuable jacket sold at auction belonged to Jimi Hendrix (USA) and was sold to the Hard Rock Cafe chain for $49,185 (£35,000) at a Sotheby's sale at the London branch of the Hard Rock Cafe on September 19, 2000.

**Most valuable boxing memorabilia** A black and white robe worn by Muhammad Ali (USA) before the 1974 "Rumble in the Jungle" fight against George Foreman (USA) fetched $157,947 (£94,000) at a sale in Los Angeles, USA, in October 1997.

**Most valuable Christmas card** The world's most valuable Christmas card was sold at auction in Devizes, Wiltshire, UK, on November 24, 2001 for $28,158 (£20,000) to an anonymous bidder. Measuring 5 × 3 in. (13 × 8 cm), it was sent by Sir Henry Cole (UK) to his grandmother in 1843 and is hand-colored by the London illustrator John Calcott Horsley. It is considered to be the world's first Christmas card.

**Most valuable carpet** A 16th-century tabriz medallion carpet from northwest Persia was sold for $2,487,178 (£1,596,500) at the Rothschild Sale, Christie's, London, UK, on July 8, 1999.

**Most valuable book** An original four-volume subscriber set of J. J. Audubon's (Haiti) *The Birds of America* was auctioned for $8,802,500 (£5,567,573) by Christie's, New York, USA, on March 10, 2000.

# LARGER THAN LIFE

**Largest fan** A hand-painted fan made of chintz and wood measuring 26 ft. 3 in. (8 m) when unfolded and 14 ft. 8 in. (4.5 m) high was made by Victor Troyas Osés (Spain) in October 1994.

**Largest Christmas bauble ornament** The largest Christmas bauble ornament in the world measures 13 ft. 9 in. (4.2 m) in diameter and was made of galvanized steel by Sergio Rodriguez (Mexico) in December 2000.

**Largest crayon** A red crayon standing 10 ft. (3 m) tall and weighing 332 lb. (150.6 kg) was unveiled on May 28, 1997. Made as part of a promotional campaign by the Dixon Ticonderoga Company, Heathrow, Florida, USA, it contained enough soy bean to make 34,527 standard-sized crayons.

**LARGEST CONTAINER OF BODY CREAM** The world's largest container of body cream is 6 ft. 6.75 in. (2 m) in diameter, 1 ft. 8.75 in. (53 cm) high, and holds 323.48 gallons (1,124.49 liters) of NIVEA Creme. It was created by Beiersdorf Hellas (Greece) and unveiled in Athens, Greece, on December 15, 2001.

**Largest pestle and mortar** The largest pestle and mortar on record was manufactured by Neftali Maldonado (Puerto Rico). The mortar (base) was carved out of a single mahogany log and is 10 ft. 4 in. (3.14 m) high, with a mouth diameter of 6 ft. (1.82 m). It weighs 4,000 lb. (1.8 tonnes). The pestle is 12 ft. (3.6 m) long with a diameter of 2 ft. (60 cm) and weighs around 800 lb. (360 kg). Maldonado says it took him 12 hours a day over four months to complete this project, using only hand tools.

**Longest pencil** The world's longest pencil was created by Faber-Castell of Selangor, Malaysia, in November 2002. It measures 64 ft. 9.5 in. (19.75 m) long and 2 ft. 7.5 in. (80 cm) in diameter, and encases a lead 6 in. (15 cm) in diameter. The giant pencil stands vertically within a protective glass structure on the new Malaysian premises of Faber-Castell. The company has been manufacturing writing instruments since 1761.

**Largest mailbox** Canada Post Corporation erected a mailbox 17 ft. 10 in. × 7 ft. 2 in. × 6 ft. 6 in. (5.43 × 2.64 × 1.98 m) in downtown Vancouver, British Columbia, Canada, in December 2000. The scaled-up version of a standard Canada Post mailbox was made of steel, and over 40,000 children used it to send their letters to Santa, by climbing a set of stairs to reach the slot at the top of the box. Many other regular letters were mailed and delivered as usual.

**Longest hammock** On June 22, 2002 The Hessenstam Hattem of the Voerman Scouting Group unveiled a giant hand-knotted hammock measuring 8 ft. 2 in. (2.5 m) wide and 424 ft. 2 in. (129.29 m) long in Hattem, The Netherlands. The hammock was so huge it had to be hung between two cranes.

**Largest wooden coat hanger** The largest wooden coat hanger ever made weighs 1,589 lb. (721 kg) and was manufactured for H&L Russel Ltd. (UK). The solid pine hanger, featuring a steel hook, is 18 ft. (5.51 m) long, 8 ft. (2.5 m) high, and 1 ft. 4.5 in. (0.42 m) wide.

**Largest chess piece** The largest chess piece is a king made by Mats Allanson (Sweden). It is 13 ft. (4 m) high and 4 ft. 6 in. (1.4 m) in diameter at the base.

**Largest sleeping bag** On July 27, 2002 in Salt Lake City, Utah, USA, Slumberjack (USA) unveiled the world's largest sleeping bag measuring 24 ft. 8 in. × 54 ft. 2.5 in. (7.51 × 16.52 m) and weighing 175 lb. (79 kg).

**Longest sofa** In September 2001 Industrie Natuzzi SPA (Italy) created the world's longest sofa (which was crescent-shaped) measuring a length of 115 ft. 2 in. (35.11 m) on the outside edge, 81 ft. 6 in. (24.86 m) on the inside edge, and with a height varying between 3 and 6 ft. (1 and 2 m).

**Largest bra** In September 1990 Triumph International Japan Ltd. developed a bra with an underbust measurement of 78 ft. 8 in. (24 m) and a bust measurement of 91 ft. 10 in. (28 m). The bra is based on the Tyrolean Cut (underwired three-quarter cup), which Triumph introduced in 1970. It was made from 230 ft. (70 m) of fabric—enough to make 1,000 "regular" bras.

**Largest electric guitar** The largest playable guitar in the world is 43 ft. 7.5 in. (13.29 m) tall, 16 ft. 5.5 in. (5.01 m) wide, and weighs 2,000 lb. (907 kg). Modeled on a 1967 Gibson Flying V and built to a scale of 1:12, it was made by students from Conroe Independent School District Academy of Science and Technology, Conroe, Texas, USA, at a cost of $3,000 (£1,975). Construction began in October 1999, and the guitar was finally played at the Cynthia Woods Mitchell Pavilion, Texas, USA, on June 6, 2000 with the opening chord of The Beatles' "A Hard Day's Night."

**Largest box of facial tissues** The world's largest box of facial tissues measures 8 × 4 ft. × 2 ft. 4.75 in. (2.45 × 1.22 × 0.73 m) and was constructed by FINE Hygienic Paper FZE and unveiled in Amman, Jordan, on October 31, 2002. The box was filled with giant sized tissues.

**Largest champagne bottle** Seven glass blowers from Demptos Glass, Jihlava, Czech Republic, created a champagne bottle 4 ft. 6.5 in. (1.39 m) tall and 4 ft. 4 in. (1.32 m) in circumference with a capacity of 25.7 gal. (117 liters) on October 15, 1998. The bottle can hold enough champagne to fill 1,000 glasses.

**Largest cigar** Jose Castelar Cairo (Cuba) took nine days to hand-roll a cigar measuring 36 ft. 2.5 in. (11.04 m). He presented his creation on April 18, 2001 at "La Triada," Tiendas Habana Universo Cubanacan SA, Havana, Cuba.

**Largest working light switch** The largest working light switch has a switch plate measuring 40 × 24 ft. (12.2 × 7.3 m) with a mechanical toggle

**LARGEST BEER MAT** The world's largest beer mat was created by Carlsberg (Denmark) in Fredericia, Denmark, on September 15, 2002. It measured 49 ft. 3 in. (15 m) in diameter and had a thickness of 2.5 in. (6 cm).

**LARGEST BASKET** The world's largest hand-woven basket was made on behalf of the Cultural Centre in Nowy Tomysl, Poland, between August 28 and 30, 2000. The basket measured 56 ft. 8.5 in. x 31 ft. 0.5 in. x 25 ft. 3.5 in. (17.29 x 9.46 x 7.71 m) and was large enough to contain trees as well as flowers.

base approximately 8 ft. (2.45 m) in height, which moves through 7 ft. 6 in. (2.3 m) in either the "on" or "off" position. It is on the Broadway-facing façade of the Marriott Marquis Hotel in Times Square, New York City, USA.

**Largest model of DNA** The largest model of DNA contained 300 base pairs and over 1,800 atoms and was roughly 40 ft. (12 m) tall. Constructed of molymod, the base pairs were assembled by more than 3,000 British school children as well as celebrities from science, politics, and the arts. The model was first assembled at the Potteries Shopping Centre in Stoke-on-Trent (UK) on March 9, 2002. Its current full length was created on July 10, 2002 in Earl's Court, London, UK.

**Largest revolver** The world's largest revolver weights 99.2 lb. (45 kg), has a length of 4 ft. 1.5 in. (1.26 m), a height of 15.75 in. (40 cm) and is a working, scaled-up copy of a Remington 1859. It was built by Ryszard Tobys (Poland) and test-fired on July 15, 2002. The gun holds six bullets, each weighing 4.7 oz. (136 g), and with a caliber of 1.1 in. (28 mm).

**Longest surfboard** Tim Mellors' (UK) surfboard is 36 ft. 6.5 in. (11.13 m) long. He first used it on August 11, 1999.

# COLLECTIONS

**Largest airline tag collection** Raghav Somani (India) has a collection of 469 airline tags from 115 worldwide airlines, which he has been collecting since 1994.

**Largest collection of hats** The record for the largest collection of hats is 20,422 and is held by residents of the Tustumena Lodge, Kasilof, Alaska, USA.

**Largest collection of bumper stickers** The largest collection of car bumper stickers is owned by Bill Heermann (USA), who has amassed 3,230 since 1984.

**Largest airplane sick bag collection** Niek Vermeulen (Netherlands) has 3,240 airline sickness bags from 740 different airlines, topping a list of over 50 serious airsickness bag collectors. Legend has it that the airsickness bag was invented sometime in the 1920s after a particularly turbulent flight from Moscow to Berlin.

**Largest collection of same brand soft drink cans** Christian Cavaletti (Italy) has a collection of 3,284 different Pepsi cans from 71 different countries, which he has been collecting since 1989.

**LARGEST NODDY COLLECTION** Betty and Johnny Hopton (UK) have collected 1,351 different Noddy items, devoting every room in their home to the Enid Blyton character. Their most valuable item, a Noddy car, is worth about $1,275 (£1,100).

**LARGEST MODEL AIRPLANE COLLECTION** The largest collection of hand-made model airplanes is owned by Robert Humphrey (USA). Robert's collection consists of 1,728 plastic airplane models, all of which he has assembled himself.

**Largest unopened beer bottle collection** Peter Broeker (Germany) has a collection of 8,131 unduplicated full beer bottles from 110 countries.

**Largest autographed drumstick collection** Peter Lavinger (USA) has collected over 1,300 drumsticks since 1980, all of which have been played and handed to him by drummers from various popular bands, including Ringo Starr (UK) of The Beatles. His collection has been valued at over $1 million (£635,700).

**Largest collection of hotel baggage labels** Over the past 40 years, Robert Henin (USA) has collected 1,067 hotel baggage labels from different countries around the world. Hotel labels date back to the 19th century when fewer people traveled abroad. Labels were created as a means of advertising each hotel, and they were stuck to travelers' suitcases as a testimony to places they had visited.

**Largest pencil collection** Emilio Arenas (Uruguay) has a collection of 6,885 different pencils, each printed with a distinct design, logo, or brand. He also owns impressive collections of key rings, ashtrays, soft drink cans, beer cans, perfume bottles, pencil sharpeners, pins, matchboxes, and phone cards.

**Largest fruit sticker collection** Antoine Secco (France) has collected over 26,875 different fruit stickers.

**Collections**

**Largest bottled water label collection** Lorenzo Pescini (Italy) has a collection of 3,709 different bottled water labels, which he has amassed since 1992. The oldest label in Lorenzo's collection is from a bottle of Acqua Roveta (1922), and his favorite is a rare label from a bottle of Acqua di Carnia (1971) produced for export to Saudi Arabia.

**Largest mug collection** The largest collection of mugs is owned by Harold Swauger (USA), who has amassed 4,567 since 1972.

**Largest bandage collection** Brian Viner (UK) has 3,750 different types of unused bandages varying in color, shape, and size.

**Largest collection of "Do Not Disturb" signs** Jean Francois Vernetti (Switzerland) has collected 2,915 "Do Not Disturb" signs from hotels in 131 different countries since 1985. His objective is to cover 191 countries.

**Largest private collection of sports photographs** The record for the largest private collection of sporting photographs belongs to Alex McFadyen (Canada). All of his 11,811 photos relate to ice hockey and are kept in a book of 678 pages, weighing a total of 165 lb. (74 kg). The collection began in October 1977 and is still growing.

**LARGEST COLLECTION OF MODEL COACHES AND BUSES** Geoff Price (UK) has been collecting model coaches and buses since 1959 and now has a total of 7,143. Because of his huge collection, Geoff and his wife have had to move three times.

**Largest *Star Wars* memorabilia collection** Jason Joiner (UK), a special effects expert who worked on the recent *Star Wars* films, has a collection of over 20,000 *Star Wars* toys. In addition, Joiner has one of the original C-3PO robots, an original R2-D2, and an original Darth Vader costume.

**Largest dragon collection** Charlene Leatherman (USA) has a collection of 793 dragon items, which she has been collecting since 1991, when she received one as a Christmas gift.

**Largest collection of nail clippers** André Ludwick (South Africa) has collected 505 different nail clippers since 1971. His collection began on a visit to Israel, when he bought some as souvenirs, and is now housed in a massive display cabinet. His favorite clipper is also one of the oldest—it was handmade by a blacksmith in 1935.

**Largest lipstick print collection** The largest collection of lipstick prints was accumulated by Breakthrough Breast Cancer and Avon Cosmetics. A total of 39,537 prints were collected in aid of the "Kiss Goodbye to Breast Cancer" campaign between July and October 2001.

**Largest hobby-horse collection** Dan Cavanah (USA) has amassed 381 hobby-horses since 1990.

**Largest matchbook cover collection** Ed Brassard (USA) has a collection of 3,159,119 matchbook covers.

**Largest pig collection** Anne Langton (UK) has a collection of 9,130 pig items, which she has been collecting for the past 20 years.

# TOYS

**Largest kite flown** The largest kite ever flown has a total area (when laid flat) of 7,320 ft.$^2$ (680 m$^2$). Called the "Megabite," it was designed by Peter Lynn (New Zealand) and is 210 ft. (64 m) long, including its tails, and 72 ft. (22 m) wide.

**Fastest time to solve a Rubik's Cube when blindfolded** Ralf Laue (Germany) solved a Rubik's Cube puzzle while blindfolded in a time of 5 min. 42 sec. on the set of *Guinness World Records: Primetime,* Los Angeles, USA, on March 11, 2001.

**Largest kaleidoscope** Glassblower Kazuhiko Kamiya (Japan) constructed a kaleidoscope that measured 24 ft. 1 in. × 10 ft. 2 in. × 8 ft. 4 in. (7.36 × 3.1 × 2.55 m) on February 11, 2000.

**SMALLEST RADIO-CONTROLLED CAR** The record for the smallest radio-controlled car is held by a 0.98-in.-long (25-mm) model (pictured, 1:90 perfect scale) of a Smart car developed by Michihiro Hino, Tokyo, Japan, in 2002.

## Most hoops when hula-hooping

The record for hula-hooping the most hoops simultaneously is 83, set by Cia Grangér (Finland) at the studios of *Guinness World Records,* Helsinki, Finland, on October 25, 1999. She sustained three full revolutions of the standard size and weight hula-hoops between her shoulders and her hips.

**Largest hula-hoop** The largest hula-hoop had a diameter of 11 ft. 10 in. (3.6 m), and Laura Rico Rodriguez (Spain) successfully rotated it three times around her waist on the set of *El Show de los Records* in Madrid, Spain, on December 14, 2001.

**Largest tin soldier** The largest tin soldier is 32 ft. (9.75 m) in height and weighs approximately 9,900 lb. (4.5 tons). It was constructed by the Sheet Metal Workers International Association and the British Columbia Sheet Metal Association (Canada). It is now on permanent display at New Westminster, British Columbia, Canada.

**Longest LEGO structure** The longest LEGO structure, built in the shape of a millipede, was 3,329 ft. 4.68 in. (1,014.8 m) long and was made from over 2,000,000 bricks. It was assembled by pupils from 23 primary schools at Myer, Westfield Southlands, Melbourne, Australia, between September 21 and 22, 2002.

**Largest LEGO logo** The largest LEGO logo in the world measures 25 ft. 4 in. × 34 ft. 1.5 in. (7.72 × 10.4 m) and was made at The Franklin Institute Science Museum on August 22, 2001 in celebration of hosting the ESPN X Games in Philadelphia, Pennsylvania, USA. The logo consisted of nearly 180,000 LEGO bricks and took members of the public five days to make from start to finish.

**Longest swing** A wooden swing measuring 439 ft. 7 in. (133.99 m) long was constructed from 132 poles and 4,921 ft. (1,500 m) of rope in two days by eight volunteers from the village of Havelte, The Netherlands. The swing can accommodate 288 children seated individually and was especially made for the Havelte village fête held on September 2, 1998. The children sat in special safety jackets to prevent them from falling off.

**Most valuable antique toy** A hand-painted tin-plate replica of the "Charles" hose reel, a piece of fire-fighting equipment, measuring 15 × 23 in. (38.1 × 58.4 cm) was sold at auction for $231,000 (£128,333) to a telephone bidder at Christie's, New York City, USA, on December 14, 1991. It was built c. 1870 by George Brown & Co. (USA).

### Smallest hand-made teddy bear

The record for the smallest hand-made teddy bear is held by Utaho Imaoka (Japan) who made a 0.25-in. (6-mm-tall) bear on July 31, 2001 in Fuji, Shizuoka, Japan. The bear has six main body parts, movable joints, and is made of ultra-suede filled with a polyester/cotton stuffing.

### Smallest sound-activated self-powered toy

The record for the smallest sound-activated self-powered toy is held by TOMY (Japan) who launched MicroPets at the Tokyo Toy Fair, Japan, in May 2002. Micropets are a range of different characters measuring up to 1.37 in. (3.5 cm) tall, which react to sound.

### Largest yo-yo

A yo-yo measuring 10 ft. 4 in. (3.17 m) in diameter and weighing 897 lb. (407 kg) was devised by J. N. Nichols (Vimto) Ltd. and made by students at Stockport College, Stockport, Greater Manchester, UK. It was launched from a crane at a height of 188 ft. 7 in. (57.5 m) at Wythenshawe, Greater Manchester, UK, on August 1, 1993 and yo-yoed four times.

### Longest pool toy

The longest pool toy ever made was a 5,280 ft.-m-long

**LONGEST SKATEBOARD** Rhyn Noll (USA) built a 20-ft.-3-in.-long (6.17-m) skateboard called the "Super Streetsurfer" and rode it for a distance of 0.7 miles (1.1 km) at Crescent City, California, USA, on May 16, 2002. The board was built to a standard, albeit lengthened, design.

**LARGEST MODEL RAILROAD ENGINE** The largest model railroad engine is a model of the *Thomas the Tank Engine* character "James" which measures 104.05 x 58.59 x 256.69 in. (2.64 x 1.50 x 6.52 m) and weighs nearly 3,300 lb. (1.5 tonnes). The electric, battery-powered model was built by BBC Visual Effects (UK) for a *Thomas the Tank Engine* tour in 2003.

(1,609.34) "pool-noodle" produced by Industrial Thermo Polymers Ltd. of Brampton, Ontario, Canada, on July 1, 2001.

**Fastest radio-controlled model car** The top speed ever reached by a radio-controlled model car is 111 mph (178.63 km/h), set by the 1:10 scale Team Associated RC10L3 Oval Racer car at the Irwindale Speedway, California, USA, on January 13, 2001. The car was driven and built by Cliff Lett (USA) of Associated Electronics.

**Most valuable toy soldier** A 1963 prototype G.I. Joe action figure, made by Hasbro (USA), was purchased by Matt Babek (USA) on an eBay online auction on December 3, 1999 for $14,000 (£8,747). This particular G.I. Joe is the only one ever made from resin, with hands and feet of diecast metal. His camouflage clothing is hand painted. Matt now keeps the figure locked up in a bank vault.

**Longest Hot Wheels track** The longest Hot Wheels track measured 1,650 ft. (502.92 m) and consisted of 2,100 pieces of track, held together by 2,150 connectors. The attempt was organized by Mattel Canada Inc. for Big Brothers Big Sisters of Canada and was completed on July 7, 2002 at Thunder Alley, Toronto, Ontario, Canada. A car successfully completed the full length of the track.

**Highest Hot Wheels gravity speed** The greatest speed reached under the power of gravity by a Hot Wheels car on a standard track is 28.465 mph (45.811 km/h) by Denis Yüksek (Germany) at Toys "R" Us, Hamburg, Germany, on October 5, 2002.

**Most valuable teddy bear** A Steiff bear named Teddy Girl was sold for $170,830 (£110,000)—more than 18 times the estimated value and twice the previous world record—at Christie's, London, UK, on December 5, 1994 to Japanese businessman Yoshihiro Sekiguchi. The bear was made in 1904, a year after Steiff (Germany) made the first jointed plush teddy bear, and had a particularly well-documented history. She had previously belonged to prominent collector Col. Bob Henderson (UK), who took her everywhere with him—even to his landing on the D-Day (June 6, 1944) beaches during World War II, where he was a small-arms adviser to Field Marshal Montgomery (UK).

**Most stunt kites simultaneously flown by one person** Mix McGraw (USA) flew 219 stunt kites simultaneously at Caesar Chavez Park, Berkeley, California, USA, on July 27, 2002. McGraw was unanchored and managed to keep the dual-control kites airborne for a period of eight minutes.

# GAMES & PASTIMES

**Highest total *Scrabble* score in 24 hours** The record for the highest *Scrabble* score in 24 hours by two players is 162,171 and is held by Chris Hawkins and Austin Shin (both UK). It was set on August 17–18, 2002 in Milton Keynes, Buckinghamshire, UK.

**Youngest *Scrabble* world champion** The youngest person to win a World *Scrabble* Championship is Mark Nyman (UK), who was 26 years 320 days old when he won in 1993.

**Highest overall *Scrabble* score** The highest *Scrabble* score is 1,049 accomplished by Phil Appleby (UK). The winning match was played on June 25, 1989, at Wormley, Hertfordshire, UK. His opponent scored 253, and the margin of victory, 796 points, is also a record.

**Most consecutive footbag singles** The world record for footbag singles is 63,326 consecutive kicks in 8 hr. 50 min. 42 sec. by Ted Martin (USA) at Lions Park, Mount Prospect, Illinois, USA, on June 14, 1997.

**Fastest 100-m men's space-hopper race** The men's record for the fastest 100-m space-hopper race is 45.1 seconds and was set by William Sadler (UK) at Framptons, Kings Langley, Hertfordshire, UK, on September 1, 2002.

**Most dominoes toppled by a group** The record for the most dominoes toppled by a group is 3,847,295 (from a possible 4,000,000). The attempt was organized by Endemol Netherlands and took place at the FEC EXPO exhibition center, Leeuwarden, The Netherlands, on November 15, 2002.

**Largest bridge tournament** The Epson World Bridge Championship, held between June 20 and 21, 1992, was contested by more than 102,000 players playing the same hands at over 2,000 centers worldwide.

**Largest *Twister* board** The largest single *Twister* sheet measured 60 × 20 ft. (18.28 × 6 m) and was manufactured by Vision International of Salt Lake City, Utah, USA, in February 1998.

**Most participants in a game of *Twister*** The greatest-ever number of participants in a game of *Twister* is 4,160, at the University of Massachusetts at Amherst, USA, on May 2, 1987. Allison Culler (USA) won the game.

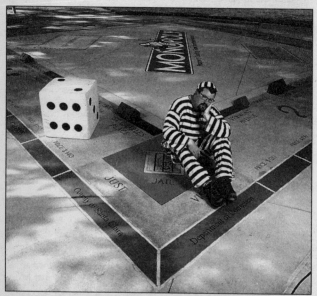

**LARGEST PERMANENT *MONOPOLY* BOARD** The largest permanent *Monopoly* board measures 31 × 31 ft. (9.44 × 9.44 m). Made of granite, it is located in San Jose, California, USA. It was opened to the public on July 26, 2002. The tokens, dice, houses, and hotels are all scaled-up proportionally.

**LARGEST GAME OF KINGYOSUKUI** The largest game of kingyosukui involved a tank 331 ft. (100.8 m) long containing 60,000 goldfish and 15,000 medaka (Japanese killifish), which are caught using a paper net. It was held on August 4, 2002 and organized by Maasaki Tanaka of Guild of Fujisawa Ginza Doyokai, Kanagawa, Japan.

**Fastest game of *Operation*** At an event held by the British Association of Urological Surgeons, Isa Isaa (Ireland) completed a game of *Operation* in 1 min. 2 sec. on June 28, 2001 in Dublin, Ireland.

**Fastest *Jenga* tower to 30 levels** The fastest time to build a *Jenga* tower 30 levels high, within the rules of the game, is 11 min. 55 sec. by Sabrina Ibrahim, John Chua, and Alex Agboola (all UK) on the BBC's "Big Toe Radio Show," London, UK, on January 28, 2003.

**Largest commercially available board game** The biggest commercially available board game is *Galaxion,* created by Cerebe Design International of Hong Kong. The board measures $33 \times 33$ in. ($83.8 \times 83.8$ cm).

**Most expensive board game** The most expensive commercially available board game is the deluxe version of *Outrage!* first produced by Imperial Games of Southport, Merseyside, UK, in 1995. The game, which is based on stealing the Crown Jewels from the Tower of London, currently retails at $12,590 (£7,995).

**Largest game of leapfrog** The largest game of leapfrog involved 675 participants from various local primary and secondary schools at the Flora Hill Stadium, Bendigo, Victoria, Australia, and took place on December 4, 2002.

**Largest sack race competition** The largest sack race involved 2,095 students from Agnieton College and primary school pupils from Zwolle, Wezep and Hattem on October 11, 2002 in Zwolle, The Netherlands.

**Most opponents in consecutive games of chess** The record for most consecutive games played with different opponents is 1,102 by Anna-Maria Botsari (Greece) at Kalavryta, Greece, on February 27–28, 2001.

**Youngest world chess champion** Gary Kimovich Kasparov (USSR, now Russia, b. April 13, 1963) won the title on November 9, 1985 at 22 years 210 days.

Maya Grigoryevna Chiburdanidze (USSR, now Georgia, b. January 17, 1961) won the women's title in 1978 when 17.

**Longest running correspondence chess rivalry** Reinhart Straszacker and Hendrik Roelof van Huyssteen (both South Africa) played their first game of correspondence chess in 1946. After 112 matches, with both men having won half the games, their record play of over 53 years ended with the death of Straszacker on October 13, 1999.

**Longest trading-card game marathon** The record for the longest trading card game playing marathon is held by Kyle Heuer, Joe Alread, Dan Bojanowski, and Kevin Reitzel (all USA) who played *The Lord of the Rings* trading card game for 32 hr. 1 min. at Virginia Beach, Virginia, USA, on May 25–27, 2002.

**Most points scored in cribbage in 24 hours** The most points scored in a cribbage game by a team of four people, playing singles in two pairs, is 139,454 by Colin Cooper, John Dunk, Peter Hyam, and John Wilson (all UK) at HM Prison Doncaster, South Yorkshire, UK, between September 16 and 17, 1995.

**Largest non-commercial jigsaw puzzle** The largest non-commercial jigsaw puzzle measured 51,484 ft.² (4,783 m²) and consisted of 43,924

**MOST PIECES IN A JIGSAW PUZZLE** Ravensburger (Germany) makes a commercially available puzzle consisting of 18,000 pieces. It depicts four world maps and measures 9 ft. 1 in. x 6 ft. 3 in. (2.76 x 1.92 m), making it the largest puzzle by area on sale.

pieces. Assembled on July 8, 1992, it was devised by Centre Socio-Culturel d'Endoume in Marseille, France, and was designed with an environmental theme.

**Fastest tiddlywink mile**   The record for the fastest tiddlywink mile is 52 min. 10 sec. and was set by Edward Wynn and James Cullingham (both UK) in Stradbroke, Suffolk, UK, on August 31, 2002.

**Longest card playing marathon**   Rolando Fasani, Ivano Pancera, Claudio Zanelli, Andrea Zanelli, Mauro Rossi, Armando von Bürer, Eros Zanelli, and Daniele Fiore played the card game *Jass* for 28 hours continuously at the Bellavista Restaurant, Sant'Abbondio, Switzerland, from March 17 to 18, 2001.

**Most bingo numbers called in one hour**   The most numbers called in one hour by an individual is 2,668 by Paul Scott (UK) at The Riva Bingo Club, Brighton, East Sussex, UK, on February 16, 1997. A total of 140 lines were completed, and the games were played by more than 800 people.

# FOOD & DRINK

**Largest bowl of pasta**   The largest bowl of pasta weighed 3,265 lb. (1,480 kg). The record was set by Nintendo of America Inc. on August 22, 2002 in Washington Square, San Francisco, California, USA. The bowl itself was made of fiberglass and was 3 ft. (91 cm) high and 10 ft. (3.05 m) wide.

**Largest box of chocolates**   A Frango mint chocolate box weighing 3,226 lb. (1,463 kg) was created by Marshall Field's, Chicago, Illinois, USA, on November 14, 2002. The box was 7 ft. (2.03 m) wide, 14 ft. (4.39 m) long, 19 in. (48 cm) deep, and contained 90,090 individual chocolates.

**Largest lollipop**   Staff of the Hershey Foods Company (USA) made a cherry-flavored lollipop weighing 4,016 lb. (1,821.63 kg) at the Hershey factory, Smithsfalls, Ontario, Canada, on June 25, 2002. The lollipop was 18.9 in. (48 cm) thick, 62.8 in. (159.5 cm) in diameter, and 190.5 in. (483.8 cm) long including the stick.

**Largest ice-cream scoop pyramid**   The Carvel Corporation (USA) made the world's largest ice-cream scoop pyramid using 3,894 scoops of ice-cream in New York, USA, on August 28, 2002.

**Largest item on a menu**   The largest item on any menu in the world is a particularly special roasted camel, which is prepared very occasionally for Bedouin wedding feasts. Cooked eggs are stuffed into fish, the fish are then stuffed into cooked chickens, the chickens in turn stuffed into a roasted sheep's carcass, and the sheep finally stuffed into a whole camel.

**Largest donut** Staff from Hemstroughts Bakeries, Donatos Bakery and the radio station WKLL-FM (all USA) made the largest American-style jelly donut weighing 3,739 lb. (1.7 tonnes) and measuring 16 ft. (4.9 m) in diameter and 16 in. (40.6 cm) high, at Utica, New York, USA, on January 21, 1993.

**Largest Jell-O** Pool Fab (Australia) organized the creation of a 9,250-gal. (35,000-liter) watermelon-flavored pink Jell-O. It was made by Paul Squires and Geoff Ross (both Australia) at Roma Street Forum, Brisbane, Queensland, Australia, on February 5, 1981.

**Largest pancake** The Co-operative Union Ltd. (UK) organized the making of a pancake 49 ft. 3 in. (15.01 m) in diameter and 1 in. (2.5 cm) deep, and weighing an incredible 6,614 lb. (3 tonnes) at Rochdale, Greater Manchester, UK, on August 13, 1994.

**Largest pizza commercially available** Paul Revere's Pizza, Mount Pleasant, Iowa, USA, bake and deliver a pizza with a diameter of 4 ft. (1.21 m) and area of 13 ft.$^2$ (1.17 m$^2$) making it the world's largest commercially available pizza. The pizza—named the "Ultimate Party Pizza"—retails at $99.99 (£61).

**Longest banana split** The residents of Selinsgrove, Pennsylvania, USA, made a banana split measuring 4.55 miles (7.32 km) in length along Market

**LARGEST PIECE OF TOFFEE** Weighing 2,940 lb. (1,333.5 kg), the largest piece of toffee was created by Susie's South Forty Confections Inc., USA, on September 17, 2002. The pecan toffee was made in the shape of Texas and contained a total of 7,056,000 calories. At its widest points, the toffee measured 10 ft. 6 in. × 8 ft. 6 in. × 2 ft. (3.2 × 2.5 × 0.6 m).

**LARGEST BAG OF COOKIES**
Loblaws Supermarkets Ltd (Canada) made a bag 10 ft. 8 in. (3.29 m) high, 7 ft. (2.13 m) deep and 45 in. (114.3 cm) wide. The bag contained a total of 100,152 cookies. It was presented at Loblaws Wonderland Market, London, Ontario, Canada, from September 6–7, 2001.

Street, Selinsgrove, on April 30, 1988. Ingredients included 24,000 bananas and 24,000 cherries.

**Longest hot dog** The longest hot dog, made by Berks Packing Company Inc., USA, measured 15 ft. 3 in. (4.64 m) and was displayed at the Feeser's 100th Anniversary Food Show at Harrisburg, Pennsylvania, USA, from October 16–17, 2001.

**Largest aluminum drinks can** The largest aluminum drinks can measured 15 ft. 3 in. (4.67 m) tall, 7 ft. 6 in. (2.32 m) wide, and weighed 9,700 lb. (4,400 kg) when empty. The can was made by the Vitalon Food Co. Ltd. and was displayed at the Chiang Kai-Shek Memorial Hall Plaza, Taipei, Taiwan, on June 2, 2002.

**Largest cocktail** The world's largest cocktail was a margarita measuring a staggering 7,038 gal. (26,645 liters). It was made on May 17, 2001 at Jimmy Buffett's Margaritaville and Mott's Inc., Universal City Walk, Orlando, Florida, USA.

**Largest chocolate bar** Elah-Dufour United Food Co. Ltd. made a scaled-up version of a Novi chocolate bar that weighed 5,026 lb. (2,280 kg) at the Eurochocolate 2000 confectionary exhibition in Turin, Italy, from March, 16–19, 2000. The chocolate bar measured 124 in. (315 cm) long, 59 in. (150 cm) wide, and 17.7 in. (45 cm) deep. It was made using approximately 1,874 lb. (850 kg) of Gianduia chocolate, 1,874 lb. (850 kg) of milk chocolate, and 1,323 lb. (600 kg) of whole Piedmont hazelnuts.

**Largest curry** Abdul Salam (UK), owner and chef of the Eastern Eye restaurant, Lichfield, Staffordshire, UK, cooked a vegetable curry weighing 6,848 lb. 11 oz. (3,106.5 kg) at Whittington Barracks, near Lichfield, on July 17, 2000. The curry fed about 7,500 people, and the event raised an estimated $6,700 (£4,500) for charity.

**Largest ice-cream boat** The largest ice-cream boat weighed 1,310 lb. 8 oz. (594.5 kg) and was made by SIA Glass AB, Sweden, on August 25, 2001. The ingredients consisted of 298 lb. (135 kg) of cream, 163 lb. (74 kg) of sugar, 159 lb. (72 kg) of strawberry cream, 119 lb. (54 kg) of chocolate, 555 lb. (252 kg) of milk, and 16 lb. 8 oz. (7.5 kg) of wafers and biscuits.

**Largest tea bag** The world's largest tea bag was made by Lipton Yellow Label of Lever Brothers Pakistan Ltd. on June 22, 2002. It measured 10 ft. 5 in. (3.18 m) long and 7 ft. 3 in. (2.21 m) wide, and weighed 19 lb. 10 oz. (8.9 kg). Attached to the bag was a string measuring 14 ft. (4.26 m) long. The giant bag was made from original filter paper and contained 15 lb. 7 oz. (7 kg) of black tea. It is estimated that 3,500 cups of tea can be made using it. It was displayed at the Avari Towers Hotel, Karachi, Pakistan.

**Largest serving of fish and chips** The largest serving of fish and chips combined weighed 28 lb. 1 oz. (12.72 kg) and was made in conjunction with Asda Stores Ltd., Simpsons Seafish, and McCain Foods Ltd. (all UK) on October 4, 2002. Individually, the fish weighed 13 lb. 6 oz. (6.06 kg), and the chips weighed 14 lb. 11 oz. (6.66 kg).

**Tallest champagne pyramid** A 56-story champagne fountain using 30,856 traditional glasses was constructed and successfully filled with champagne from the top at the Steigenberger Kurhaus Hotel, Scheveningen, The Netherlands. The record was achieved by Luuk Broos (The Netherlands) between December 28, and 30, 1999.

**Largest milkshake** The Comfort Diners, Parmalat USA, and the American Dairy Association (all USA) made the world's largest milkshake at

**LARGEST HOT CROSS BUN** The largest hot cross bun was made by staff at Pegrums Bakery, Rustington, West Sussex, UK, on March 28, 2002. The bun weighed 94.35 lb. (42.8 kg), with a diameter of 4 ft. 3 in. (1,303 m) and a height of 5 in. (13 cm).

6,000 gal. (22,712 liters) in New York, USA, on August 1, 2000. The holders of this record chose to make a Black and White Shake—vanilla with chocolate syrup—as it is a classic New York flavor.

**Largest slab of fudge**   Northwest Fudge Factory.com, Ontario, Canada, created a slab of fudge that weighed 2,002 lb. (908.09 kg). The chocolate-and-vanilla-swirl fudge was displayed at the New Sudbury Mall, Ontario, Canada, on May 4, 2002. The fudge measured 166 ft. (50.5 m) in length, 9 in. (23 cm) wide, and 3 in. (7.5 cm) high. It took 86 hours to prepare and mold the fudge.

# FEATS OF ENGINEERING

# TALL TALES

**TALLEST HOTEL** The Burj Al Arab ("The Arabian Tower,"), in Dubai, UAE, is the world's tallest hotel, standing 1,052 ft. (320.94 m) high when measured on October 26, 1999. The hotel is shaped like a sail, has 202 suites, and covers a total floor area of 1.2 million ft.$^2$ (111,480 m$^2$).

**HIGHEST HABITABLE BUILDING FLOOR** Chicago's Sears Tower has the highest habitable floor of any skyscraper at 1,430 ft. (435.8 m), and the highest roof at 1,454 ft. (443 m).

**TALLEST ROLLER COASTER**
Top Thrill Dragster, a hydraulically launched out-and-back "strata-coaster" at Cedar Point, Sandusky, Ohio, USA, reaches a height of 420 ft. (128 m) and has a maximum design speed of 120 mph (193 km/h). It opened in 2003 and cost $25 million (£16.6 million).

**TALLEST PYRAMID** The Pyramid of Khufu (pictured, also known as the Great Pyramid) at Giza, Egypt, is the world's tallest. It was 481 ft. 4.8 in. (146.7 m) high when completed around 4,500 years ago, but erosion and vandalism have reduced its height to 451 ft. 4.8 in. (137.5 m) today.

**Tall Tales**

**TALLEST OFFICE BUILDING** In March 1996 the Petronas Towers in Kuala Lumpur, Malaysia, overtook the Sears Tower's record as the world's tallest office building. Stainless steel pinnacles 241 ft. (73.5 m) long placed atop the 88-story towers brought their height to 1,482 ft. 8 in. (451.9 m).

**TALLEST FREE-STANDING TOWER** The tallest free-standing tower (as opposed to a guyed mast) is the $63-million (£28-million at 1975 rate) CN Tower in Toronto, Ontario, Canada, which rises to 1,815 ft. 5 in. (553.34 m). Work began on February 12, 1973 and it was "topped out" on April 2, 1975.

**TALLEST OBELISK** The world's tallest obelisk (a tapered four-sided column) is the Washington Monument in Washington DC, USA. It stands 555 ft. (169 m) tall and was completed in 1884 to honor George Washington.

# FACT

Compare the world's mightiest structures . . .

| 420 ft | 481 ft 4.8 in | 555 ft | 1052 ft | 1454 ft | 1482 ft 8 in | 1815 ft 5 in |

# BIG BUILDINGS

**Largest amphitheater** The Flavian amphitheater or Colosseum of Rome, Italy, completed in A.D. 80, covers 5 acres (2 ha) and has a capacity of 87,000 people. It has a maximum length of 612 ft. (187 m) and a maximum width of 515 ft. (157 m).

**Largest theater** The world's largest building used for theater is the National People's Congress Building (*Ren min da hui tang*) on the west side of

**LARGEST PLANT CONSERVATORY** The Eden Project, near St. Austell, Cornwall, UK, consists of two giant transparent domes ("biomes"), the larger of which (the humid tropics biome, left in the photo) is 180 ft. (55 m) tall, covers 273,295 ft.$^2$ (25,390 m$^2$), and has a total volume of 14.681 million ft.$^2$ (415,730 m$^2$). The smaller warm-temperate biome has 70,395 ft.$^2$ (6,540 m$^2$) of floor space and a volume of 3.02 million ft.$^3$ (85,620 m$^3$). The full project—which aims to tell the story of humankind's dependence on plants—has been open to the public since 2001.

Tiananmen Square, Beijing, China. Completed in 1959, it covers an area of 12.9 acres (5.2 ha). When used as a theater, the building seats 10,000, as it did in 1964 for the play *The East is Red.*

The most capacious custom-built theater is the Perth Entertainment Centre, Western Australia, with 8,500 seats and a main stage area measuring 70 × 45 ft. (21.3 × 13.7 m). It was opened on December 26, 1974.

**Largest train station building** With 4.413 million ft.$^2$ (410,000 m$^2$) of floor space the JR Central Towers, Nagoya, Japan, is the world's largest train station building. The complex was completed on December 20, 1999, and was built by the Central Japan Railway Company to replace the existing Nagoya Station.

**Largest theater stage** The world's largest stage is in the Hilton Theater at the Reno Hilton, Reno, Nevada, USA. It measures 175 × 241 ft. (53.3 × 73.4 m). The stage has three main lifts, each capable of raising 1,200 performers, and two turntables each with a circumference of 62 ft. 6 in. (19.1 m).

**Largest "living" roof** The roof of the Ford Motor Company's Rouge factory in Dearborn, Michigan, USA, has had 454,000 ft.$^2$ (42,180 m$^2$) of low-growing vegetation called sedum planted on it, making it the world's largest "living" roof. Planted in a 3-in.-thick (7.6-cm) mat-like material, the vegetation insulates the roof, saving on heating costs. It also lasts longer than conventional roofing as it doesn't expand or contract when temperatures change.

**Largest stadium roof** The transparent acrylic glass "tent" roof over the Munich Olympic Stadium, Germany, covers an area of 915,000 ft.$^2$ (85,000m$^2$) and rests on a steel net supported by masts.

**Largest football stadium** The Maracanã Municipal Stadium in Rio de Janeiro, Brazil, has a normal capacity for 205,000 spectators, of whom 155,000 can be seated. It was built for the 1950 World Cup, and a record crowd of 199,854 was accommodated for the Brazil v. Uruguay final match on July 16, 1950. The oval stadium is 105 ft. (32 m) high, and the distance between the middle of the field and the farthest spectator is 413 ft. (126 m). A dry moat, 7 ft. (2.13 m) wide and more than 5 ft. (1.5 m) deep, protects players from spectators and vice versa.

**Largest administrative building** The largest ground area covered by any office building is that of the Pentagon in Arlington, Virginia, USA. Built to house the US Defense Department's offices, each of the outermost sides is 921 ft. (281 m) long and the perimeter is about 4,610 ft. (1,405 m). Its five stories enclose a floor area of 6.5 million ft.$^2$ (604,000 m$^2$), the corridors total 17.5 miles (28 km) in length and there are 7,754 windows to be cleaned. It was completed on January 15, 1943 at an estimated cost of $83 million (£20.5 million).

**Largest shopping center** West Edmonton Mall in Edmonton, Alberta, Canada, covers an area of 5.3 million ft.$^2$ (492,386 m$^2$). The mall cost CAN$1.2 billion ($927 million or £700 million) to build and features over 800 stores and services, as well as 11 major department stores. Over 20,000 vehicles can be accommodated in its parking lot—the world's largest.

**Largest cathedral** St. John the Divine, the gothic cathedral church of the Diocese of New York, USA, has a floor area of 121,000 ft.$^2$ (11,240 m$^2$), equivalent to 43 tennis courts or more than two American football fields. The nave is the world's longest at 601 ft. (183.2 m) and the vaulted roof is

**LARGEST MOUND** The largest artificial mound was built as a memorial to the Seleucid King Antiochus I (reigned 69–34 B.C.). It stands on the summit of Nemrut Dagi (7,565 ft. or 2,306 m), southeast of Malatya, Turkey. It is 197 ft. (59.8 m) tall and covers an area of 7.5 acres (3 ha).

**LARGEST UNIVERSITY BUILDING** The largest existing university building is the MV Lomonosov Moscow State University, Moscow, Russia, which was built between 1949 and 1953. It is 787.5 ft. (240 m) high, has 32 stories, and 40,000 rooms.

124 ft. (37.8 m)—around 10 stories—above floor level. Although construction began in 1892, the building is only two-thirds complete.

**Largest Hindu temple** Srirangam Temple at Tiruchirappalli, Tamil Nadu, India, is the world's largest Hindu temple. Dedicated to the Hindu god Vishnu, the temple covers an area of 156 acres (63.1 ha) with a perimeter of 32,592 ft. (9,934 m). This is nearly 50% larger than the Vatican City, which at 108.73 acres (44 ha) is the world's smallest country and the center of Roman Catholicism.

**Largest surviving ziggurat** The largest partially surviving ziggurat (rectangular stepped pyramid) is the Ziggurat of Ur (now Muqayyar, Iraq), which has a base measuring $200 \times 150$ ft. ($61 \times 45.7$ m). It had three stories and was probably surmounted by a temple. The first story and part of the second story now survive to a height of 60 ft. (18 m). Ziggurats were the dominant form of religious building of the Mesopotamian civilization between the fourth millennium and 600 B.C.

**Largest Buddhist temple** The largest Buddhist temple is Borobudur, near Yogyakarta, Central Java, Indonesia, built between 750 and A.D. 842. The 645,835-ft.$^2$ (60,000-$^2$) stone structure is 113 ft. (34.5 m) tall, and its base measures $403 \times 403$ ft. ($123 \times 123$ m).

**Largest synagogue** Temple Emanu-El on Fifth Avenue at 65th Street, New York City, USA, has an area of 37,922 ft.$^2$ (3,523 m$^2$). Up to 5,500 people can be accommodated when all sanctuaries are in use.

**Largest mosque** The Shah Faisal Mosque, near Islamabad, Pakistan, has a total area of 46.87 acres (18.97 ha), with the covered area of the prayer hall covering 1.19 acres (0.48 ha). It can accommodate 100,000 worshippers in the prayer hall and courtyard and 200,000 more in the adjacent grounds.

**Largest religious structure** Angkor Wat (City Temple) in Cambodia covers a 401-acre (162.6-ha) site. Its curtain wall measures 4,200 ft. (1,280 m), and, before it was abandoned in 1432, its population was 80,000. Begun c. 900, the whole complex of 72 major monuments extends over 15.4 miles (24.8 km).

# CONSTRUCTIONS

**Longest wooden footbridge** The Hōrai Bridge, a wooden toll bridge across the Oi River in the Shizuoka Prefecture, Japan, measures 2,944 ft. 3 in. (897.42 m). It was built in 1867 and rebuilt in the 1960s because of flooding.

**Deepest railway line** The Seikan Tunnel, which crosses the Tsugaro Strait between Honshū and Hokkaidō, Japan, reaches a depth of 786 ft. (240 m) below sea level. Opened on March 13, 1988, the tunnel is a record 33.46 miles (53.85 km) long. Trains stop in the middle so that passengers can take photos through windows on the tunnel walls. By comparison, the Channel Tunnel linking Dover, UK, to Calais, France, is at an average depth of 148 ft. (45 m) below the sea floor.

**Highest causeway** The Bailey bridge erected in August 1982 over the Khardungla Pass, Ladakh, India, was, at 18,380 ft. (5,602 m), the road bridge at the highest altitude in the world. It was replaced by a causeway in the mid 1990s because of constant damage from avalanches.

**Longest cantilever bridge** The Québec Bridge (Pont de Québec) over the St. Lawrence River in Canada has the longest cantilever truss span of any in the world, measuring 1,800 ft. (549 m) between the piers and 3,239 ft. (987 m) overall. It carries a railway track and two roadways. Work began in 1900, and it was finally opened to traffic on December 3, 1917, having cost CAN$22.5 million ($22.5 million or £4.7 million) and 87 lives.

**Longest floating bridge** The second Lake Washington Bridge, Seattle, Washington, USA, has a total length of 2.39 miles (3,839 m), with its floating section measuring 1.42 miles (2,291 m). The bridge cost $15 million (£5.35 million) to build and was completed in August 1963.

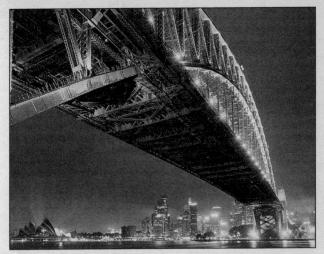

**WIDEST BRIDGE** The widest long-span bridge is the 1,650-ft.-long
(503-m) Sydney Harbour Bridge, Australia, which is 160 ft. (48.8 m) wide.
It carries two electric overhead railroad tracks, eight lanes of roadway, a
bike track, and a footway. It was officially opened on March 19, 1932.

**Oldest electric-opening bridge** The Pyrmont Bridge over Cockle Bay
in Sydney, Australia, opened in 1902 and is still in use today. Nineteen
levers have to be pulled to open the 2.2-million-lb. (1,000-tonne) swinging
section of the 1,210-ft.-long (368.8-m) bridge.

**Longest bridging** The second Lake Pontchartrain Causeway, which joins
Mandeville and Metairie, Louisiana, USA, is 23.87 miles (38.42 km) long.
It was completed in 1969.

**Longest span suspension bridge** The Tsing Ma Bridge in Hong
Kong, China, has a main span of 4,518 ft. (1,377 m), a width of 131 ft.
(40 m) and a length of 1.36 miles (2.2 km). Its shipping clearance reaches
203 ft. (62 m), and the tower height is 675 ft. (206 m). The bridge carries
both road and rail traffic.

**Longest steel arch bridge** The New River Gorge Bridge, near Fayette-
ville, West Virginia, USA, was completed in 1977 and has a span of 1,700 ft.
(518 m).

**Highest bridge** The world's highest bridge is over the Royal Gorge of the
Arkansas River in Colorado, USA, at 1,053 ft. (321 m) above the water
level. It is a suspension bridge with a main span of 880 ft. (268 m), and construction took six months, ending on December 6, 1929.

**Longest bridge-tunnel** The Chesapeake Bay bridge-tunnel, which opened to traffic on April 15, 1964, extends 17.65 miles (28.4 km) from the Eastern Shore region of the Delmarva Peninsula to Virginia Beach, Virginia, USA. The longest bridged section is Trestle C at 4.56 miles (7.34 km) long; the longest tunnel is the Thimble Shoal Channel Tunnel, at 1.09 miles (1.75 km).

**Longest sewage tunnel** The Chicago TARP (Tunnels and Reservoir Plan) in Illinois, USA, when complete, will involve 131 miles (211 km) of machine-bored sewer tunnels between 9 and 33 ft. (2.7 and 10 m) in diameter. Phase I comprises 109 miles (175.4 km), and as of June 2002, 92 miles (148 km) were operational, 8 miles (12 km) are under construction, and the rest are unfunded. The system provides pollution control (Phase I) and flood control (Phase II) and will service 3.9 million people in 52 communities over an area of 375 miles$^2$ (971 km$^2$). The estimated cost is $3.7 billion. (£2.3 billion).

**Deepest road tunnel** The Hitra Tunnel, Norway, links the mainland to the island of Hitra. It reaches a depth of 866 ft. (264 m) below sea level. It is 3.4 miles (5.6 km) long, with three lanes, and was opened in December 1994.

**Largest road tunnel by diameter** The largest diameter road tunnel is that blasted through Yerba Buena Island, San Francisco, California, USA. It is 79 ft. (24 m) wide, 56 ft. (17 m) high, and 541 ft. (165 m) long. More than 280,000 vehicles pass along its two decks each day.

**Largest tunnel-boring machine** The largest tunnel-boring machine in the world measures 48 ft. 9.4 in. (14.87 m) in diameter by 393 ft. (120 m) long and weighs 7,760,200 lb. (3,520 tonnes). It is being used to carve the 4.3-mile (7-km) Groene Hart Tunnel from Amsterdam to Rotterdam, The Netherlands, and will be completed in February 2005.

**Longest road tunnel** The tunnel between Aurland and Lærdal on the main road between Bergen and Oslo, Norway, measures 15.2 miles (24.5 km) in

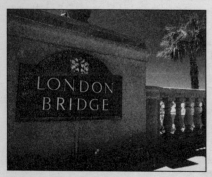

**FURTHEST DISTANCE TO MOVE A BRIDGE** London Bridge, unable to handle London's increasing traffic volume, was auctioned in 1962 to Robert McCulloch (USA) for $2,460,000 (£876,000). It was dismantled and moved brick-by-brick to Lake Havasu City, Arizona, USA, where it was reassembled and opened in 1971. The bridge was moved 5,300 miles (8,530 km) in total. It turned out that McCulloch had bought the wrong bridge: he thought he was buying Tower Bridge.

**LARGEST ROTATING BOAT LIFT** The Falkirk Wheel, Falkirk, UK, is the largest rotating boat lift in the world. It is 114 ft. (35 m) high, 114 ft. (35 m) wide, and 98 ft. (30 m) long. It was officially opened by Queen Elizabeth II on May 24, 2002. The boat lift can transfer more than eight boats at a time from the Forth and Clyde Canal to the Union Canal. The journey takes around 15 minutes.

length. The two-lane Lærdal Tunnel was ceremonially opened by King Harald on November 27, 2000 and opened to the public in 2001. It cost a reported $113.1 million (£78.5 million) to construct.

**Largest canal system** The seawater cooling system associated with the Madinat Al-Jubail Al-Sinaiyah construction project in Saudi Arabia is believed to be the world's largest canal system. It currently carries 388 million ft.³ (11 million m³) of seawater per day to cool the industrial establishments and ultimately will bring 689 million ft.³ (19.5 million m³) of water when industry consumption peaks.

**Longest canal** The Belomorsko-Baltiysky Kanal, also known as the White Sea-Baltic Canal, from Belomorsk to Povenets, Russia, is 141 miles (227 km) long and has 19 locks. It was made using forced labor between 1930 and 1933.

**Oldest navigable canal tunnel** The Malpas Tunnel on the Canal du Midi in southwest France was completed in 1681 and is 528 ft. (161 m) long. Its completion enabled vessels to navigate from the Atlantic Ocean to the Mediterranean Sea.

**Longest wall**  The Great Wall of China is the longest in the world and has a main-line length of 2,150 miles (3,460 km)—nearly three times the length of the UK—plus 2,195 miles (3,530 km) of branches and spurs. Construction of the wall began during the reign of Qin Shi Huangdi (221–210 B.C.). The wall runs from Shanhaiguan, on the Gulf of Bohai, to Yumenguan and Yangguan.

# HOMES, HOUSES, HOTELS

**Highest-altitude hotel**  The Hotel Everest View above Namche Bazar, Nepal—the village closest to Mt. Everest's base camp—is at a record height of 13,000 ft. (3,962 m).

**Tallest residential building**  The Trump World Tower in New York City, USA, is the world's tallest purely residential building, standing 861 ft. (262.5 m) tall. It has 72 stories, although the luxuriously high ceilings make it taller than most other buildings with a similar number of floors.

**Most theme hotels**  There are more than 16 theme hotels on the Strip in Las Vegas, Nevada, USA. Luxor has a sphinx, a black pyramid and an obelisk; New York-New York features a one-third-scale New York skyline; and Paris Las Vegas has a half-scale Eiffel Tower. Other themes include Treasure Island and Venice. Las Vegas boasts an incredible 120,000 hotel rooms, nearly one for every four of its inhabitants. The city accounts for roughly one-thirtieth of all hotel rooms in the USA and has the highest density of hotel rooms in the world.

**Largest hotel**  The MGM Grand Hotel and Casino in Las Vegas, Nevada, USA, consists of four 30-story towers on a site covering 112 acres (45.3 ha). The hotel has 5,005 rooms, with suites of up to 6,000 ft.$^2$ (560 m$^2$), a 15,200-seat arena, and a 33-acre (13.3-ha) theme park.

**Largest hotel presidential suite**  The largest hotel presidential suite is the Villa Salaambo attached to the Hasdrubal Thalassa Hotel, Yasmine Hammamet, Tunisia. It has a total floorspace of 16,597 ft.$^2$ (1,542 m$^2$).

**Largest inhabited castle**  The royal residence of Windsor Castle at Windsor, Berkshire, UK, is originally of 12th-century construction and measures 1,890 × 540 ft. (576 × 164 m).

**Largest hotel chain**  Best Western International Inc. is the world's biggest hotel chain, with more than 4,000 hotels in 81 countries and territories. The company, which is based in Phoenix, Arizona, USA, says it has 308,627 rooms available in its establishments, which, although part of the Best Western group, are independently owned and operated.

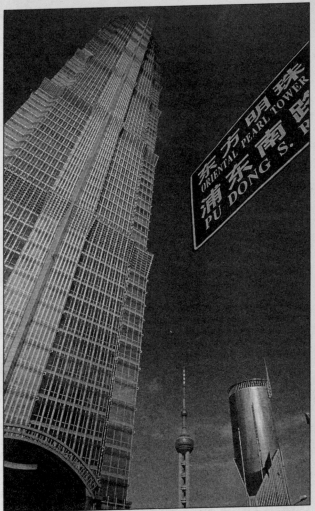

**HIGHEST HOTEL** The Grand Hyatt Shanghai in Pudong, China, is the highest hotel in the world. It occupies floors 53 to 87 of the 88-story Jin Mao Tower, the tallest building in China and at 1,377 ft. 10.8 in. (420 m) one of the tallest buildings in the world. The hotel, is around 295 ft. (90 m) higher than the pinnacle of the Burj Al Arab in Dubai (UAE)—the world's tallest hotel.

Home, Houses, Hotels

**Most expensive hotel suite** The Imperial Suite at the President Wilson Hotel in Geneva, Switzerland, can be reserved for CHF 45,000 ($33,000 or £20,907) per night.

**Largest hotel rooms** Standard suites at the Venetian, Las Vegas, Nevada, USA, measure on average 700 ft.² (65 m²).

**Northernmost hotel** The world's most northerly hotel is the Radisson SAS Polar Hotel in Longyearbyen, Svalbard, Norway. Svalbard consists of several islands from Bjærnæya in the south to Rossæya in the north, Europe's northernmost point. About 60% of the archipelago is covered by ice.

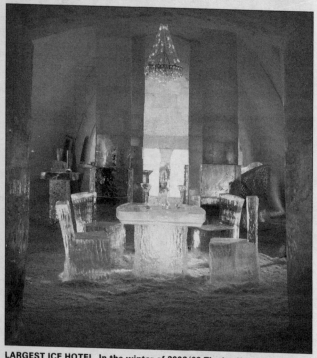

**LARGEST ICE HOTEL** In the winter of 2002/03 The Ice Hotel in Jukkasjärvi, Sweden, had a total floor area of 54,000 ft.² (5,000 m²), with 25 suites and 60 bedrooms. Lying 120 miles (200 km) north of the Arctic Circle, it has been rebuilt every December since 1990 and increases in size each year. It featured ice sculptures, a cinema, a pillared ice hall, an ice bar, and an ice chapel. Guests' ice beds are covered with thick reindeer pelts, and the interior temperature is around 20°F (-6°C).

Feats of Engineering

**Highest habitation** In April 1961 a three-roomed dwelling believed to date from the late pre-Columbian period c. 1480 was discovered perched at 21,650 ft. (6,600 m) on Cerro Llullaillaco. This 22,057-ft. (6,723-m) active volcano sits on the Argentine-Chile border.

**Northernmost inhabited place** The Canadian Forces Station Alert on Ellesmere Island, Northwest Territories, Canada, lies at Lat. 82°30′N, Long. 62°W. Set up in 1950, it is around 500 miles (800 km) from the geographic North Pole, and was an important "listening post" for spying on the former USSR (now Russia).

The Danish scientific station set up in 1952 in Pearyland, northern Greenland, is over 900 miles (1,450 km) north of the Arctic Circle and is manned every summer, making this site the northernmost habitation.

**Southernmost inhabited place** The most southerly permanent human habitation is the USA's Amundsen-Scott South Pole Station, completed in 1957 and replaced in 1975. Currently undergoing further expansion, the base, open to tourists during the summer months, now has a shop, bank, and a post office.

**Longest continuous house construction** Winchester House in San Jose, California, USA, was under continuous construction for 38 years. Originally an eight-room farmhouse on a 161-acre (65-ha) estate, its transformation into a mansion was begun in 1886 by the widowed Sarah Winchester (USA), heiress to the Winchester rifle fortune. It is also called the Winchester Mystery House because of its many oddities, such as closets opening into blank walls, a window in the floor, and staircases leading nowhere. Some believe that after the death of her husband, the widow was convinced by a medium that endless remodeling would confuse and appease the ghosts of all the people killed by the "gun that won the West." The house has 13 bathrooms, 52 skylights, 47 fireplaces, 10,000 windows, 40 staircases, 2,000 doorways and trapdoors, and three elevators.

**Highest inhabited building** The highest inhabited buildings in the world are those in the Indo-Tibetan border fort of Basisi by the Mana Pass (Lat. 31°04′N, Long. 79°24′E) at c.19,700 ft. (6,000 m). Because of lower air pressures at high altitudes and the corresponding decrease in the amount of oxygen in each breath taken, many people begin to feel the effects of altitude sickness at heights above 8,200 ft. (2,500 m). It would take several days to acclimatize to the altitude at Basisi, and most people would become very ill if they were airlifted directly to that height.

**Oldest hotel** The Hōshi Ryokan at the village of Awazu in Japan is reputed to be the world's oldest hotel. It dates back to 717, when Taicho Daishi built an inn near a hot-water spring that was said to have miraculous healing powers. The waters are still celebrated for their recuperative effects, and the Ryokan now has 100 bedrooms.

**LARGEST PALACE** The Imperial Palace in the center of Beijing, China covers a rectangular area measuring 3,150 x 2,460 ft. (960 x 750 m) within its 178-acre (72-ha) site. The outline dates from the early 15th century, but because of constant reconstruction work, most of the intramural buidings (five halls and 17 palaces) are from the 18th century.

**Most expensive house sale** The home belonging to Hong Kong businessman and philanthropist Eric Hotung at 610 Black's Link, Hong Kong, sold for HK$778.88 million ($101,909,312 or £62,767,500) on May 12, 1997. It was bought by an anonymous buyer.

**Longest residency** Virginia Hopkins Phillips (USA) resided in the same house at Onancock, Virginia, USA, from the time of her birth in 1891 until shortly after her 102nd birthday in 1993.

**Largest hotel lobby** The lobby at the Hyatt Regency in San Francisco, California, USA, is 350 ft. (107 m) long, 160 ft. (49 m) wide, and, at 170 ft. (52 m) tall, is the height of a 15-story building.

**Most expensive non-palatial house built** Hearst Castle at San Simeon, California, USA, was built between 1922 and 1939 for William Randolph Hearst (USA) at a total cost of more than $30 million (then £6.5 million), which is the equivalent today of $350 million (£250 million). It has more than 100 rooms, a heated swimming pool 104 ft. (32 m) long, an assembly hall 83 ft. (25 m) long, and a garage for 25 limousines. The house required 60 servants to maintain it.

**Largest casino** Foxwoods Resort Casino in Ledyard, Connecticut, USA, includes a total gaming area of 193,000 ft.² (17,900 m²). The complete complex covers an area of 4.7 million ft.² (436,000 m²) and includes three separate hotels, 24 restaurants, a theater, and a performance arena. The casino itself features more than 5,800 slot machines, 17 different table games, and a 3,200-seat bingo hall. Foxwoods employs more than 8,000 people.

**Largest area of polished marble floor tiles** The Venetian Resort-Hotel-Casino, Las Vegas, Nevada, USA, has a total floor area of 1.5 million ft.² (139,354 m²) covered in marble tiles shipped from Italy and Spain. This is equivalent to the area of 535 tennis courts.

# CARS

**Earliest full-scale automobile** The earliest full-scale automobile was a military steam tractor made by Nicolas-Joseph Cugnot (France) at the Paris Arsenal in October 1769. It had a maximum speed of 2.5 mph (4 km/h). Cugnot's second, larger tractor, completed in May 1771, survives in the Conservatoire Nationale des Arts et Métiers in Paris, France.

**Earliest passenger car** The world's first passenger-carrying automobile was a steam-powered road vehicle carrying eight passengers, built by Richard Trevithick (UK). The car made its first run at Camborne, Cornwall, UK, on December 24, 1801.

**Earliest internal combustion car** The first successful gas-driven car, the Motorwagen, built by Karl Friedrich Benz (Germany), ran at Mannheim

**LARGEST AUTOMOTIVE SHOW** The biennial International Motor Show for Passenger Cars (IAA), held in Frankfurt, Germany, is the world's largest automotive exhibition. The 2001 event, held from September 13 to 23 attracted over 1,000 exhibitors (including Porsche, shown) from 39 countries and covered an area of 2.5 million ft.² (235,000 m²). The show was attended by around 13,600 journalists from 75 countries and more than 800,000 other visitors.

in late 1885. The three-wheeler weighed 560 lb. (254 kg) and could reach 8–10 mph (13–16 km/h). Its single-cylinder engine delivered 0.85 hp (0.63 kW) at 400 rpm. It was patented on January 29, 1886.

**Largest production car** Of cars produced for private use, the largest was the Bugatti "Royale" Type 41, known in the UK as the "Golden Bugatti," which was assembled at Molsheim, France, by the Italian Ettore Bugatti. First built in 1927, it measured over 22 ft. (6.7 m) in length. The hood was over 7 ft. (2.13 m) long.

**Longest car** A 100-ft.-long (30.5-m), 26-wheeled limo was designed by Jay Ohrberg (USA). It has many unique features, including a swimming pool with diving board and a king-sized water bed. It is designed to drive as a rigid vehicle, but it can be changed to bend in the middle. It was designed for use in films and displays.

**Most powerful production car** The Koenigsegg CC (Sweden) has a maximum power output of 655 hp (488 kW), making it the most powerful car ever to enter series production. The car has a claimed top speed of 243.5 mph (392 km/h) and a 0–60 mph (0–100 km/h) acceleration time of under 3.5 seconds. The Bugatti Veyron, with a claimed power output of 987 hp (736 kW), was due to be launched in 2003 but had not entered production at the time of going to press.

**BIGGEST VEHICLE PRODUCER** In 2002 the General Motors Corporation (USA) produced an estimated 8,274,000 motor vehicles, making it the world's largest automobile producer. The company, whose brands include Buick, Cadillac, Chevrolet, Opel (Vauxhall), Isuzu, and Saab, made profits of $1.7 billion (£1.1 billion) that year, up from $600 million (£416 million) in 2001.

**Largest engine of a production car** The greatest engine capacity of a production car was 823.8 in³ (13.5 liters), for the US Pierce-Arrow 6-66 Raceabout of 1912–18, the US Peerless 6-60 of 1912–14, and the Fageol of 1918.

**Fastest production car** The highest speed ever attained by a standard production car is 240.1 mph (386.7 km/h) for a McLaren F1, driven by Andy Wallace (UK) at the Volkswagen Proving Ground, Wolfsburg, Germany, on March 31, 1998.

**Fastest reverse driving** Darren Manning (UK) reached a speed of 102.58 mph (165.08 km/h) going backwards in a Caterham 7 Fireblade at Kemble airfield, Gloucester, UK, on October 22, 2001.

**Blindfold land-speed record** Alistair Weaver (UK) reached a speed of 141 mph (226.91 km/h) while driving an Audi S8 blindfolded and guided by radio at Elvington airfield, N Yorks, UK, on April 8, 2002.

**Fastest electric car** The highest speed achieved for an electric vehicle over a two-way flying kilometer is 245.523 mph (395.821 km/h), by Dempsey's World Record Associates *White Lightning Electric Streamliner.* The car was driven by Patrick Rummerfield (USA) at the Bonneville Salt Flats, Utah, USA, on October 22, 1999.

**Greatest distance driven in one hour using an internal combustion engine** The greatest distance driven in one hour by a car with an internal combustion engine is 219.598 miles (353.409 km), by Helmut Henzler (Germany) and Keke Rosberg (Finland) in a prototype Volkswagen diesel-powered car on October 18, 1980, at the Nardo circuit in Italy.

**Greatest distance driven in one hour by an electric vehicle** The greatest distance covered in one hour by an electric car is 124.2 miles (199.881 km), by Oscar De Vita (Italy) driving the Bertone *ZER* (Zero Emission Record) prototype at the Nardo circuit, Italy, on October 2, 1994. The streamlined car was also the first electric vehicle to break the 186-mph (300-km/h) barrier.

**Highest car mileage** The highest recorded mileage for a car is in excess of 2 million miles (3.2 million km) for a 1966 Volvo P-1800S owned by Irvin Gordon (USA). He reached the 2-million-mile mark in the NBC Studios at Times Square, New York, USA, on March 27, 2002.

**Most fuel-efficient vehicle** The best fuel consumption ever recorded is 10,240 mpg (3,624.5 km/liter) for a vehicle by team Fancy Carol-Nok (Japan) in the Scottish Eco Marathon on August 12, 2001. The minimum speed allowed was 10 mph (16.1 km/hr).

**Fastest rocket car** The highest speed attained in a rocket-powered four-wheeled vehicle over a measured kilometer is 631.367 mph (1,016.086

**SMALLEST PRODUCTION CAR** Smaller than a fairground "dodgem" car, the Peel P50 was 53 in. (134 cm) long, 39 in. (99 cm) wide, and 53 in. (134 cm) high, and weighed just 130 lb. (59 kg). The vehicle was made by Peel Engineering Co., Peel, Isle of Man, UK, between 1962 and 1965.

km/h). This was achieved by *The Blue Flame*, driven by Gary Gabelich (USA) on the Bonneville Salt Flats, Utah, USA, on October 23, 1970. Momentarily, Gabelich exceeded 650 mph (1,046 km/h).

**Fastest road race** The fastest road race in the world is the Silver State Classic on Route 318, Nevada, USA, in which drivers maintain average speeds in excess of 190 mph (305 km/h) over the 90-mile (145-km) course. The highest ever average speed was 207.78 mph (334.38 km/h), set by Chuck Shafer and Gary Brockman (both USA) in May 2000.

**Longest ownership of vehicle from new** Eugene Stenger (USA) bought his white 1954 Chevrolet Corvette on April 5, 1954 and has owned it ever since. The original price was $3,577.85 (then £1,270).

# TRAINS, TRAMS & BUSES

**Fastest speed on a rail system** The highest speed recorded on any national rail system is 320.2 mph (515.3 km/h) by a French SNCF high-speed TGV (Train à Grande Vitesse) "Atlantique" train between Courtalain and Tours, France, on May 18, 1990.

**Fastest average-speed train trip** The West Japan Railway Company operates its 500-Series Nozomi bullet trains or *shinkansen* at an average speed of 162.7 mph (261.8 km/h) on the 119-mile (192-km) line between Hiroshima and Kokura on the island of Honshu, Japan.

**Fastest steam locomotive** The highest speed ever ratified for a steam locomotive is 125 mph (201 km/h) over 1,319 ft. (402 m) by the London North Eastern Railway "Class A4" (4–6–2) No. 4468 *Mallard* (later numbered 60022), which hauled seven coaches weighing 535,722 lb. (243 tonnes) gross down Stoke Bank, near Essendine, (now) Rutland, UK, on July 3, 1938.

**Most powerful steam locomotive** The world's most powerful steam locomotive measured by tractive effort (the force exerted at the rim of the driving wheel) was No. 700, a triple-articulated or triplex six-cylinder 2-8-8-8-4 tank engine built by the Baldwin Locomotive Works in 1916 for the Virginian Railway, USA. It had a tractive force of 166,300 lb. (75,433 kg) when working compound and 199,560 lb. (90,519 kg) when working simple.

**Fastest diesel train** The former British Rail (UK) inaugurated its HST (High Speed Train) daily service between London, Bristol and South Wales on October 4, 1976 using InterCity 125 trains. One of these holds the world speed record for diesel trains, at 148 mph (238 km/h), set on a test run between Darlington, Durham, and York, N Yorks, UK, on November 1, 1987.

**Fastest Maglev train** The highest speed by a manned magnetically levitated vehicle (Maglev) is 343 mph (552 km/h) by the MLX01, run by the Central Japan Railway Company and Railway Technical Research Institute on a test line between Otsuki and Tsuru, Japan, on April 14, 1999.

**Earliest public electric railway** The first public electric railway was opened on May 12, 1881, at Lichtervelde near Berlin, Germany. It was 2.5 km (1.5 miles) long, ran on 100V current and carried 26 passengers at up to 48 km/h (30 mph).

**FASTEST TRAIN IN REGULAR PUBLIC SERVICE** The magnetically levitated (Maglev) train linking China's Shanghai International Airport to the city's financial district reaches a top speed of 267.8 mph (431 km/h) on each 18-mile (30-km) run. The train, built by Germany's Transrapid International, had its maiden run on December 31, 2002.

**Largest steam locomotive**  The largest steam locomotives are generally considered to be the 4-8-8-4 "Big Boys," built by the American Locomotive Company from 1941 to 1944. They are 39.852 m (130 ft. 9 in.) long and weigh 508.02 tonnes (1.12 million lb.) with their tenders.

**Longest passenger train**  A passenger train created by the National Belgian Railway Company (NMBS) in aid of a Belgian cancer research charity measured 1.07 miles (1.73 km) and consisted of 70 coaches. The train, which weighed 6.14 million lb. (2,786 tonnes), was pulled by one electric locomotive and traveled 38.9 miles (62.5 km) from Ghent to Ostend, Belgium, on April 27, 1991. It made the journey in 1 hr. 11 min. at an average speed of 32.8 mph (52.8 km/h).

**Oldest steam locomotive in use**  The *Fairy Queen* was built in 1855 by Kitson Thompson Hewitson of Leeds, West Yorkshire, UK. Between October 1997 and February 1998 she was put into service hauling a twin-coach train between Delhi Cantonment, Delhi, and Alwar, Rajasthan, India.

**Highest railway line**  At La Cima, Peru, the standard-gauge (56.5-in. or 1,435-mm) track on the main line between Lima and La Oroya reaches 15,806 ft. (4,818 m) above sea level as it crosses the Andes, making it the highest in the world. There are 67 tunnels and 59 bridges on the line. However, in 2001, China began building the Qinghai-Tibet railway, which is planned to reach a height of 16,640 ft. (5,072 m).

**Country with shortest railway**  The country with the shortest length of railway track is the Vatican City. It only has a 2,828-ft. (862-m) spur, which is used just for goods and supplies, that enters the Holy See from Italy.

**Largest railway station by platforms**  The world's largest station by number of platforms is Grand Central Terminal, Park Avenue and 42nd Street, New York, USA, built between 1903 to 1913 and has 44 platforms. They are located on two underground levels with 41 tracks on the upper level and 26 on the lower. The station covers 47 acres (19 ha) and some 550 trains and 200,000 commuters use it daily.

**Most trains "spotted"**  Bill Curtis (UK) is acknowledged as the world champion "train spotter." His totals include some 85,000 locomotives, clocked up over a period of 40 years in 31 different countries.

**Longest model train**  The longest model train consisted of 650 1:87-(HO) scale wagons hauled by four locomotives and measured 228 ft. (70.2 m) in length. It was run by the Arid Australia model railroad group in Perth, Australia, on June 3, 1996.

**Longest miniature hobby railroad**  Train Mountain Railroad Museum near Chiloquin, Oregon, USA, has a total of 117,610 ft. (35,847 m) of 7.5-in. (19-cm) gauge track, with 67,366 ft. (20,533 m) of "mainline" track and the remainder comprising yards and sidings.

**EARLIEST BUSES** The first municipal motor omnibus service in the world was inaugurated on April 12, 1903 and ran between Eastbourne railway station and Meads, East Sussex, UK.

**Longest monorail** The Osaka Monorail, Osaka, Japan, has a total operational length of 13.8 miles (22.2 km). Fully operational since August 1997, it runs between Osaka International Airport and Hankyu Railway Minami Ibaraki Station, with the second stage running between Hankyu and Keihan Railway Kadomashi Station. The Chiba Urban Monorail near Tokyo, Japan, is the longest suspended monorail train system in the world, measuring 9.45 miles (15.2 km). The first 1.99 mile (3.2 km) stretch opened on March 20, 1979, and the line has been expanded three times since.

**Most extensive underground rail system** America's New York City subway system is the most extensive in the world, with a total track distance of 842 miles (1,355 km) and some 468 stations.

**Least extensive underground rail system** The shortest operating underground system is the Carmelit in Haifa, Israel. Opened in 1959, the Carmelit is just 1.12 miles (1,800 m) long. The only subway/metro in Israel, the Carmelit is a funicular running at a gradient of 12 degrees. Running from Paris Square to Carmel Central, it has six stations.

**Oldest trams in revenue service** The oldest trams in revenue service in the world are cars 1 and 2 of the Manx Electric Railway, dating from 1893. These still run regularly on the 17.75-mile (28.5-km) railway between Douglas and Ramsey, Isle of Man, UK.

**Most extensive tram system** The city of St. Petersburg, Russia, has the world's most extensive tramway system, with approximately 2,400 cars on routes with over 430 miles (690 km) of track. The first electric locomotive in Russia was tested in St. Petersburg in 1880, and the first electrical tramlines on the city streets were opened in September 1907.

**Largest bus fleet** The largest fleet of buses is owned by the Andhra Pradesh State Road Transport Corporation (India). As of October 31, 1999 the company owned a total of 18,397 buses. The bus network consists of 8,745 routes between 209 depots, 703 stations, and 1,801 bus stops spread over the 106,204-mile$^2$ (275,068-km$^2$) state.

**Longest bus** The articulated DAF Super CityTrain buses of the Democratic Republic of the Congo measure 105 ft. 8 in. (32.2 m) long and can carry 350 passengers comfortably (sitting and standing). They weigh 61,729 lb. (28 tonnes) unladen.

# BIKES & MOTORBIKES

**Earliest bicycle** The earliest machine propelled by cranks and pedals with connecting rods was built between 1839 and 1840 by Kirkpatrick Macmillan (UK). A copy of the machine is now in the Science Museum, London, UK.

**Largest bicycle** The largest rideable bicycle, (measured by wheel diameter) is *Frankencycle,* built by David Moore (USA) and first ridden by Steve Gordon (USA) on June 4, 1989. The giant pennyfarthing has a front wheel diameter of 10 ft. (3.05 m) and is 11 ft. 2 in. (3.4 m) high.

**Smallest bicycle** The world's smallest-wheeled rideable bicycle is one with wheels of a diameter of 0.43 in. (11 mm) at the front and 0.51 in. (13 mm) at the rear. The bicycle was ridden by its constructor Zbigniew Rózanek (Poland) for a distance of 16 ft. (5 m) on August 11, 1999.

**Largest pedal-powered vehicle** Roger Dumas (USA) created a 55-seater "bicycle" 140 ft. 8 in. (42.875 m) long, consisting of multiple bicycle frames welded together and supported by wheels at regular intervals along its length. It was pedaled by 52 people for 3,236 ft. (986 m) in Augusta, Maine, USA, on July 29, 2000 (although there were 55 seats, three were for children who were unable to pedal).

**Longest bicycle** The longest true bicycle ever built (i.e., with only two wheels) is 84 ft. 11 in. (25.88 m) long and was built by Super Tandem Club Ceparana (Italy). Forty club members cycled a distance of 368 ft. (112.2 m) at Ceparana, Italy, on September 20, 1998. Cornering proved a problem.

**LONGEST UNICYCLE RIDE** Lars Clausen (USA) covered a distance of 9,125.97 miles (14,686.82 km) by unicycle between April 22 and November 12, 2002. His double crossing of the USA started in Tillamook, Oregon, and finished in Los Angeles, California, taking in 39 states. The 202.78 miles (326.34 km) covered in a 24-hour period, from Martin, South Dakota, to a point near Highmore, South Dakota, from June 5–6, 2002, was also a record. He used a 36-in. (91-cm) Coker unicycle.

**Largest tricycle** The world's largest rideable tricycle was constructed at Bay de Noc Community College, Escabana, Michigan, USA, in July 1998. The trike was 23 ft. 4 in. (7.13 m) high, had a front wheel 15 ft. 4 in. (4.67 m) in diameter, and back wheels 7 ft. 4 in. (2.23 m) in diameter.

**Lightest full-size racing bicycle** Dionisio Coronado (Spain) constructed a full-size racing bicycle weighing just 9.903 lb. (4.492 kg) in 2001. The secret behind the hi-tech machine's weight is its beryl-alloy frame, which measures $19.6 \times 23.6 \times 18.9$ in. ($50 \times 60 \times 48$ cm).

**Pennyfarthing stack** The Colorado chapter of bicycle historians, "The Wheelmen" created a self-supporting line of 83 pennyfarthing bicycles and riders at Clear Creek History Park near Golden, Colorado, USA, on July 27, 2002.

**PRODUCTION MOTORCYCLE WITH LARGEST ENGINE** Honda's Goldwing GL1800 and Valkyrie Rune models both have a horizontally opposed 6-cylinder engine with a capacity of 111.7 in.³ (1832 cc)—the largest available on any standard production motorcycle. However, at the time of going to press, Triumph had an even larger three-cylinder c. 134.25 in.³ (2200 cc) motorcycle planned for production.

**Fastest 100 miles on a unicycle**  Takayuki Koike (Japan) set the unicycle record for 100 miles (160.9 km) in 6 hr. 44 min. 21.84 sec. on August 9, 1987—an average speed of 14.83 mph (23.87 km/h).

**Fastest human-powered vehicle**  Sam Whittingham (Canada) reached a speed of 80 mph (130.36 km/h) on his streamlined recumbent bike *Varna Diablo* at the World Human Powered Speed Challenge near Battle Mountain, Nevada, USA, on October 5, 2002.

**Longest front-wheel wheelie on a motorcycle**  Craig Jones (UK) covered 738 ft. (225 m) on the front wheel of his Buell XB9S motorcycle at Naples, Florida, USA, on November 23, 2002.

**Blindfold motorcycle speed record**  Blind motorcyclist Mike Newman (UK) reached a speed of 89 mph (143.2 km/h) at Elvington airfield, N. Yorks, UK, on August 7, 2001.

**Fastest motorcycle speed**  Dave Campos (USA), riding a 23-ft. (7-m) streamliner named *Easyriders* powered by two 91.5-in.³ (1500-cc) Ruxton Harley-Davidson engines, set American Motorcyclist Association (AMA) and Fédération Internationale de Motorcyclisme (FIM) absolute records with an average speed of 322.15 mph (518.45 km/h) over two 1-mile (1.6-km) runs at Bonneville Salt Flats, Utah, USA, on July 14, 1990.

**Greatest distance on a motorcycle in 24 hours**  A team of 19 riders from Suzuki and Metzeler covered a total distance of 3,666.355 miles (5,900.426 km) in 24 hours on a Suzuki RF900R at Nardo racetrack, Italy, from June 4 to 5, 1994.

**Highest speed on a quadbike**  Graham "G-Force" Hicks, a deaf-blind daredevil from Peterborough, Cambs, UK, reached a speed of 104.02 mph (167.4 km/h) on a quadbike at Bruntingthorpe Proving Ground, Leics, UK, on June 22, 2002. Hicks received instructions from his pillion rider, Rob Hall, who told him where to steer using a system of touch-based commands. The quadbike was a custom-built machine powered by a 67-in.³ (1100-cc) Honda Blackbird motorcycle engine.

**Longest motorcycle**  Douglas and Roger Bell (both Australia) designed and built *Big Ben*, a 24-ft. 11-in.-long (7.6-m) motorcycle weighing nearly 4,400 lb. (2,000 kg). It is powered by three 317-in.³ (5.2-liter) V12 Jaguar car engines, connected by a solid crankshaft to synchronize their running. *Big Ben* is so large that it needs power steering to maneuver it.

**Tallest rideable motorcycle**  The tallest rideable motorcycle is *Bigtoe,* built by Tom Wiberg (Sweden), which at its highest point is 7 ft. 6 in. (2.3 m) tall. The bike has a top speed of 60 mph (100 km/h) and is powered by a Jaguar V12 engine. *Bigtoe* cost $80,000 (£50,000) to build and features hydraulic steering and a 500-W stereo.

**FASTEST BACKWARDS MOTORCYCLING** Szabolcs Borsay (Hungary) reached a speed of 124.725 mph (200.726 km/h) riding his Suzuki GSX-R 1000 sitting backwards at Balaton Airport, Sármellék, Hungary, on July 2, 2002. Borsay started by riding forward, then turned around so he was sitting on the gas tank holding the handlebars behind him. Once through the speed trap, he turned back around to brake.

**Longest motorcycle wheelie** Yasuyuki Kudo (Japan) covered 205.7 miles (331 km) non-stop on the rear wheel of his Honda TLM220R motorcycle at the Japan Automobile Research Institute proving ground, Tsukuba, near Tsuchiura, Japan, on May 5, 1991.

**Largest scooter by engine capacity** The Suzuki Burgman 650 scooter has a 40-in.³ (638-cc) four-stroke, two-cylinder engine, the largest available on a production model today. The 524-lb. (238-kg) Burgman went on sale in 2003.

**Longest snowmobile journey** Tony Lenzini (USA) drove his 1986 Arctic Cat Cougar snowmobile a total of 7,211 miles (11,604.6 km) in 60 riding days between December 28, 1985 and March 20, 1986.

**Greatest distance on a snowmobile in 24 hours** The greatest distance covered on a snowmobile in 24 hours is 1,405.67 miles (2,262.2 km), by Vince Lofquist (USA) from January 9 to 10, 2001. Lofquist completed 304 laps of a 4,624-mile (7.44-km) course at an average speed of 58.57 mph (94.2 km/h).

**Farthest distance traveled on a snowmobile on water** On June 18, 2000, Jani Anttila (Finland) traveled a distance of 11.18 miles (18 km) along a lake near Toivakka, Finland, on his standard snowmobile.

# BOATS, YACHTS & FERRIES

**Largest floating crane ship** The world's largest floating crane ship is *Thialf,* a 661.5-ft.-long (201.6-m) semi-submersible barge, which has two 311-ft. (95-m) cranes that, when operating in tandem, have a lifting capacity of 31.3 million lb. (14,200 tonnes).

**Largest hospital ship** United States Navy Ship USNS *Mercy* and her sister ship USNS *Comfort* each have a total patient capacity of 1,000, with 80 intensive-care beds and 12 operating rooms, making them the largest floating hospitals in the world. They are 894 ft. (272.5 m) long, 105 ft. 8 in. (32.2 m) across, and have a full-load displacement of 138.72 million lb. (62,922 tonnes).

**Largest sailing ship by weight** The largest vessel ever built in the era of sail was the *France II,* a steel-hulled, five-masted barque launched at Bordeaux, France, in 1911. Her hull measured 418 ft. (127.4 m) overall, and she had a deadweight tonnage (cargo-carrying capacity) of 17.6 million lb. (8,000 tonnes). Although principally designed as a sailing vessel, she was also fitted with two auxiliary engines. However, these were removed in 1919 and she became a pure sailing vessel. *France II* was wrecked off the island of New Caledonia on July 12, 1922.

**FASTEST CIRCUMNAVIGATION IN A POWERED BOAT** On July 3, 1998 the *Cable & Wireless Adventurer* circumnavigated the world in 74 days, 20 hr., 58 min., 30 sec. The powered, 115-ft.-long (35.05-m) stabilized monohull vessel, equipped with state-of-the-art navigation and communications equipment, traveled more than 26,000 miles (41,841 km).

**Tallest mast on a sailing ship** The 246-ft. 8-in.-long (75.2-m) luxury yacht *Mirabella V,* which was due to be commissioned in the second half of 2003, has a single carbon-fiber mast 295 ft. (90 m) tall. The largest ever single-masted yacht, *Mirabella V* was built by Vosper Thornycroft in Southampton, UK, and is available for rent at a reported rate of $300,000 (£200,000) per week.

**Longest sailing ship** The French-owned sister ships *Club Med I* and *II* are the largest sailing ships afloat, with a length of 613 ft. (187 m). They have five aluminum masts and 30,100 ft.$^2$ (2,800 m$^2$) of computer-controlled sails. Each caters to around 400 passengers, with roughly 200 crew members. With their relatively small sail area and powerful engines, the ships are strictly motor-sailers.

**Most powerful tug** The 27,900-hp (20,800-kW) tug/supply vessel *Normand Progress* achieved a bollard pull (a test of a ship's pulling power) of 670,200 lb. (304 tons)—believed to be the greatest ever—on October 15, 1999 at Osneset, Norway. The 311-ft.-long (95-m) vessel was built by Ulstein Verft (Norway) in 1999 and is owned by Solstad Rederi AS (Norway).

**Fastest propeller-driven boat** Russ Wicks (USA) achieved a speed of 178.61 knots (205.494 mph or 330.79 km/h) in his hydroplane *Miss Freei* on June 15, 2000, at Lake Washington, Seattle, USA, the highest ever speed in a propeller-driven boat. *Miss Freei* was powered by a Lycoming L-7C turbine engine taken from a Chinook helicopter, generating 3,000 hp (2,237 kW) at 10,000 rpm. Featuring a canopy from an F-16 jet fighter, the 28-ft. (8.5-m) 6,600-lb. (3-ton) boat shoots a 200-ft. (60-m) jet of water out behind it at speed.

**Fastest sailing vessel** On October 26, 1993 the trifoiler (three-hulled hydrofoil) *Yellow Pages Endeavour* reached a speed of 46.52 knots (53.57 mph or 86.21 km/h) while on a timed run of 1,640 ft. (500 m) at Sandy Point near Melbourne, Victoria, Australia.

**Fastest trans-Atlantic sailing** The fastest ever Atlantic crossing, made between Ambrose Light Tower, New York, USA, and Lizard Point, Cornwall, UK, is 4 days 17 hr. 28 min. 6 sec. by the catamaran *Playstation,* captained by Steve Fossett (USA) in October 2001.

**Fastest Atlantic crossing** The fastest crossing of the Atlantic is 2 days, 10 hr., 34 min., 47 sec. by the 222-ft. (68-m) luxury yacht *Destriero,* skippered by Cesare Fiorio (Italy), from August 6 to 9, 1992. The gas-turbine-propelled vessel maintained an average speed of 45.7 knots (52.6 mph or 84.6 km/h) despite weighing nearly 440 tons (400 tonnes). The turbines generate 18,000 hp (13,420 kW) each and burn nearly 11 tons (10 tonnes) of fuel per hour, take in water and expel it from the rear at a rate of 13,200 gal. (60,000 liters) per second.

**LARGEST EVER ICEBREAKER** The largest icebreaker was the SS *Manhattan,* a 1,007-ft.-long (306.9-m) oil tanker specially converted in 1968. With protective steel armor 9 ft. (2.7 m) thick, 30 ft. (9.1 m) deep, and 670 ft. (204 m) long, she weighed 335 million lb. (152,407 tonnes).

**Greatest distance sailed in 24 hours** The greatest distance ever covered under sail in 24 hours is 694.78 nautical miles (799.5 miles or 1,286.73 km) by the 110-ft. (33.5-m) maxi catamaran *Maiden 2,* in the North Atlantic on June 12–13, 2002. The yacht was sailed by Brian Thompson, Helena Darvelid, Adrienne Cahalan (all UK), and a crew of seven. The average speed was 28.95 knots (33.31 mph or 53.61 km/h).

**Fastest circumnavigation by a crewed yacht** The fastest ever circumnavigation by crewed yacht is 64 days, 8 hr., 37 min., by the 108-ft. (33-m) catamaran *Orange,* skippered by Bruno Peyron (France). The record voyage, which ended on May 5, 2002, started and finished at Brest, France, and took the 12-man crew into the South Atlantic and around Antarctica.

**Largest cargo vessel** The world's largest ship of any kind is the oil tanker *Jahre Viking* (formerly the *Happy Giant* and *Seawise Giant),* with a deadweight tonnage (cargo-carrying capacity) of 1.24 billion lb. (564,763 tonnes). The tanker is 1,504 ft. (458.45 m) long, has a beam of 226 ft. (68.8 m) and a draught of 80 ft. 9 in. (24.61 m).

**Largest car ferry** The ferry with the greatest car-carrying capacity is Irish Ferries' *Ulysses,* launched on September 1, 2000. The ship can carry 1,342 cars or 240 trucks, is 685 ft. 8 in. (209 m) long and 104 ft. 6 in. (31.84 m) wide and has full-load displacement of 60.46 million lb. (27,425 tonnes).

**Fastest car ferry** Designed in Australia by Advanced Multi-Hull Designs PTY Ltd, the *Luciano Federico L* is powered by two 21,500-hp

(16,000-kW) gas turbines and has a loaded speed of 57 knots (65.5 mph or 105.5 km/h), with a top speed of 60 knots (69 mph or 111 km/h). She sails between Buenos Aires, Argentina, and Montevideo, Uruguay.

**Largest passenger ship** The Cunard Line's *Queen Mary II,* which is due to make her maiden voyage in January 2004, is 1,132 ft. (345 m) long and 135 ft. (41 m) wide. At approximately 150,000 grt (gross registered tons), *Queen Mary II* is nearly three times larger than *Titanic* (46,000 grt) and has space for 2,620 passengers and 1,253 crew. She is estimated to have cost around $800 million (£498 million) to build.

**Earliest scheduled public hovercraft service** The first public hovercraft service was run across the Dee estuary between Rhyl (Wales) and Wallasey (England), UK, by the 60-knot (69-mph or 111-km/h) 24-passenger Vickers-Armstrong VA-3 from July to September 1962.

**Largest civilian hovercraft** The SRN4 Mk III, a British-built civil hovercraft formerly employed for ferrying passengers and cars across the English Channel, weighs 341 tons (310 tonnes) and can hold 418 passengers and 60 cars. It is 185 ft. (56.38 m) in length and is powered by four Bristol-Siddeley Marine Proteus engines, giving a maximum speed in excess of 65 knots (75 mph or 120 km/h).

**Oldest active sailing ship** The oldest square-rigged sailing vessel that is still sea-going is thought to be the 1,320-ton (1,200-tonne) iron barque *Star of India,* built at Ramsey, Isle of Man, UK, in 1863 as the full-rigged ship *Euterpe.* She is now preserved as a museum ship in San Diego, California, USA, but makes occasional day-trips under sail.

# AIRCRAFT

**Fastest circumnavigation by balloon** Steve Fossett (USA) flew around the world alone in 13 days 8 hr., 33 min. in *Bud Light Spirit of Freedom* from June 19 to July 2, 2002. He took off from Northam, Western Australia, and landed at Eromanga, Queensland, Australia. This was only the second ever non-stop circumnavigation of the globe by balloon, and the first ever solo.

**Highest altitude in a hot-air balloon** Per Lindstrand (Sweden) achieved the altitude record of 64,997 ft. (19,811 m) in a Colt 600 hot-air balloon over Laredo, Texas, USA, on June 6, 1988.

**Highest balloon altitude record** The greatest altitude ever reached by a manned balloon is 113,740 ft. (34,668 m), by Commander Malcolm D. Ross and Lieutenant Commander Victor A. Prather (both USA) of the US Navy over the Gulf of Mexico, USA, on May 4, 1961. Their non-pressurized, gas-filled polyethylene balloon was called *Lee Lewis Memorial.*

**Largest balloon** The largest balloon ever made, known by its model number of SF3-579.49-035-NSC-01, had an inflatable volume of 70,732,718 ft.³ (2,003,192 m³) and was 785 ft. 9.36 in. (239.49 m) in gore length. The giant unmanned balloon, manufactured by Winzen Research, Inc. (now Winzen Engineering, Inc.) of South St. Paul, Minnesota, USA, was prepared for flight at the National Scientific Balloon facility in Palestine, Texas, USA, on October 1, 1975. There were no photographs of the attempt and, unfortunately, due to problems, the launch was "aborted on launch pad."

**Longest helicopter flight** On April 6, 1966, Robert Ferry (USA), in accordance with Fédération Aéronautique Internationale (FAI) rules, piloted his Hughes YOH-6A helicopter from Culver City, California, to Ormond Beach, Florida, USA, without refueling—a distance of 2,213.1 miles (3,561.6 km).

**Highest altitude for a helicopter** The highest recorded altitude in a helicopter is 40,820 ft. (12,442 m) by Jean Bouletan (France) flying an Aérospatiale SA315B Lama over Istres, France, on June 21, 1972.

**Helicopter speed record** Under FAI rules, the world speed record for helicopters was set by John Trevor Eggington with co-pilot Derek J. Clews (UK), who averaged 249.09 mph (400.87 km/h) over Glastonbury, Somerset, UK, on August 11, 1986 in a Westland Lynx demonstrator.

**Largest helicopter** The Russian Mil Mi-12 had a rotor diameter of 219 ft. 10 in. (67 m), a length of 121 ft. 4.8 in. (37 m), and a weight of 114 tons (103.3 tonnes). It was powered by four 6,500-hp (4,847-kW) turboshaft engines. A prototype was shown in 1971 at the Paris Air Show but never went into production.

**Largest helicopter in production** The largest helicopter currently produced is the five-man-crewed Russian Mil Mi-26, which has a maximum take-off weight of 123,460 lb. (56,000 kg). Unladen, it weighs 62,170 lb. (28,200 kg) and its overall length is 131 ft. (40 m). The eight-bladed main rotor has a diameter of 105 ft. (32 m) and is powered by two 11,240-hp (8500-kW) turbine engines.

**Fastest aerial circumnavigation** The fastest flight under Fédération Aéronautique Internationale (FAI) rules, which permit flights that exceed the length of the Tropic of Cancer or Capricorn (22,858.8 miles or 36,787.6 km), was one of 31 hr. 27 min. 49 sec. by an Air France Concorde flown by Captains Michel Dupont and Claude Hetru (both France) from JFK airport in New York, USA, eastbound via Toulouse, Dubai, Bangkok, Guam, Honolulu and Acapulco, from August 15–16, 1995. In total, there were 80 passengers and 18 crew on board flight AF1995.

**Lightest airplane to cross the South Atlantic** The lightest airplane to cross the South Atlantic is the RWD-5bis, powered by a De Havilland Gipsy Moth engine. It set the Fédération Aéronautique Internationale world record for straight line distance in Category II (single-seater aircraft with a max. weight of 992 lb.) on May 7, 1933, traveling 2,226 miles (3,582 km). The plane was flown by Captain Stanislaw Skarzynski (Poland) from St. Louis, Senegal, to Maceio, Brazil, in 20 hr. 30 min.

**Fastest propeller-driven aircraft** The former Soviet Tu-95/142 (NATO code-name Bear) long-range bomber is the fastest propeller-driven aircraft in standard production, with a maximum speed of Mach 0.82 or 575 mph (925 km/h). First produced in the 1950s, it remains in service with several air forces around the world. It has four 14,795-hp (11,033-kW) engines driving eight-blade contra-rotating propellers.

**Highest flying propeller-driven aircraft** The highest ever altitude reached by a propeller-driven aircraft is 96,500 ft. (29,413 m), by the

**HEAVIEST AIRCRAFT** The aircraft with the highest standard maximum take-off weight is the Antonov An-225 Mriya (Dream) at 1.32 million lb. (600 tonnes). The An-225 also has the longest wingspan of any aircraft to have flown more than once, at 290 ft. (88.4 m), but only one was ever built. Another Anatov aircraft, the An-124, has the largest wing span of any series-produced aircraft, measuring 240 ft. 6 in. (73.3 m).

unmanned, solar-powered *Helios* prototype flying wing over the Hawaiian Island of Kauai on August 13, 2001. Commissioned by NASA and developed by AeroVironment, Inc. of Monrovia, California, USA, *Helios* is one of a new breed of slow-flying, high-altitude aircraft that experts believe may offer a viable alternative to communications satellites in the future.

**Largest airplane propeller** The largest airplane propeller ever to fly was the 22-ft. 7.5-in.-diameter (6.9-m) Garuda propeller, fitted to the Linke-Hofmann R II, which was built in Breslau, Germany (now Wroclaw, Poland) and flown in 1919. It was driven by four 260-hp (195-kW) Mercedes engines and turned at only 545 rpm. Today, typical single-engine aircraft have propellers of roughly 7 ft. (2 m) diameter that turn at 2,500 rpm.

**Largest propeller-driven aircraft** The largest propeller-driven aircraft ever to enter production is the Russian Antonov An-22. It has a wing span of 211 ft. (64.4 m) and a maximum take-off weight of 550,000 lb. (250 tonnes). Still in service with the Russian military, the An-22 is powered by four 14,791-hp (11,030-kW) contra-rotating turboprop engines and has a cruising speed of 422 mph (680 km/h).

**Fastest airliner** On December 31, 1968 the Tupolev Tu-144, Russia's version of Concorde, became the first airliner to fly supersonic. It was reported

**GREATEST SPEED IN A MANNED AIRCRAFT** The greatest speed ever reached by an air-launched manned aircraft is 4,520 mph (7,274 km/h), or Mach 6.7, by the X-15A-2 rocket plane flown by USAF test pilot Major William "Pete" Knight over California, USA, on October 3, 1967. Although this is nearly twice the official FAI air speed record, the X-15's flights are not eligible because the aircraft did not take off using its own power.

to have reached Mach 2.4 (1,600 mph or 2,587 km/h)—the fastest speed of any airliner—although its normal cruising speed was Mach 2.2. The aircraft was retired in 1978.

**Largest passenger aircraft** The Boeing 747-400 is the largest passenger aircraft flying today, with a wingspan of 211 ft. 4 in. (64.4 m), a length of 231 ft. 7 in. (70.6 m) and a maximum take-off weight of 437 tons (396.89 tonnes). Thanks to the "bubble" above its nose, the 747 also has a higher capacity than its nearest competitor, the Airbus A340-600—typically 524 passengers, compared with 419 in the A340.

**Longest passenger aircraft in service** At 246 ft. 11 in. (75.3 m) the Airbus A340-600 is the longest passenger aircraft currently in service. It has a maximum take-off weight of 804,700 lb. (365 tonnes), a wingspan of 208 ft. 2 in. (63.45 m), and a passenger capacity of 419.

**Largest volume cargo aircraft** The aircraft with the largest cargo hold by volume is the Airbus Beluga A300-600ST Super Transporter. The cargo deck has a volume of 49,440 ft.$^3$ (1,400 m$^3$). It is 123 ft. 8 in. (37.7 m) long, with a maximum height and width of 23 ft. 3 in. (7.1 m). Its maximum payload weight is 103,616 lb. (47 tonnes).

**Fastest jet** The USAF Lockheed SR-71 "Blackbird," a reconnaissance aircraft, is the world's fastest non-experimental airplane, with a top speed in excess of Mach 3. First flown in its definitive form on December 22, 1964, it is capable of attaining an altitude of close to 100,000 ft. (30,000 m). Its range at Mach 3 is 3,000 miles (4,800 km) at 79,000 ft. (24,000 m).

**First supersonic flight** The first ever supersonic flight was achieved on October 14, 1947 by Captain (later Brigadier General) Charles "Chuck" Elwood Yeager (USA) over Lake Muroc, California, USA, in a Bell XS-1 rocket aircraft. Yeager reached Mach 1.015 (670 mph or 1,078 km/h) at an altitude of 42,000 ft. (12,800 m). The XS-1 is now in the Smithsonian Institution, Washington, DC, USA.

# LARGE VEHICLES

**Tallest mobile crane** The Demag CC 12600, made by Mannesmann Dematic, is 649 ft. 7 in. (198 m) high. It has a 393-ft. 8-in. (120-m) "fixed jib" attached to a 374-ft. (114-m) near-vertical boom and has a maximum lifting capacity of 3.53 million lb. (1,600 tonnes) at 72 ft. (22 m) radius. This monster crane requires 100 trucks to transport all its different parts to a site.

**Largest bulldozer** The Komatsu D575A "Super Dozer" is the world's largest bulldozer weighing in at 336,000 lb. (152.6 tonnes). Its 24.27 ×

10.66-ft. (7.4 × 3.25-m) blade has a capacity of 2,437 ft.³ (69 m³). The 38-ft. 5-in.-long (11.72-m) pusher moves on tank-style tracks and is powered by a 1,150-hp (858-kW) turbocharged diesel engine.

**Longest trucks on public roads** Australian road trains, which consist of powerful semi-trucks pulling up to three trailers, are permitted by national legislation to be up to 175.5 ft. (53.5 m) long and weigh up to 276,000 lb. (125.2 tonnes), although some states set the limits lower. Such vehicles, which are the main form of freight transportation in remote areas of the country, are permitted to travel only on designated routes.

**Largest tower crane** The world's largest tower crane (or construction crane) is the Danish made Kroll K-10000 which, in standard configuration, is capable of lifting 264,554 lb. (120 tonnes) at 269 ft. (82 m) radius (i.e., the distance from the central supporting column). It stands 393 ft. (120 m) high on a rotating cylinder just 39 ft. 3 in. (12 m) in diameter without any support wires, but has 491,630 lb. (223 tonnes) of counterweights to balance out its 275-ft.-long (84 m) load-carrying boom. In comparison, a typical tower crane stands 262 ft. (80 m) tall and is capable of lifting only around 7,700 lb. (3.5 tonnes) at a radius of 269 ft. (82 m).

**LARGEST LAND VEHICLE** The largest machine capable of moving under its own power is the 31.3-million-lb. (14,196-tonne) RB293 bucket wheel excavator, an earthmoving machine manufactured by MAN TAKRAF of Leipzig, Germany. It is 722 ft. (220 m) long, 310 ft. (94.5 m) tall, and is capable of shifting 8.475 million ft.³ (240,000 m³) of earth per day. The bucket wheel, is 71 ft. (21.6 m) in diameter, which means it stands as tall as a five-story building.

**LARGEST HYDRAULIC SHOVEL EXCAVATOR** The RH 400-2000 hydraulic shovel excavator manufactured by O & K Mining (Germany) is the largest of its kind in the world. The giant crawler weighs 1.984 million lb. (900 tonnes) and is capable of filling the world's largest dump truck in just six passes. It has a shovel capacity of 1,825.7 ft.³ (51.7 m³). The top of the driver's cab is 33.5 ft. (10.2 m) high, and the machine is powered by a 4,002-hp (2,984-kW) Cummins diesel engine fed by a 4,230-gal. (16,000-liter) fuel tank.

**Largest revolving pedestal crane** The revolving pedestal crane at the Yantai Raffles shipyard in Yantai, China, is thought to be the most powerful of its kind. It can lift 4.4 million lb. (2,000 tonnes) to a height of 311 ft. (95 m) from its main hook, and 44,000 lb. (200 tonnes) to 443 ft. (135 m) from its secondary arm. It was designed for use in the construction of oil rigs.

**Largest fork-lift truck** In 1991 Kalmar LMV of Lidhult, Sweden, manufactured three counterbalanced fork-lift trucks capable of lifting loads up to 198,415 lb. (90 tonnes) at a load center of 7 ft. 6 in. (2.4 m). They were built to handle the great man-made river project comprising two separate pipelines, one 620 miles (998 km) long from Sarir to the Gulf of Sirte, and the other 557 miles (897 km) from Tazirbu to Benghazi, Libya.

**Largest dump truck** The T-282, manufactured by the Liebherr Mining Equipment Co. of Virginia, USA, is the world's largest two-axle dump truck, with a payload capacity of 720,900 lb. (327 tonnes). The diesel-electric-powered vehicle is 47 ft. 6 in. (14.47 m) long, 28 ft. 7 in. (8.7 m) wide, and 24 ft. (7.3 m) high, and weighs 443,100 lb. (201 tonnes).

**Largest monster truck** "Bigfoot 5" is 15 ft. 6 in. tall (4.7 m) with 10-ft.-tall (3-m) tires and weighs 38,000 lb. (17.23 tonnes). It is one of a fleet of 17 Bigfoot trucks created by Bob Chandler (USA) and was built in the summer of 1986. Now parked in St. Louis, Missouri, USA, it makes occasional appearances at local shows.

**Fastest monster truck** On September 11, 1999 at Smyrna Airport, Nashville, Tennessee, USA, Dan Runte reached a speed of 69.3 mph (111.5 km/h) in "Bigfoot 14," the highest ever recorded speed in a monster truck. The speed was clocked during the run-up to the longest ever monster truck jump of 202 ft. (61.57 m).

**Fastest truck wheelie** Patrick Bourny (France) drove his modified truck cab in a wheelie at 55.92 mph (90 km/h) at Lure on October 21, 2000 for *L'Émission des Records,* Paris, France.

**Largest trailer** The largest trailer was built in 1990 for HE Sheik Hamad Bin Hamdan Al Nahyan of Abu Dhabi, UAE. A two-wheeled, five-story vehicle, it is 66 ft. (20 m) long, 39 ft. (12 m) wide and weighs 240,303 lb. (109 tonnes). There are eight bedrooms and bathrooms, four garages, and water storage for 6,340 gal. (24,000 liters).

**Largest dragline excavator** "Big Muskie," a walking earthmoving machine weighing 29.1 million lb. (13,200 tonnes) was the largest ever dragline excavator and among the largest mobile machines ever made, weighing as much as nearly 10,000 sedans. It stood at Central Ohio Coal Co.'s Muskingham open-cast coal mine in Ohio, USA, but was dismantled in 1999.

**Largest land transport vehicle** The two 6-million-lb. (2,721-tonne) crawler-transporters used to move Space Shuttles to their launch pad at Kennedy Space Center, Florida, USA, are the largest vehicles used to transport other objects. Each crawler is 131 ft. (40 m) wide and 114 ft. (35 m) long and runs on eight tank-style tracks. Each of the 57 links that make up these tracks weighs around 2,000 lb. (900 kg).

**Longest vehicle** The longest land vehicles ever made are the overland supply train built by R. G. Le Tourneau Inc. of Longview, Texas, USA, for

**LARGEST FRONT-END LOADER The largest wheel-driven front-end loader is the LeTourneau L-2350, which weighs 578,000 lb. (262,176 kg) and can lift up to 160,000 lb. (72,574 kg) in its 1,431-ft.³ (40.52-m³) capacity bucket. This massive earthmover is powered by a giant diesel engine that develops 2,300 hp (1,715 kW).**

the U.S. Army. One example, the *Arctic Snow Train,* later owned by the famous wire-walker Steve McPeak (USA), had 54 wheels and was 572 ft. (174.3 m) long. Its gross train weight was 880,000 lb. (400 tonnes), with a top speed of 20 mph (32 km/h).

**Largest tire**  Standing 13 ft. 1 in. (4 m) tall and weighing over 8,800 lb. (4 tonnes), the world's largest tires are built by Michelin to fit onto specialized dump trucks, including Caterpillar's largest model, the 797.

**Heaviest load transported by road**  Between July 14 and 15, 1984, John Brown Engineers & Contractors BV moved the Conoco Kotter Field oil production deck, which has a roll-out weight of 8.38 million lb. (3,805 ton), for the Continental Netherlands Oil Co. of Leidsenhage, The Netherlands.

# SCIENCE & TECHNOLOGY

# SCIENCE ADVANCES

**Darkest man-made substance** The darkest man-made substance is a black coating composed of a nickel-phosphorus alloy. It reflects just 0.16% of visible light, around 25 times less than conventional black paint. The principle was first developed by researchers in the USA and India in 1980. In 1990 Anritsu (Japan) further refined this method to produce the darkest version so far.

**Smallest piece of ice** The smallest piece of ice was created by Roger Miller and Klaus Nauta of the University of North Carolina, USA, in 1999. Consisting of just six water molecules arranged in a hexagon, the ice crystal is the smallest theoretically possible, as a minimum of six molecules are required for the formation of ice. In comparison, the average water droplet contains around 100,000,000,000,000,000,000 molecules of water.

**Largest vacuum chamber** The Space Power Facility at NASA's Glenn Research Center, Plum Brook Station, Sandusky, Ohio, USA, measures 100 ft. (30.4 m) in diameter and 122 ft. (37 m) in height. It can sustain a high vacuum of $10^{-6}$ torr and simulate solar radiation using a 4 megawatt quartz heat-lamp array, as well as temperatures as low as -320°F (-195.5°C). It is used to test the performance of spacecraft and space hardware prior to launch.

**Smallest thermometer** On February 7, 2002, Yihua Gao and Yoshio Bando (both Japan) of the National Institute for Materials Science announced that they had created a thermometer from a single carbon nanotube. Measuring just 75 nanometers wide (one nanometer equals one billionth of a meter) and with a length of around 10,000 nanometers, the tube contains liquid gallium with linear expansion properties that allow the measurement of a wide range of temperatures, from 122–932°F (50–500°C).

**SMALLEST LASER SCULPTURE** On August 15, 2001 researchers at Osaka University, Japan, made a three-dimensional bull measuring seven thousandths of a millimeter high and ten thousandths of a millimeter long—the same size as a single red blood cell. The bull was sculpted from resin with two focused laser beams using a technique called two-photon micropolymerization. The bull is so small that 30 of them could be placed side by side across the period at the end of this sentence.

**DEEPEST OPERATING NEUTRINO OBSERVATORY** The Sudbury Neutrino Observatory is located 6,800 ft. (2,072 m) below ground in the Inco Creighton Mine, Ontario, Canada. It consists of a 39-ft.-diameter (2-m) vessel containing around 1.9 million lb. (900 tonnes) of heavy water. It is designed to detect neutrinos, the neutral particles produced by nuclear fusion in the Sun. The depth of the observatory facilitates detection.

**Shortest flash of light** On August 16, 2002, a team of European physicists, led by Ferenc Krausz at the Vienna Institute of Technology, Austria, announced that they had created bursts of X-ray light lasting just 500 billion billionths of a second (or 500 attoseconds). The technique will allow detailed studies of how electrons behave within atoms.

**Heaviest element** The undisputed heaviest chemical element discovered to date is 110. Its "discovery" was reported on November 19, 1994 by researchers at the Heavy Ion Research Center at Darmstadt, Germany. They used an ion accelerator to bombard lead atoms with nickel nuclei to create the new element, which existed for less than one thousandth of a second before decaying into lighter elements. The name darmstadtium (with the symbol Ds) has been proposed, following the tradition of naming elements after their place of discovery.

**Longest running agricultural experiment** The Broadbalk Experiment, Rothamsted, Hertfordshire, UK, which aims to measure the effects of fertilizer on crops, has continuous data from 1843 to the present day.

**Most powerful pulsed neutron source** ISIS, at the Rutherford Appleton Laboratory, Chilton, Oxfordshire, UK, is the world's most powerful pulsed neutron source. Covering the size of a football field, it produces $4 \times 10^{16}$ fast neutrons per second. These are focused into beams in a "neutron microscope," allowing scientists to study, at a microscopic scale, the atomic and molecular arrangements that give materials their unique properties.

**Highest-intensity focused laser** The Vulcan laser at the Rutherford Appleton Laboratory, Chilton, Oxfordshire, UK, is the highest-intensity focused laser in the world. Following its 2002 upgrade, it is now capable of producing a laser beam with an irradiance (focused intensity) of $10^{21}$ watts per $cm^2$.

**Longest laser ranging experiment** The McDonald Laser Ranging Station near Fort Davis, Texas, USA, uses a laser to measure the distance between the Earth and the Moon to an accuracy of 0.39 in. (1 cm). It bounces a laser off the reflective targets left on the lunar surface by five US and Soviet missions. The distance between the centers of the Earth and the Moon is 239,000 miles (385,000 km), and the laser ranging has shown that the Moon is receding from us at a rate of 1.5 in. (3.8 cm) per year. This is one of the most accurate distance measurements ever made.

**Most accurate value of pi** As continuation of a long-running project, mathematician Yasumasa Kanada (Japan) of the University of Tokyo has calculated the number pi to 1,241,100,000,000 decimal places. This calculation has been achieved using a HITACHI SR8000/MPP computer.

**Least dense solid** The least dense solid in the world is an aerogel with a density of just 0.47 grains/inch³ (1.9 mg/cm³). It is made by Lawrence Livermore National Laboratory (USA).

**MOST POWERFUL X-RAY GENERATOR** The Z Machine at the Sandia National Laboratories, USA, can, very briefly, give out X-rays with a power output roughly the same as 80 times that of all the world's electrical generators. The Z machine is used by scientists to study extreme conditions in physics, such as the nature of black holes.

**Lowest man-made temperature** The lowest man-made temperature achieved to date is 0.000000003 Kelvin, or 3 nanoKelvin above absolute zero, the coldest temperature theoretically possible. It was reached using rarified gas composed of atoms of 85 rubidium, which, at these low temperatures, form a Bose-Einstein condensate—where the atoms behave as one "superatom." It was achieved by a team of scientists led by Elizabeth Donley from the University of Colorado, Boulder, Colorado, USA, and the National Institute of Science & Technology, Boulder, Colorado, USA.

**Largest lens** The largest refracting optical lens in the world measures 5 ft. 11.93 in. (1.827 m) in diameter. It was constructed by a team led by Thomas Peck (USA) at the Optics Shop of the Optical Sciences Center of the University of Arizona in Tucson, Arizona, USA, and completed in January 2000. It was built as a test for the secondary mirror of the 21-ft. 3.9-in.-diameter (6.5-m) MMT Telescope on Mt. Hopkins, Arizona, USA.

**Largest gravitational wave detector** The largest gravitational detector is the Laser Interferometry Gravitational Wave Observatory (LIGO) in the USA, which is 2.4 miles (4 km) long. LIGO consists of two almost identical L-shaped structures based in Louisiana and Washington (USA), almost 2,000 miles (3,200 km) apart. The 2.4-mile-long (4-km) arms of the facility provide LIGO with the extreme sensitivity required for the detection of gravitational waves.

**Slowest light** In January 2001 two groups of US scientists announced that they had slowed down light itself to a dead stop. Light usually travels at 186,000 miles/sec (300,000 km/sec).

# AMAZING SCIENCE

**Largest bacterium** According to a study published in the journal *Science* in April 1999, the bacterium *Thiomargarita namibiensis* ("Sulfur Pearl of Namibia") is the largest prokaryotic organism yet known, and is visible to the naked eye at around the size of the period at the end of this sentence. A typical bacterial cell is about 750 times smaller than this. Biologist Heide Schulz (Germany) from the Max Planck Institute for Marine Microbiology in Bremen, Germany, found these up-to-0.029-in.-wide (0.75-mm) microorganisms in sediments off the Namibian coast during a cruise in 1997 with the Russian research vessel *Petr Kottsov.*

**Simplest genome** *Mycoplasma genitalium* has the smallest number of genes of any organism on Earth. Its genome was sequenced in 1995 and found to have just 480 genes compared with around 40,000 for humans. This organism lives in the genital tracts of humans.

**WEAKEST FORCE** Of the four fundamental forces in the universe—the strong nuclear, the weak nuclear, electromagnetic, and gravitational forces—the weakest is gravity, with a strength of $10^{40}$ compared to electromagnetism, which is given the value of 1. Every single atom in the universe is "gravitationally aware" of every other atom. The gravity of this bright cluster of galaxies, for example, is acting like a huge lens in space, bending the light from more distant galaxies into distorted arcs.

**Heaviest and lightest quark** Of the six "flavors" of quarks—known as "up," and "down," "top," "bottom," "strange," and "charmed"—the "top" is the heaviest at 170 giga-electron-volts (GeV). The lightest are the "up" and "down" quarks, both at 0.15 GeV.

**Smallest entity** The smallest of the known free-living organisms are the pleuropneumonia-like organisms (PPLO) of the genus *Mycoplasma.* One of these, *Mycoplasma laidlawii,* first discovered in sewage in 1936, has a diameter during its early existence of only $10^{-7}$ m. Examples of the strain known as H.39 have a maximum diameter of $3 \times 10^{-7}$ m and weigh an estimated $10^{-16}$ g. Thus an average 420,000-lb. (190-tonne) blue whale would weigh $1.9 \times 10^{24}$ times as much.

**Most powerful reaction** When normal matter reacts with antimatter, the result is the complete annihilation of both. All mass is converted to energy as in Einstein's famous equation $E=MC^2$. Weight for weight, matter/antimatter reactions are 300 times more powerful than fusion reactions, and a thousand times more powerful than fission (as used in nuclear plants). They are also 10 billion times more powerful than conventional chemical reactions such as burning hydrogen and oxygen.

**Rarest element on Earth** The element astatine (At) is the rarest element in the Earth's crust, with around 0.9 oz. (25 g) total occurring naturally.

**Highest microbe** In April 1967 NASA reported that bacteria had been discovered at an altitude of 25 miles (41 km).

**Lowest temperature possible** Temperature is a direct result of the vibrations of the atoms or molecules that make up matter. The coldest that any substance can theoretically be is when there is no vibration in its atoms or molecules. This is referred to as absolute zero, and is at 0 K (zero Kelvin) or -459.67°F (-273.15°C). Absolute zero has never been achieved in an Earth laboratory, and even in the coldest parts of deep space, the temperature is slightly above absolute zero.

**Oldest living bacteria** Bacteria trapped in suspended animation inside salt crystals for 250 million years have been revived and cultured by US scientists. Designated Bacillus 2-9-3, this species is ten times older than the previous oldest revived bacteria.

**Deadliest natural toxin** The anaerobic bacterium of spoiled food, which causes botulism (*Clostridium botulinum*), is so deadly (more so than strychnine, arsenic, or even snake venom) that 1 oz. (30 g) could theoretically kill 33 million tons of living matter, and 1 lb. (0.5 kg) could kill the entire human population.

**Toughest microbe** The bacterium *Deinococcus radiodurans* (formerly *Micrococcus radiodurans*) can withstand atomic radiation of 6.5 million roentgens, or 10,000 times the level fatal to the average human. In March 1983, John Barras (USA) of the University of Oregon, USA, reported bacteria from sulfurous seabed vents thriving at 583°F (306°C) in the East Pacific Rise at Lat. 21°N.

**Largest microbe** The largest known protozoans in terms of volume are the extinct *Calcareous foraminifera* (Fcraminiferida) of the genus *Nummulites*. Individuals measuring up to 6 in. (150 mm) wide were found in the Middle Eocene rocks of Turkey.

The largest existing protozoan is a species of the fan-shaped *Stannophyllum* (Xenophyophora). This is also the longest known microbe, with one example found measuring 9.8 in. (25 cm).

**MOST STABLE HADRON** Hadrons are subatomic particles made up of quarks. The most stable hadron is the proton, with a lifetime of at least $10^{25}$ years. This carbon nucleus shows protons made up of one "down" and two "up" quarks, and neutrons made up of two "downs" and one "up." Quarks exist in three "colors"—red, green, and blue—and one of each color is required to make a hadron.

**SMALLEST UNIT OF LENGTH** The smallest possible size for anything in the universe is the Planck length—$1.6 \times 10^{-35}$m across (equivalent to around a millionth of a billionth of a billionth of a billionth of a cm across). This is the scale at which the quantum foam (representation shown) is believed to exist. The laws of quantum physics cause minute wormholes to open and close constantly, giving space a rapidly changing, foam-like structure. If it were possible to exploit the tremendous energy of the quantum foam, then the power contained within one cubic centimeter of empty space would be enough to boil the Earth's oceans.

**Fastest speed possible** The fastest speed possible in the universe is the speed of light. This is achieved only by light and other forms of electromagnetic radiation, i.e., radio waves, infrared radiation, X-rays, etc. The speed of light varies depending on what it is traveling through. It is fastest when traveling through a vacuum, where its velocity is 299,792,458 m/s (around 186,000 mps or 300,000 km/s). This means that when you look at the Moon, you see it as it was about 1.3 seconds ago, and the Sun around 8.3 minutes ago.

**Largest virus** The world's largest virus is "Mimivirus," which contains 900 genes. It was discovered in 1992 in a sample from a water cooling tower in Bradford, UK. It was examined by researchers at the National Center for Scientific Research in Paris, France, who released their results on March 27, 2003 in the journal *Science*.

**Longest time survived in space by bacteria** From April 7, 1984 to January 11, 1990 *E. coli* bacteria cells survived unshielded onboard NASA's Long Duration Exposure Facility satellite, in low Earth Orbit.

Hardware samples removed from the US unmanned lunar probe *Surveyor 3* were returned to Earth by the crew of *Apollo 12* in November, 1969. Upon analysis it was discovered that bacterial organisms (*Streptococcus mitis*)—which had contaminated *Surveyor 3* before its launch on April 17, 1967—had survived more than two-and-a-half years in space.

**Lightest known particle** The lightest known particles in the universe are neutrinos which have a maximum mass of 0.00000000000000000000000000000000000018 kg. Neutrinos come in three varieties—electron, muon, and tau neutrinos. The mass is an average of the three types. Neutrinos are created by radioactive decay and nuclear fusion (the same process that powers the Sun).

# MEDICAL MILESTONES

**First successful kidney transplant** The first successful human kidney transplant was performed by R.H. Lawler (USA) at Little Company of Mary Hospital, Chicago, Illinois, USA, on June 17, 1950.

**First heart transplant patient** The first heart transplant operation was performed on 55-year-old Louis Washkansky (South Africa) at the Groote Schuur Hospital, Cape Town, South Africa. The operation lasted from 1 am to 6 am on December 3, 1967 and was performed by a team led by Prof. Christiaan Barnard (South Africa). Washkansky survived for 18 days.

**First heart-lung-liver transplant patient** The first triple-transplant patient was Davina Thompson (UK). On December 17, 1986 at Papworth Hospital, Cambridge, UK, she underwent seven hours of surgery performed by a team of 15, headed by chest surgeon John Wallwork and Prof. Sir Roy Calne (both UK).

**Longest surviving kidney transplant patient** The longest surviving kidney transplant patient is Johanna Leanora Rempel (Canada), who was given a kidney from her identical twin sister Lana Blatz on December 28, 1960. The operation was performed at the Peter Bent Brigham Hospital, Boston, Massachusetts, USA. Both Johanna and her sister have continued to enjoy excellent health and both have had healthy children.

**Longest surviving heart transplant patient** Dirk van Zyl (South Africa) survived 23 years 57 days having received an unnamed person's heart at the Groote Schuur Hospital, University of Cape Town, South Africa, on May 10, 1971.

**First recipient of an artificial heart** On December 2, 1982 at the Utah Medical Center, Salt Lake City, Utah, USA, Dr. Barney B. Clark (USA) was the first recipient of an artificial heart. The surgeon was Dr. William C. De-Vries, and the heart was a Jarvik 7 designed by Dr. Robert K. Jarvik. Dr. Clark died on March 23, 1983, 112 days later.

**Youngest person with a pacemaker** Stephanie Gardiner (UK) was four hours old when she was fitted with a tiny pacemaker the size of a postage stamp on March 11, 1995 at Bristol Children's Hospital, Bristol, UK.

**MOST EYE OPERATIONS PERFORMED** Dr. Murugappa Chennaveerappa Modi (India), a pioneer of mass eye surgery, performed a total of 610,564 cataract, squint correction, and cornea transplant operations between 1943 and 1993—an average of 12,211 a year.

**Longest artificial heart transplant survival** The longest surviving recipient of an artificial heart was William J. Schroeder (USA) who lived for 620 days after his operation at Louisville, Kentucky, USA, from November 25, 1984 to August 7, 1986.

**Longest-working pacemaker** The longest-working pacemaker was a lithium-battery-powered Biotec 777 fitted into János Szilágyi (Hungary) on January 18, 1979. It was last confirmed to be operating as normal on September 2, 2002.

**Most organs transplanted in a single operation** Dr. Andreas Tzakis (USA) transplanted seven organs—a liver, pancreas, stomach, large and small intestines, and two kidneys—into a 10-month-old Italian girl during 16 hours of surgery at Jackson Children's Hospital in Miami, Florida, USA, on March 23, 1997. The girl suffered from megacystis microcolon syndrome, a rare congenital defect that interferes with the body's ability to absorb nutrients.

**Youngest multi-organ transplant patient** Sarah Marshall (Canada) became the youngest person to receive a multi-organ transplant when, on August 7, 1997, age 174 days, she was given a liver, a bowel, a stomach, and a pancreas at London's Children's Hospital of Western Ontario, Canada. Sarah was born with the rare condition known as megacystis microcolon intestinal hypoperistalis syndrome. She had an enlarged bladder, small colon, and an abnormal bowel.

**Least invasive cochlear implant surgical technique** A minimally invasive surgical technique to perform cochlear implants in children was pioneered by Prof. Gerry O'Donoghue at the Queen's Medical Centre, Nottingham, UK. Instead of cutting a long incision in the scalp, a simple 1.2-in.-long (3-cm) incision is made behind the ear and a well drilled in the skull into which the implant is then inserted. This new method to treat children with profound deafness results in less scarring, a reduced chance of infection, and significantly less trauma to the child.

**Youngest person fitted with a pair of bionic arms** Kyle Barton (UK) was eight years old when he was fitted with his second bionic arm by

Dr. Dipak Datta, a consultant at the Northern General Hospital, Sheffield, UK, in February 2002. Kyle had to have both his legs and arms amputated after he contracted meningitis in 1998, and was fitted with his first bionic arm in 2001. The arms, equipped with electrodes, can sense impulses from the brain and have a grip action in each hand.

**Youngest person to have a full limb transplanted** Chong Lih Ying (Malaysia) was only four weeks old when doctors transplanted her twin sister's left arm to her body on May 18, 2000. Chong was born with a deformed left arm and no hand. The donor arm came from Lih Ying's twin sister, who was born with the severe brain abnormality meningoencephalocele and had no hope of survival.

**First bionic arm** In 1993, Scottish hotel owner Campbell Aird, who had his right arm amputated in 1982 after doctors diagnosed muscle cancer, was fitted with the first working bionic arm, created by a team of five bioengineers at the Margaret Rose Hospital, Edinburgh, UK.

**First brain cell transplant** The first ever brain cell transplant was performed by a team of doctors from the University of Pittsburgh Medical Center, Pennsylvania, USA, on June 23, 1998. The aim of the operation was to reverse the damage that had been caused by a stroke to 62-year-old Alma Cerasini, who had suffered paralysis of her right arm and leg as well as the loss of most of her speech. The team has subsequently performed 11 more operations of this type.

**Most reconstructive surgeries by a team of traveling doctors** A team of volunteer doctors visited 18 countries and treated 5,139 patients as

**MOST DETAILED HUMAN DISSECTION** The "Visible Woman" is a real cadaver that was sliced into 5,189 slices 330 microns thick by Dr. Victor Spitzer and his team at the University of Colorado (USA). Each slice was photographed and stored in a computer to form a minutely detailed 3-D virtual human body. The team have also created a "Visible Man."

part of Operation Smile's "World Journey of Hope," which took place from February 5 to April 14, 1999. The doctors repaired cleft lips and cleft palates, as well as performing surgery on facial tumors, burns, and facial injuries.

**First successful separation of conjoined twins** The earliest successful separation of Siamese twins was performed on xiphopagus (joined at the sternum) girls at Mount Sinai Hospital, Cleveland, Ohio, USA, by Dr. Jac S. Geller (USA) on December 14, 1952.

**Longest-living human cells** The cells of Henrietta Lacks (USA) are still alive and being grown in laboratories worldwide decades after her death in October 1951. In February of that year doctors had removed cells from a malignant tumor in the 31-year-old and found them to lack chromosome 11—now known as the "tumor suppressor." As a result, "HeLa" cells have become "immortal" and are one of the most helpful tools in biomedical research.

**First test-tube baby** Louise Brown (UK) was delivered by Caesarean section in Oldham General Hospital, Lancashire, UK, at 11:47 pm on July

**LONGEST LASTING HIP REPLACEMENT** In September 1970, at age 32, Denise Poole (UK) received a complete hip replacement (shown here in an x-ray photo). The hip is still in place today—almost 34 years later.

25, 1978. She was externally conceived on November 10, 1977 and weighed 5 lb. 12 oz. (2.6 kg) at birth. Louise's birth was the result of the work of UK gynecologist Patrick Steptoe and two Cambridge doctors, Robert Edwards and Barry Bavister. The trio pioneered a new technique by which an egg could be taken from a woman's ovary, fertilized in a laboratory (*in vitro* fertilization), and then returned to the womb to develop normally. The technique has since helped thousands of women throughout the world with fertility problems to have children.

**Earliest kidneys created by cloning** In January 2001 scientists from Advanced Cell Technologies, Massachusetts, USA, announced that they had for the first time successfully grown kidneys using cloning technology. The technique took a DNA-containing nucleus from a single cow skin cell and fused it with a host egg. The egg multiplied into an embryo rich in stem cells. These cells were chemically manipulated to grow into kidney cells, using an artificial kidney-shaped scaffold. Several of these miniature kidneys were grown in this way and transplanted back into the cow, where they began to produce urine.

# INTERNET

**Largest fine for an Internet crime** US anti-abortion activists who operated a site called "The Nuremberg Files," which contained "wanted" posters listing the names and addresses of doctors who perform abortions, were ordered to pay more than $107.7 million (£65 million) in damages on February 3, 1999.

**Largest Internet advertiser by sector** According to Competitive Media Reporting/TNS Media Intelligence, in 2002 the largest internet advertisers by sector were the business and finance sectors, which, between them, spent a massive $1,216,879,196 (£810,940,465) worldwide.

**Largest Internet search engine** Google, with over three billion pages, has the largest continually refreshed index of webpages of all the world's search engines. The company was founded by Larry Page and Sergey Brin (both USA). Their first office was a garage in Menlo Park, California (USA), which opened in September 1998 with a staff of four people.

**Most comprehensive cyberspace map** American researchers Bill Cheswick and Hal Burch, working out of the Bell Laboratories, Murray Hill, New Jersey, USA, created a map of cyberspace featuring 88,000 endpoints. Colors are used to represent different Internet Service Providers (ISPs). To create the map, Cheswick sent out electronic tracers from his New Jersey-based computer, which "died" when they reached way points of terminal destinations. On the point of expiry, the messages sent back a death notice, enabling Burch's program to create the map.

**LARGEST INTERNET CAFÉ** The easyEverything Internet café, Times Square, New York, USA, opened on November 28, 2000. It has a record 648 computer terminals.

**Most popular country-level domain** According to NetNames Ltd., as of March 2001, the most popular country level domain is .uk (Britain), with over two million domain registrations. Britain is closely followed by Germany (.de). Although America has the most Internet sites, few of them use .us in their url.

**Largest Internet joke vote** Laughlab, an Internet experiment into humor, was conducted by psychologist Richard Wiseman (UK) from the University of Hertfordshire, UK, and the British Association for the Advancement of Science. Running from September 2001 to October 2002, around 40,000 jokes were submitted from people all over the world, and over two million votes cast for the funniest (which can be read at: www.laughlab.co.uk/winner).

**Earliest computer virus** The first computer program that replicates itself surreptitiously was demonstrated by Fred Cohen, a student at the Massachusetts Institute of Technology, USA, on November 11, 1983.

**Largest wireless Internet provider** NTT DoCoMo (Japan) is the world's largest wireless Internet provider, with 36,931,000 subscribers to their imode service as of February 2003.

**Internet2 land speed record** Internet2 is a consortium of 202 universities working to develop the next generation of the Internet. In November 2002 an international team sent 6.7 gigabytes of data—equivalent to nearly two feature-length DVD movies—across 6,821 miles (10,978 km) of network, from Sunnyvale, California, USA, to Amsterdam, The Netherlands, in less than one minute. The team consisted of the Nationaal Instituut voor Kernfysica en Hoge-Energiefysica (NIKHEF), the Stanford Linear Accelerator Center (SLAC), the California Institute of Technology (Caltech), and the Faculty of Science of the Universiteit van Amsterdam (UvA). This ongoing competition is judged on a combination of bandwidth and distance, using standard Internet protocols.

**Earliest email** In 1971 Ray Tomlinson (USA), an engineer at computer company Bolt, Beranek and Newman, Cambridge, Massachusetts, USA, sent the first ever email in an experiment to see if he could get two computers to exchange a message. It was Ray who decided to use the @ symbol to separate the recipient's name from their location. The first ever email message was: "QWERTYUIOP."

**Oldest electronic "spam"** The world's first "spam" (unsolicited mass email) was sent at 12:33 EDT on May 3, 1978 by Gary Thuerk (USA) who worked for Digital Equipment Corp. (USA). It was sent to 397 email accounts on the ARPAnet (Advanced Research Projects Agency Network) of the US Defense Department, inviting them to a product demonstration of the DECSYSTEM-2020, 2020T, 2060, and 2060T computers. ARPAnet is regarded as the predecessor to the Internet.

**Country with the most Internet users** In December 2002 the USA had over 160 million Internet users out of a world total of around 665 million users.

**Highest capacity intercontinental Internet route** In 2001, the Internet routes between Europe and USA/Canada had a bandwidth capacity of 162,250.1 Mbps (megabits per second). In second place was the combined routes connecting USA/Canada and Asia and Pacific, with a bandwidth capacity of 41,820.1 Mbps. The lowest capacity was between Africa and Europe, with a bandwidth capacity of 444.8 Mbps.

**Most Internet users per capita** At year-end 2001, the Computer Industry Almanac released figures that showed Sweden with the highest pro-

**FIRST HYPERTEXT BROWSER** In October 1990 Tim Berners-Lee (UK) started work on a global hypertext browser. The result—the World Wide Web—was made available on the Internet in the summer of 1991. Berners-Lee had originally proposed a global hypertext project to allow people to combine their knowledge in a web of hypertext documents in 1989.

portion of Internet users, with 554.18 people online for every 1,000 of the population. Iceland was in second place with 552.04 per 1,000. The USA came sixth with 522.1.

**Continent with the most Internet users** According to analysts Nua, as of September 2002, of the 605.6 million people online worldwide, 190.91 million were online in Europe. Asia/Pacific was second with 187.24 million users.

**Largest free web-based email provider** Microsoft's Hotmail is the world's largest free web-based email service provider, with more than 110 million subscribers as of September 2002.

**Highest Internet bandwidth connection from a commercial plane** On January 15, 2003 the first ever commercial airline flight with a broadband Internet connection left Frankfurt, Germany, and flew to Washington, DC, USA. The data transfer rates on this flight, operated by Lufthansa (Germany), was 3 Mbps (download) and 128 Kbits per second (upload). Lufthansa was the first airline to offer this service.

**Longest broadband wireless connection** The longest wireless broadband connection to date, using Wi-Fi (wireless fidelity) technology, was

**OLDEST INTERNET BENCH** On August 6, 2001 the world's first park bench with free access to the Internet was opened in Bury St. Edmunds, Suffolk, UK. The standard park bench was converted by msn.co.uk to allow four people to connect their laptops simultaneously, in an attempt to change how people use the Internet.

192.6 miles (310 km) and was achieved on November 25, 2002 by the Swedish Space Corporation. The link was between a stratospheric balloon, launched from Esrange, Sweden, and a base station near Esrange. The balloon's antenna was provided by Alvarion (Israel). A data rate of at least 1 Mbps was sustained throughout the link.

**Largest online dating service** Match.com has logged more than 17 million registrations since its launch in April 1995. As of August 2002, there were more than 3.5 million members worldwide with profiles posted on the site. Founded in the USA, Match.com is a subscription-based site that registers more than 800,000 new members each month.

**Most globally connected city on the Internet** New York City, USA, has direct Internet connections to 71 other countries and can handle almost 150 Gbps of Internet traffic at any time. London, UK, comes second with direct connections to 61 other countries.

# COMMUNICATIONS

**Busiest international telephone route** The busiest international telephone route is between the USA and Canada. In 2001 there were some 10.4 billion minutes of two-way traffic between the two countries.

**First pole-to-pole telephone call** On April 28, 1999 at 10:30 am (GMT) the first ever phone call took place between people at the North and the South Poles. The call was made by Mike Comberiate and Andre Fortin (both NASA, USA) and lasted 45 minutes.

**Country with the most telephones** The country with the greatest number of telephones is the USA, with 165 million. The USA also makes the greatest number of calls of any country, with 550 billion a year.

**Most telephones per head of population** Monaco has the most telephones per head of population with 1,994 per 1,000.

**Largest telephone vote** The record for the largest TV telephone vote belongs to Thames Television and 19 Television's (both UK) *Pop Idol,* which was broadcast on ITV on February 9, 2002. The communications firm Telescope (UK) registered 9,006,025 votes, as viewers decided who of the two finalist singers should win.

**Longest telephone cable** The world's longest submarine telephone cable is Fiber-optic Link Around the Globe (FLAG), which runs for 16,800 miles (27,000 km) from Japan to the UK. It links three continents (Europe, Africa, and Asia) and 11 countries, and can support 600,000 simultaneous phone calls.

**MOST DISTANT RADIO SIGNAL FROM ANOTHER WORLD** In August 1989 some of the 27 dishes of the Very Large Array, New Mexico, USA, joined the efforts of the Deep Space Network of radio antennae in order to boost the reception of NASA's *Voyager 2* spacecraft during its encounter with the planet Neptune, 2,794.1 million miles (4,496.7 million km) from the Sun.

**Largest switchboard** The switchboard at the Pentagon, Arlington, Virginia, USA, has 34,500 lines handling nearly one million calls per day through 100,000 miles (161,000 km) of telephone cable. Its busiest ever day was June 6, 1994—the 50th anniversary of D-Day—when there were 1,502,415 calls.

**Smallest telephone** The smallest operational telephone was created by Jan Piotr Krutewicz (USA) on September 16, 1996. It measured just 1.8 × 0.3 × 0.8 in. (47.5 × 10 × 21 mm).

**Largest carrier of international telephone calls** In 2001 the largest carrier of international telephone calls, in terms of outgoing traffic, was AT&T Corp. (USA), with 12 billion minutes of communications.

**Country with the most cell phones** The country with the greatest number of cellular telephone subscribers is China, with 170 million in mid 2001.

**Most cell phone subscribers** Vodafone Group Plc has the world's largest cell phone subscriber base, with more than 100 million subscribers worldwide as of February 2002.

**Largest telecoms company merger**  A merger between British cellular communications company Vodafone Group Plc, formerly known as Vodafone Airtouch Plc, and German telecoms company Mannesmann AG, valued at £103.4 billion ($171.1 billion), was completed on April 12, 2000.

**Largest telecom company**  In 2002 Nippon Telegraph and Telephone Corporation (NTT) based in Tokyo, Japan, had revenues of $86,734 million (£60,870 million), a recorded loss of $4,404 million (£6,276 million), and had a workforce of 213,000 employees.

**Largest digital satellite radio broadcaster**  From its two geosynchronous satellites, WorldSpace (USA) broadcasts digital radio channels to Africa, Asia, and Europe, covering a total surface area (footprint) of 30.8 million miles$^2$ (80 million km$^2$). Its first satellite, Afristar, began broadcasting in October 1999 and Asiastar was launched in March 2000. Its third satellite, Ameristar, is due for launch in the near future.

**Largest civil communications satellite**  The Astra 1-K was built by Alcatel Space (France). It had a mass of 11,576 lb. (5,250 kg) and, fully deployed, would have been 121 ft. 4 in. (37 m) in length and 21 ft. 7 in. (6.6 m)

**LOUDEST SIGNALLING DEVICE**  The Chrysler air raid sirens (being demonstrated here) are the loudest sirens ever made and are capable of producing 138 dB at a distance of 100 ft. (30 m). They are so loud that a normal person would be deafened within 200 ft. (60 m) of one during operation.

in height. Upon its launch on November 26, 2002, its Russian Proton booster failed, leaving the satellite stranded in low Earth orbit. It was safely deorbited on December 10, 2002, over the Pacific Ocean.

**Most powerful radio signal beamed into space** On November 16, 1974 scientists at the Arecibo Radio Telescope, Puerto Rico, transmitted a binary radio signal to the M13 globular cluster in the constellation of Hercules. The message, which shows basic data on humanity, lasts for 169 seconds at 2,380 MHz. When the message arrives, in around 25,000 years, any advanced alien civilization will receive the signal at a strength 10 million times the intensity of the normal radio signals from our Sun. Of course, if anyone replies, it will take another 25,000 years for us to receive it.

**Most powerful communications satellite** The Hughes Space and Communications HS702 satellite is capable of emitting a 15-kW signal, making it the most powerful commercial communications satellite in the world. To achieve such a high output, the satellite draws upon twin high-efficiency solar cells.

**Longest transmission using optical fiber** As reported in September 1994, the longest transmission distance at a data rate of 20 gigabits per second over a fiber path containing repeaters is 78,000 miles (125,000 km). This was achieved using a recirculating fiber loop at BT laboratories at Martlesham, Suffolk, UK.

**Narrowest optical fiber channels** Physicists at the University of Bath, UK, have produced a material called photonic crystal fiber that has a regular array of holes that run the fiber's entire length. These tubes are the basis

for the world's narrowest optical fiber channels for communications. The fibers could stretch to 6.2 miles (10 km) with cores just ¼₀₀₀₀₀₀₀₀ in. (0.00000001 mm) thick. The core length-to-width ratio is equivalent of the Channel Tunnel extended all the way from the Earth to Jupiter.

**FASTEST MORSE CODE TRANSMITTER The highest speed recorded for hand-key transmitting Morse Code is 175 symbols a minute (equivalent to 35 wpm) by Harry A. Turner (USA) of the US Army Signal Corps on November 9, 1942.**

**Fastest multimode optical fiber transmission** A team of scientists at Essex University, UK, led by Stuart Walker (UK), transmitted 1.02 terabits per second of data down a single 1.86-mile (3-km) strand of multimode optical fiber in March 2002. This is equivalent to around 15.9 million simultaneous phone calls.

**Earliest radio transmission** The earliest description of a radio transmission system was written by Mahlon Loomis (USA) on July 21, 1864 and demonstrated between two kites that were 14 miles (22 km) apart at Bear's Den, Loudoun County, Virginia, USA, in October 1866. Loomis received US patent No. 129,971 on July 20, 1872.

**Fastest around-the-world text message** On February 20, 2002 at the 3GSM World Congress in Cannes, France, Logica sent a text message around the world by forwarding it to cell phones in six countries in six continents. The message finally came back to the original cell phone in Cannes after 3 min. 17.53 sec.

# ROCKETS

**SMALLEST ROCKET** *Pegasus,* a three-stage booster, is 50 ft. 10 in. (15.5 m) long. It was first air-launched from a B-52 aircraft in 1990. It is designed to place light payloads into low-level orbit.

**LARGEST SOLID ROCKET BOOSTER** The two reusable boosters that assist the launch of the US space shuttle use solid fuel. Each booster measures 149 ft. (45.4 m) long and 12 ft. (3.6 m) wide and contains over 1,000,000 lb. (450,000 kg) of propellant.

**MOST POWERFUL COMMERCIAL ROCKET LAUNCHER** *Ariane 5-ESCA* is capable of placing a 22,000-lb. (10-tonne) payload into geosynchronous orbit 22,370 miles (36,000 km) above Earth.

Rockets

**MOST SUCCESSFUL COMMERCIAL ROCKET LAUNCHER** From March 1995 to February 2003 Arianespace's (France) family of *Ariane 4* rockets had 74 consecutive commercial rocket launches. Its final launch occurred on February 15, 2003.

**HEAVIEST PAYLOAD LAUNCHED TO THE OUTER SOLAR SYSTEM** On October 15, 1997 a Titan IV rocket with a Centaur upper stage launched the 12,467-lb. (5,655-kg) NASA/ESA *Cassini-Huygens* spacecraft. This robotic probe will explore Saturn and its moons in July 2004.

**LARGEST SPACECRAFT TO ORBIT AND LAND UNMANNED** *Buron* was the Soviet answer to the US space shuttle. It was launched into Earth orbit only once (on November 15, 1968) before its budget was cut. As there were no cosmonauts on board this two-orbit flight and landing was computer-controlled. The *Buron* orbiter measured 119.3 ft. (36.37 m) long and had a mass of 231,000 lb. (105,000 kg).

**MOST POWERFUL ROCKET**
The NI booster from the former USSR launched on February 21, 1969 with a thrust of 10.1 million lb. (4,620 tonnes), but exploded 70 seconds after take-off.

# SPACE EXPLORATION

**Most distant image of Earth** On February 4, 1990 NASA's *Voyager 1* spacecraft turned its camera back toward the Sun and the planets. After 12.5 years in space, traveling away from Earth, *Voyager 1*'s camera took a picture of our home planet from a distance of almost 4 billion miles (6.5 billion km).

**Longest extraterrestrial balloon flight** The twin Soviet spacecraft *Vega 1* and *Vega 2* were launched on December 15 and 20, 1984. Both probes encountered Venus in June 1985, where they dropped packages into the Venusian atmosphere. Each package split into a lander and a balloon. The *Vega 2* balloon transmitted data on the Venusian atmosphere for 46.5 hours, before contact was lost. *The Vega 1* balloon transmitted data for 56 minutes. After dropping their packages on Venus, both *Vega* spacecraft continued on their course to successful fly-bys of Halley's Comet, in March 1986.

**Longest orbital survey of an outer planet** NASA's Galileo spacecraft arrived at the planet Jupiter on December 7, 1995. This survey was the first time a probe has orbited an outer-Solar-System body. Galileo is destined to burn up in the atmosphere of Jupiter in September 2003.

**FIRST MEN ON THE MOON** Neil Armstrong (USA), commander of the *Apollo 11* mission, became the first man to set foot on the Moon when he stepped on to the Sea of Tranquility at 02:56:15 GMT on July 21, 1969 (or 22:56:15 EDT on July 20, 1969). He was followed out of the lunar module *Eagle* by Edwin "Buzz" Aldrin (USA) while the command module *Columbia,* piloted by Michael Collins (USA), orbited above.

**Greatest spacecraft collision** On June 25, 1997 an unmanned *Progress* supply vehicle weighing 15,000 lb. (7 tonnes) collided with the Russian *Mir* Space Station. Cosmonauts Vasily Tsibliev and Alexander Lazutkin (both USSR) on board *Mir* had to work quickly to seal a breach in the hull of *Mir*'s *Spektr* module, while US astronaut Michael Foale prepared *Mir*'s *Soyuz* capsule for a possible evacuation. Although loss of life was avoided, the station was left dangerously low on power and oxygen, and temporarily tumbled out of control.

**Most planets visited by one spacecraft** NASA's *Voyager 2* spacecraft, launched in 1977, visited all four of the outer gas giants, Jupiter, Saturn, Uranus, and Neptune, between 1979 and 1989.

**Smallest manned spacecraft** The Manned Maneuvering Unit (MMU) used by astronauts working outside the space shuttle is 4 ft. (1.24 m) tall, 2 ft. 8 in. (0.83 m) wide, 3 ft. 8 in. (1.12 m) deep, and weighs just 240 lb. (109 kg). Powered by nitrogen thrusters, it was first used on shuttle mission STS-41-B in February 1984 when astronaut Bruce McCandless (USA) maneuvered up to 328 ft. (100 m) away from *Challenger.*

**Most distant solar-powered spacecraft** On April 18, 2002 NASA's *Stardust* spacecraft, en route to sample comet Wild 2 in January 2004, was a distance of 253 million miles (407 million km) from the Sun. Solar-powered spacecraft are usually used to explore the inner Solar System, as the more distant planets do not receive enough sunlight to efficiently power spacecraft at those distances from the Sun.

**Closest comet fly-by by a spacecraft** On March 13, 1986 the European Space Agency's *Giotto* probe passed the icy nucleus of Halley's Comet at a distance of just 370 miles (596 km).

**Most remote man-made object** *Voyager 1,* launched from Cape Canaveral, Florida, USA, on September 5, 1977, is now the farthest man-made object from the Earth. On February 17, 1998 it surpassed the slower *Pioneer 10,* which was launched on March 2, 1972. As of February 25, 2003, *Voyager 1* was more than 8.134 billion miles (13.091 billion km) from Earth.

**Most space flights by an astronaut** On April 8, 2002 US astronaut Jerry Ross began his seventh space mission, setting the record for the most space flights. He was a crew member on the STS 110 mission of the space shuttle *Atlantis,* on a construction flight to the International Space Station. All Ross's flights have been on the space shuttle. His record has since been equaled by NASA astronaut Franklin Chang-Diaz (USA), who flew his seventh mission between June 5 and 19, 2002 on the space shuttle *Endeavour.*

**Longest surviving interplanetary spacecraft** The unmanned space probe *Pioneer 6* was launched on December 16, 1965. After achieving its Solar orbit between Earth and Venus, it was able to successfully determine the structure and flow of the Solar wind—the million-mile-an-hour stream of charged particles from the Sun. No longer used to collect science data, *Pioneer 6* is still functioning after more than 37 years.

**Most probed planet** To date there have been 28 missions to Venus. The most recent spacecraft to encounter Venus was the *Cassini-Huygens* space-craft, which flew by the planet twice (in 1998 and 1999) to pick up speed

**MOST ACCURATE MEASURE OF THE AGE OF THE UNIVERSE** Just as a map of Earth can be shown as an oval, these results from NASAs Wilkinson Microwave Anisotropy Probe (WMAP) show the whole universe. The tone variations show temperature differences of just a few millionths of a degree in the microwave "heat echo" of the "Big Bang." They provide a snapshot of the universe when it was just 380,000 years old and have allowed astronomers to calculate its current age to be 13.7 billion years, with an uncertainty of only 1%.

**MOST REUSED SPACECRAFT** NASA's space shuttle *Discovery* was first launched on August 30, 1984. It has since completed 30 space missions, more than any other spacecraft. Shown in the picture is astronaut Steven L. Smith (USA) standing on the shuttle's robot arm, preparing to replace a transmitter in the Hubble Space Telescope on *Discovery's* 27th mission in December 1999.

from gravitational slingshots. *Cassini-Huygens* is now en route to Saturn and will get there in July 2004.

**Most comets discovered by a spacecraft** The Solar and Heliospheric Observatory (SOHO) was launched on December 2, 1995. It orbits between the Sun and the Earth where it constantly monitors solar activity. As of February 15, 2003 SOHO had discovered 587 comets by chance, as they appeared close to the Sun and were imaged by the spacecraft.

**Longest time survived on Venus** Of the nine successful and partially successful robotic probes that have landed on Venus, the one that lasted the longest was *Venera 11*. This Soviet spacecraft, launched on September 9, 1978, landed on December 25, 1978. Following touchdown, it transmitted data back to Earth for 95 minutes before being crushed or incinerated by the harsh Venusian atmosphere.

**Oldest operating manned spacecraft** *Discovery,* the third of NASA's fleet of space shuttle orbiters, was first launched into space on August 30, 1984. With the losses of *Challenger* in 1986 and *Columbia* during reentry on February 1, 2003, *Discovery* is now the world's oldest operating manned spacecraft.

**First spacewalk** On March 18, 1965, Lieutenant-Colonel Alexei Arkhipovich Leonov (USSR) became the first person to engage in EVA or extra-vehicular activity, commonly known as a "spacewalk."

**Most spacewalks** The greatest number of spacewalks is ten, totaling 31 hr. 37 min. by Russian cosmonaut Aleksandr Serebrov. The first five spacewalks took place in January/February 1990 during *Soyuz* TM-8 (launched September 5, 1989). The second five took place in September/October 1993 during Soyuz TM-17 (launched July 1, 1993).

# TECHNOLOGY

**Smallest transistor** On December 9, 2002 IBM (USA) announced the development of a 6-nanometer-long transistor. This breakthrough could allow the creation of computer chips with 100 times more transistors than currently possible.

**Largest LCD television screen** The largest liquid display crystal (LCD) television has been built by Samsung (South Korea). It has a diagonal viewing area of 54 in. (137 cm) and was revealed as a prototype at the Consumer Electronics Show, Las Vegas, Nevada, USA, on January 9, 2003.

**Earliest Jpeg** Jpeg, standing for Joint Photographic Experts Group, is one of the best known digital image formats. Developed in order to standardize the techniques for digital image compression, the format is used particularly for the internet and by digital cameras. The earliest images to use Jpeg compression are four digital test images called "Boats," "Barbara," "Toys," and "Zelda," created by the Jpeg Group on June 18, 1987 in Copenhagen, Denmark.

**Highest resolution digital camera** The highest resolution digital camera is MegaCam, which has a resolution of 320 million pixels. An astronomical camera, it has been used on the 11-ft. 10-in. (3.6-m) Canada-France-Hawaii Telescope, Hawaii, USA, since June 28, 2002.

**Highest-capacity DVD disc** Blu-ray, the new format for DVDs, uses a blue laser instead of the traditional red laser seen in current CD and DVD players. The blue laser allows up to 27 gigabytes of data to be stored on a single layer of a single-sided DVD. This new format was jointly established by nine of the largest electronics companies, and announced in February 2002. DVD players using the Blu-ray format are now under development.

**SMALLEST COLOR TELEVISION SCREEN** Microemissive Displays Ltd., Edinburgh (UK) have developed a tiny color TV/video screen that measures just 0.15 x 0.11 in. (3.84 x 2.88 mm). The ME1602, which can be linked to video cameras and DVD players, has a resolution of 160 x 120 pixels. It works using organic light-emitting diode technology.

**Smallest biological computing device** A team of scientists from the Weizmann Institute of Science (Israel) has adapted molecules of DNA to act as tiny molecular computing devices. Two DNA molecules and an enzyme molecule react together, acting as input, software, hardware, and power supply. Experiments have shown that a microliter of salt solution

**LARGEST PLASMA SCREEN** The largest plasma screen produced to date is the PPM63H1 produced by Samsung (South Korea), which measures 63 in. (160 cm) diagonally. Plasma screen technology uses charged gas between two layers of glass, which operates under the same principles as fluorescent lights and neon tubes. The result is a perfectly flat, uniformly focused, high-quality image on a slim screen.

**MOST GENDER-AWARE ROBOT** Artificial intelligence company Intelligent Earth, Kirkcaldy, UK, have developed visual gender recognition software for its robotic head Doki. Based on visual data alone, Doki can recognize the gender of women with an accuracy of 100%, and men with an accuracy of 96%. Doki is also able to scientifically rate the attractiveness of women, using visual data.

containing 3 trillion self-contained DNA computing devices can perform 66 billion operations per second, with the necessary power/fuel for the computations provided by the DNA itself as it is cleaved by the hardware enzyme. The results were announced on February 24, 2003 in the Proceedings of the National Academy of Sciences. The team consisted of Rivka Adar, Yaakov Benenson, Zvi Livneh, Tamar Paz-Elizur and Ehud Shapiro (all Israel).

**Smallest PC** On April 16, 2002, OQO (USA) unveiled a fully functioning PC measuring just $4.1 \times 2.9 \times 0.9$ in. ($10.4 \times 7.3 \times 2.2$ cm) and weighing less than 9 oz. (225 g). Described as an ultra-personal computer, it runs with a 1 GHz processor, 10 or 20 GB hard drive, and 256 MB of RAM, and is capable of running the full version of Microsoft's Windows XP.

**Most powerful quantum computer** Whereas normal computers use a string of zeros and ones (bytes) to represent data, experimental quantum computers use qubits, which can be a zero, one, or both simultaneously. On December 20, 2001, IBM's Almaden Research Center in San Jose, California, USA, announced that they had used a 7-qubit quantum computer to calculate the factors of the number 15. They used a billion billion molecules that have seven nuclear spins for the calculation. Consisting of the nuclei of five atoms of fluorine and two of carbon, these molecules are able to interact with each other as qubits.

**Fastest digital signal processor** The fastest digital signal processor (DSP) is the TMS320C6416, made by Texas Instruments (USA). On March 12, 2003 a clock speed of 1 GHz was demonstrated at the Texas Instruments Laboratories, Stafford, Texas, USA. DSPs are used for real-time processing of data where no time lag is acceptable. Applications include audio signal processing, video signal processing, and telecommunications.

**Most sophisticated battlefield simulator** The most sophisticated battlefield computer simulator is the Combined Arms Tactical Trainer. Situated at Warminster, UK, and Sennelager, Germany, it is capable of training more than 850 military personnel at once in an integrated, realistic combat scenario involving vehicles, aircraft, soldiers, and commanders. Simulated combat arenas of more than 3,800 miles$^2$ (10,000 km$^2$) are used. It was constructed for the UK's Ministry of Defence by Lockheed Martin, and became operational on September 1, 2002.

**Most emotionally responsive robot** Kismet, created by Cynthia Breazeal at the Massachusetts Institute of Technology, USA, is a robotic head powered by 15 networked computers and 21 motors. It is designed to recognize and respond to different emotions while interacting with humans. Nine of the computers are used to control Kismet's vision alone.

**Largest consumer electronics show** The International Consumers Electronics Show (CES) 2003, which ran from January 9 to 12, 2003 in Las Vegas, Nevada, USA, was the largest ever consumer electronics show. A total of 116,687 people attended the event, which had 2,283 exhibitors and 124,800 million ft.$^2$ (11,600 m$^2$) of exhibition space.

**Largest-distributed computing project** SETI@home, launched on May 17, 1999 by the University of California at Berkeley, California, USA, is a free downloadable software package that activates instead of a screensaver when a computer is idle. It uses the computer's processor to analyze radio radiation data from the universe (downloaded when the user logs on to the Internet) in the search for extraterrestrial intelligence. The astronomical data is collected from the Arecibo radio telescope, Puerto Rico. As of March 18, 2003 there were a total of 4,320,471 users around the world. Since its launch, SETI@home has amassed more than one million years of computing time.

# INVENTIONS

**EARLIEST USE OF THE WHEEL** The earliest documented use of the wheel as a means of transport dates back 5,500 years to Mesopotamia (modern Iraq). Previously, humans had moved heavy objects by rolling them over logs.

**EARLIEST TELESCOPE** In 1608 three Dutch eyeglass-makers claimed that they had each invented a telescope and actually produced refracting telescopes. Credit is given to Hans Lippershey, but Galileo Galilei (Italy) brought the invention to the notice of the scientific world in 1609. However, recent evidence suggests that Leonard Diggers (UK) invented a refractor 50 years earlier.

**EARLIEST GRAMOPHONE** The gramophone or phonograph was first conceived by Charles Cros (France), who described his idea in papers deposited in the French Academy of Sciences on April 30, 1877. Thomas Edison (USA) achieved the first practical device. The picture shows an Edison Standard Phonograph.

**EARLIEST COLOR TELEVISION TRANSMISSION** On July 3, 1928 John Logie Baird (UK) demonstrated color television transmission for the first time at his studios in London, UK. The picture shows an early portable television.

**EARLIEST MICROWAVE** In 1946 Percy Spencer (USA), an engineer at the Raytheon Company, Lexington, Massachusetts, USA, demonstrated the first microwave, named a Radarange. Shown here is an early microwave at the 1947 Ideal Home Exhibition at Olympia, London, UK.

**EARLIEST PORTABLE TELEPHONE** The concept of a portable telephone (a radio-telephone from the early 1970s shown here) first appeared in 1947 at Lucent Technologies' Bell Labs, New Jersey, USA. The first actual portable telephone handset was invented by Martin Cooper (USA), of Motorola, who made the first call on April 3, 1973 to his rival, Joel Engel, head of research at Bell Labs.

**Inventions**

**MOST PATENTS** Thomas Edison (USA) holds the record for the most patents held by a single person with 1,093, either on his own or jointly. They include the microphone, the motion-picture projector, and the incandescent electric lamp.

**EARLIEST COMPACT DISC** The standard for the compact disc (CD, DVD shown) was first proposed by Philips (Netherlands) and Sony (Japan) in 1980, and agreed upon in 1981 by the Compact Disc Standard Digital Audio Disc Committee. The first CDs became available to the public in Europe and Japan in the autumn of 1982, and the USA in 1983—where 800,000 discs were sold in the first year alone.

**EARLIEST "CLAMSHELL" LAPTOP** Regarded as the first "true" laptop, the GRiD Compass was designed in 1979 by William Moggridge (UK) for GRiD Systems Corporation (USA). It was introduced in 1982 with a RAM of 512K. The picture shows a 2003 Apple Mac Titanium G4.

# WEAPONS

**Earliest use of a crossbow**  The earliest reliable record of the use of a crossbow is from 341 B.C. at the Battle of Ma-Ling, Linyi, China. Historians believe these weapons were single-shot and held with a pistol-style grip. The earliest (non-recorded) use of crossbows was probably by the Stone Age people in Africa and southeast Asia.

**Largest-caliber cannon**  The largest-caliber cannon ever constructed is the *Tsar Pushka* (Emperor of Cannons), used by the Turks against the walls of Constantinople (now Istanbul, Turkey) in 1453 and now housed in the Kremlin, Moscow, Russia. This 86,641-lb. (39.3 tonne) cannon has a barrel 17 ft. 6 in. (5.34 m) long with a bore of 35 in. (89 cm) and fires a 1,200-lb. (540-kg) stone shot. The cannon was pulled by 60 oxen and 200 men.

**Largest gun**  In the siege of Sevastopol, USSR (now Ukraine), in July 1942, the Germans used a gun of a caliber of 31 in. (80 cm) with a barrel 94

**MOST HEAVILY ARMED TANK**  The most heavily armed tanks in recent times have been the Russian T-64, T-72, T-80 and T-90 tanks, all of which have a 4.92-in. (12.5-cm) gun-missile system. The American Sheridan light tank mounts a 6-in. (15.2-cm) weapon, which is both a gun and a missile launcher combined, but this is not a long-barreled, high-velocity gun of the conventional type. The British AVRE (Armoured Vehicle Royal Engineers) Centurion tank had a 6.5-in. (16.5-cm) low-velocity demolition gun.

ft. 8.5 in. (28.87 m) long. It was named *Schwerer Gustav* and was built by Krupp (Germany). The whole assembly of the gun was 141 ft. (42.9 m) long and weighed 2,963,000 lb. (1,344 tonnes).

**Greatest range of a gun** The famous long-range gun that shelled Paris, France, in World War I (1914–18), the *Paris-Geschütz,* or Paris Gun, had a caliber of 8.25 in. (21 cm) and a range of 76 miles (122 km). The little-known V3 static underground firing tubes built in 50 shafts during World War II (1939–45) near Mimoyecques, not far from Calais, France, to bombard London, UK, never actually became operative; but they would have fired projectiles a distance of some 95 miles (150 km).

**Highest rate of fire of a machine gun in service** Designed for use in helicopters and armored vehicles in the late 1960s, the 0.3-in.-caliber (7.62-mm) M134 Minigun is based on the multiple-barreled Gatling design. It has six barrels revolved by an electric motor and fed by a 4,000-round link belt. This allows for a firing rate of 6,000 rounds per minute, or 100 per second—about ten times that of an ordinary machine gun.

**Highest rate of fire for a ballistic weapon** The fastest firing ballistic weapon is a prototype 36-barrel gun built by Metal Storm of Brisbane, Australia, which has a firing rate in excess of one million rounds per minute. This is possible because the gun has no moving parts. Instead, numerous bullets are stacked in the barrels of the gun, separated by packages of primer and propellant (gunpowder) connected to a computer-controlled firing system. Although the weapon's rate of fire is in excess of one million rounds per minute, the magazine has a capacity of just 540 rounds. This means that when fired at its maximum rate the weapon will be out of ammunition in a fraction of a second.

**Earliest tank** The first tank was No. 1 Lincoln, modified to become *Little Willie,* built by William Foster Co. Ltd. of Lincoln, Lincolnshire, UK. It first ran on September 6, 1915. Tanks first saw action with the Heavy Section Machine Gun Corps (later the Tank Corps), at the Battle of Fiers-Courcelette, France, on September 15, 1916. The Mark I Malé tank, armed with a pair of 6-pounder guns and four machine guns, weighed 62,611 lb. (28.4 tonnes) and was powered by a 105-hp (78.2-kW) motor, giving a maximum speed of 3–4 mph (4.8–6.4 km/h).

**Lightest tank** The entire hull of the Advanced Composite Armored Vehicle Platform (ACAVP) tank is manufactured from E-glass epoxy, a plastic/fiberglass composite material strong enough to protect its crew from rifle fire and shrapnel while making it 10% lighter than an equivalent metal-hulled tank. To provide protection from heavier fire, additional metal armor can be mounted. The ACAVP was developed by the British Defence Evaluation and Research Agency (DERA) and first demonstrated in March 2000.

**First atomic bomb used in battle** The first atom bomb was dropped on Hiroshima, Japan, by the United States at 8:16 am on August 6, 1945. It

**MOST ACCURATE BOMB** The US-built Joint Direct Attack Munition (JDAM) is the world's most accurate air-drop munition. JDAMs are steerable tailkits attached to existing "dumb bombs" (shown here, nearest on wing). The tailkits have internal navigation systems that continually check the bomb's position by satellites. Upon impact JDAMs are accurate to plus/minus 6 ft. 7 in. (2 m).

had an explosive power equivalent to that of 15 kilotons of trinitrotoluene (TNT). Code-named *Little Boy,* the bomb was 10 ft. (3.04 m) long and weighed 9,000 lb. (4,080 kg).

**Heaviest conventional bomb** The heaviest conventional bomb ever used operationally was the British Royal Air Force's Grand Slam, which weighed 22,000 lb. (9,980 kg) and measured 25 ft. 4 in. (7.74 m) long. It was first dropped on Bielefeld railroad viaduct, Germany, on March 14, 1945. The US Air Force tested an even larger bomb, weighing 42,000 lb. (19,050 kg), in 1949.

**Largest non-nuclear conventional bomb in existence** The world's largest non-nuclear conventional bomb is the Massive Ordnance Air Blast (MOAB), a precision-guided weapon weighing 21,500 lb. (9,752 kg). It was first tested by the US Air Force at the Eglin Air Force Armament Center, Florida, USA, on March 11, 2003. Rather than exploding on impact with the ground, the bomb deploys a parachute and detonates just above the ground, directing its blast more effectively into the enemy target.

**Earliest successful test of a high-powered microwave weapon** High-powered microwave (HPM) weapons are designed to disable electrical systems. The earliest recorded successful testing of an HPM occurred in April 1999 under the observation of the Joint Command and Control Warfare Center of San Antonio, Texas, USA. HPMs discharge a powerful energy pulse of around two billion watts, which destroys any electronics within a 984-ft. (300-m) range. Their aim is to cause maximum destruction to any military or civilian power and electrical systems, and thereby partially disable the enemy.

**Earliest use of a graphite bomb** The earliest use of a graphite bomb (G-bomb) in battle occurred in 1991 when Allied forces used it to disable

85% of Iraq's power supplies during the Gulf War. The bomb explodes a cloud of ultra-fine carbon-fiber wires over electrical installations, short-circuiting electrical systems.

**Earliest use of infrared equipment in battle** The earliest use of infrared technology in battle was during World War II (1939–45), when the USA, the UK, and Germany were all developing the new technology. Electric sniperscopes mounted on top of rifles converted the infrared light of enemy soldiers into visible light, enabling accurate nighttime firing. However, few of these early sniperscopes were actually used in battle as they had heavy batteries and a low range.

**Most powerful nerve gas** S-2-(diisopropylamino) ethyl O-ethyl methylphosponothioate, or VX, developed at the Chemical Defence Experimental

**SMALLEST NUCLEAR WEAPON** The W54 fission bomb, deployed by the USA in the 1960s, is the smallest confirmed nuclear weapon ever made. Its warhead was 30 in. (76 cm) long, 11 in. (27 cm) in diameter at its widest point, weighed 51 lb. (23.13 kg), and had a yield of 0.1 kilotons. It was designed to be used by commando teams to destroy harbors or bridges, or else deployed as a battlefield weapon, shot from a custom-made bazooka.

Establishment, Porton Down, Wiltshire, UK, in 1952, is lethal with an airborne dosage of 10 mg-minute/m³, or an oral dosage of 0.3 mg—about one fifth the size of a raindrop. VX gas affects the nervous system by bonding with the chemicals that transmit signals to the nerves and disrupting them. Symptoms of VX begin to occur two hours after contact and include loss of muscle control, slurred speech, convulsions and then death.

**Largest torpedo** The Russian Type 65, a 25.5-in.-diameter (65-cm) torpedo, carries a warhead of nearly 2,200 lb. (1 tonne) of conventional explosive, or a 15-kiloton nuclear warhead—slightly less powerful than the bombs dropped on Hiroshima and Nagasaki. It can home in on a ship more than 50 miles (80 km) away and close at 43.5 knots (50 mph or 80 km/h)—far in excess of the speed of the fastest surface ships.

# AIR & SEA WARFARE

**Largest battleship ever** The largest battleships ever commissioned were the Japanese vessels *Yamato* (commissioned in December 1941 and sunk southwest of Kyushu, Japan, on April 7, 1945) and *Musashi* (commissioned in August 1942 and sunk in the Philippine Sea on October 24, 1944). The Imperial Japanese Navy's super battleships, they were designed to be the most heavily armed in the world. Both ships had a full-load displacement of 156.7 million lb. (71,111 tonnes), an overall length of 863 ft. (263 m), and a full-load draught of 35.5 ft. (10.8 m). They were armed with nine 18.1-in. (460-mm) guns.

**Fastest destroyer** The highest speed attained by a destroyer was 45.25 knots (52 mph or 83.42 km/h) by the 6.4 million-lb. (2,900-tonne) French ship *Le Terrible* in 1935. Built in Blainville, France, and powered by four Yarrow small tube boilers and two Rateau geared turbines giving 100,000 hp (74,570 kW), she was decommissioned at the end of 1957.

**Largest aircraft carrier** The nine US Navy Nimitz class nuclear-powered aircraft carriers are the largest warships afloat. Fully loaded, each ship displaces 217.2 million lb. (98,550 tonnes) and, when battle-ready, can carry around 5,680 personnel and 80 aircraft.

**Fastest warship** The world's fastest ever warship was the US Navy's 78-ft.-long (23.7-m), 220,000-lb. (100-tonne) experimental surface-effect ship SES-100B. The hovercraft attained a world record 91.9 knots (105 mph or 170 km/h) on January 25, 1980 on Chesapeake Bay, Maryland, USA.

**Largest navy** The largest navy in the world in terms of manpower is the United States Navy. In March 2003 there were 383,427 uniformed personnel on active duty, supported by 185,371 civilian employees. This does not

**OLDEST AIR FORCE** The earliest autonomous air force is the UK's RAF (Royal Air Force), whose origins date back to 1878 when the War Office commissioned a military balloon. The RAF itself came into existence on April 1, 1918, to take on a growing flying role previously undertaken by the army.

include the 170,000 uniformed members of the US Marine Corps, which is, strictly speaking, a separate part of the armed forces.

**Earliest aircraft carrier** Although platforms for takeoffs and landings had been fitted to warships as early as 1910, the first ship with a runway running the full length of its deck was the British Royal Navy's HMS *Argus*, launched in 1918. She had a flight deck 565 ft. (172 m) long and space for 20 aircraft.

**Earliest stealth ship** The earliest known ship incorporating stealth technology is the US Navy's *Sea Shadow*, which was completed in the mid 1980s but revealed to the public only in 1993. The bizarre-looking twin-hulled ship is 164 ft. (49.98 m) long, 68 ft. (20.72 m) wide, and has a full-load displacement of 1.25 million lb. (569 tonnes). It has a crew of ten and a top speed of 11.5 mph (18.52 km/h).

**Largest amphibious ship** With a full-load displacement of 80.47 million lb. (36,500 tonnes) and a length of 844 ft. (257.3 m), the US Navy's Wasp-class vessels are the largest amphibious ships afloat today. Primarily designed for landing troops on shore, they are also capable of carrying aircraft, and various smaller landing vessels.

**Largest surface-effect ship** Similar to hovercraft, surface-effect ships travel on a cushion of air but also have two sharp, rigid hulls that remain in the water. The largest surface-effect ships currently in operation are two Russian Bora-class guided-missile corvettes, which have a displacement of 2.31 million lb. (1,050 tonnes) and a claimed cruising speed of 54 knots (62 mph or 100 km/h). The Bora are 215 ft. (65.6 m) long, 59 ft. (18 m) wide, and have a crew of 68.

**Largest submarine** The world's largest submarines are those of the Russian 941-Akula class (code-named Typhoon by NATO). The launch of the first Akula submarine, at the secret covered shipyard at Severodvinsk in the White Sea, was announced by NATO on September 23, 1980. The vessels are believed to have a submerged displacement of 58.4 million lb. (26,500 tonnes), to measure 562.6 ft. (171.5 m) overall and to be armed with 20 multiple-warhead SS-N-20 missiles with a range of

4,500 nautical miles (8,300 km). It is thought that less than five remain in service.

**Most submarines** The United States Navy has 74 armed submarines, the greatest number of any country. The entire submarine fleet is nuclear-powered, and includes more than 50 Seawolf- and Los Angeles-class attack ships, as well as 18 Ohio-class ballistic missile carriers.

**Earliest sinking of a ship by a submarine** The US Civil War Confederate ship *H. L. Hunley* became the first submarine ever to sink another vessel during wartime, when she successfully "torpedoed" the Union Navy's *Housatonic* off Charleston Harbor, South Carolina, USA, on February 17, 1864. The 40-ft.-long (12-m) sub was powered by a propeller turned by a crew of seven, who inhabited a cabin just 4 ft. (1.2 m) tall and 3 ft. 6 in. (1.06 m) wide. The "torpedo" consisted of a barrel of gunpowder attached to a 20-ft. (6-m) spear at the front of *Hunley*. The sub would ram an enemy ship, embedding the spear, then back off and detonate the charge remotely by pulling a rope.

**Largest naval hovercraft** The largest naval hovercraft, and the largest hovercraft currently in operation anywhere, are the Russian Zubr ships (code-named Pomornik by NATO), which are 187 ft. (57 m) long, 73.1 ft. (22.3 m) wide, and have a full-load displacement of 1.17 million lb. (535 tonnes). Zubr ships are amphibious landing craft able to deliver 360 troops or three battle tanks onto beaches at speeds of up to 60 knots (69 mph or 111 km/h). They have a crew of between 21 and 31 and are heavily armed, with two multiple-rocket launchers, four portable air-defense missile systems, and two 30-mm machine guns.

**EARLIEST NUCLEAR SUBMARINE** The world's first nuclear-powered submarine was USS *Nautilus* of the United States Navy, launched on January 21, 1954. *Nautilus* was 324 ft. (98.7 m) long, with a beam of 88 ft. (26.8 m). She had a crew of 95 enlisted men and 10 officers, and was capable of reaching speeds of over 20 knots (23 mph or 37 km/h).

**NAVY WITH THE LARGEST NUMBER OF AIRCRAFT** The United States Navy currently has over 4,000 aircraft in service, the greatest number of any world navy. It operates around 20 different types of fixed-wing aircraft, including carrier-based F-14 Tomcat and F/A-18 Hornet fighters, and reconnaissance, transport, anti-submarine and airborne-command-post aircraft. It also has six different types of helicopters.

**Greatest wingspan for a bomber** The American ten-engined Convair B-36J "Peacemaker" had a wingspan of 230 ft. (70.1 m), the longest ever for a bomber. The aircraft, which had a maximum take-off weight of 410,000 lb. (185 tonnes), has been out of service since the late 1950s, when it was replaced by the Boeing B-52. Its top speed was 435 mph (700 km/h).

**Most widely used military helicopter** Over 16,000 Bell Helicopter Textron (USA) UH-1 Iroquois ("Huey") helicopters have been produced since 1959, making it the most widely used military helicopter in the world. The general-purpose UH-1 became the workhorse of the US forces during the Vietnam War (1959–75), and it is claimed that over 5,000 UH-1s still remain in service in over 45 countries.

**Fastest combat jet** The fastest combat jet is the Russian Mikoyan MiG-25 fighter (code-named "Foxbat" by NATO), which has been tracked by radar at about Mach 3.2 (2,110 mph or 3,395 km/h). The MiG-25 was designed as a high-altitude interceptor but is also used as a reconnaissance aircraft. A MiG-25 can take off and climb to an altitude of 114,000 ft. (35,000 m) in a little over four minutes.

**Greatest airborne assault** The largest airborne assault was the World War II Anglo-American Operation Market Garden, when three divisions (34,000 men) landed near Arnhem, The Netherlands, starting on September

17, 1944. The operation involved 2,800 aircraft and 1,600 gliders, but failed in its objectives.

**Largest air force ever**  The largest air force of all time was the United States Army Air Corps (now the United States Air Force), which had 79,908 aircraft in July 1944 and 2,411,294 personnel in March 1944.

# ART & MEDIA

# ART & INSTALLATIONS

**Largest matchstick mosaic** In 1998 M. Schumann (Netherlands) constructed a mosaic of the Town Hall in Haarlem, The Netherlands, comprising 80,000 wooden matchsticks. The finished picture measured 3 ft. 6 in. × 2 ft. 4 in. (110 × 75 cm). Schumann spends hours constructing the world's famous buildings out of thousands of matchsticks.

**Largest finger painting** The largest finger painting in the world measures 2,766.5 ft.$^2$ (257 m$^2$) and was created by students from Lawrence Technological University, Southfield, Michigan, USA, on September 10, 2002. The final image was that of an American flag in memory of those lost in the September 11, 2001 tragedy.

**Most visited modern art gallery** The Tate Modern, London, UK, is the world's favorite modern art museum with 5.25 million visitors in the year 2000. This is more than double the visitors to the Museum of Modern Art in New York, USA, and Paris's Pompidou Centre, France.

**LONGEST MODERN ART SCULPTURE** The longest modern art sculpture is *Marsyas,* which measures 492 ft. (150 m) long and approximately 10 stories high. It was created by Turner Prize-winning artist Anish Kapoor (India). The giant sculpture was displayed in the Turbine Hall of the Tate Modern, London, UK, from 2002 to 2003. *Marsyas* comprises three steel rings joined together by a single span of red PVC membrane.

Art & Media

**Largest batik** The largest batik painting measures 150 ft.$^2$ (13.93 m$^2$) and was created by Satish Ryali (India) in April 2002. It took Satish around 206 hours over 35 days to complete the batik. The batik's theme is derived from Indian mythology in the Hoysala art tradition.

**Largest man-made crop picture** Crop artist Stan Herd's (USA) largest work to date was a 160-acre (65-ha) portrait of the 1930s Hollywood star Will Rogers (USA) created on the plains of southwest Kansas, USA, in 1983.

**Largest needlepoint** Beginning in August 2000, Vahid Saadati (Canada), along with a team of 650 volunteers, created the largest needlepoint, measuring 14 ft. 7 in. × 24 ft. 7 in. (4.44 × 7.49 m). It depicts the word "welcome" in 103 languages.

**Most valuable sculpture by a living artist** *Michael Jackson and Bubbles,* a porcelain sculpture created by the artist Jeff Koons (USA) in 1988, sold for $5,616,750 (£3,945,344) at Sotheby's, New York, USA, on May 15, 2001. The piece measures 42 × 70.5 × 32.5 in. (106.7 × 179.1 × 82.6 cm) and is described as a mix of pop culture and high art that perfectly captures the decade of the eighties. The gold-and-white-colored sculpture shows Michael Jackson (USA) reclining with his arm around his pet primate.

**Largest permanent coin mural** Eduardo D. Henriques (Portugal) has produced a number of permanent "nautical" murals made from Portuguese coins, the largest of which, *Império Português,* measures 6 × 16 ft. 4 in. (1.83 × 5 m) and uses 37,121 coins. An admiration for the tradition of Portuguese naval adventures inspired Eduardo's artwork.

**Largest painting by numbers** The largest painting by numbers measures 957 ft.$^2$ (88.95 m$^2$) and was created by nearly 300 students and staff from Portmead Primary School, Swansea, UK, on July 24, 2002. The giant painting depicts an underwater scene.

**Most visited traveling art exhibition** Since it opened in Japan in 1996, *Body Worlds,* an exhibition of posed, plastinated (plastic-preserved) human bodies by Gunther von Hagens (Germany), has traveled to 11 major cities. As of September 2002, the exhibition had received more than 9.57 million visitors.

**Tallest sculpture** The *Windwand,* at Canary Wharf, London, UK, is a 166-ft.-4-in.-tall (50.7-m) red flexible wand made from glass-fiber composite with an outer layer of carbon-fiber. Designed by Ron Arad Associates, it was built by Carbospars Ltd. (UK). Weighing 1,543 lb. (700 kg), it measures 15 in. (40 cm) in diameter at its base and narrows to 3.1 in. (8 cm) with red high-density LED lights at the tips, making it visible from 2 miles (3.21 km) away.

**Largest ice sculpture** An ice palace completed in January 1992 during the Winter Carnival at St. Paul, Minnesota, USA, used 18,000 blocks of ice.

**LARGEST TOAST MOSAIC** The largest toast mosaic was created by Maurice Bennett (New Zealand, shown here with a mosaic depicting Elvis Presley). It measured 39 ft. 4 in. × 13 ft. 5 in. (12 × 4.1 m) and used 2,724 slices of bread, toasted to different tones to create skin color and shadow. It portrayed Mark Blumsky, former mayor of Wellington, and was displayed in Wellington, New Zealand, from February to March 1999.

Built by TMK Construction Specialties, Inc. (USA), it was 166 ft. 8 in. (50.8 m) high and contained 10.8 million lb. (4,900 tonnes) of ice.

**Largest linoprint** The world's largest linoprint measures 438 ft.² (40.7 m²) and was created by the Stiching Grafisch Collectief Thoets (Netherlands), on October 28, 2000.

**Largest simultaneous photography exhibition** A photography exhibition showing photographer Martin Parr's (UK) work entitled *Common Sense* was held simultaneously in 44 venues around the world, with 41 of them opening on April 1, 1999. The aim of the exhibition, which had already toured the world, was to highlight details of day-to-day life. Although the intensely colorful pictures were taken with a 35-mm camera, their high quality meant they could be successfully reproduced by a laser copier. This meant that Parr's work could be shown in a number of public spaces simultaneously.

**Largest sand painting**   The world's largest sand painting measures 32 ft. 6 in. × 27 ft. 2 in. (9.9 × 8.3 m) and was created by a team from Procter & Gamble on October 23, 2002 at the Le Meridien Limassol Spa & Resort, Cyprus. The design depicts the company's logo.

**Greatest art robbery**   On April 14, 1991, 20 paintings, estimated to be worth $500 million (£280 million), were stolen from the Van Gogh Museum in Amsterdam, The Netherlands. However, only 35 minutes later they were found in an abandoned car not far from the museum.

**Largest 3D balloon sculpture**   The world's largest three-dimensional balloon sculpture used 58,942 balloons and was constructed by a team from the Balloon Express Shop, Rovigo, Italy, in the shape of a giant diplodocus dinosaur named "DinoBigo." The sculpture was 88 ft. 6 in. (27 m) long and displayed in La Fattoria shopping center, Rovigo, Italy, in November and December 2001.

**Largest picture mosaic**   The world's largest picture mosaic was created by 15,550 British children as part of Persil's *Big Mummy* project. It measured 643.65 m² (6,928 ft. 2 in.²), and was completed on 30 August 2002, at Alexandra Palace, London, UK.

**Largest scrap-metal sculpture**   The world's largest scrap-metal sculpture, completed by Gary Greff (USA) in August 2001, stands 110 ft. (33.5 m) tall, is 154 ft. (46.9 m) wide, and weighs 157,659 lb. (71,513 kg). Entitled *Geese in Flight,* the sculpture resembles Canadian geese flying against a backdrop of sky and prairie and is one of a series of metal sculptures located along the Enchanted Highway between Gladstone and Regent, North Dakota, USA.

**Largest brick sculpture**   Entitled *Train,* the world's biggest brick sculpture cost £760,000 to build and used more than 180,000 housebricks by the time it was unveiled on June 23, 1997, just a few steps from where the world's first train passenger service ran 170 years ago. The life-size structure depicting the *Mallard* steam engine is 130 ft. (39.6 m) long and was made in Darlington, Co., Durham, by David Mach (UK) and a team of 20 apprentice bricklayers.

# FASHION

**Most expensive tiara**   The world's most expensive tiara was designed by Italian fashion designer Gianni Versace and had an estimated retail value of $5 million (£3.2 million) in 1996. The tiara was decorated with 100-carat diamonds, set in yellow gold, and weighed approximately 10.5 oz. (300 g).

**Largest neck tie** A tie measuring 264 ft. (80.46 m) and made from 1,161 ft. (354 m) of fabric using 125,128 stitches was displayed at Shoppers Stop, Bangalore, India, from November 15 to December 14, 1997. The tie took 12 men 120 hours to make.

**Most popular sunglasses** Ray-Ban sunglasses sold 10 million units worldwide in 1998. Ray-Ban's best-known model, the Wayfarer, has been available since 1953 and is reported to be the best-selling style in history. The Luxottica Group, the Italian company that acquired Ray-Ban in 1999, reported for the fiscal year ending December 2002 an increased net income of 18% to 372.1 million ($390.7 million or £242.7 million).

**MOST VALUABLE ANTIQUE DRESS** An 1888 court dress designed by Charles Frederick Worth (UK) was sold at auction by Monica Seggos and Robert von Kampen (both USA) on May 3, 2001 at Doyle New York, USA, to an anonymous buyer for $101,500 (£70,894). It was worn by Esther Maria Lewis Chapin (USA) when presented to Queen Victoria in 1889. The gown has a 23-in. (58.4-cm) waist and a 10-ft. 6-in. (3.1-m) train.

**Most expensive bikini** The jewelers Prestons of Windsor, Berkshire, UK, made a diamond-encrusted bikini valued at $194,458.97 (£123,409.90) and unveiled it on March 22, 2000 at Windsor Fashion Week. Modeled by Naomi Campbell look-alike Susan Sangster, the plain black bikini was hand-sewn with individual pieces of jewelry to form a design that used a staggering total of 66 carats' worth of diamonds.

**Largest jeans** The world's largest pair of jeans are 94 ft. (28.6 m) long and 62 ft. (18.8 m) wide and were constructed by Levi Strauss Co., Inc. (Canada). The giant jeans were unveiled on July 30, 2001 and were inflated by a hot-air device to raise them to their full three-dimensional height. They are based on a pattern for a size 32 waist and 36 leg—yet enlarged to more than 20 times the normal pattern size. The jeans weigh 543 lb. (246.3 kg), use more than 7,805 ft.$^2$ (725 m$^2$) of 10-oz. denim, and have a working 13-ft.-long (3.96-m) zipper and an embossed metal button.

**Highest annual earnings for a model** The world's top-earning model is currently Gisele Bundchen (Brazil), who earned $12.5 million (£8.3 million) in 2001, according to the *Forbes* Celebrity 100 list released on June 21, 2002.

**Longest sari** A silk sari created by Vikas Chajjer (India) in May 1998 measured 396 ft. 11 in. (121 m) long and 45 in. (114 cm) wide. Taking 19 days to complete (11 to weave, three to hand-paint, and one day each to bleach, spray, print, embroider, and finish) the sari has two hand-painted designs: one with the seven wonders of the world and the other portraying Mahatma Gandhi.

**Largest knickers** The largest pair of knickers were manufactured by Cunning Stunts (UK) from acrylic and lace, and measured 14 ft. × 29 ft. 7 in. (4.26 × 8.97 m). The giant pair of pants was devised by advertising agency Bartle Bogle Hegarty (UK) to promote *FHM* magazine's lingerie special and hung across Oxford Street, London, UK, in October 1999.

**Largest g-string** The world's largest g-string was unveiled at the Body Shop's UK headquarters in Littlehampton, West Sussex, on March 15, 2001. The giant white and red cotton thong, measuring approximately 30 ft. 2 in. × 15 ft. (9.2 × 4.6 m), was presented by the Body Shop in conjunction with the charity Comic Relief's "Pants to Poverty" fundraising campaign.

**Highest heeled shoes commercially available** The highest heels commercially available boast a combination of 11-in. (27.9-cm) platforms and 16-in. (40.6-cm) heels. Available in red or black leather, these "Vertigo" shoes sell for $1,092 (£725). Produced by Leatherwork London Ltd. (UK), they are sold by LadyBWear (UK). The company takes no responsibility for anyone who falls while wearing the shoes.

**Fastest sheep to sweater** The Exeter Spinners Audrey Felton, Christine Heap, Eileen Lancaster, Marjorie Mellis, Ann Sandercock, and Maria

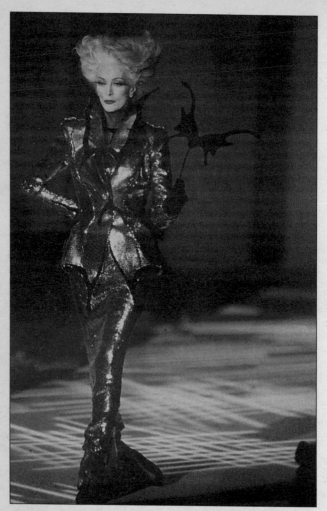

**LONGEST WORKING CAREER FOR A CATWALK MODEL** Born in 1931, model Carmen Dell'Orefice (USA) has been modeling for the Ford Agency (USA) since the 1940s. At the age of 72 she is still in demand for contracts and international shows. Daphne Self (UK) is 73 years old but has had an intermittent modeling career. She is signed to Models 1 in London, UK, and has been photographed for *Vogue* and *Marie Claire*.

Scott (all UK) produced a sweater by hand from raw fleece in 1 hr. 55 min. 50.2 sec. on September 25, 1983, at BBC Television Centre, London, UK.

**Longest modeling contract** The Japanese actress and model Shima Iwashita has been a house model for the Japanese cosmetic company Menard since she first signed with them on April 1, 1972. Her contract is renewed every year.

**Largest beret** José Antonio Basteguieta (Spain) made a beret *(boina)* measuring 11 ft. 5.76 in. (3.5 m) in diameter, which was displayed on *El Show de los Récords,* Madrid, Spain, on October 13, 2001.

**Largest evening jacket** The world's largest evening jacket is 32 ft. 6 in. (9.9 m) long and 17 ft. 9 in. (5.4 m) wide, and was created by Michael Voronin (Ukraine). Constructed with the help of 26 people in 106 hours, the jacket was made to celebrate the Ukrainian fashion holiday on September 8, 2002 in Kiev, Ukraine.

**Most valuable natural pearl necklace** A single-strand pearl necklace reputedly worn by French queen Marie-Antoinette fetched $1,476,345 (£910,313) at Christie's, Geneva, Switzerland, on November 16, 1999—the highest price ever paid for a natural pearl necklace. Consisting of 41 large and graduated pearls and held together by a diamond cluster clasp, the necklace was once owned by Woolworth heiress Barbara Hutton (USA). It was sold to an anonymous European buyer.

**Largest men's suit** Between February 14 and March 7, 2001 tailors from Raymond Ltd. (India) constructed the world's largest men's suit at their factory in Mumbai (Bombay), India. From shoulder to trouser hem the suit measured 64 ft. (19.5 m) long. The suit was made from 1,263 ft. (385 m) of polywool sapphire fabric, 787 ft. (240 m) of polyester lining, and a total of 4.8 miles (7.8 km) of thread.

**Largest dress** A dress measuring 39 ft. 6 in. (9.6 m) long with a diameter of 65 ft. 6 in. (20 m) was made for the 1998 Junta Central Fallera de Valencia in Spain. The dress was made from 7,532 ft.$^2$ (700 m$^2$) of fabric and was an exact, scaled-up replica of a dress worn by the first Miss Spain in 1929.

**Most valuable dress** A flesh-colored, beaded, silk Jean Louis gown, worn by the actress Marilyn Monroe (USA) when she sang "Happy Birthday" to President Kennedy (USA) on May 19, 1962, was sold at auction on October 27, 1999 for $1,267,000 (£782,340) at Christie's, New York, USA, to New York dealers Robert Schagrin and Peter Siegel (both USA) of Gotta Have It! Collectibles. The dress originally cost $12,000 (£7,410) and was such a tight fit for the actress that she had to be sewn into it.

**Largest canvas sports shoe** The world's largest canvas sports shoe measures 13 × 5 × 4 ft. (3.9 × 1.5 × 1.2 m), made by Michelle Nagy (Canada) in conjunction with the Juvenile Diabetes Research Foundation

**LARGEST LEATHER BOOT** In 2001, Pasquale Tramontana (Italy) completed the largest leather boot, which measures 13 ft. 7 in. x 8 ft. 10 in. (4.16 x 2.7 m) and is 31 in. (80 cm) wide. The boot took five years to make at a cost of 25 million lire ($11,416 or £8,884). It weighs 617 lb. (280 kg), and used 40 hides of leather.

and Shopper's Drug Mart in Toronto, Ontario, Canada, on September 16, 2001. Made of canvas with cotton stitching, aluminum grommets, and a rubber sole, the shoe's lace is 50 ft. (15.2 m) long.

**Most Oscar dresses sold at a charity auction** A record 56 evening gowns worn to Academy Awards ceremonies by actresses Elizabeth Taylor, Sharon Stone, and Uma Thurman were auctioned at "Unforgettable: Fashion of the Oscars" at Christie's, New York, USA, on March 18, 1999. A record $786,120 (£488,820) was donated to the American Foundation for AIDS Research (AmFAR). The most valuable item in the auction was a blue and violet faille-crepe dress worn by Elizabeth Taylor to the 1969 Academy Awards. It sold for $167,500 (£104,154).

# MOVIE CLASSICS

**Earliest motion picture** Louis Aimé Augustin Le Prince (France) was attested to have achieved dim moving outlines on a whitewashed wall at the Institute for the Deaf, Washington Heights, New York, USA, as early as 1885–87.

**First talkie** The earliest sound-on-film motion picture was achieved by Eugene Augustin Lauste (France), who patented his process on August 11, 1906 and produced a workable system using a string galvanometer in 1910 at Benedict Road, Stockwell, London, UK.

**Highest gross for a film series** The 20 James Bond movies made by Eon Productions Ltd. (UK), from *Dr. No* (UK, 1962) to *Die Another Day*

(UK/USA, 2002), have grossed over $3.6 billion (£2.25 billion) worldwide. *Die Another Day,* starring Pierce Brosnan (Rep. of Ireland) as James Bond, is the highest earner of the series, with a worldwide gross of over $393 million (£246 million).

**Most expensive film**  Paramount's *Titanic* (USA, 1997) cost just over $200 million (then £118.9 million) to make. Originally given a $125-million (£74.3-million) budget, it was due for release in July 1997, but post-production problems set the date back to December 1997 and added to the cost.

With production costs adjusted for inflation, the most expensive film ever made was *Cleopatra* (USA, 1963), whose $44-million (then £15.7-million) budget would be equivalent to $307 million (£175.4 million) today.

**Highest box-office gross**  The film with the highest box-office earnings is *Titanic* (Paramount, USA), which was released on December 19, 1997. It became the first film ever to take $1 billion at the international box office, with a total gross of $1.8 billion (£1.3 billion).

**Highest box-office gross (inflation adjusted)**  Rising cinema ticket prices mean that the all-time top-grossing movies are nearly all recent films. However, *Gone with the Wind* (USA, 1939), based on the best selling novel by Margaret Mitchell (USA), took a massive $393.4 million (then £88 million) at the international box office—a sum that, accounting for inflation, places the film top with a total gross equivalent to $3,785,107,801 (£2,365,692,376) today. In the USA alone, *Gone with the Wind* had 283,100,000 admissions compared to 130,900,000 for *Titanic* (USA, 1997)—the film with the highest box-office gross to date.

**Highest box-office gross for an animated movie (inflation adjusted)**  Walt Disney's (USA) first full-length feature film, *Snow White and the Seven Dwarfs* (USA, 1937), took $184.9 million (£37.4 million) at the box office worldwide, equivalent to $1.6 billion (£1 billion) today. The film took four years

**MOST APPEARANCES AS JAMES BOND**  Sean Connery (pictured) and Roger Moore (both UK) have both starred as British secret agent "007" seven times. Connery starred in the first Bond movie, *Dr. No* (UK, 1962), and Moore made his debut as Bond in *Live and Let Die* (UK, 1973).

**MOST EXTENSIVE SCREEN TEST** To find the actress to play the role of Scarlett O'Hara in *Gone with the Wind* (USA, 1939), film makers MGM shot 149,000 ft. (45.415 m) of black-and-white test film and another 13,000 ft. (3,962 m) of color film with 60 actresses, none of whom got the part. Vivien Leigh's (UK shown here with Clark Gable) successful test was actually made after the movie shoot had begun—perhaps the only instance of a major motion picture going into production before the star role had been cast.

to make at a cost of $1.5 million (then £303,398)—equivalent to $13.3 million (£8.3 million) today.

**Highest box-office gross for a western** *Dances with Wolves* (USA, 1990), directed by and starring Kevin Costner (USA), has grossed $424.2 million (£297.6 million) at the international box office. The film won seven Oscars from 12 nominations in 1991, including Best Director for Costner.

**Highest box-office gross for a silent film** King Vidor's (USA) *The Big Parade* (USA, 1925), set during World War I and starring John Gilbert (USA), had a box-office gross of $22 million (then £4.6 million).

**Highest box-office gross for a horror movie** *The Exorcist* (USA, 1973), directed by William Friedkin (USA) with a budget of $12 million (then £4.89 million), has taken $292.7 million (£205.3 million) at the international box office to date.

**Highest box-office gross for a science fiction film (inflation adjusted)** In an inflation-adjusted list, *Star Wars* (USA, 1977) has an international box-office gross of $2.65 billion (£1.62 billion). The film originally took $513.7 million (£294.29 million) worldwide before its re-issue in 1997.

**Most Oscars won by a film** Two films have both won a record 11 Oscars (American Academy Awards). The first to achieve the record was *Ben-Hur* (USA, 1959), which won its Oscars from 12 nominations in 1960. *Titanic* (USA, 1997) won its Oscars from 14 nominations in 1998.

**Most film Oscar nominations without winning** *The Turning Point* (USA, 1977) starring Shirley MacLaine and Anne Bancroft (both USA) and *The Color Purple* (USA, 1986) starring Danny Glover and Whoopi Goldberg (both USA) were each nominated 11 times for an Academy Award, but neither film won an Oscar.

**Most Best Director Oscar wins** John Ford (USA) won an Oscar for Best Director on four occasions, for *The Informer* (USA, 1936), *The Grapes of Wrath* (USA, 1940), *How Green was My Valley* (USA, 1941), and *The Quiet Man* (USA, 1952).

**Most edited single sequence in a movie** The chariot-race scene in *Ben-Hur* (USA, 1925), starring Ramon Novarro (Mexico), for which editor Lloyd Nosler (USA) had to compress 200,000 ft. (60,960 m) of film into a sparse 750 ft. (228.6 m), was the most edited scene in cinema history, with a ratio of 267:1.

**Longest screen partnership for a comedy duo** Actors Stan Laurel (UK) and Oliver Hardy (USA) starred in 106 films together (including 50 shorts) between 1917 and 1950. They first appeared together in *Lucky Dog* (USA, 1917—released 1922) and starred together for the last time in *Atoll K* (France/Italy, 1950).

**Most prolific actor/singer/film star** Bing Crosby (b. Harry Lillis Crosby, USA) made 104 films for cinema and was producer to six during his singing and acting career, which began in 1930. For ten years Bing was continually among the top ten box-office stars, and for five consecutive years (1944–49) he remained at the No. 1 spot—a feat no other film star has bettered. He won the Oscar for Best Actor in 1944 for the film *Going My Way* (USA, 1943) and was nominated for Best Actor in *The Country Girl* (USA, 1954) and *Man on Fire* (USA, 1957).

**Most leading roles** John Wayne (b. Marion Michael Morrison, USA) acted in 153 movies from *The Drop Kick* (USA, 1927) to *The Shootist* (USA, 1976). In 142 of these he played the lead.

**Most film extras** It is believed that over 300,000 extras appeared in the funeral scene of *Gandhi* (UK, 1982), the epic film directed by Richard Attenborough (UK). Eleven camera crews shot 20,000 ft. (6,096 m) of film for that scene, more than the total footage of the 188-minute released film. The edited funeral sequence ran for only 125 seconds of screen time.

**MOST FILMS BY A DANCING PARTNERSHIP** Fred Astaire (USA) and Ginger Rogers (USA) appeared as a dancing partnership in ten films, starting with *Flying Down to Rio* (USA, 1933) in which they had a brief dance number called the Carioca, and ending with *The Berkleys of Broadway* (USA, 1949).

**Longest interval between an original film and a sequel** A record 46 years elapsed before Walt Disney Production's *Return to Oz* (USA, 1985) was made, which resumed the story six months after Dorothy's return to Kansas in MGM's *The Wizard of Oz* (USA, 1939).

**Film star with the most biographies** Charlie Chaplin (UK) has had his life and art expounded in 259 book-length works. He began his career on the music-hall stage, and while a member of a troupe touring the USA he was recruited by Mack Sennet to create his Little Tramp character for the big screen. Chaplin refused to use sound until 1940.

# WORLD CINEMA

**Most nominations for best foreign language film** France has been nominated for the Best Foreign Language Film Oscar 34 times between 1948 and 2002. The last nomination in this category was for *Le Fabuleux destin d'Amélie Poulain* (*Amélie* from Montmartre, France, 2001) in 2002. France has won the category 12 times.

**Longest film commercially shown in its entirety** Edgar Reitz's *Die Zweite Heimat* (*The Second Homeland,* Germany, 1992), lasted 25 hr. 32 min. and premiered in Munich, Germany, in September 1992.

**Longest film title** The official title of Lina Wertmüller's (Italy) film is *Un Fatto di sangue nel commune di Sculiana fra due uomini per causa di una vedova si sospetano moventi politici. Amore-Morte-Shimmy. Lugano belle. Tarantelle. Tarallucci é vino* (Italy, 1979). It has 179 characters, including punctuation. The English language title was simply *Revenge.*

**Highest box-office gross for a foreign language film** The martial arts film *Wo hu zang long* (*Crouching Tiger, Hidden Dragon,* Taiwan, 2000) was first released on June 30, 2000. Directed by Ang Lee (Taiwan) and starring Yun-Fat Chow (Hong Kong) and Michelle Yeoh (Malaysia, p. 303), it became the highest grossing foreign language film, taking $209,136,710 (£144,501,285) by April 2002 in the USA and UK.

**Highest box-office gross for a French film** Directed by Jean-Pierre Jeunet and starring Audrey Tautou (both France), *Le Fabuleux destin d'Amélie Poulain* (*Amélie from Montmartre,* France, 2001), first released in France on April 25, 2001, took the foreign box office by storm and amassed a total of $144,488,955 (£101,005,911).

**Highest box-office gross for an Italian film** *La Vita è Bella (Life is Beautiful,* Italy, 1977), released by Miramax and starring Roberto Benigni (Italy), had a worldwide gross of $229 million (£143 million). It also became the highest grossing foreign language film in North America, making $57.6 million (£36 million), and overtaking the previous record of $21.8 million (£13.62 million) set by *Il Postino* (*The Postman,* Italy, 1994).

**Highest box-office gross for an Australian film** Directed by Peter Fairman, *Crocodile Dundee* (Australia, 1986), starring Paul Hogan (Australia) and Linda Kozlowski (USA), grossed $328 million (£218 million).

**Highest box-office gross for a Bollywood film** *Hum Aapke Hain Koun . . . !* (*Who Am I To You?,* India, 1994), starring Madhuri Dixit and Salman Khan (both India), is the highest grossing Bollywood film of all time taking more than $63.8 million (£40.4 million) in its first year, and breaking the record set by the curry western, *Sholay* (*Embers,* India, 1975).

**LARGEST ANNUAL FILM OUTPUT** India produces more feature-length films than any other country. A record 948 films were produced in 1990, and in 1994 a total of 754 films were produced in a record 16 languages at its three major centers of production: Bombay (Mumbai), Calcutta, and Madras. Actress Aishwarya Rai (pictured) is one of India's biggest film stars.

**Highest box-office gross for a German film** *Das Boot* (*The Boat*, Germany, 1981), the story of a WW II U-boat crew, is the highest grossing German film in cinema history. The film took $84.915 million (£41.933 million) at the international box office.

**Oldest film director** Manoel de Oliveira (Portugal), who began directing films in 1931, made his most recent film, *O Principio da Incerteza* (*The Principle of Uncertainty,* Portugal, 2002), at the age of 94. The film was presented at the Cannes film festival, France, on May 18, 2002.

**Largest production crew for a feature film** The largest number of craftsmen and technicians employed on a dramatic feature was 532 for the WWI flying story *Gunbus* (*Sky Bandits,* UK, 1986), directed by Zoran Perisic (Yugoslavia) and starring Nicholas Lyndhurst (UK).

**Longest film shot on a single camera** Written and directed by Fabrizio Prada (Mexico), *A Day in Paradise* (Mexico, 2001) was shot in real time at 15 different locations on December 16, 2001 on a single camera for 82 minutes. The final running time was 88 minutes, and the film was shown without any cuts on July 5, 2002 at the El Ágora de Xalapa, Xalapa, Veracruz, Mexico.

**Fastest movie produced from script to screen** The shortest time ever taken to make a feature-length film from scripting to screening is 13

**MOST OSCAR NOMINATIONS FOR A FOREIGN LANGUAGE FILM** The martial arts film *Wo hu zang long* (*Crouching Tiger, Hidden Dragon,* Taiwan, 2000) was nominated for a record ten Oscars in 2001, including Best Picture, Best Director, Music (Song), Costume Design, Film Editing and Writing (Adapted Screenplay). It won Oscars for Best Foreign Language Film, Art Direction, Music (Score) and Cinematography.

days for *The Fastest Forward* (UK, 1990), produced by Russ Malkin and directed by John Gore (both UK). The cast, crew, technicians, and cinematographic suppliers accepted a charity challenge and the 75-minute thriller was given a gala premiére at the Dominion Theatre, London, UK, on May 27, 1990.

**Longest film series with the same star** Kiyoshi Atsumi (Japan) appeared in the lead role of all the Torajiro Kuruma (more commonly known as Tora-san) comedy movies produced by Shockiki studios, Japan, between August 1969 and December 1995.

**Longest screen partnership** The stars of India's Malayalam cinema, Prem Nazir and Sheela (both India), played opposite each other in a total of 130 movies until Sheela retired in 1975. Prem Nazir, who was the quintessential male lead, starred in over 700 films in total, while the actress Sheela starred in 370.

**Longest close-up on film** *Daera* (*The Division,* India, 1953), has a close-up of actress Meena Kuman (India), who plays the lead female character Sheetal, that lasts for 6 min. 30 sec. Written and directed by Kamaal Amrohi (India), the film was made in black and white, and has a running time of 139 minutes.

**Longest working career of a film actor** The German comedian and character actor Curt Bois (1901–91), who made his film debut at the age of seven in *Der Fidele Bauer* (*The Jolly Peasant,* Germany, 1908), had a film

**MOST OSCARS WON FOR BEST FOREIGN LANGUAGE FILM** Italy has won 13 Oscars for Best Foreign Language Film, the most recent being for *La Vita é Bella (Life is Beautiful,* 1997) in 1999, at the 71st Academy Awards. *Cinema Paradiso* (1989) won an Oscar in 1990.

career lasting 79 years, with his final role being as Homer in *Der Himmel über Berlin* (*Wings of Desire,* Germany, 1987). Bois left Germany in 1933 on the accession of the Nazis and made his way to the USA via Prague, Vienna, Paris, and London, arriving in Hollywood in 1938. He appeared in such films as *Caught* (USA, 1949) and *Casablanca* (USA, 1942), before returning to Germany in the early 1950s.

**Longest working career of a film actress**  Maxine Elliot Hicks (USA) made her debut in *The Borrowed Finery* (USA, 1914) for the Thomas Edison Company, leading to a career spanning 78 years. Her last film for the big screen was *Beethoven* (USA, 1992).

# HOLLYWOOD

**Busiest Hollywood star**  In terms of the most movies completed during a limited period of time, comedienne Joan Blondell (USA) starred in 32 feature films in 27 months between 1930 and 1933.

**Highest annual earnings for a film actor**  According to the 2002 *Forbes* Celebrity 100 list, the top-earning actor is currently Adam Sandler (USA) who earned an estimated $47 million (£31.3 million) in 2001.

**Highest annual earnings for a film producer**  Screenwriter, film director, producer and media entrepreneur George Lucas (USA) topped the 2002 *Forbes* Celebrity 100 list having earned an estimated $200 million (£133.5 million) in 2001.

**Highest salary per film for an actress**  For her roles in both *Erin Brockovich* (USA, 2000) and *The Mexican* (USA, 2001) Julia Roberts (USA) commanded a fee of $20,000,000 (then £12,500,000 and £13,750,430 respectively).

**Highest salary per film for an actor**  Arnold Schwarzenegger (USA, b. Austria) was paid a basic wage of $30 million (then £20.9 million) in 2001 for his role as "The Terminator" in *Terminator 3: Rise of the Machines* (USA, 2003).

**Most Golden Globe film awards**  The Golden Globe Awards have been presented annually since 1944 by the Hollywood Foreign Press Association. The most Golden Globes awarded to a single film is five, and five films share this record: *Doctor Zhivago* (USA, 1965), *Love Story* (USA, 1970); *The Godfather* (USA, 1972); *One Flew Over the Cuckoo's Nest* (USA, 1975); and *A Star is Born* (USA, 1976).

**Most Oscar nominations for an actor**  Since beginning his career in the film *The Cry Baby Killer* (USA, 1958), Jack Nicholson (USA) has been

**MOST GOLDEN GLOBE AWARDS WON BY AN ACTOR** The most Golden Globes won by an individual is six, achieved by Jack Nicholson (USA) between 1975 and 2003. His most recent win was for *About Schmidt* (USA, 2002).

nominated for 12 Oscars, four as Best Supporting Actor and the rest as Best Actor. His first nomination was in 1970 for Best Supporting Actor in *Easy Rider* (USA, 1969).

**Most Golden Globe awards won by an actress** Shirley MacLaine (USA) won six Golden Globe awards between 1955 and 2003, as well as a Special Award in 1959 for most versatile actress, and a Cecil B. DeMille Award in 1998 for outstanding contribution in the entertainment world.

**Most Oscars won in a year by an individual** Walt Disney (USA) won the most Oscars at a single presentation with four in 1953 for Best Cartoon: *Toot, Whistle, Plunk and Boom;* Best Documentary Short: *The Alaskan Eskimo;* Best Documentary Feature: *The Living Desert;* and Best Two-Reel Short: *Bear Country.*

**Most Oscar nominations for a living person** Between 1968 and 2003 the composer John Williams (USA) received 42 Oscar nominations. His first nomination was for Best Music, Scoring of Music, Adaptation or Treatment for *Valley of the Dolls* (USA, 1967), and his most recent for Best Original Score for *Catch Me If You Can* (USA, 2002).

**Earliest posthumous Oscar awarded** The first posthumous Oscar was awarded at the 1939 Academy Awards on February 29, 1940 to Sidney Howard (USA, d. August 23, 1939) for his screenplay of *Gone With The Wind* (USA, 1939).

**Most Oscars won for individual creative achievement** MGM filmmaker Cedric Gibbons (USA) won 11 Oscars for Art Direction from a total of 40 nominations from 1930 to 1957. The most won by a woman is eight, by costume designer Edith Head (USA).

**Most Oscar nominations for an actress** Between 1979 and 2003 Meryl Streep (USA) was nominated for 13 Oscars, three as Best Actress in a Supporting Role and the rest for Best Actress. She won the Best Actress in a Supporting Role Oscar in 1980 for *Kramer vs. Kramer* (USA, 1979) and Best Actress in 1983 for *Sophie's Choice* (USA, 1982).

**Only tie for Best Actress Oscar** The only tie for Best Actress was between Barbra Streisand (USA), honored for *Funny Girl* (USA, 1968), and

**MOST GENERATIONS OF PRINTS AT MANN'S CHINESE THEATRE** Actor Kirk Douglas (USA) left his mark on Hollywood Boulevard, Los Angeles, USA, in 1962, when his footprints were set in stone. His actor/producer son Michael (USA, shown) left his handprints in September 1997. Their prints sit side by side—the first time one family has had two generations of prints at the famous theater.

Katharine Hepburn (USA), for *The Lion in Winter* (UK, 1968), at the 1969 Academy Awards.

**Most Oscars won for Best Actress** With four Best Actress Oscars, Katharine Hepburn (USA) holds the record. She won for *Morning Glory* (USA, 1933), *Guess Who's Coming to Dinner* (USA, 1967), *The Lion in Winter* (UK, 1968), and *On Golden Pond* (USA, 1981).

**Most Oscar nominations for an actor without winning** Both Richard Burton (UK) and Peter O'Toole (Rep. of Ireland) have been nominated seven times for the Best Actor award, but neither has won. Richard Burton's span lasted 25 years: the first nomination in 1953 for *My Cousin Rachel* (USA, 1952) and the last for *Equus* (UK, 1977) in 1978. Peter O'Toole's no-win span has so far lasted 20 years, from a nomination for *Lawrence of Arabia* (UK, 1962) in 1973 to one for *My Favorite Year* (USA, 1982) in 1983. In 2003 he was presented with an Honorary Award.

**Most Oscars for Best Supporting Actor** Walter Brennan (USA) won three Oscars for Best Actor in a Supporting Role, for *Come and Get It* (USA, 1936), *Kentucky* (USA, 1938), and *The Westerner* (USA, 1940). He also gained a fourth nomination in the same category for *Sergeant York* (USA, 1941).

**Most Oscars won for Best Supporting Actress** The record is shared by two actresses: Shelley Winters (USA), who won Oscars for her roles in *The Diary of Anne Frank* (USA, 1959) and *A Patch of Blue* (USA, 1965); and Dianne Weist (USA), who won for *Hannah and Her Sisters* (USA, 1986) and *Bullets Over Broadway* (USA, 1994).

**Youngest Oscar winner** The youngest Oscar winner is Tatum O'Neal (USA) who was 10 years 148 days on April 2, 1974 when she received the Best Supporting Actress award for *Paper Moon* (USA, 1973).

In 1934 Shirley Temple (USA) was awarded an honorary Oscar for her achievements at the age of 6 years 310 days.

**Youngest Best Actor Oscar winner** Richard Dreyfuss (b. October 29, 1947, USA) won the Best Actor Oscar on April 13, 1978, at the age of 29 years 166 days, for his performance as Elliot Garfield in *The Goodbye Girl* (USA, 1977).

**Youngest Best Actress Oscar winner** Marlee Matlin (b. August 24, 1965, USA) won the Best Actress award on March 31, 1987, at the age of 21 years 219 days, for her role as Sarah Norman in *Children of a Lesser God* (USA, 1986).

**Most Tony and Oscar award wins for the same role** A total of eight performers have won the Tony and the Oscar for the same role: José Ferrer (USA) in the title role of *Cyrano de Bergerac* (Tony in 1947 and the Oscar in 1950); Shirley Booth (USA) in *Come Back, Little Sheba*

**HIGHEST ANNUAL EARNINGS FOR A FILM ACTRESS** The world's top-earning actress is currently Cameron Diaz (USA) who earned an estimated $40 million (£26.7 million) in 2001, according to the 2002 *Forbes* Celebrity 100 list.

(1950/1953); Yul Brynner (Russia) in *The King and I* (1952/1956); Rex Harrison (UK) in *My Fair Lady* (1957/1964); Anne Bancroft (USA) in *The Miracle Worker* (1960/1962); Paul Schofield (UK) in *A Man for All Seasons* (1962/1966); and Joel Grey (USA) in *Cabaret* (1967/1973). The American Theatre Wing's Tony Awards are given in recognition of achievement in a theater performance. The Tony was named after Broadway actress and director Antoinette Perry (USA, d. 1946).

# AT THE MOVIES

**Largest current movie attendance** In India, 1999 figures show movie admissions reaching 3.1 billion, over twice as much as the USA, which in 2001 had 1.48 billion admissions. In third place is France, with 185.4 million admissions in 2001. The largest movie audience ever in one given year was 4.49 billion in the USA in 1929.

**Cinema complex with most screens** The largest cinema multiplexes have 30 screens and are known within the industry as "megaplexes." There are currently around a dozen such complexes in the world, operated by several cinema companies, mostly in North America and Western Europe. The first megaplex theater (defined as 16 screens or more)—an AMC Grand—opened in May 1995 in Dallas, Texas, USA.

**Largest cinema by seating capacity** The Roxy, on 7th Avenue and 50th Street, New York City, USA, was built at a cost of $12

**HIGHEST OPENING WEEKEND BOX-OFFICE GROSS FOR A COMEDY** *Austin Powers in Goldmember* (USA, 2002), starring Mike Myers (Canada, shown here in the poster as Austin Powers), opened at 3,613 cinemas in the USA on July 26, 2002, taking $71.5 million (£45.7 million) over its first three days. In comparison, the original "Austin" debuted with $9.5 million (£5.7 million) in May 1997 and the first sequel opened at $54.92 million (£33.14 million) in June 1999.

million (then £2.4 million) and had an original seating capacity of 6,214 when it opened on March 11, 1927. It employed 16 projectionists, an orchestra of 110 musicians led by four conductors, and three organists who played simultaneously on Kimball organ consoles rising from the orchestra pit. It closed on March 29, 1960 and was demolished later that year.

The largest cinema in the world today by seating capacity is the Radio City Music Hall, New York City, USA, which opened on December 27, 1932 with 5,945 (now 5,910) seats.

**Largest cinema complex by seats**  Kinepolis Madrid, which opened in Madrid, Spain, on September 17, 1998, is the world's largest cinema complex, with a seating capacity of 9,200 in its 25 screens, which each seat between 211 and 996 people.

**Oldest continuously running cinema**  The Duke of York's Cinema in Brighton, East Sussex, UK, has been running continuously as a cinema since it first opened as The Duke of York Premier Picture House on September 22, 1910. When new, it seated an audience of 800, but it only seats 330 today.

**LARGEST DRIVE-IN THEATER**  The largest drive-in theater measured by capacity was the All-Weather Drive-In of Copiague, New York, USA. It had space for 2,500 cars plus an indoor 1,200-seat viewing area on its 28-acre (11.33-ha) site. The largest drive-in theaters by car capacity were the Troy Drive-in, Detroit, Michigan, USA, and the Panther Drive-in, Lufkin, Texas, USA, which were each able to hold 3,000 cars.

**Oldest custom-built cinema in operation** The oldest custom-built cinema still in operation is the Electric on Portobello Road in London, UK. It first opened on February 24, 1911 as a 600-seater. It was closed in the 1980s but re-opened on February 22, 2001 with a seating capacity of 240.

**Oldest drive-in theater** The oldest drive-in theater still in operation is Shankweiler's Drive-in Theater, Orefield, Pennsylvania, USA, which has opened for every season (April to September) since April 15, 1934. It was only the second drive-in theater to open in the USA and then held 275 cars. It now has a 300-car capacity.

**First drive-in theater** The first patent for the Drive-in Theater (US Patent no. 1909537) was issued on May 16, 1933 to Richard Hollingshead (USA). He opened the first drive-in on June 6, 1933 on a 400-car site in Camden, New Jersey, USA. The film shown was *Wife Beware* (USA, 1933).

**Earliest public screening of sound on film** The earliest showing of a "talkie" was *The Arsonist,* (Germany/USA, 1922), which was screened at the Alhambra cinema, Berlin, Germany, on September 17, 1922.

**Longest cinematic release** *Titanic* (USA, 1997) stayed in the US movie charts from December 19, 1997 to September 25, 1998, a duration of 281 days.

**Widest film release** Heyday Films and Warner Bros' *Harry Potter and the Chamber of Secrets* (USA/Germany 2002) had the widest release of any film in history when it opened on November 17, 2002 in the USA on 8,500 screens (3,682 cinemas).

**Longest first run of a film in one cinema** *Romance in Lushan* (China, 1980) first opened at the Jiangxi Movie Circulation & Screening Company, Lushan, China, on July 12, 1980, and has been shown four times a day ever since. As of December 8, 2001, the film had been seen by 1,336,638 movie-goers.

**Longest commercially made film in general release** *The Burning of the Red Lotus Temple* (China, 1928–31), adapted by the Star Film Co. from the newspaper serial *Strange Tales of the Adventurer in the Wild Country* by Shang K'ai-jan, was released in 18 feature-length parts over a period of three years. Although never shown publicly in its 27-hour entirety, some theaters put on all-day performances of six parts in sequence.

**Highest box-office gross for an opening day** *Spider-Man* (USA, 2002) took a record $43.6 million (£29.8 million) in box-office receipts on its opening day in the USA on May 3, 2002 and a record-breaking $114.8 million (£78 million) for its opening weekend from a total of 3,615 screens.

**Most valuable film poster** A one-sheet poster for the Universal film *The Mummy* (USA, 1932), starring Boris Karloff (UK), sold for $453,500

**FASTEST BOX-OFFICE GROSS OF $100 MILLION** *Spider-Man* (USA, 2002) opened on May 3, 2002 at 3,615 theaters. It passed the $100 million (£62,244 million) mark faster than any other movie, in just three days.

(then £282,431) at Sotheby's, New York, USA, on March 1, 1997. The sale of this poster surpassed the previous high of $198,000 for a *Frankenstein* (USA, 1931) one-sheet in 1993.

**First in-flight movie** The first in-flight movie was First National's *The Lost World* (USA, 1925), shown during an Imperial Airways flight in a converted Handley-Page bomber, from London, UK, to Paris, France, in April 1925.

# STUNTS & SPECIAL EFFECTS

**Most prolific movie stuntman** Vic Armstrong (UK) has doubled for every actor playing James Bond, and in a career spanning three decades has performed stunts in more than 200 films, including *Superman* (USA, 1978) and *Raiders of the Lost Ark* (USA, 1981). He has also coordinated stunts for movies such as *Tomorrow Never Dies* (UK/USA, 1997). Armstrong was awarded the Oscar for Technical Achievement in 2001 for "the refinement and application to the film industry of the Fan Descender for accurately and safely arresting the descent of stunt persons in high freefalls."

**Most stunts by a living actor** Jackie Chan, the Hong Kong actor, director, writer, producer, and stunt co-ordinator, has appeared in more than 90 films, including *The Big Brawl* (USA, 1980) and *Highbinders* (HK/USA, 2002). He made his debut in *Big and Little Wong Tin Bar* (HK, 1962) at the age of eight. No insurance company will underwrite Chan's productions, in which he performs all his own stunts.

**Highest free fall on film** The greatest height from which a stuntman has leaped in a free fall was 1,100 ft. (335 m), a stunt performed for *Highpoint* (Canada, 1979) by Dar Robinson (USA) from a ledge at the summit of the CN Tower, Toronto, Canada. His parachute opened just 300 ft. (91 m) from the ground after six seconds of free falling.

**Highest jump without a parachute on film** The highest jump without a parachute by a movie stuntman was 232 ft. (70.71 m) by A.J. Bakunas (USA) doubling for Burt Reynolds in *Hooper* (USA, 1978). He fell onto an air mattress. A specialist in such dangerous high falls, Bakunas tragically died on September 9, 1980 doing a stunt for the film *Steel* (USA, 1980).

**Highest ski base jump on film** For the pre-title sequence of *The Spy Who Loved Me* (UK, 1977), Rick Sylvester (USA) skied off the edge of a 2,000-ft. (610-m) cliff on Asgard Peak, Baffin Island, Canada, before opening his Union Jack round canopy.

**Highest bungee jump from a structure in a movie** James Bond's bungee jump off a dam during the opening sequence of *GoldenEye* (UK/USA, 1995), performed by Wayne Michaels (UK), was a drop of over 722 ft. (220 m). The sequence, orchestrated by Michaels, Simon Crane, and the Oxford Stunt Factory (all UK), took place at the Verzasca hydroelectric dam in Switzerland. Taking two weeks to prepare, Michaels jumped from a suspended platform to avoid banging into the steel-peg-studded face of the dam.

**Most expensive aerial stunt** Simon Crane (UK) performed one of the most dangerous ever aerial stunts when he moved between two jets at an al-

**LARGEST "BREAKAWAY GLASS" STRUCTURE MADE FOR A FILM** Eight panels of "breakaway glass," each measuring 8 ft. 3.5 in. × 5 ft. 4.5 in. × 1.125 in. (2.525 × 1.635 × 0.03 m), were built for the stunt sequence in *Die Another Day* (UK/USA, 2002) in which James Bond drives his Aston Martin car through the closed doors of an ice palace. Created at Pinewood Studios (UK), each panel weighed 352.7 lb. (160 kg) and was made of SMASH! urethane liquid plastic.

titude of 15,000 ft. (4,572 m) for *Cliffhanger* (USA, 1993). The stunt, performed only once because it was so risky, cost a record $1 million (£568,000). Sylvester Stallone (USA), the film's star, is said to have offered to reduce his fee by the same amount to ensure that the stunt was made.

**Largest co-ordinator of filmed aerial stunts** Flying Pictures of Surrey, UK, has planned and co-ordinated aerial stunts for more than 200 feature films, including *Cliffhanger* (USA, 1993) and *GoldenEye* (UK/USA, 1995), as well as co-ordinating stunts for hundreds of television shows and commercials.

**Longest leap in a car** The longest leap in a car propelled by its own engine was performed by stunt driver Gary Davis (USA) in *Smokey and the Bandit II* (USA, 1980). Davis raced a stripped-down Plymouth at 80 mph (128 km/h) up a ramp placed against the back of a double-tiered car carrier and described a trajectory of 163 ft. (49.6 m) before landing safely on the desert floor.

**Longest speedboat jump in a movie** A stunt sequence by Jerry Comeaux (USA) in *Live and Let Die* (UK, 1973), in which James Bond is chased through a Louisiana bayou in a Glastron GT-150 speedboat and leaps over a road, set a then world-record distance of 120 ft. (36.5 m).

**Largest car pile-up on film** The climax of the film *Blues Brothers 2000* (USA, 1998) is marked by a car chase resulting in a pile-up that involves 50 cars. The crash sequence lasts just over two minutes but took four months to film.

**Largest film stunt explosion** An explosion staged for the movie *Blown Away* (USA, 1994) on September 24, 1993 incorporated a scuttled ship be-

**MOST COMPUTER-GENERATED EFFECTS IN A MOVIE** The film *Pleasantville* (USA, 1998) had 1,700 digital visual-effect shots, compared with the average Hollywood film, which has 50.

**MOST DEVELOPED DIGITAL CHARACTER ON FILM** The character Gollum in *The Lord of the Rings: The Two Towers* (NZ/USA, 2002) was created by WETA Digital (NZ) to have 250 facial expressions and 300 moving muscles. His body movements were based on those of the actor Andy Serkis (UK), who, to facilitate the creation of the computer graphics, was filmed wearing both a body stocking and a motion-capture suit for every scene in which Gollum appears.

side an old wharf in East Boston, USA, filled with 720 gal. (2,727 liters) of fuel and 32 bombs each weighing 16 oz. (453 g). The explosion lasted nine seconds.

**Most expensive explosion sequence in a movie** An explosion sequence involving the destruction of six ships during the bombing scene at the end of the film *Pearl Harbor* (USA, 2001) cost $5.5 million (then £3,850,000). The blast used 700 sticks of dynamite, 2,000 ft. (610 m) of primer cord and 4,800 gal. (18,185 liters) of gasoline.

**Highest special-effects budget** A total of $6.5 million (then £2,246,023) was budgeted for the special effects in *2001: A Space Odyssey* (UK/USA, 1968), which represented over 60% of the total production cost of $10.5 million (then £3,628,191). At today's exchange rates, this figure is more like $33.1 million (£23 million).

**Largest film stunt budget** More than $3 million (then £1.87 million) of the $200-million (then £125-million) budget for *Titanic* (USA, 1997) went toward stunts.

**Largest camera crane used on a film** To be able to cover all angles of the 775-ft.-long (236.22-m) set of the film *Titanic* (USA, 1997), an Akela crane with a normal reach of 80 ft. (24.38 m) was adapted to have an expanded reach of almost 200 ft. (61 m). A gyro-stabilized camera was then mounted on the crane basket, and the crane was moved along the side of the set on tracks.

**Most digital artists on a film** Sony Pictures Imageworks (USA) had a team of 200 visual-effect artists working on *Spider-Man* (USA, 2002). During the 121 minutes of film, 450 digital shots were produced.

**Most Oscars won for visual effects** Dennis Muren (USA) won a total of six Oscars for Visual Effects between 1983 and 1994. He also won a Technical Achievement Award in 1982 and two Special Achievement Awards: one in 1981 for *Star Wars: Episode V—The Empire Strikes Back* (USA, 1980) and another in 1984 for *Star Wars: Episode VI—Return of the Jedi* (USA, 1983).

# THE PRINTED WORD

**All-time best selling book** Excluding non-copyright works such as the Bible and the Koran, the world's all-time best selling book is *Guinness World Records* (formerly *The Guinness Book of Records.*) Since it was first published in October 1955, global sales in some 37 languages have exceeded 94,767,083 copies (to June 30, 2002).

**Best selling diary** *The Diary of Anne Frank* (1947) has sold more than 25 million copies worldwide and has been translated into 67 languages. It is the true autobiographical account of events that took place while the Frank family hid in an attic in Amsterdam, The Netherlands, to escape Nazi persecution during World War II.

**Best selling work of non-fiction** Although it is impossible to obtain exact figures, there is little doubt that the Bible is the world's best selling and most

**MOST SYNDICATED COMIC STRIP** "Garfield," created by Jim Davis (USA) and circulated by Universal Press Syndicate, is the world's most syndicated comic strip, appearing in 2,570 journals throughout the world.

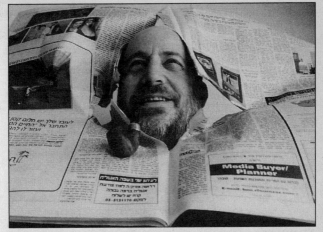

**MOST LETTERS TO EDITORS PUBLISHED IN ONE YEAR** Ehud Buch (Israel) had 131 of his letters published by four prominent Israeli national newspapers—namely *Ma'ariv, Yediot Achronot, Ha'aretz,* and *Globes*—during the year 2001.

widely distributed book. A survey by the Bible Society concluded that around 2.5 billion copies were printed between 1815 and 1975, but more recent estimates put the number at more than 5 billion.

**Best selling children's book series in a single year** In 1999 the *Harry Potter* series by JK Rowling (UK) sold more than 18.5 million copies in the USA and over 4.5 million copies in the UK and Commonwealth. In the same year, Rowling became the first novelist to have three titles occupying the top four slots (both hardback and paperback) of the *New York Times* bestseller list for 16 weeks *(Harry Potter and the Sorceror's Stone, Harry Potter and the Chamber of Secrets* and *Harry Potter and the Prisoner of Azkaban).* The first title hit the bestseller list on September 27, 1999 and was still there in April 2000. The second and third books in the series both debuted at number one on the list and by April 2000 were still in the top five.

**Best selling author** The world's best selling fiction writer is the late Agatha Christie (UK), whose 78 crime novels have sold an estimated two billion copies in 44 languages. She also wrote 19 plays and penned six romantic novels under the pseudonym Mary Westmacott. Annual royalty earnings from her works are estimated to be in the millions.

**Fastest selling Booker Prize-winning novel** In 1993, on the day after the Booker Prize was announced, Roddy Doyle's (Republic of Ireland) winning novel *Paddy Clarke Ha Ha Ha* sold 27,000 copies in hardback within half an hour of bookstores opening.

**Most Booker Prize nominations** Iris Murdoch (UK) was nominated for the Booker Prize six times over 18 years for *The Nice and the Good* (1969), *Bruno's Dream* (1970), *The Black Prince* (1973), *The Good Apprentice* (1985) and *The Book and the Brotherhood* (1987). She won in 1978 with *The Sea, the Sea.* Both J.M. Coetzee (South Africa) and Peter Carey (Australia) have won a record two Booker Prizes.

**Largest advance for a non-fiction book** Former US President Bill Clinton (USA) sold the worldwide publishing rights to his memoirs to Alfred A. Knopf Inc. (USA) for an advance of more than $10 million (£7.1 million)—the largest ever advance for a non-fiction book.

**Longest novel** *A la Recherche du Temps Perdu (Remembrance of Things Past)* by Marcel Proust (France) contains an estimated 9,609,000 characters (every letter and space counts as one character). Proust produced the first volume of his 13-volume masterpiece in 1912 (it was first published in 1913). His second volume won international awards as soon as it was published. This long novel explores the power of the unconscious and the nature of writing itself.

**Largest encyclopedia** The largest encyclopedia in current use is *The Arabic Legislations Encyclopaedia* compiled by Mohamed Abu Baker Ben Younis (Libya). Its 164,000 pages are contained in 200 volumes weighing 925 lb. (420 kg). The general index is contained in six additional volumes, and there are also additional annexes. It claims to contain every piece of legislation from all Arab countries.

**Largest book** The *Super Book* measures 9 ft. × 10 ft. 0.84 in. (2.74 × 3.07 m) and weighs 557 lb. (252.6 kg). Consisting of 300 pages, it was published in Denver, Colorado, USA, in 1976.

**Largest dictionary** *Deutsches Wörterbuch* (German Dictionary), begun in 1854 by German brothers Jacob and Wilhelm Grimm (best known for their collection of fairy tales), was completed in 1971 and consists of 34,519 pages in 33 volumes. It is available as a special order at Amazon.com for $1,695 (£1,200).

**Earliest cartoon strip** The first cartoon strip ever printed was "The Yellow Kid," which first appeared in the *New York Journal* on October 18, 1896. He was a New York character who excelled at making fun of upper-class customs and who wore a characteristic yellow gown. Although it was the first comic strip to be published, single satirical cartoons had been published in journals for many years.

**Longest running comic book** *The Dandy* comic has been published by DC Thomson & Co. (UK) continuously since its first edition on December

**LARGEST POP-UP BOOK** The largest pop-up book is a revised edition of *Aesop's Fables* measuring 48 x 30 in. (122 x 76 cm) and weighing 28.5 lb. (13 kg). The book was designed by Roger Culbertson (USA) using the original illustrations by Peter de Sève (USA). Published in 1993, the original book was 4 x 2.5 in. (10 x 6 cm). It is now out of print.

4, 1937. The weekly comic's best known character is Desperate Dan, an unshaven cowboy whose favorite food is cow pie. The only time publication varied from its weekly schedule was during World War II, when it was published bi-weekly.

**Magazine with the largest circulation** *Parade,* the syndicated color magazine, is distributed with 330 newspapers across the USA every Sunday and currently has a circulation of around 35.9 million. It has a readership of 77.6 million and in 2001 had advertising revenues of $570 million (£400 million). *Parade*'s first issue was published on May 31, 1941 with an initial print run of 125,000 copies.

**Largest weekly magazine sales** In 1974 the US *TV Guide* became the first weekly periodical to sell a billion copies in a year. It has the highest circulation of any weekly magazine with 11.8 million copies per week and an estimated reach of 35 million readers.

**Most translated document** A six-page document entitled *Universal Declaration of Human Rights,* produced by the United Nations (UN) in 1948, has been translated into 321 languages and dialects from Abkhaz to Zulu. The revelations after the horrors of World War II prompted the newly formed UN to produce a document in recognition "of the inherent dignity and of the equal and inalienable rights of the human family" and to guarantee peace, justice, dignity, respect, tolerance, equality, and freedom to all individuals.

# TV SHOWS & PEOPLE

**Longest time in same TV series role** The record for the longest time playing the same role in a television series is held by William Roache (UK). He has been playing the character Ken Barlow in ITV's *Coronation Street* continuously since the first episode of the British soap on December 9, 1960. The character was first seen as a student and since then has had three wives and numerous girlfriends, been a newspaper editor and a teacher, and survived a suicide attempt.

**Most enduring TV host** The monthly *Sky at Night* (BBC, UK) has been presented by Patrick Moore (UK) without a break or a miss since April 24, 1957. By December 2002 a total of 600 shows had been broadcast. This makes the *Sky At Night* the world's longest running TV program with the same host.

**Most TV variety shows hosted by the same host** As of April 5, 2002 the record for the highest number of live variety TV shows hosted by the same person is 5,000. Fuji Television Network Inc.'s (Japan) *Waratte Iitomo!* has been hosted by Kazuyoshi Morita, aka Tamori (Japan), since its first episode on October 4, 1982.

**Longest career as a cartoon voice-over artist** In its first few weeks, the original cinema series *Popeye* was voiced by William Costello (USA), but in 1934, for the film *Let You and Him Fight* (USA), Jack Mercer (USA) took over the role and continued in it for the next 45 years and 294 productions—also recording the voice-overs for the TV cartoons.

**Most enduring commercial stars** The PG Tips tea advertising campaign starring chimpanzees began in December 1956, the second year of commercial television in the UK. Since the first installment (voiced by Peter Sellers, UK) was televised, the campaign ran to more than 100 ads, with the final one made in 1994. The chimpanzees, who are said to have earned more than $1,530 (£1,000) each per commercial, have a retirement fund set up by the company. PG Tips teabags came on the market in 1930.

**Most prolific TV scriptwriter** The most prolific television writer in the world was Ted (later Lord) Willis (UK), whose total output since 1942 is estimated to be 20 million words. From 1949 until his death in 1992 he wrote 41 TV series, including the first seven years and 2.25 million words of *Dixon of Dock Green,* which ran on BBC Television (UK) from 1955 to 1976. He also wrote 37 stage plays and 39 feature films.

**HIGHEST PAID TV GUEST STAR** The world record for the highest amount paid to an actor to guest star on a TV show is $765,900 (£500,000), paid to Matthew Perry (USA) for appearing in an episode of *Ally McBeal* (FOX, USA). In the 2-hour show, broadcast on April 15, 2002, Perry played the character of Todd Merrick. The record is based on money earned per minute.

**Most celebrities featured in a cartoon TV series** Since first appearing in 1987 as a series of 30-second spots produced by Matt Groening (USA) for the FOX network's *The Tracey Ullman Show* (USA), *The Simpsons* cartoon series has featured 340 guests as of episode 300, "Barting Over." Celebrities have included Barry White, Elizabeth Taylor, Britney Spears, and U2.

**Highest annual earnings for a TV news broadcaster** The world's highest paid TV news broadcaster is Katie Couric (USA), who earns $13 million (£8 million) per year as the host of NBC's *Today* (USA) news program. She signed a 4.5-year contract in December 2001 that is reported to be worth $65 million (£40 million). Katie overtook fellow newscaster Barbara Walters (USA) on the *Forbes* list of 2002.

**Highest earnings by a child TV actor** The child TV actors with the highest earnings are the twins Mary-Kate and Ashley Olsen (USA). Their TV career began when they were just nine months old when they appeared in *Full House* (ABC, USA). By the age of nine they could command a total of $79,000 (£56,000) per episode. Now 17, they are currently staring in ABC Family Channel's *So Little Time*.

**Highest paid TV actor per episode** Kelsey Grammer (USA) was paid a salary of $1.6 million (£1.1 million) per show for playing psychoanalyst Frasier Crane in the 2002/03 series of *Frasier* (NBC, USA). Grammer is also executive producer on the show and on occasion has directed episodes.

**MOST PRIME-TIME EMMY AWARD NOMINATIONS IN A SEASON** The world record for the most Prime-time Emmy Award nominations in a season is 23, for HBO's *Six Feet Under* (USA) in 2002. *Six Feet Under* is a dark comedy-drama series about brothers running a funeral home.

**LONGEST WORKING CAREER OF A TV NATURALIST** The longest
working career as a writer and host of TV nature programs belongs to
Sir David Attenborough (UK), whose first series, *Zoo Quest* (BBC), was
broadcast in 1954. He most recently presented the BBC's *The Life of
Mammals* in 2003.

**Highest-paid TV drama actor per episode** The world's highest-paid
actor in a TV drama series is Noah Wyle (USA), who will earn approximately $400,000 (£258,530) per episode of *ER* (NBC, USA) for the
2003/04 series. Wyle plays the character of the head doctor, Dr. John Carter.

**Highest earnings for an actress for a current TV series** Jennifer Aniston, Lisa Kudrow, and Courteney Cox Arquette (all USA), who have played the female leads in NBC's *Friends* (USA) since 1994, were earning $1 million (£703,330) each per episode of the 2002/03 series. At the time of going to press the series was still running. There are typically 24 episodes in a series, meaning that each of the actresses will earn $24 million (£16.88 million) overall.

**Most Emmy awards won by a TV series in a season** NBC's (USA) drama series *The West Wing*, which is set behind the scenes at the White House, won a record nine awards for a single season at the 52nd Annual Prime-time Emmy Awards held on September 9 and 10, 2000.

**Most awards won by a TV commercial** The international commercial that has won the most awards is the 1995 Levi "Drugstore" 501 jeans television advertisement, which won a total of 33 awards. It was directed by Michel Gondry (France) who won a Lion D'Or for this at Cannes in 1994.

**First virtual TV host** The world's first virtual TV presenter is Maddy, who on March 27, 2002 co-hosted *Tomorrow's World* (BBC, UK) for the first time and in real-time alongside the human hosts. Maddy was created by Digital Animations Group, Glasgow, UK.

**Most TV quiz appearances by a contestant** Since March 1986 Marc Vanacker, of Kortrijk-Heule, Belgium, has appeared on an impressive 29 television quiz shows, broadcast in Belgium, Germany, The Netherlands, and the UK. As a result of appearing on these shows, which included *Going for Gold* (Grundy Television), *Risiko* (ZDF), and *Einstein* (NCRV), he won BFr 1,520,326, ($34,577 or £23,721), trips to the USA, Paris, and Vienna, a car, and two encyclopedias.

**Most TV links hijacked by a campaigner** As of March 28, 2002 the record for the most television links hijacked is 16,335 and belongs to Gabriele Paolini (Italy). He regularly sabotages presenter links on national TV in Italy, encouraging the use of condoms as part of his personal battle against the spread of the disease AIDS.

# TV ENTERTAINMENT

**Longest running children's magazine program** *Blue Peter*, the BBC's (UK) magazine program for children, was first transmitted from London's Lime Grove Studios on October 16, 1958 and is still broadcast today. Originally hosted by Christopher Trace and Leila Williams (both UK), it has so far seen 29 hosts, the longest serving being John Noakes (1965–78). As of March 28, 2003, 3,682 shows have been broadcast.

**LARGEST MUSIC TV NETWORK** MTV is beamed into 340 million households in 140 countries around the globe, which means it can be seen by one in three of the world's total TV audience. MTV began broadcasting in the USA in 1981. The most watched and highest rated show in the history of MTV is *The Osbournes*, a "reality TV" show that follows the bizarre real life of rock star Ozzy Osbourne (UK) and his family.

**Longest running reality TV show** The world's longest running reality TV show is *The Real World*, which first aired on MTV (USA) in May 1992.

The series follows the lives of seven strangers living together for six months. The first series was set in Chicago, USA. The show is now in its 12th season and set in Las Vegas. This "live soap-opera" style of television, in which cameras have no limits, led to many other shows, including *Survivor*, *Big Brother*, and *The Osbournes*.

**Longest running TV drama** Procter & Gamble Productions' *Guiding Light* (USA), which was first aired on CBS on June 30, 1952, and is currently aired each weekday, is the longest running TV drama. Originally a 15-minute radio serial on WLW Radio in Cincinnati, USA, it was first broadcast on January 25, 1937. The show celebrated its 50th anniversary in June 2002.

**Longest running prime-time animated series** *The Simpsons,* created by cartoonist Matt Groening (USA), is the longest running prime-time animated television show, with 300 episodes having been aired on the FOX network (USA) as of February 16, 2003. *The Simpsons* originally featured as a series of 30-second spots for FOX's *The Tracey Ullman Show* in 1987.

**LONGEST RUNNING TV CHAT SHOW** NBC's *The Tonight Show* (USA) was first aired on September 27, 1954. In 1992 the show was renamed *The Tonight Show With Jay Leno,* and has been hosted continually since then by Jay Leno (USA), pictured with guest Steve Irwin (Australia). Although the show's name and hosts have changed over the years, the essential format of late-night celebrity interviews, with the host behind a desk has remained the same.

After 50 cartoons were aired on the show, Groening was offered his own series, which premiered as a half-hour Christmas special on December 17, 1989 and began as a regular series on January 14, 1990. The show has won 17 Emmy awards and is watched in over 70 countries worldwide. It is also the longest running prime-time series still releasing new episodes.

**Most watched TV network** The state-owned station China Central Television (CCTV) is transmitted to 90% of all Chinese viewers in China. It is estimated that more than 1.1 billion people have access to television in China. The total broadcasting time of its 12 channels each day is 240 hours, in Mandarin, Fujian dialect, and English. The single most watched show is the daily *Xin Wen Lian Bo* news program, which attracts 315 million viewers.

**Largest TV audience for a wedding** On July 29, 1981 the marriage of HRH Prince Charles to Lady Diana Spencer was seen by an estimated 750 million people in 74 countries. At the time the largest outside broadcast in British history, it had an audience in the UK of 39 million.

**Largest TV audience for a series** At its peak of popularity, *Baywatch* (USA) was the most widely viewed TV series in the world ever, with an estimated weekly audience of more than 1.1 billion in 142 countries in 1996. Shown in every continent bar Antarctica, the show has since been seen in 148 countries and translated into 44 languages.

**Largest TV audience for a live broadcast** The broadcast of the funeral of Diana, Princess of Wales (1961–97) on September 6, 1997 had the largest worldwide audience for a live broadcast with 2.5 billion viewers. The event was simultaneously shown by six television stations in the UK as well as by many other stations around the world.

**Largest TV audience for a comedy program** The final episode of the US TV comedy series *Seinfeld*, starring Jerry Seinfeld (USA), was screened on May 14, 1998 and attracted 108 million viewers. Described commonly as being about nothing in particular, the show offered weekly vignettes from the lives of four New Yorkers.

**Largest audience for a TV documentary** The world's highest audience for a TV documentary is 39 million, for CBS's (USA) program *9/11* about the September 11, 2001 terrorist attacks in America, which was shown in the USA on March 10, 2002.

**Most successful TV soap** The American TV series *Dallas* began quietly in 1978 with just five episodes. By 1980, it was watched by an estimated 83 million Americans, giving it a then record 76% share of the television audience. It was also seen in more than 90 other countries, often in locally dubbed versions.

**Largest number of TV program episodes sold** The greatest number of episodes from one TV program ever sold was 1,144 episodes of *Coronation*

**MOST POPULAR CHILDREN'S EDUCATIONAL PROGRAM**
*Sesame Street,* produced since November 10, 1969 by the Children's Television Workshop, New York, USA, is sold to 180 countries around the world. *Sesame Street* was created as an experiment in 1968, designed to use the medium of television to reach and teach preschoolers. *Sesame Street* has received the most Emmys in television history.

*Street* sold by Granada Television (UK) to CBKST (Canada) on May 31, 1971. This constituted 20 days 15 hr. 44 min. of continuous viewing.

**Longest TV talk-show marathon** The world record for the longest TV talk-show marathon is 30 hours, held by Vador Lladó (Spain) of Flaix TV, who continually interviewed and hosted from May 3 to 4, 2002 in Barcelona, Spain.

**Deepest live TV broadcast by a host** The world's deepest underwater live TV broadcast was hosted by Alastair Fothergill (UK) at a depth of 1.5 miles (2.4 km) on the BBC's *Abyss Live.* The dive was broadcast on September 29, 2002 from inside a MIR submersible off the east coast of the USA.

**Longest TV documentary on a single subject** The six-part documentary film series *7 Up* shown on ITV (UK) has followed, every seven years, the lives of 14 children who were selected in 1963 at the age of seven from different social groups in the UK. The first film in the series, *7 Up* (1963), was followed by *7 times 7* (1970), which filmed the children aged 14, and by four additional installments so far. The most recent was *42 Up* (1998).

**Most expensive TV program** In January 1998 Warner Brothers (USA), the makers of the hospital drama *ER*—America's number one prime-time show, with a then weekly audience of 33 million—agreed to a three-year deal with NBC (USA), who paid a record $13.1 million (£8.2 million) per episode for 22 of the one-hour shows.

**Most expensive TV documentary series per minute** Depicting how dinosaurs lived, reproduced, and became extinct, the BBC's (UK) documentary series *Walking with Dinosaurs* (1999) cost over £37,654 ($61,112) per minute to produce. The six-part series took over two years to make and cost a total of £6.1 million ($9.9 million).

# BRANDS & ADVERTISING

**Largest global brand** According to a recent study by leading market research company AC Nielsen, the largest global brand based on sales is Coca-Cola, which in 2002 had sales of over $19 billion (£13 billion). The Coca-Cola Company, which has its global headquarters in Atlanta, Georgia, USA, is the world's foremost manufacturer, marketer, and distributor of non-alcoholic beverage concentrates and syrups, with markets in nearly 200 countries worldwide.

**Best selling brand of clothing** Levi Strauss & Co. (USA) is the world's biggest brand-named clothing manufacturer and sells under the Levis, Dockers, and Slates brands in more than 30,000 retail outlets in 100 countries. As of November 2002 the company's sales had totalled $4.1 billion (£2.6 billion).

**Best selling underwear** Marks & Spencer (UK) sells more underwear globally than anyone else, selling 50 million pairs (counting multi-packs as a pair) of their own-brand women's panties each year alone. The company operates almost 700 stores in some 30 countries worldwide.

**Largest bra manufacturer** In 2002 US clothing and food giant Sara Lee controlled 30% of the US bra market. The company, which had total sales of $17,628 million (£11,504 million) and profits of over $1,010 million (£659 million), owns the Wonderbra, Playtex, Berlei, and Gossard brands.

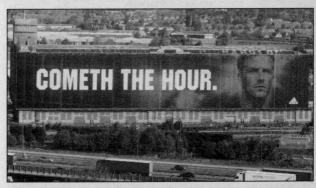

**LARGEST ADVERTISING BILLBOARD** The largest advertising billboard measures 77.7 ft. (23.7 m) high and 433 ft. (132 m) long, has a surface area of 33,673.8 ft.² (3,128.4 m²) and weighs 4,400 lb. (2 tonnes). The billboard, owned by Mega Profile Ltd. (UK), is on the side of Fort Dunlop next to the M6 motorway near Birmingham, West Midlands, UK.

**BEST SELLING DESIGNER UNDERWEAR** The most popular designer underwear brand is Calvin Klein (USA, Calvin Klein model Travis, also USA, shown). In 1998 the company sold 30 million pairs of ladies' and gentlemen's briefs with a total retail value of $425 million (£256 million).

**Earliest existing advertising** The earliest existing advertisement to be found was discovered in the ruins of Pompeii, near Naples, Italy, and is for a bookseller. It dates from around A.D. 79.

**Earliest public TV advertisement** The first public TV advertisement ever broadcast was shown on June 27, 1941 on NBC's WNBT station in New York, USA. The ad was for a Bulova watch.

**Earliest advertising agency** James White's advertising agency was established in London, UK, in 1800.

**Most expensive advertising campaign** The most expensive advertising campaigns are to be found in the pharmaceutical industry. Both Johnson & Johnson-Merck Consumer Pharmaceuticals Co. (USA) and SmithKline Beecham (UK) unleashed $100-million-plus (£62.3 million) marketing campaigns to introduce Pepcid AC and Tagamet HB respectively, which act as acid reducers. The advertising category for heartburn, acid indigestion, and sour stomach remedies is worth $1.12 billion (£700 million).

**Most expensive TV advertising campaign** The most expensive TV advertising campaign cost $8.1 million (£5.7 million) and was produced for Pepsi-Cola (USA) in 2002. The 90-second commercials cost $90,000 (£63,333) per second and starred the pop star Britney Spears (USA). The ads were first aired during Super Bowl XXXVI, held on February 3, 2002.

**Largest simultaneous TV ad premiere** On November 1, 1999, at 9 pm local time, the Ford Motor Company (USA) aired their 2-minute "Global

**BIGGEST SELLING DESIGNER CLOTHING LABEL** The biggest selling designer clothing brand in the world is Ralph Lauren (USA), which had annual global sales of $2.3 billion (£1.4 billion) in the 2002 fiscal year. The company has 236 Polo shops worldwide, and also sells its designs through approximately 1,600 department stores and specialty shops.

Anthem" advertisement on over 140 pan-regional or local market networks in 190 countries. The commercial was shot in nine countries and featured singer Charlotte Church (UK) and all seven of Ford's automobile brands.

**Highest TV advertising rate** The highest TV advertising rate was $2.4 million (£1.6 million), paid for each 30-second slot of NBC network's (USA) prime airtime during the transmission of Super Bowl XXXV on January 28, 2001.

**First advertisement filmed in space** An advertising campaign for Tnuva Milk, showing cosmonaut Vasily Tsibliyev (Russia) drinking milk aboard the Russian Mir space station, was first broadcast on August 22, 1997.

**Shortest TV commercial** The world's shortest TV commercial is half a frame (one field) long and lasts for ⅟₆₀ of a second. Twelve different versions of the commercial were produced, all advertising MuchMusic (a Canadian music and video TV channel), and the first was aired on January 2, 2002. The creator, producer, and editor of the commercial was Tharanga Ramanayake (Canada).

**Largest advertising budget** General Motors Corporation (USA) spent $2,876,242,400, (£1,810,369,345) on advertising within the media industry in 1999, according to marketing information company CMR's report released in March 2000.

**Largest ad on a roof** A logo for The Big Fresh Company (NZ) measuring 157 ft. 5 in. (48 m) wide and 475 ft. 8 in. (145 m) long was put on the roof of the Woolworths Distribution Centre, Manukau City, New Zealand, in March 1998. The sign, with each capital letter measuring 98 ft. 5 in. (30 m) high, is visible to 2.5 million people annually sitting at window seats in planes landing at and taking off from Auckland Airport.

**Largest ad on a building** An advertisement measuring 47,385 ft.² (4,402 m²) was erected on a building next to the M4 motorway near Chiswick, London, UK, to promote international airline Gulf Air. It was displayed during May and June 1995.

**Largest illuminated advertising sign** The Las Vegas Hilton Hotel in Nevada, USA, has a sign that is 197 ft. (60 m) in length and 32 ft. 10 in. (10 m) high. Lit by 16,000-W metal-halide projectors, it was constructed by Abudi Signs Industry Ltd. at Ramat Gan, Israel.

**Longest moving advertising billboard** To launch the South African Broadcasting Corporation's Channel 2 on May 11, 1998, an 880-ft. 1-in. (268.2-m) billboard covering an area of 11,541 ft.² (1,072.19 m²) was created along the sides of a train, which then traveled between cities in Gauteng province.

**Largest freestanding advertising sign** The largest and tallest freestanding advertising sign is at the Hilton Hotel and Casino in Las Vegas, Nevada, USA, and was unveiled in November 1996. Its two faces have a total area of 70,100 ft.² (6,512.3 m²), and it is 279 ft. (85.03 m) high. It also features more than 6 miles (9.65 km) of lights.

# MUSIC &
# ENTERTAINMENT

**FASTEST SELLING RAP ARTIST** Eminem's (USA) album *The Marshall Mathers LP* sold a record 1.76 million copies in its first week on release in the USA in May 2000.

**BIGGEST ARTIST PAY-OFF** Mariah Carey (USA) received a reported $28-million (£17.3-million) pay-off to end her recording contract with EMI/Virgin (UK) in January 2002. The company lost an estimated $54.3 million (£33.5 million) on the deal.

**MOST BRIT AWARDS WON BY AN INDIVIDUAL** Robbie Williams (UK) has won a total of 14 BRIT (British Record Industry Trust) Awards during his career—more than any other artist or act.

**BIGGEST FIRST CHART WEEK**
UK, *Pop Idol* winner Will Young's (UK) debut single "Anything Is Possible"/"Evergreen" sold 1,108,269 copies in its first chart week from February 25 to March 2, 2002, including 385,000 on its first day. Young went on to sell an unprecedented two million singles in the UK in just 15 weeks.

**YOUNGEST FEMALE TO TOP UK ALBUM CHART** Canadian singer/songwriter Avril Lavigne (b. September 27, 1984) topped the UK album chart on January 11, 2003 at the age of 18 years 106 days. The album *Let Go* reached No.1 in its 18th chart week.

**BIGGEST ALBUM ACT IN JAPAN** Utada Hikaru (Japan) is the only Japanese act to sell over two million copies of three consecutive albums.

**MOST PERFORMERS ON ONE SINGLE** The largest number of people to sing on one single is 275,000 on S Club 7's (UK) "Have You Ever." The single was released on November 19, 2001 as part of BBC's Children in Need appeal and features contributions from 3,616 schools in the UK.

**MOST SUCCESSFUL REMIX ALBUM** In February 2002 Jennifer Lopez's (USA) album *J To Tha Lo!: The Remixes* became the first album solely featuring remixes to top the US charts, with sales over 156,000 in its first week.

**YOUNGEST MALE SOLO ARTIST TO ENTER THE UK SINGLES CHART AT NO.1** Gareth Gates (UK, b. July 12, 1984) was 17 years 262 days old when his single "Unchained Melody" entered the chart at No.1 on March 30, 2002.

# POP CLASSICS

**Biggest selling group** The Beatles (UK) recorded the greatest sales for any group, with all-time sales estimated by EMI at over one billion discs and tapes to date. In 2001 the band was certified for album sales of 163.5 million in the USA alone.

**Most No.1 albums by a group on the US charts** The Beatles (UK) have had a record 19 No.1 albums on the US album charts—more than double that of Elvis Presley (USA) and the Rolling Stones (UK), who have both had nine albums at the top spot.

**Biggest selling album series** As of November 2002 the *Now!* series was the biggest selling album series with worldwide sales of over 60 million. It was first launched in the UK in 1984, where 52 of the 53 albums released made No.1.

**MOST GRAMMY AWARDS WON IN A SINGLE YEAR BY AN INDIVIDUAL**
The record for the most Grammy Awards won in a year is eight, by
Michael Jackson (USA) in 1984. He won Best New R&B Song and Best
Male R&B Vocal Performance with "Billie Jean;" Best Male Rock Vocal
Performance and Record of the Year with "Beat It;" and Best
Recording for Children with "E.T. The Extra-Terrestrial." He also won
Album of the Year and Best Male Pop Vocal Performance with *Thriller*,
as well as jointly winning Producer of the Year with Quincy Jones
(USA).

**Biggest selling debut album** *Boston* by Boston (USA), released in
1976, has sold over 16 million copies worldwide, making it the best selling
debut album of all time.

**Biggest selling album on UK chart** The biggest selling album on the UK chart is *Sgt. Pepper's Lonely Hearts Club Band* by the Beatles (UK), with a reported 4.5 million sales since its release in June 1967.

**Most albums simultaneously on the US charts** The most albums in the US Top 200 at the same time by the same artist is seven. The Beatles (UK), The Monkees (USA), and U2 (Rep. of Ireland) all share the record.

**Greatest advance sales for a single** "Can't Buy Me Love" by The Beatles (UK) had 2.7 million advance orders before its release on March 21, 1964.

**Fastest selling album** The Beatles' (UK) album entitled *1,* released on November 13, 2000, sold a record 13.5 million copies around the world in its first month—3.6 million on the first day alone. It was No.1 in 35 countries, earning over 100 platinum albums around the globe.

**Most no.1 albums by a male soloist on the US charts** Elvis Presley (US) had a record nine No.1 solo albums. They were: *Elvis Presley* (1956), *Elvis* (1956), *Loving You* (1957), *Elvis Christmas Album* (1957), *GI Blues* (1960), *Something For Everybody* (1961), *Blue Hawaii* (1961), *Roustabout* (1964) and *Elvis—Aloha From Hawaii* (1973).

**MOST SUCCESSFUL FAMILY POP GROUP** The Bee Gees—brothers Maurice (1949–2003), Robin and Barry Gibb (all UK)—had 24 Top 20 singles in the USA and the UK between 1968 and 2000, plus 13 Top 20 albums in the USA and 12 in the UK, including the best selling film soundtrack ever—*Saturday Night Fever.* They were inducted into the Rock and Roll Hall of Fame in 1996 and won a BRIT award for Lifetime Achievement the following year.

**Most consecutive UK No.1 singles**  The Beatles (UK) hold the record for the most consecutive No.1 hits. They had 11 in a row between 1963 and 1966 (from "From Me to You" through to "Yellow Submarine").

**Longest time on the UK singles charts**  "My Way" by Frank Sinatra (USA) spent 124 weeks on the UK charts. It entered and re-entered the charts no fewer than 10 times between April 2, 1969 and April 1994.

**Most hit singles on the UK charts**  Cliff Richard (UK) holds the record for the most UK chart hit singles, with 126 to March 2003.

**Most No.1 singles on the US charts**  The Beatles (UK) have had the most No.1 hits on the US singles charts, with 20.

**Most consecutive weeks on the UK singles charts**  Elvis Presley (USA) spent the most consecutive weeks on the UK singles charts. His 13

**MOST US TOP 40 SINGLES ENTRIES BY A FEMALE ARTIST**  In November 2002 Madonna (USA) made the US Top 40 for a record 44th time with the James Bond theme, "Die Another Day"—overtaking Aretha Franklin (USA) as the female with the most US Top 40 entries. The same single was also her 35th US Top 10 entry—thus overtaking The Beatles (UK) who were on 34, and just one short of Elvis Presley's (USA) record 36 entries.

hit singles from "A Mess of Blues" in 1960 to "One More Broken Heart for Sale" in 1963 spent an unbroken 144 weeks on the charts.

**Biggest selling single by a female group**  The best selling single by a female group is "Wannabe" by The Spice Girls (UK) in July 1996. It topped the charts in the UK for seven weeks, selling over 1.2 million copies, and hit No.1 in 31 other countries, selling a reported 4 million worldwide.

**Biggest selling Christmas song**  The 1942 recording of "White Christmas" by Bing Crosby (USA) has sold over 100 million units around the world, with about half the sales being singles. The song has been reissued annually since 1942. Its latest chart success was in December 1998, when it charted for four consecutive weeks in the UK, reaching No. 29.

**Most hits by a solo artist**  Bing Crosby (USA) started his solo career in 1931 and accumulated 396 chart entries, including 38 No.1s, in the USA alone. During his lifetime he recorded an estimated 2,600 songs.

**Most Grammy Awards won by a solo pop performer**  Stevie Wonder (USA) ha won 19 Grammy Awards since 1973 including Best Male R&B Vocal Performance six times. Stevie Wonder's career was launched by his first hit, the US No.1 "Fingertips—Part 2" in 1963, and he remains one of pop and soul's top artists.

**City with the most UK No.1 hits per capita**  According to *Guinness World Records Book of BRITISH HIT SINGLES,* the city that has provided the most No.1 hit singles, (from Lita Roza in 1953 to Atomic Kitten in 2002) on the UK chart per head of population is Liverpool (pop. 439,473) with local acts achieving 56 hits—1 per 7,847 of the city's population.

# ROCK & COUNTRY

**Largest paying rock-band concert attendance**  An estimated 195,000 people paid $16.50 (then £10) each to attend a performance by A-Ha at the Rock In Rio festival, Maracanã Stadium, Brazil, in April 1990.

**Most performers in a concert**  The largest single rock concert, in terms of participants and organization, was Roger Waters' production of Pink Floyd's *The Wall* staged on July 21, 1990 in Potsdamer Platz, straddling East and West Berlin, Germany. Over 600 people performed on stage, and an estimated 200,000 others made up the production crew.

**Largest rock-star benefit concert**  A concert held at Wembley Stadium, London, UK, on April 20, 1992 in memory of Freddie Mercury (UK) of Queen, raised £20.1 million (then $35 million) for AIDS charities. The concert was attended by 75,000 people and is estimated to have been seen

**LONGEST STAY AT NO.1 IN US ROCK SINGLES CHART** Canadian band Nickelback's single "Too Bad" held top spot on the US Mainstream Rock chart for a record-breaking 20 weeks between January and May 2002. Lead singer Chad Kroeger is shown here.

by almost 1 billion people in more than 70 countries. It featured artists such as U2 (Rep. of Ireland), David Bowie (UK), and Liza Minnelli (USA).

**Most concerts by a group in 50 days** The most musical performances by a group in 50 days is 101, by the rock band Jackyl (USA) as they toured the USA from September 12 to October 31, 1998. The band appeared in 59 cities in 26 states.

**Most concerts performed in 12 hours**  The Bus Station Loonies (UK), a four-piece punk act, played twenty five 15-minute gigs in 12 hours at venues in and around Plymouth, Devon, UK, on September 29, 2001. The band, supported by two road crews, raised $1,894 (£1,200) for charity.

**Highest grossing country music tour**  Garth Brooks' (USA) three-year "Sevens" tour starting in March 1997 grossed $105 million (then £65.6 million), playing 350 shows in 100 cities with an average attendance of 55,000 people per show.

**Highest grossing country music tour per show**  George Strait's (USA) 45-date 1998 to 2000 tour grossed $90 million (then £56.25 million)—an average of $2 million £1.25 million) per show. The final ten dates in 2000 grossed $24 million (£15 million)—an average of $2.4 million (£1.5 million) per show—and were attended by 475,000 people.

**Highest annual earnings by a country music artist**  Shania Twain (Canada) earned $36.6 million (then £23.2 million) for her tours during 1999, more than any other country performer and $3.1 million (£2 million) more than she earned from touring in 1998. Overall in the 1990s, the top-earning act on the road was George Strait (USA), who grossed $158 million (then £100.1 million). The most popular live act, Garth Brooks (USA) always kept his seat prices lower and therefore did not out-earn George Strait.

**Most No.1 albums by a country music artist**  Since 1981 George Strait (USA) has had 15 of his 26 released albums go to No.1 in the charts—a total unbeaten by any other act. In terms of box-set editions, his *Strait Out of the Box* has sold 7 million copies, more than any other artist.

**Biggest selling country album in USA by a solo artist**  The best selling country album in the USA by a solo artist is Shania Twain's (Canada) *Come On Over,* which sold a record 19 million copies after its release on November 4, 1997. The sales of Shania Twain's album overtook those of Garth Brooks' (USA) album *No Fences* (1990), which had sold just over 16 million copies as of June 15, 2000.

**Most successful male country artist in the USA**  Garth Brooks is the most successful country recording artist of all time, with album sales of over 100 million since 1989. He also has the highest certified album sales of any solo artist in the USA. Brooks has won many awards, including Entertainer of the Year at the 1997 Country Music Awards.

**Most platinum RIAA albums for a country music artist**  Since 1981 George Strait (USA) has released 26 albums, with all but one of them (a Christmas album) earning RIAA (Recording Industry Association of Amer-

**LONGEST STAY IN A SINGLES CHART** "How Do I Live" by LeAnn Rimes (USA) entered the Top 25 US Country singles sales chart on June 21, 1997 and was still there in February 2003, a record 291 weeks (five and a half years) later.

ica) platinum certificates for sales of over one million copies in the USA. In all, his albums have sold over 55 million copies.

**Most multi-platinum RIAA certificates** The recording artist with the most multi-platinum RIAA certificates is Elvis Presley (USA), who has a total of 33. This figure excludes certificates for videos.

**Biggest selling live album** *Double Live* by Garth Brooks (USA) is the top-selling live album in the USA with certified sales of 14 million (7 million double LPs) since its release on November 17, 1998.

**Biggest selling single album in the USA by a British act** The best-selling album in the USA by a British group is *Led Zeppelin IV* by Led Zeppelin, with estimated sales of 22 million. In the world's biggest album market, the USA, *The Wall* by Pink Floyd has certified sales of 23 million (11.5 double albums) and *The Dark Side of the Moon* (also Pink Floyd) 15 million single albums. The latter continues to sell well worldwide and may well have outsold the other two on a global basis—its accredited world sale being 23 million—the same figure claimed by The Beatles' *1*.

**Biggest selling album in USA for a female solo artist** Canadian country singer Shania Twain's album *Come On Over* has sold 19 million copies in the USA and 30 million worldwide since its release on November 4, 1997.

**Biggest selling Australian album** *Back in Black* by AC/DC (Australia) has had estimated global sales of 19 million copies since 1980. The band—currently Bon Scott (UK), Angus and Malcolm Young (UK), Cliff Williams (UK), and Phil Rudd (Australia)—formed in 1973 in Sydney, NSW, Australia, and took their name at the suggestion of Angus and Malcolm's sister, who saw it on a vacuum cleaner.

**Earliest million-selling CD** The first CD to sell one million copies worldwide was Dire Straits' (UK) *Brothers in Arms* album in 1986. It went on to sell more than a million in Europe alone, including over 250,000 in Britain.

**Most simultaneous album entries in a week in the US chart** Rock group Pearl Jam (USA) had seven different albums enter the US Top 200 chart on March 17, 2001. They were part of a series of 23 albums recorded live at different venues around the USA, breaking their own record of five entries from a series of 25 simultaneously released live albums from previous concerts held during their highly successful world tour.

# URBAN BEATS

**Rapper with the most US No.1 albums** When *The Blueprint 2* topped the US album charts in November 2002, Jay-Z (USA) became the only rap act to have scored five No.1 albums. Eminem (USA) is the only MC to have sold more albums.

**Best selling rap/R&B album in the USA** The best selling rap/R&B album ever in the USA is *CrazySexyCool* by TLC (USA), which has recorded 11 million sales. This surpasses MC Hammer's *Please Hammer Don't Hurt 'Em* album, which has sold 10 million.

**Biggest selling rap artist** Rap legend 2Pac (born Tupac Shakur, USA) has certified US album sales of 33.5 million, and has now had more hits after his death (at the age of 25 in September 1996) than he achieved while he was alive. His posthumous hits include two US No.1 albums, *The Don Killuminati* (1997) and *Until the End of Time* (2001) (both produced after his death), and a dozen US R&B chart singles.

**Largest rap group** Hip-Hop outfit Minority Militia (USA) is the world's largest rap group, with 124 members. Each member either raps, sings, plays an instrument, or produces on the group's 2001 album *The People's Army,* released on Low Town Records.

**Youngest solo rap artist** Jordy (Lemoine, France) was at No.1 in the French singles chart with techno/house rap "Dur dur d'être bébé" (It's Hard to be a Baby) at the age of four years six months in September 1993. The song later entered the US Billboard chart.

**Fastest rap artist** Rebel XD (Seandale Price) from Chicago, Illinois, USA, beat his own record when he rapped 683 syllables in 54.501 seconds on the set of *Guinness World Records: Primetime* in Los Angeles, California, USA, on June 24, 1998.

**Longest stay on the US rap singles chart** "Hot Boyz" by Missy "Misdemeanor" Elliott, featuring Nas, Eve, and Q-Tip (all USA), spent a record 18 weeks at the top of the US Rap Chart in 1999/2000.

**OLDEST MOBO WINNER The oldest MOBO (Music Of Black Origin) award winner is BB King (USA) who was 73 in 1998 when he picked up the Lifetime Achievement award.**

**FASTEST SELLING FEMALE DEBUT ALBUM** Ashanti's (USA) debut album *Ashanti* sold 503,000 copies in its first week on release in the USA in April 2002. In the same week, she became the first female performer to simultaneously hold the top two places on the Hot 100 Singles Chart with "Foolish" and "What's Luv" (with Fat Joe).

**Youngest solo rap artist at No.1 on the US R&B and rap charts** In July 2000 Lil' Bow Wow (aka Shad Lamar Moss, USA), aged 13 years 4 months, went to No.1 on the US rap and R&B charts with "Bounce with Me" (featuring Xscape).

**Youngest R&B chart entrant** Hailie Jade Mathers (USA) became the youngest performer to be credited with an R&B hit when, at age 6 years 210 days, "My Dad's Gone Crazy" charted in August 2002. She performed on the track with her father, Eminem (USA).

**Longest span on the US R&B chart**  Ray Charles (USA) has appeared on the US R&B Singles Chart for seven decades. He first charted as leader of the Maxine Trio with "Confession Blues" in April 1949, and his latest entry came in July 2002 with "Mother," making a span of 53 years.

**Best selling drum 'n' bass album**  The best selling drum 'n' bass album is *New Forms* by Reprazent (UK), which has sold a total of 763,910 albums around the world. The band sold 250,000 albums in the UK and 513,910 worldwide.

**Best selling big-beat album**  The best selling big-beat album is Fatboy Slim's (UK) *You've Come a Long Way Baby,* which was released in October 1998 and has sold over three million copies worldwide, one million in the UK alone.

**Best selling reggae album**  *Legend* (1984), by the late Bob Marley (Jamaica), is the biggest selling reggae album of all time. In the UK, where it topped the album charts, it has had certified sales of 1.8 million, and although it never reached the Top 40 in the USA, it sold more than 10 million copies there.

**Best selling raï artist**  Algerian raï singer Khaled has sold over 3 million albums worldwide, including *Khaled* (1992), which featured his first international hit "Didi." Khaled also appeared in concert with fellow Algerian stars Rachid Taha and Faudel in 1999. Their live album, *1, 2, 3 Soleils,* sold one million copies worldwide.

**Best selling world music album**  The 1998 Grammy-award-winning album *Buena Vista Social Club* (1997) has sold over four million copies, with 1.5 million sold in the USA alone. The album brought some of Cuba's best musicians together, including Rubén González, Ibrahím Ferrer, and Compay Segundo.

**Biggest selling album by a Latin artist**  Mexican-born Carlos Santana's *Supernatural* album (1999) has sold 14 million copies in the USA alone, and many millions more worldwide.

**Biggest selling solo bhangra artist**  Malkit Singh (India) has sold an average of 260,000 copies of each of his albums, totaling sales of over 4.9 million records since he began his career in 1985.

**Fastest selling rap album**  Rap artist Eminem's (USA) album *The Marshall Mathers LP* sold a record 1.76 million copies in its first week in the USA when it was released in June 2000.

**Oldest artist at No.1 on the US charts**  Louis Armstrong (USA) was almost 63 years old when his single "Hello Dolly!" reached No.1 in 1964.

**Oldest artist to have a million-seller** Cuban singer/guitarist Company Segundo (born Francisco Repilado) has sold over one million albums around the world since his 88th birthday in 1995. The entertainer, who first recorded in the 1930s, found new fame as a member of the group Buena Vista Social Club in 1996.

**Most consecutive weeks at No.1 by the same producer** Hip-Hop producer Irv Gotti (USA) produced the No.1 single on the US Hot 100 Pop Chart for a record 19 successive weeks between February 23 and June 22,

**MOST SIMULTANEOUS R&B HITS** In 2001 US R&B artists R Kelly and Jay-Z equaled the record set by both DMX and Juvenile (both USA) in 1999 of achieving six simultaneous entries on the Billboard Hot R&B/Hip-Hop Singles and Tracks charts.

2002. Some of the major artists Gotti has worked with include Ja Rule, Ashanti, Jay-Z, DMX, and Fat Joe (all USA).

**Most music videos made for one song** Five different videos were made for the track "Timber" (1998) by UK dance act Coldcut: the original mix, the EBN remix (New York), the LPC remix (Sweden), the Clifford Gilberto remix (Germany), and the Gnomadic remix (UK).

**Largest international music festival** The largest international music festival is WOMAD (World of Music, Arts and Dance), which has staged more than 90 events in 20 different countries since 1982. Originally inspired by musician Peter Gabriel (UK), WOMAD's worldwide profile has grown quickly, with annual events in Australia, North America, Japan, and Europe. The central aim of WOMAD is to bring together and celebrate music, arts, and dance drawn from all over the world.

# CLASSICAL & JAZZ

**Most prolific conductor** Herbert von Karajan (Austria) made over 800 recordings encompassing all the major works. During his career, he conducted the London Philharmonia Orchestra, the Vienna State Opera, and La Scala Opera Orchestra of Milan, and founded the Satzburg Festival in 1967. He was principal conductor of the Berlin Philharmonic Orchestra for 35 years before his retirement, which was shortly before his death in 1989.

**Longest career as a conductor** As of September 2002, Torstein Grythe (Norway, b. November 24, 1918), age 84, had been conducting the Silver Boys Choir of Oslo, Norway, for 62 years, since he started in 1940.

**Oldest orchestra** The first modern symphony orchestra—four sections consisting of woodwind, brass, percussion, and string instruments—played at the court of Duke Karl Theodor (Germany) at Mannheim, Germany, in 1743. The oldest existing symphony orchestra, the Gewandhaus Orchestra of Leipzig, Germany, was also established in 1743. Originally known as the Grosses Concert and later as the Musik bende Gesellschaft, its current name dates from 1781.

**Most prolific composer** Georg Philipp Telemann (Germany) wrote 12 complete sets of services for the church year (with one cantata for every Sunday), 78 services for special occasions, 40 operas, between 600 and 700 orchestral suites, 44 passions, plus concertos, sonatas, and other pieces of chamber music.

**Longest operatic encore** The longest encore listed in the *Concise Oxford Dictionary of Opera* was the whole of Domenico Cimarosa's (Italy)

**LONGEST OPERA** The longest of the commonly performed operas is *Die Meistersinger von Nürnberg* by Richard Wagner (Germany). A normal uncut version as performed by the Sadler's Wells company (UK) between August 24 and September 19, 1968 entailed 5 hr. 15 min. of music. The photo shows John Tomlinson and Thomas Allen (both UK) in a recent production at the Royal Opera House, Covent Garden, London, UK.

opera *Il Matrimonio Segreto* at its premiere in 1792. This was at the command of the Austro-Hungarian Emperor Leopold II.

**Shortest opera** The shortest published opera is *The Sands of Time* by Simon Rees and Peter Reynolds (both UK), which was 3 min. 34 sec. long when performed under Reynolds' direction at BBC TV Centre, London, UK, on September 14, 1993.

**Youngest opera singer** On March 24, 1950 Ginetta Gloria La Bianca (USA, b. May 12, 1934) sang Gilda in *Rigoletto* at Velletri, Italy, aged 15 years 316 days.

**Oldest opera singer** The Ukrainian bass Mark Reizen sang the role of Prince Gremin in Tchaikovsky's *Eugene Onegin* at the Bolshoi Theatre in Moscow, Russia, on his 90th birthday in 1985.

**Most costume changes in a live operatic performance** On November 2, 1997 Natalie Choquette (Canada) wore a total of 15 costumes during a recital at the Wilfred-Pelletier Hall, Montreal, Canada. During the first part of the show she wore seven costumes, and after the interval, she donned eight more.

**Biggest selling classical album** The best selling classical album is *In Concert,* with global sales of 10.5 million to date. It was recorded by José Carreras, Placido Domingo (both Spain), and Luciano Pavarotti (Italy) in Rome, Italy, on July 7, 1990. The recording was made for the soccer World Cup finals, held that year in Italy.

**Longest interval between composition and performance** The longest interval between a composer writing a piece of music and its performance in the manner intended is from March 3, 1791 until October 9, 1982 (over 191 years). Mozart's *Organ Piece for a Clock* was finally performed at Glyndebourne, East Sussex, UK, with the assistance of organ builders William Hill & Son and Norman & Beard Ltd.

**Most people to share a Grammy award** The greatest number of people to share a Grammy award is 46, by the Chicago Symphony Orchestra, (CSO). The CSO won the first of its Grammy awards in February 1978 for Best Choral Performance–Classical with its recording of Verdi's *Requiem.* The Orchestra has been involved in 56 wins since, including 24 by conductor Sir Georg Solti (UK) and nine by chorus director Margaret Hillis (USA).

**Youngest person at No.1 in the classical charts** In November 1998 Charlotte Church (UK, b. February 21, 1986) entered the UK classical album charts with her debut *Voice of an Angel* at the age of 12 years 9 months. The album went double platinum in the UK within four weeks of its release.

**Most valuable jazz instrument** The most valuable jazz instrument is a saxophone once owned by Charlie Parker (USA) that sold for $144,500 (£93,500) at Christie's, London, UK, on September 7, 1994.

**Best selling jazz artist** The best selling jazz artist is Kenny G (USA), who has sold an estimated 55 million albums worldwide to date. This in-

**LARGEST OPERA HOUSE The Metropolitan Opera House at Lincoln Center, New York City, USA, has a combined seating and standing capacity of 4,065. The auditorium, which seats 3,800, is 451 ft. (137 m) deep, and the stage measures 230 ft. (70 m) wide by 148 ft. (45 m) deep. It was completed in September 1966 at a cost of $45.7 million (then £16.3 million).**

**MOST EXPENSIVE HIT** The most expensive hit was the CD set *Miles Davis at Montreux* (Miles Davis, USA), which entered the US Top 20 Jazz Chart in November 2002, and was priced at $250 (£154).

cludes 12 million copies of *Breathless,* the best selling jazz album of all time, which was released in 1992.

**Longest working career as a recording artist** Adelaide Hall (USA) is the artist with the longest recording career, having released material over eight consecutive decades. The jazz singer's first record, *Creole Love Call,* was recorded with Duke Ellington (USA) on October 26, 1927, and her last was made on June 16, 1991 at the Cole Porter Centennial Gala.

**Earliest jazz record made** The first jazz record made was of *Indiana* and *The Dark Town Strutters' Ball,* recorded for the Columbia label in New York, USA, on or about January 30, 1917, by the Original Dixieland Jazz Band. It was released on May 31, 1917.

**Largest pipes and drums band** The Millennium Pipes event, held in aid of Marie Curie Cancer Care, took place in Edinburgh, UK, on August 5, 2000, with 10,000 bagpipers and drummers from around the world playing many pipe-music classics.

**Largest drum ensemble** A drum ensemble numbering 2,208 participants gathered to play at Mydonose Showland, Istanbul, Turkey, on March 17, 2002. The ensemble consisted of members of Türk Otomobil Fabrikasi AS (TOFAS) and was led by the popular Turkish rhythm band Harem.

**Largest ehru ensemble** Conducted by Yan Huichang (China), 938 ehru (a Chinese stringed instrument) players aged between 6 and 76 years performed with the Hong Kong Chinese Orchestra at the opening of the Huqin Festival of Hong Kong at Hong Kong's Cultural Festival Centre on February 11, 2001.

**Oldest piano** The earliest pianoforte in existence is one built in Florence, Italy, in 1720 by Bartolommeo Cristofori (Italy) and now preserved in the Metropolitan Museum of Art, New York City, USA.

# PERFORMANCE ARTS

**Largest dance festival** The Festival de Dança de Joinville in Santa Catarina, Brazil, is the world's largest dance festival. First produced in 1983, the festival is held over a minimum of 10 days and is attended by 4,000 national and international dancers from 140 amateur and professional dance groups. It is watched by more than 200,000 people annually.

**Largest chorus line** On September 28, 1997, 593 people from The Roy Castle Foundation (UK) performed a routine for the finale of *The Roy Castle Record Breaking Extravaganza* at the Royal Liverpool Philharmonic Hall, Liverpool, UK.

**Most grands jetés** On November 28, 1988 Wayne Sleep (UK) completed 158 grands jetés along the length of Dunston Staiths, Gateshead, Tyne & Wear, UK, in 2 minutes.

**Most ballet kicks** Emma Smith (USA) performed 587 continuous *grand battements* on alternating legs on February 26, 2002 at the New Hanover County Senior Center, Wilmington, N. Carolina, USA.

**THICKEST MAKE-UP** The thickest three-dimensional make-up is Chutti, unique to the southwest Indian Kathakali dance-theater tradition. The villainous redbeard characters have mask-like attachments, built up using rice paste and paper, that extend 6 in. (15 cm) from the face. The make-up takes hours to apply, and the colors and costume styles used denote the different nature of each of the characters.

**FASTEST THEATRICAL PRODUCTION** Velvet Jacket Ltd.'s musical production of *Oklahoma!* performed by Act 24 at The Playhouse, Edinburgh, UK, at 8 pm on May 6, 2000, was produced in a time of 23 hr. 55 min. from first receiving the script. The time in production includes auditions, casting, rehearsals, publicity design, rigging, stage and set design, and construction.

**Most flamenco taps in a minute** The most flamenco taps in a minute is 734, achieved by Alberto Hidalgo (Germany) at the JHQ Rheindahlen International Golden Jubilee Show, Monchengladbach, Germany, on June 9, 2002.

**Oldest surviving ballet** *The Whims of Cupid and the Ballet Master* was choreographed in 1786 by Vincenzo Galeotti (Italy) for the Royal Danish Ballet. *La Fille Mal Gardée* is sometimes regarded to be the oldest, but it appeared three years later, and the original choreography is lost.

**Longest play** The longest recorded theatrical production has been *The Warp* by Neil Oram (UK) directed by Ken Campbell (UK), a 10-part play cycle performed at the Institute of Contemporary Art, The Mall, London, UK, between January 18 and 20, 1979. Russell Denton (USA) was on stage for all but 5 min. of the 18 hr. 5 min. play.

**Longest Shakespeare play** Of William Shakespeare's (UK) 37 plays, *Hamlet* (1604), comprising 4,042 lines and 29,551 words, is the longest. Within the play is the longest speech of Shakespeare's 1,277 speaking parts, with Hamlet having 1,569 lines containing 11,610 words.

**Largest simultaneous performance of one show** The children's musical *The Rainbow Juggler* was performed in 56 different theaters across the UK, Ireland, Germany, USA, and Australia by 4,568 Stagecoach Theatre Arts students on November 20, 1999.

**Longest running off-Broadway musical** *The Fantasticks* by Tom Jones and Harvey Schmidt (both USA) opened on May 3, 1960 and finally closed on January 13, 2002 having been performed a record 17,162 times at the Sullivan Street Playhouse, Greenwich Village, New York, USA.

**Longest theatrical run** The longest continuous run of any show in the world is *The Mousetrap* by Agatha Christie (UK), with its 50th anniversary and the 20,807th performance held on November 25, 2002 at the St. Martin's Theatre, London, UK. The thriller opened on November 25, 1952 at the Ambassadors Theatre, London, UK, and moved after 8,862 performances to the St. Martins Theatre next door on March 25, 1974. The box office has grossed $33.3 million (£20 million) from more than ten million theatergoers in its 50 years.

**Most expensive stage production** The stage adaptation of Disney's 1994 film *The Lion King* is the most expensive theatrical production ever, with the Broadway production, which opened on November 13, 1997, costing an estimated $15 million (£9.3 million).

**Longest theatrical run for a comedy** The longest running comedy was *No Sex, Please, We're British,* written by Anthony Marriott and Alistair Foot and presented by John Gale (all UK). It opened at the Strand Theatre, London, UK, on June 3, 1971, transferred to the Duchess Theatre on August 2, 1986 and finally ended on September 5, 1987 after 16 years 3 months and 6,761 performances.

**Longest period as an understudy in the same role** On March 12, 1994 Nancy Seabrooke (UK) retired from the Company of *The Mousetrap* at the age of 79 after having understudied the part of Mrs. Boyle for 15 years and 6,240 performances. She performed the part on 72 occasions.

**Greatest theatrical loss** The largest loss sustained by a theatrical show was borne by the American producers of the Royal Shakespeare Company's musical *Carrie,* which closed after five performances on Broadway on May 17, 1988 at a cost of $7 million (then £3,744,516).

**Longest theatrical run for a revue** The greatest number of performances of any theatrical presentation is 47,250 (to April 1986) for *The Golden Horseshoe Revue,* a show staged at Disneyland Park, Anaheim, California, USA, from July 16, 1955 to October 12, 1986. It was seen by over 16 million people.

**Longest running musical** Andrew Lloyd Webber's *Cats* is the longest running musical in the history of both London's West End and Broadway, New York, USA. In London it opened in 1981 at the New London Theatre, Drury Lane, and when it closed after its 8,950th and final West End per-

**MOST EXPENSIVE STAGE PROP** For the musical stage version of *Chitty Chitty Bang Bang,* which opened on April 16, 2002 at the London Palladium, London, UK, the magical flying car of the title cost an estimated $1.07 million (£750,000) to make. The complete set, designed by set designer Anthony Ward (UK), cost an estimated $8.9 million (£6.2 million) to stage. The show is the most expensive British production ever seen in the West End.

formance on May 11, 2002—its 21st birthday—it had been seen by over eight million people. On Broadway, it opened at the Winter Garden Theater on October 7, 1982, and the 7,485th and final performance was held on September 10, 2000.

**Most theater performances in the same role** Kanbi Fujiyama (Japan) played the lead role in 10,288 performances by the comedy company Sochiku Shikigeki from November 1966 to June 1983.

**Longest theater performance** A team of 15 people from Thisaigal Cultural Troupe (India) performed 12 plays on a stage outside Karuna Hospital, Madurai, India, from July 9 to 11, 1999 for a total of 57 hr. 30 min.

# SPORTS

# AMERICAN FOOTBALL

**Most points in a Super Bowl career**  Jerry Rice (USA) has scored 48 points in Super Bowl games, in 1989–90, 1995, and 2003 for the San Francisco 49ers and the Oakland Raiders.

**Youngest coach to win a Super Bowl**  At age 39 years 161 days, Jon Gruden (USA) led the Tampa Bay Buccaneers to victory at Super Bowl XXXVII in San Diego, California, USA, on January 26, 2003.

**Highest Super Bowl aggregate score**  The highest aggregate score in a Super Bowl was 75, when the San Francisco 49ers beat the San Diego Chargers 49–26 at the Super Bowl XXIX in 1995.

**Most secure Super Bowl**  Super Bowl XXXVI at the Louisiana Superdome in New Orleans, USA, on February 3, 2002 had the tightest security measures ever for a Super Bowl. The match, in which the New England Patriots beat the St. Louis Rams 20–17, was granted National Security Special Event status. The US Secret Service coordinated security and many government resources were used.

**Most yards gained receiving in a Super Bowl career**  Jerry Rice (USA) has caught passes for a record 589 yards over four Super Bowl appearances in 1989, 1990, 1995, and 2003, playing for the San Francisco 49ers and the Oakland Raiders.

Jerry Rice also holds

**MOST TEAM INTERCEPTIONS IN A SUPER BOWL**  In Super Bowl XXXVII, played in San Diego, California, USA, on January 26, 2003, the Tampa Bay Buccaneers (player Dexter Jackson shown) made a record five interceptions, returning them 172 yards for three touchdowns.

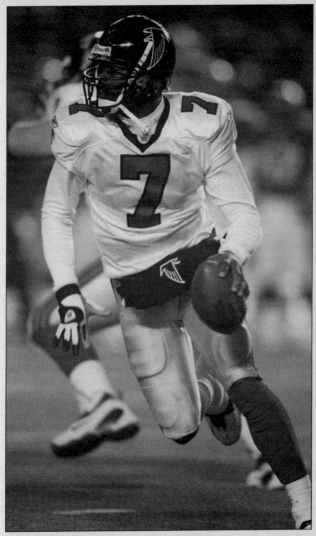

**MOST RUSHING YARDS MADE BY A QUARTERBACK IN AN NFL GAME**
Quarterback Michael Vick (USA) rushed a record 173 yards in a single
NFL game playing for the Atlanta Falcons against the Minnesota
Vikings at Minneapolis, Minnesota, USA, on December 1, 2002.

American Football

the record for the most receiving yards at a single Super Bowl, with 215 yards for the San Francisco 49ers against the Denver Broncos in 1989.

**Most yards gained rushing in an NFL career** Emmitt Smith (USA) of the Dallas Cowboys rushed for a total of 17,162 yards over his NFL career, between 1990 and 2002.

**Most yards gained receiving in an NFL career** Jerry Rice (USA) of the San Francisco 49ers and the Oakland Raiders gained 21,597 yards pass receiving between 1985 and 2002.

In addition to the career record, Jerry Rice also holds the record for the most yards earned receiving in an NFL season, with 1,848 yards for the San Francisco 49ers in 1995.

**Most interceptions in an NFL season** The most interceptions made in an NFL season is 14 by Dick "Night Train" Lane (USA) playing for the Los Angeles Rams in the first fully professional season in 1952. He returned them for 298 yards and two touchdowns.

**Most passes completed in an NFL season** The most passes completed in a regular NFL season is 418 by quarterback Rich Gannon (USA) for the Oakland Raiders in 2002.

**Most passes received in an NFL season** Marvin Harrison (USA) of the Indianapolis Colts caught a record 143 passes in 2002.

**Most passes completed in an NFL career** Dan Marino (USA) of the Miami Dolphins completed a total of 4,967 passes between 1983 and his retirement from the game in 2000. He holds many other records, including most yards gained passing in both a career (61,631) and a season (5,084 in 1984).

**Most touchdowns in an NFL career** Multiple NFL record holder Jerry Rice (USA) has scored 192 touchdowns in his career to date, playing for the San Francisco 49ers and the Oakland Raiders since 1985.

**Highest combined kick-off return yardage in an NFL season** Michael Lewis (USA) of the New Orleans Saints set an NFL combined punt/kick-off return record with 2,432 yards in the 2002 season.

**Longest field goal** The longest ever field goal in an NFL game is 63 yards by Tom Dempsey (USA) of the New Orleans Saints on November 8, 1970 against the Detroit Lions; and by Jason Elam (USA) of the Denver Broncos against the Jacksonville Jaguars on October 25, 1998.

**Longest run from scrimmage** Tony Dorsett (USA) scored on a touchdown run of 99 yards playing for the Dallas Cowboys against the Minnesota Vikings on January 3, 1983.

**Longest return of a missed field goal**  The longest return of a missed field goal for a touchdown is 107 yards by Chris McAlister (USA) playing for the Baltimore Ravens against the Denver Broncos on September 30, 2002.

**Most field goals in an NFL career**  Gary Anderson (USA) scored 494 field goals during his NFL career (Pittsburgh Steelers, 1982–94; Philadelphia Eagles, 1995–96; San Francisco 49ers, 1997; Minnesota Vikings, 1999–2002).

**Most safeties in an NFL game**  Fred Dryer (USA) made two safeties in a single game, playing for the Los Angeles Rams against the Green Bay Packers on October 21, 1973.

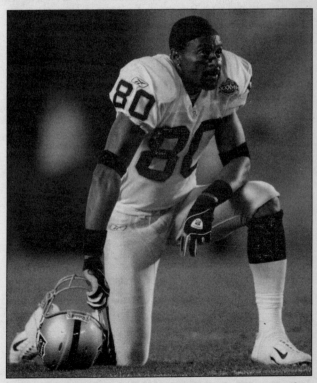

**MOST PASSES RECEIVED IN AN NFL CAREER**  The most pass receptions in an NFL career is 1,456 by Jerry Rice (USA) of the San Francisco 49ers and the Oakland Raiders (1985–2002).

**Highest score in an NFL game**  The highest score in any NFL game is 73 by the Chicago Bears against the Washington Redskins (0) in the 1940 NFL Championship game at Washington DC, USA, on December 8.

**Most NFL titles**  The Green Bay Packers have won a record 12 NFL titles—in 1929–31, 1936, 1939, 1944, 1961–62, 1965–67, and 1996.

**Most consecutive NFL games played**  Jim Marshall (USA) played 282 consecutive NFL games, for the Cleveland Browns in 1960 and the Minnesota Vikings in 1961–79.

**Most NFL games**  Quarterback George Blanda (USA) played a record 340 games in a record 26 seasons. He played for the Chicago Bears in 1949–58, the Baltimore Colts in 1950, the Houston Oilers in 1960–66, and the Oakland Raiders in 1967–75, and was the first player to score more than 500 points for three different teams. He was voted player of the year in 1961.

**Most consecutive NFL wins**  The Chicago Bears achieved a record 17 consecutive NFL wins in 1933–34. The most consecutive games without defeat is 25 by Canton Bulldogs (22 wins and 3 ties) from 1921–23.

**Largest attendance at an NFL regular season game**  The largest crowd numbered 102,368 for the Los Angeles Rams against the San Francisco 49ers at the LA Coliseum, Los Angeles, California, USA, on November 10, 1957.

**Shortest NFL player**  Jack Shapiro (USA), who played for the Staten Island Stapletons in 1929, was 5 ft. 0.5 in. (1.54 m) tall. He played just one game at halfback, rushing for seven yards (in two attempts) and returning a punt 12 yards.

# BASEBALL

**Longest hit for a home run in an MLB game**  The longest measured hit for a home run in a Major League Baseball (MLB) game is 634 ft. (193 m) by Mickey Mantle (USA) on September 10, 1960 for the New York Yankees against the Detroit Tigers at Briggs Stadium, Detroit, USA.

**Most base hits in an MLB career**  The most base hits in a Major League career is 4,256 by Peter Rose (USA) who played for the Cincinnati Reds, the Philadelphia Phillies, and the Montreal Expos between 1963 and 1986.

**Most base hits in an MLB season**  The most base hits in a Major League Baseball season is 257 by George Sisler (USA) playing for the St. Louis Browns in 1920.

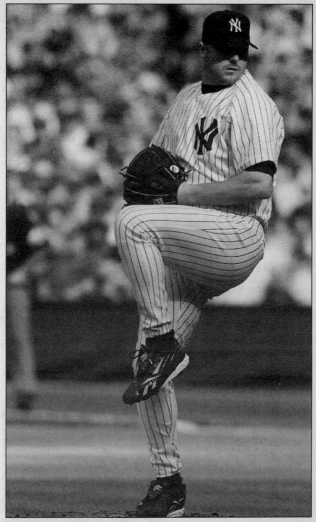

**MOST CY YOUNG PITCHING AWARDS** The Cy Young Award is presented each season to the League's outstanding pitcher. Roger Clemens (USA, Houston Astros) has received the award six times, with the Boston Red Sox (1986–87 and 1991), the Toronto Blue Jays (1997–98), and the New York Yankees (2001).

**Highest batting average in an MLB season** The highest batting average in a Major League season is .438 by Hugh Duffy (USA) playing for the Boston Beaneaters in 1894.

**Most consecutive hits in the MLB** The most consecutive hits in the Major League is 12, and the record is shared by two players. The first to achieve the feat was Pinky Higgins (USA) of the Boston Red Sox in June 1938. He was followed by Walt Dropo (USA) playing for the Detroit Tigers in July 1952.

**Most hits by an MLB rookie in a season** The most hits by a rookie (a first year player) in an MLB season is 242 by Ichiro Suzuki (Japan) playing for the Seattle Mariners in 2001. Ichiro broke the 90-year record set by "Shoeless" Joe Jackson (USA) for the Cleveland Naps (later renamed the Cleveland Indians) in 1911.

**Most runs in an MLB career** The most runs scored in a Major League career is 2,288 by Rickey Henderson (USA) up to the end of the 2002 season. He began the first of his 28 seasons to date on June 24, 1979 with the Oakland Athletics. He then played for eight other franchises before finishing the 2002 season with the Boston Red Sox.

**Most RBIS in an MLB career** The most runs batted in (RBIs) in an MLB career is 2,297 by Hank Aaron (USA), between 1954 and 1976.

**MOST CONSECUTIVE MAJOR LEAGUE GAMES BATTED SAFELY**
The most consecutive Major League games batted safely is 56 by Joe DiMaggio (USA) between May 15 and July 16, 1941.

**Most doubles hit in an MLB career** The most doubles hit in a Major League career is 792 by Tris Speaker (USA) who played for the Boston Red Sox, the Cleveland Indians, the Washington Senators, and the Philadelphia Athletics from 1907 to 1928.

**Most triples hit in an MLB career** The most triples hit in a Major League career is 309 by Sam Crawford (USA) for the Cincinnati Reds and the Detroit Tigers from 1899 to 1917.

**Most grand slam home runs in the same inning** On April 23, 1999 Fernando Tatis (Dominican Republic), batting for the St. Louis Cardinals, became the first player in Major League history to hit two grand slam home runs in the same inning. He set the record against the Los Angeles Dodgers' pitcher Chan Ho Park (South Korea) in the 3rd inning of the game, which was won by the Cardinals 12–5.

**Most strikeouts in an MLB career** Nolan Ryan (USA) pitched a total of 5,714 strikeouts during his Major League career with the New York Mets, the California Angels, the Houston Astros, and the Texas Rangers from 1966 to 1993. In 1979 Ryan became the first player in Major League history to sign a contract worth $1 million (then £472,660) when he joined the Houston Astros.

**Most strikeouts in an MLB game** Roger Clemens (USA) playing for the Boston Red Sox, pitched a record 20 strikeouts in one game (nine innings) against the Seattle Mariners on April 29, 1986 and the Detroit Tigers on September 18, 1996. Kerry Wood (USA) playing for the Chicago Cubs equaled this record on May 6, 1998 against the Houston Astros.

**Most strikeouts in an MLB season** The most strikeouts in a Major League season is 383, pitched by Nolan Ryan (USA) of the California Angels in 1973. The record for American League baseball is 513 strikeouts in one season, by Matt Kilroy (USA) for the Baltimore Orioles in 1886.

**Most shutouts in an MLB season** The most shutouts achieved by a pitcher in one season is 16, by George Bradley (USA) for the St. Louis Brown Stockings in 1876 and Pete Alexander (USA) for the Philadelphia Phillies in 1916.

**Most total bases in an MLB season** The most total bases in a season is 457 by Babe Ruth (USA) for the New York Yankees in 1921.

**Most stolen bases in an MLB season** The most stolen bases in a season is 130 by Rickey Henderson (USA) playing for the Oakland Athletics in 1982.

**Most consecutive MLB games** Cal Ripken, Jr. (USA) of the Baltimore Orioles played a record 2,632 consecutive Major League games between May 30, 1982 and September 19, 1998.

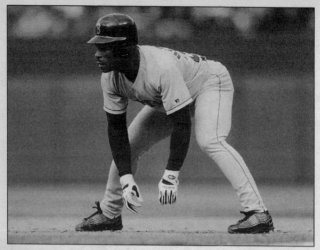

**MOST STOLEN BASES IN A CAREER** The most bases stolen in a career is 1,403 by Rickey Henderson, (USA, Boston Red Sox), known as the "Man of Steal," from 1979–2002.

**Most MLB MVP awards** Barry Bonds (USA) has won a record five Major League Most Valuable Player (MVP) awards. He won his fifth while playing with the San Francisco Giants in the 2002 season. Bonds won his previous awards in 1990, 1992, 1993, and 2001.

**Most World Series MVP awards** The most World Series Most Valuable Player (MVP) Awards received by a player is two. Several people have won this award twice: Sandy Koufax (USA) of the Los Angeles Dodgers in 1963 and 1965; Bob Gibson (USA) of the St. Louis Cardinals in 1964 and 1967; and Reggie Jackson (USA) with the Oakland Athletics in 1973 and the New York Yankees in 1977.

**Most home runs in a minor league season** Joe Bauman (USA) of the Roswell Rockets scored a record 72 home runs in one season in 1954.

**Youngest World Series player** Fred Lindstrom (USA) played for the New York Giants on October 24, 1924 at age 18 years and 339 days.

**Longest baseball throw** Glen Gorbous (Canada) threw a baseball a record 445 ft. 10 in. (135.88 m) on August 1, 1957.

**Largest baseball game attendance** An estimated 114,000 spectators watched a game between Australia and an American Services team in a demonstration event during the Olympic Games at Melbourne, Australia, on December 1, 1956.

**Largest wooden baseball bat** The largest wooden baseball bat is 13 ft. 5 in. (4.089 m) long with a circumference of 3 ft. 4 in. (1.016 m) and is owned by the Fargo-Moorhead RedHawks baseball club (Fargo Baseball LLC) of Fargo, North Dakota, USA.

# BASKETBALL

**Most NBA championship titles** The most NBA Championship titles won is 16 by the Boston Celtics, in 1957, 1959–66, 1968–69, 1974, 1976, 1981, 1984, and 1986.

**Most wins in an NBA season** The most wins in an NBA season is 72 by the Chicago Bulls in the 1995/96 season.

**Most points in an NBA season** The most points scored in an NBA season is 4,029 by Wilt "The Stilt" Chamberlain (USA) for the Philadelphia Warriors in 1961–62.

**Most points scored by a player in an NBA game** The most points scored by one player in an NBA game is 100 by Wilt Chamberlain (USA) playing for the Philadelphia Warriors against the New York Knicks on March 2, 1962.

**Most points by a team in an NBA game** The highest team score in an NBA game is 186 by the Detroit Pistons against the Denver Nuggets (184) at Denver, Colorado, USA, on December 13, 1983.

**Most field goals in an NBA season** The most field goals scored by one player in an NBA season is 1,597 by Wilt Chamberlain (USA) in 1961–62 for the Philadelphia Warriors.

**MOST FREE THROWS IN AN NBA CAREER** The most free throws in an NBA career is 9,443 in 1,405 games by Karl Malone (USA) playing for the Utah Jazz from 1985 to 2003.

**Most field goals in an NBA game** The most field goals scored by an individual in an NBA game is 36 by Wilt Chamberlain (USA) when he played for the Philadelphia Warriors against the New York Knicks on March 2, 1962.

**Most three-point field goals in an NBA season** The most three-point field goals scored by an individual in an NBA season is 267 by Dennis Scott (USA) for the Orlando Magic in 1996 to 1997.

**Highest scoring average in an NBA season** The highest scoring average in a NBA season is 50.4 points per game by Wilt Chamberlain (USA) for the Philadelphia Warriors in 1961 to 1962.

**Highest aggregate score in an NBA match** The highest aggregate score in an NBA match is 370, when the Detroit Pistons (186) beat the Denver Nuggets (184) at Denver, USA, on December 13, 1983. Overtime was played after a 145–145 tie in regulation time.

The record for the highest aggregate score in regulation time is 320, when the Golden State Warriors beat Denver 162–158 on November 2, 1990.

**Greatest NBA game-winning margin** The greatest winning margin in an NBA game is 68 points, when the Cleveland Cavaliers beat Miami Heat 148–80 on December 17, 1991.

**Most points in NBA all-star games** The most points scored in NBA All-Star games is 262 by Michael Jordan (USA). He scored 20 points in his 14th appearance in Atlanta, Georgia, USA, on February 9, 2003.

**Most points scored in an NBA career** The most points scored in an NBA career is 38,387 (at an average of 24.6 points per game) by Kareem

Abdul-Jabbar (USA) from 1969 to 1989. This includes 15,837 field goals scored in regular season games and 5,762 points, including 2,356 field goals, scored in playoff games.

**Most consecutive NBA games played** The most consecutive NBA games played is 1,177 by A.C. Green (USA) for the Los Angeles Lakers,

**HIGHEST POINTS-SCORING AVERAGE IN AN NBA CAREER** The highest points-per-game scoring average for players exceeding 10,000 points is 30.1 by Michael Jordan (USA), who scored 32,292 points in 1,072 games for the Chicago Bulls (1984–98) and the Washington Wizards (2001–03).

**MOST STEALS IN AN NBA CAREER** The most steals in an NBA career is 3,216 in 1,475 games by John Stockton (USA) playing for the Utah Jazz from 1984 to 2003.

Phoenix Suns, Dallas Mavericks, and Miami Heat from November 19, 1986 to March 20, 2001.

**Longest basketball marathon** The longest basketball marathon lasted for 26 hr. 42 min. The record was set by Warwick Academy (Bermuda) at the Bermuda College gym, Paget, Bermuda, from March 15 to 16, 2003. In all, 27 games were played.

**Most consecutive free throws** Ted St. Martin (USA) scored 5,221 consecutive free throws at Jacksonville, Florida, USA, on April 28, 1996.

**Most consecutive free throws in an NBA season** Mike Williams (USA), of the Minnesota Timberwolves, made 97 consecutive free throws in NBA matches between March 24 and November 9, 1993.

**Farthest headed basketball shot**  Eyal Horn (Israel) shot a basketball with his head while standing a distance of 25 ft. (7.62 m) from the backboard in Los Angeles, USA, on November 10, 2000.

**Farthest basketball dribble**  The greatest distance covered in 24 hours while dribbling a basketball is 97.37 miles (156.71 km) by Suresh Joachim (Australia) at Vulkanhallen, Oslo, Norway, from March 30 to 31, 2001.

**Most basketballs dribbled simultaneously**  On August 15, 2000 at his home in Mesa, Arizona, USA, Joseph Odhiambo (USA) dribbled six basketballs simultaneously, beating his previous record of five.

**Most assists in an NBA career**  The most assists in an NBA career is 15,585 in 1,475 games by John Stockton (USA) playing for the Utah Jazz from 1984 to 2003.

**Most rebounds in an NBA career**  The most rebounds in an NBA career is 23,924 in 1,045 games by Wilt Chamberlain (USA) playing for the Philadelphia Warriors (1959–62), San Francisco Warriors (1962–65), Philadelphia 76ers (1965–68), and Los Angeles Lakers (1968–73).

**Most blocks in an NBA career**  The most blocks in an NBA career is 3,830 in 1,238 games by Hakeem Olajuwon (USA) playing for the Houston Rockets (1984–2001) and the Toronto Raptors (2001–02).

**Tallest NBA player**  The tallest ever NBA player was Gheorghe Muresan (Romania) of the Washington Bullets, who was 7 ft. 7 in. (2.31 m). His first game was in 1994.

**Youngest NBA player to start a game**  The youngest player to start an NBA game is Kobe Bryant (USA), who played for the Los Angeles Lakers against the Dallas Mavericks on January 28, 1997 at age 18 years 158 days.

# ICE HOCKEY

**Most points scored in an NHL career**  The most points scored in an NHL career is 2,857, by Wayne Gretzky (Canada) for the Edmonton Oilers, Los Angeles Kings, St. Louis Blues, and New York Rangers between 1979 and 1999. The points total comprises 894 goals and 1,963 assists achieved in 1,487 games.

**Most points scored in the Stanley Cup**  The most points scored in the Stanley Cup is 47, by Wayne Gretzky (Canada) for the Edmonton Oilers in 1985. The points scored comprise 17 goals and 30 assists, which are in themselves records.

**MOST HAT-TRICKS IN A CAREER** The greatest number of hat-tricks scored in a National Hockey League (NHL) career is 50, by Wayne Gretzky (Canada, shown here with the 1999 All-Star trophy). He played in the NHL between 1979 and 1999.

**Most men's Olympic ice hockey wins** The most men's Olympic ice hockey titles won is eight by the USSR in 1956, 1964, 1968, 1972, 1976, 1984, 1988, and 1992 (as the CIS).

**Most wins in an NHL season** The most wins in an NHL season is 62 by the Detroit Red Wings (USA) in the 1995/96 season.

**Most losses in an NHL season** The most losses in an NHL season is 71 by the San Jose Sharks (USA), who managed this in the 1992/93 season, despite playing a record 32 games at home.

**Longest NHL winning streak** The longest run of winning games home and away in NHL history is 17 by the Pittsburgh Penguins (USA) between March 9 and April 10, 1993.

**Longest ice hockey game** The longest game of ice hockey lasted 62 hr. 15 min. and was played by the Moosomin Moose Hockey Team, at Moosomin Communiplex, Saskatchewan, Canada, from January 9 to 12, 2003.

**Most team goals in an NHL season** The most goals scored by a team in an NHL season is 446 by the Edmonton Oilers (Canada) in 1983/84. In the same season they also achieved a record 1,182 points.

**Most goals in an NHL season by a rookie** Teemu Selanne (Finland) scored a total of 76 goals in his first season for the Winnipeg Jets in 1992/93.

**Most games in a professional ice hockey career** The most games played in a professional career is 2,421 by Gordon "Gordie" Howe (Canada) from 1946 to 1979. This includes 1,767 regular season games and 157 play-off games for the Detroit Red Wings and the Hartford Whalers in the NHL, and 419 regular season games and 78 playoff games for the Houston Aeros and the New England Whalers in the World Hockey Association.

**Quickest NHL goal** The fastest time for a goal to be scored in an NHL match is five seconds. This record is shared by three players: Doug Smail (Canada) for the Winnipeg Jets against the St. Louis Blues in Winnipeg, Manitoba, Canada, on December 20, 1981; Bryan John Trottier (Canada) for the New York Islanders against the Boston Bruins in Boston, Massachusetts, USA, on March 22, 1984; and Alexander Mogilny (Russia) for the Buffalo Sabres against the Toronto Maple Leafs in Toronto, Ontario, Canada, on December 21, 1991.

**Quickest ice hockey goal** Per Olsen (Denmark) scored two seconds after the start of the match for Rungsted against Odense in the Danish First

**MOST WOMEN'S ICE HOCKEY WORLD CHAMPIONSHIPS The women's ice hockey World Championships have been held since 1990 and have been won on each occasion—a total of seven times—by Canada (in 1990, 1992, 1994, 1997, 1999, 2000, and 2001). In winning the seven titles, Canada (shown here winning Olympic gold in 2002) have not lost one game.**

Division at Hørsholm, Denmark, on January 14, 1990. Jørgen Palmgren Erichsen (Norway) scored three goals in 10 seconds for Frisk against Holmen in a junior league match in Norway on March 17, 1991.

**Most ice hockey targets shot in 30 seconds**  Daniel Wågström (Sweden) hit four goal targets in 30 seconds on the set of the *Guinness Rekord TV* program in Stockholm, Sweden, on November 5, 2001.

**Most assists in an NHL career**  The most assists in an NHL career is 1,963 by Wayne Gretzky (Canada), for the Edmonton Oilers, the Los Angeles Kings, the St. Louis Blues, and the New York Rangers between 1979 and 1999.

**Most goaltending shutouts in an NHL career**  The most goaltending shutouts in an NHL career is 103 achieved by Terry Sawchuk (USA) for the Detroit Red Wings, the Boston Bruins, the Toronto Maple Leafs, the Los Angeles Kings, and the New York Rangers between 1949 and 1970.

**Most goaltending shutouts in NHL playoffs**  The most shutouts by a goaltender in NHL playoff history is 22 by Patrick Roy (Canada) playing for the Montreal Canadiens and the Colorado Avalanche between 1985 and 2002.

**Most career wins by an NHL goaltender**  At the end of the 2002 regular season, the most NHL career wins by a goaltender was 516 by Patrick Roy (Canada) of the Colorado Avalanche. Roy began his NHL career with the Montreal Canadiens in 1985.

**Most consecutive NHL games played**  The most consecutive NHL games played is 964 by Doug Jarvis (Canada) playing for the Montreal Canadiens, the Washington Capitals and the Hartford Whalers from October 8, 1975 to October 10, 1987.

**Most NHL playoff penalty minutes**  The most penalty minutes amassed in NHL playoff games is 729 by Dale Hunter (Canada) playing for the Quebec Nordiques, Washington Capitals, and Colorado Avalanche from 1980 to 1999.

**Most penalty minutes in an NHL career**  The player with the most penalty minutes in NHL history is Dave "Tiger" Williams (Canada) with 3,966, amassed over 17 seasons between 1971 and 1988, playing for the Toronto Maple Leafs, the Vancouver Canucks, the Detroit Red Wings, the Los Angeles Kings, and the now defunct Hartford Whalers.

**Most penalties in an NHL game**  The most penalties awarded in an NHL game is 85 when the Edmonton Oilers played the Los Angeles Kings in Los Angeles, California, USA, on February 28, 1990.

**Longest NHL infraction suspension**  The longest suspension handed to a player for an on-ice incident is 23 games to Marty McSorley (Canada)

**MOST NHL ALL-STAR SELECTIONS** Gordie Howe (Canada) was selected 21 times for National Hockey League All-Star games while playing for the Detroit Red Wings between 1946 and 1979. He was selected for the first team on 12 occasions and the second team nine times.

of the Boston Bruins in February 2000. McSorley had struck Vancouver Canucks' Donald Brashear (Canada) on the head with his stick during a game at Vancouver, British Columbia, Canada, on February 21, 2000.

**Most overall goals in a winter paralympics ice sledge hockey competition** The most goals scored overall in the ice sledge hockey competition at the Winter Paralympics is 16 by Jens Kask (Sweden); four in 1994, seven in 1998 and five in 2002.

**Most overall assists in a winter paralympics ice sledge hockey competition** The most overall assists in an ice sledge hockey competition at the Winter Paralympics is 16 by Helge Bjoernstad (Norway); one in 1994, five in 1998, and 10 in 2002. The total for 2002 is a record for a single Games.

# SOCCER

**Most countries in FIFA World Cup qualifiers** A record 198 federations registered to play in the qualifiers for the 2002 FIFA World Cup, held jointly in South Korea and Japan. The football federations of Afghanistan, Burundi, New Guinea, Niger, and North Korea were the exceptions.

**Most goals in a World Cup Finals** The most goals scored by a player in a single World Cup Finals tournament is 13 by Just Fontaine (France) in Sweden in 1958.

**Most World Cup clean sheets** The goalkeeper to have kept the most clean sheets in World Cup Finals matches is Peter Shilton (UK), who played for England in a total of 10 matches in three tournaments between 1982 and 1990 without conceding a single goal.

**Fastest World Cup red card** The fastest time to be sent off in a World Cup Finals soccer match is 3 minutes by Ion Vladoiu (Romania) playing against Switzerland on June 22, 1994 at the Pontiac Silverdome, Detroit, Michigan, USA.

**Most Olympic titles won** The most Olympic soccer titles won is three, by Great Britain in 1900 (unofficial competition), 1908, 1912; and Hungary, in 1952, 1964, 1968.

**Most women's Olympic soccer titles** Women's soccer was introduced to the Olympic Games in 1996. The winners have been the USA in 1996 and Norway in 2000.

**Most Futsal World Cup titles** Since it was first held in 1989, the Futsal (indoor soccer) World Cup has been won three times by Brazil, in 1989, 1992, and 1996. The fourth tournament, held in 2000 in Guatemala, was won by Spain, who beat Brazil in the final.

**Most European Cup wins** The most European Champions Cup (instituted 1956) wins is nine by Real Madrid (Spain), in 1956–60, 1966, 1998, 2000, and 2002.

**Most African Cup of Nations wins** The record for the most wins at the African Cup of Nations is four, held jointly by Ghana (1963, 1965, 1978,

1982), Egypt (1957, 1959, 1986, 1998) and Cameroon (1984, 1998, 2000, 2002).

**Most Asian Cup wins** The most wins in the Asian Cup is three, by Iran in 1968, 1972, and 1976, and Saudi Arabia in 1984, 1988, and 1996.

**Highest score in an international soccer match** The highest score ever achieved in an international match is 31-0 by Australia against Ameri-

**MOST WORLD CUP WINS** The Fédération Internationale de Football Association (FIFA), which was founded on May 21, 1904, instituted the first World Cup on July 13, 1930, in Montevideo, Uruguay. The tournament is held quadrennially. Brazil has won five times, in 1958, 1962, 1970, 1994, and 2002. Brazil's captain Cafu lifted the trophy in 2002 in Yokohama, Japan.

**MOST WORLD CUP FINALS GOALS** The most goals scored in World
Cup Finals tournaments is 14 by Gerd Müller (West Germany), who
scored 10 in 1970 in Mexico and four in West Germany in 1974, when
the host nation went on to lift the trophy.

can Samoa. It occurred in a World Cup qualifying match at Coffs Harbour,
New South Wales, Australia, on April 11, 2001. During the match, Archie
Thompson (Australia) scored an international record 13 goals.

**Most expensive soccer player** The highest transfer fee quoted for a
player is a reported 13 billion Spanish pesetas ($66.36 million or £47 mil-
lion) for Zinedine Zidane (France) for his transfer from Juventus (Italy) to
Real Madrid (Spain) on July 9, 2001.

**Oldest soccer ground** The first competitive game was played on December 26, 1860 at Sandygate, owned by Hallam FC, Sheffield, South Yorkshire, UK.

**Oldest cup competition** The oldest soccer trophy is the Youdan Cup,
first won in 1867 by Hallam FC in Sheffield, South Yorkshire, UK.

**Highest score in a women's international match** In a women's inter-
national, the record score is 210 and has occurred on four occasions: Japan
against Guam at Guangzhou, China, on December 5, 1997; Canada against
Puerto Rico at Centennial Park, Toronto, Canada, on August 28, 1998; and
Australia against American Samoa, and New Zealand against Samoa, both at
Mt. Smart Stadium, Auckland, New Zealand, on October 9, 1998.

**Most league titles** The record number of successive national league championships is eleven by Al-Ansar Sporting Club of Lebanon, who were top of their league between 1988 and 1999.

**Fastest hat-trick** The fastest time to score three goals is 2 min. 13 sec. by Jimmy O'Connor (Ireland) for Shelbourne against Bohemians at Dallymount Park, Dublin, on November 19, 1967.

**Fastest hat-trick in an international** Japanese international masashi "Gon" Nakayama scored a hat-trick in 3 min. 15 sec. against Brunei during an Asian Cup qualifying match on February 16, 2000. Nakayama netted on 1 min., 2 min. and 3 min. 15 sec., bettering the 62-year-old mark set by England's George Hall, who scored three goals in 3 min. 30 sec. against Ireland.

**Most World Cup hat-tricks** Four players have scored two hat-tricks in World Cup tournaments: Sándor Kocsis (Hungary) at the 1954 tournament in Switzerland; Just Fontaine (France) in Sweden in 1958; Gerd Müller (West Germany) at the 1970 tournament in Mexico; and Gabriel Batistuta (Argentina) on his World Cup debut against Greece in the USA in 1994, and against Jamaica in France in 1998.

**Most goals in a career** The most goals scored in a specified period is 1,279 by Edson Arantes do Nascimento (known as Pelé, Brazil), from September 7, 1956 to October 1, 1977 in 1,363 games. His best year was 1959 with 126 goals, and the *Milésimo* (1,000th) came from a penalty for his club Santos at the Maracanã Stadium, Rio de Janeiro, Brazil, on November 19, 1969 when playing his 909th first-class match. He later added two more goals in special appearances.

**Most goals scored direct from corner kicks** The most goals scored in a single match by an individual direct from corners is three by Steve Cromey (UK) for Ashgreen Utd. against Dunlop FC on February 24, 2002 at Bedworth, Warwickshire, UK, and by Daniel White (UK) for Street and Glastonbury under-11s against Westfield Boys on April 7, 2002.

**Most penalties missed by a player in an international** Martin Palermo (Argentina) missed three penalties during his team's defeat by Colombia in the 1999 Copa América in Paraguay. His first shot hit the crossbar, the second landed in the stands, and the third was saved.

**Fastest soccer kick** The fastest soccer kick is 80.1 mph (129 km/h) achieved by Francisco Javier Galan Màrin (Spain) at the studios of *El Show de los Récords,* Madrid, Spain, on October 29, 2001.

**Most undisciplined soccer match** In the local cup match between Tongham Youth Club, Surrey, UK, and Hawley, Hampshire, UK, on Novem-

**FASTEST GOAL IN A WORLD CUP FINALS MATCH** The quickest goal scored in a World Cup Finals match, as recognized by FIFA, is 11 seconds, by Hakan Sukur for Turkey against South Korea at Daegu, South Korea, on June 29, 2002.

ber 3, 1969, the referee booked all 22 players, including one who went to the hospital, and one of the linesmen. The match, won by Tongham 2-0, was described by a player as "a good, hard game."

**Fastest goal** Goals scored in three seconds and under, following kickoff, have been claimed by a number of players. From video evidence, Ricardo Olivera (Uruguay) scored in 2.8 seconds for Rio Negro against

Soriano at the José Enrique Rodó stadium, Soriano, Uruguay, on December 26, 1998.

**Youngest player in all four English soccer divisions** The youngest person to play in all four divisions of the soccer league is Melvyn John Rees (UK, b. January 25, 1967). Rees achieved this feat during the 1987/88 season, at just 20 years of age, playing for Watford. The goalkeeper previously turned out for Cardiff City and went on to play in the inaugural season of the Premiership in 1992/93 for Sheffield United, following a spell at West Bromwich Albion. Having already fought off one attack of cancer, he succumbed to a recurrence in 1993, aged 26.

**Most goals in a Major League Soccer game** The most goals scored in a Major League Soccer (MLS) game by a player is five by Clint Mathis (USA) for the MetroStars against the Dallas Burn on August 26, 2000. Mathis' team went on to win the game with a final score of 6–4.

**Most assists in a Major League Soccer season** The most assists by one player in an MLS season is 26 by Carlos Valderama (Colombia) for the Tampa Bay Mutiny in 2000.

**Most Major League Soccer goals** The most goals scored in MLS is 88 by Ray Lassiter (USA) for the Tampa Bay Mutiny, DC United, Miami Fusion, and Kansas City Wizards in 1996–2001.

**Most Major League Soccer titles** DC United of Washington DC, USA, has won three MLS titles, in 1996, 1997, and 1999.

**Most goals scored by a goalkeeper in one game** Paraguayan José Luis Chilavert scored a hat-trick of penalties for Vélez Sarsfield in their 6–1 defeat of Ferro Carril Oeste in the Argentine professional league. A penalty and free kick specialist, Chilavert also holds the record for the most goals scored by a goalkeeper, with 56 league and international goals from July 1992 to October 2001 for Paraguay and Strasbourg, France. He is the only goalkeeper to score in a World Cup qualifier.

**Highest score in a national soccer Cup Final** In 1935 Lausanne-Sports beat Nordstern Basel 10–0 in the Swiss Cup Final. Two years later they were beaten by an identical margin by Grasshopper-Club (Zurich) in the same Cup Final.

**Most soccer matches played** Peter Shilton (UK) made a record 1,389 senior appearances, including a record 1,005 league appearances—comprising 286 for Leicester City (1966–74), 110 for Stoke City (1974–77), 202 for Nottingham Forest (1977–82), 188 for Southampton (1982–87), 175 for Derby County (1987–92), 34 for Plymouth Argyle (1992–94), one for Bolton Wanderers (1995), and nine for Leyton Orient (1996–97)—one League play-off, 86 FA Cups, 102 League Cups, 125 internationals, 13 Under-23s, four Football League XIs, and 53 various European and other club competitions.

**MOST EXPENSIVE DEFENDER**  Rio Ferdinand (UK, left in picture) continued to be the world's most expensive defender in July 2002 after joining Manchester United from Leeds United (both UK) in a deal worth a reported $46.9 million (£30 million).

**Longest clean sheet**  The longest that any goalkeeper has succeeded in preventing goals being scored past him in top class competition is 1,275 minutes (just over 14 matches) by Abel Resino (Spain) of Atlético Madrid. The record in international matches is 1,142 minutes (nearly 13 matches) by Dino Zoff (Italy) from September 1972 to June 1974.

**Most European Championships** Germany has won the European Championship three times, in 1972, 1980 and 1996 (the first two as West Germany). A women's version was first held in 1984, and the most wins is four by Germany, in 1989, 1991, 1995 and 1997.

**Most Champions League victories** Real Madrid (Spain) has won the most UEFA Champions League matches with 49 victories between 1992 and 2003, scoring a record 176 goals in the process. With 46 wins and 162 goals, Manchester United (UK) is second.

**Most Champions League appearances** The most UEFA Champions League appearances by an individual player is 76 by Gary Neville (UK) for Manchester United between 1993 and 2003, having made his debut against Galatasaray in Istanbul, Turkey, in a second round tie.

**Most Champions League goals** Raúl González Blanco (Spain) has scored 39 goals in UEFA Champions League matches, playing for Real Madrid from 1992 to date.

**Largest soccer ball** A soccer ball made from artificial leather PV-PVC and sewn by hand, made by Ihsan Sports (Pakistan), had a diameter of 13 ft. 1 in. (4 m) when measured on June 30, 2002.

**Most consecutive soccer passes** The most consecutive soccer passes is 557 by members of the McDonald's Youth Football Scheme at Tsing Yi,

**FASTEST CHAMPIONS LEAGUE GOAL** The fastest goal in a Champions League match was scored by Gilberto Silva (Brazil) in 20.07 seconds playing for UK club Arsenal against Dutch side PSV Eindhoven in Eindhoven, The Netherlands, on September 25, 2002. Arsenal went on to win the game 4–0.

**MOST INTERNATIONAL CAPS**
The most international appearances for a national team by a player is 170 by Claudio Suarez (Mexico) between 1992 and 2002.

Hong Kong, China, on May 4, 2002. The event lasted four and a half hours, and 1,250 children aged 6 to 14 took part.

**Longest time spinning a ball on the forehead** On November 25, 2001 Tommy Baker (UK) spun a FIFA-approved soccer ball on his forehead for a record 11.9 seconds after transferring it from his finger at the studios of *Guinness Rekord TV* in Stockholm, Sweden.

**Longest time heading a ball** The world record for heading a soccer ball without it dropping is 8 hr. 12 min. 25 sec. by Goderdzi Makharadze (Georgia) at the Boris Paichadze National Stadium, Tbilisi, Georgia, on May 26, 1996.

**Farthest distance traveled keeping a soccer ball in the air** Jan Skorkovsky (Czechoslovakia) kept a soccer ball in the air without it dropping while traveling 26.219 miles (42.195 km) as a competitor in the Prague City marathon on July 8, 1990. He finished the marathon in a time of 7 hr. 18 min. 55 sec.

**Most people juggling a soccer ball simultaneously** The most individuals each keeping a soccer ball in the air at the same time is 446 by teams of girls taking part in the Football Association National Centres of Excellence Festival at the University of Warwick, Coventry, UK, on June 19, 1999.

**Most touches of a soccer ball in 30 seconds** The most touches of a soccer ball in 30 seconds, while keeping the ball in the air, is 136 by Ferdie Adoboe (USA) at Fort Lowell Park, Tucson, Arizona, USA, on January 22, 1999. He also completed 262 touches in one minute, a record that he went on to break in July 2000 with 266 touches.

# RUGBY

**Most conversions in 12 hours**  The most rugby conversions kicked in 12 hours is 1,782 by members of Braintree (UK) under-15s rugby squad on July 13, 2002 at Braintree Rugby Club, Braintree, Essex, UK. The kicks were taken from three positions along the 22-meter line.

**Most consecutive Rugby League appearances**  Keith Elwell (UK) played in 239 consecutive games for Widnes from May 5, 1977 to September 5, 1982.

**Most consecutive hat-tricks in Rugby League**  The most consecutive matches in which an individual player has scored a hat-trick of tries is 12 by Richard Lopag of Deighton New Saracens, Huddersfield, West Yorkshire, UK, during the 2000/01 season.

**Most Rugby League World Cup wins**  Australia has won the World Cup eight times, in 1957, 1968, 1970, 1977, 1988, 1992, 1995, and 2000, as well as a win in the International Championship of 1975. The competition was first held in 1954.

**Most Rugby League Challenge Cup wins**  The Rugby League Challenge Cup (inaugurated 1896/97 season) has been won 17 times by

**MOST INTERNATIONAL APPEARANCES BY A RUGBY UNION FORWARD**
Jason Leonard (UK) has played 102 times for England. The prop was awarded his first cap in July 1990 against Argentina in Buenos Aires, and he won his 100th against France in the Six Nations Championship at Twickenham, UK, in February 2003.

**MOST WORLD SEVENS SERIES TITLES** The World Sevens Series, which began in 1999, has been won every year by New Zealand (team captain Eric Rush pictured) in 2000, 2001, and 2002. The series is a competition consisting of between nine and eleven separate sevens tournaments played around the world each season.

Wigan, in 1924, 1929, 1948, 1951, 1958–59, 1965, 1985, 1988–95, and 2002.

**Highest score in an international Rugby League match** The highest score in an international league match is Australia's 110–4 defeat of Russia during the Rugby League World Cup at Hull, East Yorkshire, UK, on November 4, 2000.

**Most points scored by an individual in an international Rugby League match** Hazem El Masri (Lebanon) scored a record 48 points (16 goals, 4 tries) against Morocco in a World Cup qualifying match at Avignon, France, on November 17, 1999.

**Most Super League titles** The most Super League titles won by a team is four by St. Helens, in 1996, 1999, 2000, and 2002. The Super League is the UK's premier rugby league competition, instituted in 1996.

**Highest attendance at a Rugby Union match** The largest paying attendance for an international match is 109,874 on July 15, 2000 for New Zealand's 39–35 Tri-Nations victory over Australia at Stadium Australia, Sydney, NSW, Australia.

**Most points scored by an individual in a Rugby Union season** The first class season scoring record is 581 points by Samuel Arthur Doble

(UK) for Moseley in 52 matches in 1971/72. He also scored 47 points for England in South Africa out of season.

**Most international Rugby Union appearances** Philippe Sella (France) played in 111 internationals for France between 1982 and 1995.

**Most Rugby Union World Cup wins** The most wins of the Webb Ellis Trophy (instituted 1987) is two by Australia, in 1991 and 1999.

**Highest combined score in a professional cross-code rugby match** The highest combined points score in a professional cross-code rugby match is 80 points scored between St. Helens (Rugby League) and Sale Sharks (Rugby Union) at Knowsley Road, St. Helens, Merseyside, UK, on January 27, 2003. Sale Sharks won the match 41–39.

**Most women's Rugby Union World Cup titles** The women's World Cup has been contested four times (1991, 1994, 1998, and 2002). New Zealand has won the title twice, in 1998 and 2002, while USA and England have one win apiece.

**Most points in an international Rugby Union career** Neil Jenkins (UK) has scored 1,052 points in 86 matches for Wales (1,011 points in 83

**MOST NRL TITLES** The most National Rugby League (NRL) titles won by a team is two by the Brisbane Broncos, in 1998 and 2000. The NRL is Australia's premier rugby league competition, instituted in 1998. Broncos fullback Darren Lockyer (Australia) is pictured.

matches) and the British Lions (41 points in three matches), between 1991 and March 2001.

**Most Tri-Nations titles** The Tri-Nations, inaugurated in 1996 and played annually between Australia, New Zealand and South Africa, has been won a record four times by New Zealand, in 1996–97, 1999, and 2002.

**Most consecutive international Rugby Union appearances** The most consecutive international appearances is 63 by hooker Sean Fitzpatrick (New Zealand) between 1986 and 1995.

**Most points scored by a team in the Six Nations Tournament** England scored a record 229 points in their five games in 2001.

**Most Six Nations Championships** England has won more Six Nations Championships than any other country, with three wins in 2000, 2001, and 2003. Their 2003 campaign was also a grand slam win. The Six Nations replaced the Five Nations tournament in 2000 when Italy was invited to join the historic competition.

**Most international grand slams** The most grand slams—winning all matches in what was the Five and is now the Six Nations Championship—is 12 by England between 1913 and 2003.

**Highest Rugby Union posts** The posts at the Roan Antelope Rugby Union Club, Luanshya, Zambia, are the world's highest, at 110 ft. 0.5 in. (33.54 m).

# CRICKET

**Fastest Test double century** The fastest 200 scored in a Test match was by Nathan Astle (New Zealand) playing against England in the first Test at Jade Stadium, Christchurch, New Zealand, on March 17, 2002. He reached the 200 mark in 153 balls and proceeded to score 222 of 168, including 28 fours and 11 sixes. England, however, went on to win the game by 98 runs, making Astle's effort the highest individual innings in a lost game.

**Most runs in Test cricket** Allan Border (Australia) scored 11,174 runs in 156 Tests (av. 50.56) between 1978 and 1994.

**Most centuries in Test cricket** Sunil Gavaskar (India) scored 34 centuries (in 214 innings) playing for India between 1971 and 1987.

**Highest individual Test innings** Brian Lara (Trinidad) scored 375 in 12 hr. 48 min. for the West Indies against England at Recreation Ground, St. John's, Antigua, on April 16–18, 1994.

**HIGHEST BATTING AVERAGE IN TEST CRICKET** Don Bradman (Australia, pictured on right of photo with Australian captain Bill Woodfull), holds the record for the highest batting average with 99.94, playing for Australia in 52 Tests (6,996 runs in 80 innings) from 1928–1948.

**Most catches in Test cricket** Mark Waugh (Australia) made 181 catches in 128 Tests for Australia between 1991 and 2002.

**Most extras conceded in a Test innings** The West Indies conceded a total of 71 sundries in Pakistan's first innings at Georgetown, Guyana, on April 3–4, 1988. This figure was made up of 21 byes, eight leg byes, four wides, and 38 no-balls.

**Highest Test score** Sri Lanka scored 952 for 6 against India at Colombo, Sri Lanka, between August 4 and 6, 1997.

**Highest maiden Test century score** Garfield Sobers (Barbados) scored 365 not out for the West Indies against Pakistan at Kingston, Jamaica, on February 27–28 and March 1, 1958.

**Biggest Test partnership** On August 4–6, 1997, Sanath Jayasuriya (340) and Roshan Mahanama (225) scored 576 for the second wicket for Sri Lanka against India at Colombo, Sri Lanka.

**Lowest innings total** The lowest innings total in Test cricket is 26 by New Zealand against England at Auckland, New Zealand, on March 28, 1955.

**Lowest Test bowling average** George Lohmann (England) had a bowling average of 10.75 playing for England. He appeared in 18 tests between 1886 and 1896 and took 112 wickets.

**Most catches by a wicketkeeper** Ian Healy (Australia) made 366 catches in 119 Tests playing for Australia between 1988 and 1999.

**Oldest Test cricket player** The oldest man to play in a Test match was Wilfred Rhodes (UK), age 52 years 165 days, for England against the West Indies at Kingston, Jamaica, on April 12, 1930. Rhodes made his debut in the last Test captained by WG Grace (UK) who, at 50 years 320 days old on June 3, 1899, was the oldest ever Test captain.

**Most "ducks" in Test matches** The player who has the dubious honor of scoring the most "ducks" (or zeros) in Test cricket is Courtney Walsh (Jamaica) with 43 in 185 innings for the West Indies, between November 1984 and April 2001.

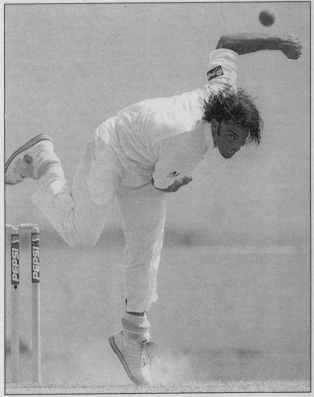

**FASTEST BOWLING** The highest electronically measured speed for a ball bowled by any bowler is 100.23 mph (161.3 km/h) by Shoaib Akhtar (Pakistan) against England on February 22, 2003 in a World Cup match at Newlands, Cape Town, South Africa.

**Best one-day international bowling start** The best bowling start to a match was made by Chaminda Vass (Sri Lanka) playing in a World Cup game for Sri Lanka against Canada at Pietermaritzburg, South Africa, on February 15, 2003. He took a hat-trick with the first three balls of the game and then claimed a fourth victim in his opening over before finishing with 6 for 25. Sri Lanka went on to win the match by 10 wickets.

**FASTEST WORLD CUP CENTURY** The fastest World Cup 100 runs scored by an individual was made in 67 balls by John Davison (Canada) playing against the West Indies at Centurion Park, Northern Transvaal, South Africa, on February 23, 2003. The innings contained eight fours and six sixes.

**Lowest one-day international team score**  The lowest completed innings total is 36 by Canada against Sri Lanka at Boland Park, Paarl, South Africa, on February 19, 2003.

**Most wickets in a one-day international career**  The most wickets taken in a one-day career is 502 (at an average of 23.52) by Wasim Akram (Pakistan) in 356 matches between 1985 and 2003.

**Highest batting average in a season**  The highest batting average for a season is 330 by Colin Gill (UK) for Plymstock 2nd XI playing in the Devon Cricket League in 1998. Gill batted 10 times and was dismissed just once in the season.

**Highest individual innings score**  Brian Lara (Trinidad) scored 501 not out in 7 hr. 54 min. for Warwickshire against Durham at Edgbaston, West Midlands, UK, between June 3 and 6, 1994. His innings included the most runs in a day (390 on June 6) and the most runs from boundaries (308–62 fours and 10 sixes).

**Highest innings in a limited overs match**  The highest innings by an individual in a limited overs match is 268 by Surrey's Alistair Brown (UK) against Glamorgan on June 19, 2002 at The Oval, London, UK, in a Cheltenham and Gloucester Trophy match. During his stay at the wicket, Brown hit 12 sixes and 30 fours.

The highest score by a team in a limited overs match is 438 by Surrey against Glamorgan in the same match.

**Longest individual innings**  On November 1–3, 1999 Rajiv Nayyar (India) batted for 16 hr. 55 min. when scoring 271 for Himachal Pradesh against Jammu and Kashmir at Chamba, India.

**Most World Cup wins**  The most tournament wins is three by Australia in 1987, 1999 and 2003.

**Highest and lowest World Cup team scores**  The highest innings total in a cricket World Cup match is 398–5 by Sri Lanka against Kenya at Kandy, Sri Lanka, on March 6, 1996.

The lowest cricket World Cup score is 36 by Canada against Sri Lanka at Boland Park, Paarl, South Africa, on February 19, 2003.

**Most runs off a ball**  Garry Chapman (Australia) scored 17 (all run, with no overthrows) off a single delivery for Banyule against Macleod at Windsor Reserve, Victoria, Australia, on October 13, 1990. Chapman had pulled the ball to mid-wicket where it disappeared into 10-in-high (25-cm) grass.

**Youngest Test player**  Hasan Raza (Pakistan, b. 11 March 1982) made his debut at 14 years 227 days, against Zimbabwe at Faisalabad, Pakistan, on October 24, 1996.

# BALL SPORTS

## HOCKEY

**Most appearances in men's hockey** By January 2001 Jacques Brinkman had represented The Netherlands 337 times since his debut in 1985.

**Most appearances in women's hockey** Karen Brown made a record 355 international appearances for England and Great Britain between 1984 and 1999.

**Most goals scored in a hockey career** David Ashman (UK) scored a record 2,326 goals in hockey, having played for UK sides Hampshire, Southampton, Southampton Kestrals, and Hamble Old Boys (for whom he scored 2,165 goals, a record for one club) between 1958 and 1999.

**Most goals scored by a player in a hockey game** M.C. Marckx (UK) scored 19 goals playing for Bowdon 2nd XI against Brooklands 2nd XI (final score 23–0) on December 31, 1910. He was selected for the England team in March 1912 but declined because of business priorities.

**MOST MEN'S WORLD CUP HOCKEY WINS** The FIH hockey World Cup for men was first held in 1971. The most wins by a team is four by Pakistan, in 1971, 1978, 1982, and 1994. Pakistan's current captain, Muhammad Nadeem, is shown.

**MOST MEN'S OLYMPIC BEACH VOLLEYBALL WINS** Beach volleyball has been part of the Olympic Games since 1996, and the USA has won the men's competition on both occasions. Karch Kiraly and Kent Steffes won in Atlanta in 1996, and Dain Blanton and Eric Fonoimoana won in Sydney in 2000.

**Highest score in international men's hockey** The highest score in a men's international hockey match was achieved when India defeated the USA 24–1 in Los Angeles, California, USA, in the 1932 Olympic Games.

**Highest score in international women's hockey** The highest score in an international women's hockey match was by England when they beat France 23–0 at Merton, Greater London, UK, on February 3, 1923.

**Most wins in World Cup women's hockey** The *Fédération Internationale de Hockey* (FIH) World Cup for women was first held in 1974. The most wins is five by The Netherlands, in 1974, 1978, 1983, 1986, and 1990.

## HANDBALL

**Most handball targets hit in 30 seconds** Jonas Källman (Sweden) hit a record eight handball targets in 30 seconds on the set of *Guinness Rekord TV* in Stockholm, Sweden, on November 27, 2001.

**Highest score in an international handball match** The highest score in an international handball match was recorded when the USSR beat Afghanistan 86–2 in the "Friendly Army Tournament" at Miskolc, Hungary, in August 1981.

**Highest men's Olympic handball score** The highest handball score in a match at the Olympic Games is 44 by Yugoslavia against Kuwait in 1980 and by Sweden against Australia in 2000.

**Highest women's Olympic handball score** The highest score by a women's handball team in an Olympic match is 45 by Austria against Brazil at Sydney, Australia, in 2000.

**Most men's Olympic handball titles** The USSR has won the men's Olympic handball title three times, in 1976, 1988, and 1992 as the Unified Team from the republics of the former USSR.

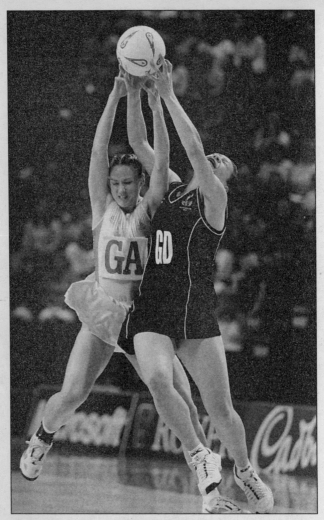

**MOST COMMONWEALTH GAMES NETBALL TITLES** Netball has been
contested twice at the Commonwealth Games—first in Kuala Lumpur,
Malaysia, in 1998 and in Manchester, UK, in 2002. Australia won on
both occasions. Sherelle McMahon (Australia) battles Sherly Clarke
(New Zealand, on the right) for the ball in the 2002, New Zealand v.
Australia final, above.

**Most men's European Cup handball titles** Two teams have won the men's European Cup five times: Vfl Gummersbach (West Germany) in 1969–71, 1974, and 1983; and Barcelona (Spain) in 1991 and 1996–99. Vfl Gummersbach is the only club team to win all three European trophies: the European Champions' Cup, the European Cup Winners' Cup, and the IHF Cup.

# KORFBALL

**Largest korfball tournament** On June 12, 1999 a total of 1,796 players participated in the *Kom Keukens/Ten Donck* international youth korfball tournament in Ridderkerk, The Netherlands. The games were played by the rules of the Royal Dutch Korfball Association

**Most korfball World Games titles** First held as part of the World Games in 1985, the korfball World Games title has been won five times (the total number of times that the event has been held) by The Netherlands, in 1985, 1989, 1993, 1997, and 2001. In winning these five titles, the Dutch team has never lost a match.

**Highest final score in World Championship korfball** The highest team score in the final of the Korfball World Championships is 23 by The Netherlands against Belgium (11) in 1999. The margin of victory was the greatest in a final.

# LACROSSE

**Most women's international lacrosse appearances** Vivien Jones (UK) played in 97 internationals (85 for Wales, nine for the Celts, and three for Great Britain) between 1977 and 2001.

**Most women's lacrosse World Cup titles** The women's lacrosse World Cup replaced the World Championships in 1982. The USA has won six times, in 1974, 1982, 1989, 1993, 1997, and 2001.

**Most men's lacrosse World Championships** The USA has won eight of the nine men's lacrosse World Championships, in 1967, 1974, 1982, 1986, 1990, 1994, 1998, and 2002.

# STICKBALL

**Longest stickball hit** Josue Rodriguez (USA) hit a self-pitched ball a distance of 315 ft. (96 m) with a stickball bat in New York, USA, on September 30, 2000.

# VOLLEYBALL

**Most men's Olympic volleyball titles** Introduced into the Olympic Games in 1964 for men and women, volleyball has been dominated by teams from the former USSR, the men's team winning a record three titles, in 1964, 1968, and 1980.

**Most women's Olympic volleyball titles**  The USSR women's volleyball team has won four gold Olympic medals, in 1968, 1972, 1980, and 1988.

**Most men's World volleyball titles**  The USSR won six World Championship titles, in 1949, 1952, 1960, 1962, 1978, and 1982.

**Highest beach volleyball career earnings**  Karch Kiraly (USA) amassed a record $2,929,158 (£1,872,708) in official AVP Tour earnings through the end of the 2002 season.

## CANADIAN FOOTBALL

**Most touchdowns scored in a CFL season**  Cory Philpot (USA) scored a record 22 touchdowns for the BC Lions in the 1995 Canadian Football League season.

**Most touchdowns scored in a CFL career**  George Reed (USA) scored 137 touchdowns for the Saskatchewan Roughriders from 1963 to 1975.

**Most CFL games played**  Lui Passaglia (Canada) played a record 408 Canadian Football League games for the BC Lions between 1976 and 2000.

**Most points scored**  The most points scored in a game is 36 by Bob McNamara (Canada) for the Winnipeg Blue Bombers versus the BC Lions on October 13, 1956.

**Longest rush in Canadian football**  Two players have gained 109 yards rushing from the line of scrimmage: George Dixon (Canada) for the Montreal Alouettes against the Ottawa Roughriders on September 2, 1963; and Willie Fleming (Canada) for the BC Lions against the Edmonton Eskimos on October 17, 1964.

**Longest field goal**  The longest field goal was 60 yards by Dave

**MOST POINTS SCORED IN A CANADIAN FOOTBALL CAREER** Lui Passaglia (Canada, far right, receiving the 88th Grey Cup), who played for the BC Lions, scored a record 3,984 points in his career, which lasted from 1976 to 2000.

Ridgeway (UK) for the Saskatchewan Roughriders against the Winnipeg Blue Bombers on September 6, 1987.

**Most yards receiving in a season**  Allen Pitts (Canada) gained a record 2,036 yards receiving for the Calgary Stampeders in the 1994 season.

**MOST AUSTRALIAN FOOTBALL LEAGUE PREMIERSHIP TITLES**  The greatest number of AFL Premiership titles won is 16—by Carlton between 1906 and 1995, and Essendon between 1897 and 2000. (Near right: Essendon player Michael Long in the 2000 Grand Final versus Melbourne.)

**Most yards rushing in a game** The most yards gained rushing in a game is 287 by Ron Stewart (Canada) for the Ottawa Roughriders against the Montreal Alouettes on October 10, 1960.

**Most interceptions in a career** The most interceptions made in a Canadian football career is 396 by Ron Lancaster (Canada) for Ottawa and Saskatchewan in 1960–78.

# AUSTRALIAN FOOTBALL

**Highest team score in an AFL match** The record score by one team in an Australian Football League game is 239 (37–17) by Geelong against Brisbane on May 2, 1992.

**Most AFL Grand Final goals** The Australian Football League Grand Final scoring record is nine goals. This has been achieved by two players: Gordon Coventry (Australia) for Collingwood versus Richmond in 1928, and Gary Ablett (Australia) for Geelong versus Hawthorn in 1989.

**Most goals in an AFL career** The most goals scored in an Australian Football League career is 1,357, by Tony Lockett (Australia), between 1983 and 1999.

Peter Hudson (Australia) holds the senior career goal-scoring record with 2,191, scored from 1963 to 1981 in the Victorian Football League (VFL) and in Tasmania.

**Most AFL games played** The career record for the greatest number of Australian Football League games played is 426, by Michael Tuck (Australia), who played for Hawthorn between 1972 and 1991.

**Longest AFL winning streak** The most consecutive games won in the Australian Football League Premiership is 23 by Geelong between 1952 and 1953.

**Highest attendance at an AFL League Grand Final** A record 121,696 spectators attended the Melbourne Cricket Ground, Melbourne, Victoria, to see Carlton versus Collingwood in the Grand Final on September 26, 1970.

# SHINTY

**Highest individual score in a Shinty Cup final** In 1938 John Macmillan Mactaggart (UK) scored ten hails, or goals, for Mid Argyll in a Camanachd Cup match.

**Most Shinty Challenge Cup individual wins** David Ritchie and Hugh Chisholm (both UK) of Newtonmore have won a record 12 Challenge Cup winners' medals each.

**LARGEST ATTENDANCE AT A GAELIC FOOTBALL MATCH** The record crowd for a Gaelic Football game is 90,556, for the Down v. Offaly final at Croke Park, Dublin, Ireland, in 1961. The ground, as it is today, is shown here.

## HURLING

**Longest hit in a hurling contest** The greatest distance for a "lift and stroke" hit is 129 yds. (118 m) credited to Tom Murphy of Three Castles, Kilkenny, Ireland, in a "long puck" contest held in 1906.

**Most wins of the all-Ireland hurling championship** The greatest number of All-Ireland Championships won by one team is 28. These were won by Cork between 1890 and 1999.

**Largest attendance for a hurling match** The largest crowd ever to attend a hurling match was 84,865 for the All-Ireland final between Cork and Wexford at Croke Park, Dublin, in 1954.

## OTHER BALL SPORTS

**Most Pelota Vasca world championship titles** The *Federación Internacional de Pelota Vasca* holds world championships every four years. The most world titles won is 13 by Aaron Sehter (Argentina) from 1952 to 1982. The most successful pair has been Roberto Elias and Juan Labat (both Argentina), who won the *Trinquete Share* four times—in 1952, 1958, 1962, and 1970. The most wins in the long court game, *Cesta Punta,* is three, by José Hamuy (Mexico) with two different partners, in 1958, 1962, and 1966.

**Fastest moving ball in a sport** On August 3, 1979, at a game of jai-alai at Newport Jai-Alai, Rhode Island, USA, a throw from Jose Ramon Areitio was measured at a speed of 188 mph (302 km/h)—the fastest projectile speed in any ball sport.

# TENNIS

**Longest tennis match**  The longest competitive tennis match, lasting 24 hr. 24 min., was played between Paul Jessop and Lee Marks (both UK) on June 22–23, 2002 at the David Lloyd Leisure Club in Birmingham, West Midlands, UK.

**Most Davis Cup ties in a season**  In reaching the Challenge Round in 1965, Spain played a record eight Davis Cup ties in a single year, more than any other nation.

**Most Davis Cup appearances**  The most Davis Cup appearances by an individual player is 164 matches in 66 ties by Nicola Pietrangeli (Italy) between 1954 and 1972. His win-loss record for singles is 78–32 and 42–12 for doubles.

**Most Davis Cup final appearances**  The most Davis Cup final appearances by a player is 11 by Bill Tilden (USA) between 1920 and 1930. He played 28 matches with a win-loss record of 21–7.

**Most consecutive Davis Cup wins**  The most consecutive Davis Cup tournament wins is seven by the USA between 1920 and 1926. Their reign was brought to an end in 1927 by France, who went on to

**YOUNGEST MALE WIMBLEDON CHAMPION**  The youngest male Wimbledon champion is Boris Becker (West Germany) who won the men's singles title in 1985 at the age of 17 years 227 days. He was also the first unseeded player and the first German to become champion.

keep the title for six years. Theirs was the second longest winning streak before losing to Great Britain in 1933.

**Oldest tennis player**   The oldest tennis player is José Guadalupe Leal Lemus (Mexico), who began playing tennis in 1925 and has been playing regularly ever since. At the age of 99 he continues to play every week at the Club Campestre Morelia, Morelia, Mexico, with a group of players over 20 years his junior.

**Longest rally**   The longest contrived tennis rally is one of 17,062 strokes between Ray Miller and Rob Peterson (both USA) at Alameda, California, USA, as part of the United States Tennis Association's Tennis Festival on July 4, 2001. The attempt lasted 9 hr. 6 min.

**Most Wimbledon women's singles titles**   The most Wimbledon singles titles won by a woman is nine by Martina Navrátilová (USA) in 1978–79, 1982–87, and 1990.

**Most Wimbledon men's singles titles**   The most Wimbledon men's singles titles won is seven by Pete Sampras (USA) in 1993–95 and 1997–2000.

**Oldest Wimbledon champion**   The oldest Wimbledon tennis champion is Margaret Evelyn Du Pont (USA). She won the mixed doubles with Neale Fraser (Australia) in 1962 at the age of 44 years 125 days.

**Youngest female Wimbledon champion**   The youngest female Wimbledon champion is Martina Hingis (Switzerland), who was 15 years 282 days old when she won the women's doubles in 1996.

**Best wildcard performance at Wimbledon**   The best performance by a wildcard entrant at Wimbledon is that of Goran Ivanisevic (Croatia) in 2001. Invited to play in the competition by the All England Club, Ivanisevic was ranked 125th in the world. He won the Men's singles title, beating Pat Rafter (Australia) 6–3, 3–6, 6–3, 2–6, 9–7 in the final. It was his fourth Wimbledon final. He also served a record 213 aces throughout the tournament, including 27 in the final.

**Women's Grand Slam winners**   Four women have achieved the grand slam, and the first three won six successive grand slam tournaments: Maureen Connolly (USA), in 1953; Margaret Court (Australia) in 1970; and Martina Navrátilová (USA) in 1983–84. The fourth was Steffi Graf (Germany) in 1988, when she also won the women's singles Olympic gold medal. Pam Shriver (USA), with Navrátilová, won a record eight successive grand slam tournament women's doubles titles and 109 successive matches in all events from April 1983 to July 1985.

**Earliest men's Grand Slam winner**   The first man to have won all four of the world's major singles championships—Wimbledon and the US, Australian and French Opens—was Fred Perry (UK), when he won the French title in 1935.

The first man to hold all four championships simultaneously was Don Budge (USA) in 1938. He also won Wimbledon and the US Open in 1937, giving him six successive grand slam wins.

The first man to win the grand slam twice was Rod Laver (Australia) as an amateur in 1962 and again in 1969, when the tournaments were opened to professionals.

**Most Grand Slam singles titles** Margaret Court (Australia) won 24 grand slam singles titles between 1960 and 1973.

**Most Grand Slam men's singles titles** The most grand slam singles tennis titles won by a man is 14 by Pete Sampras (USA) between 1990 and 2002.

**Most US Open men's singles titles** The most US Open singles titles won by a man is seven. The record is shared by three players: Richard Sears (USA) in 1881–87; William Larned (USA) in 1901, 1902, and 1907–11; and Bill Tilden (USA) in 1920–25 and 1929.

**Most US Open women's singles titles** Molla Mallory (Norway, *née* Bjurstedt) won eight US Open women's singles titles in 1915–18, 1920–22, and 1926.

**YOUNGEST MALE NUMBER ONE TENNIS PLAYER** Marat Mikhailovich Safin (Russia) was 20 years 234 days old when his victory at the President's Cup Tournament in Tashkent, Uzbekistan, on September 17, 2000, made him the number one ranked player in the world.

**YOUNGEST WIMBLEDON MATCH WINNER** The youngest person to win a match at Wimbledon is Jennifer Capriati (USA) who was 14 years 89 days old when she played her first match on June 26, 1990. She was also the youngest seeded Wimbledon player.

### Most US Open titles won by a man

The most US Open titles won by a man is 16, by Bill Tilden (USA), including seven men's singles, in 1920–25 and 1929.

### Most US Open titles won by a woman

Margaret Du Pont (USA) won 25 US Open titles. She won 13 women's doubles, nine mixed doubles, and three singles titles between 1941 and 1960.

### Most consecutive serves

The most consecutive "good" serves (without a double fault) is 8,017 by Rob Peterson (USA) at Port Aransas, Texas, USA, on December 5, 1998. The attempt lasted 10 hrs. 7 min.

**Most French Open men's singles titles** The most French Open singles tennis titles won by a man is six by Björn Borg (Sweden) in 1974–75 and 1978–81.

**Most French Open women's singles titles** The most French Open singles titles won by a woman is seven, by Chris Evert (USA) in 1974–75, 1979–80, 1983, and 1985–86.

**Longest tennis coaching marathon** Butch Heffernan (Australia) coached tennis for a record 52 hours on November 23–25, 2001 at the Next Generation Club in Brierley Hill, Dudley, West Midlands, UK.

**Most Federation Cup wins** The most wins in the Federation Cup, the women's international team championship instituted in 1963 and known as the Fed Cup from 1995, is 17 by the USA between 1963 and 2000. Virginia Wade (UK) played each year from 1967 to 1983 in a record 57 ties, playing 100 rubbers. Her win-loss record for singles is 36–20 and 30–14 for doubles.

# RACKET SPORTS

## *TABLE TENNIS*

**Most men's team World Championships** The Chinese men's table tennis team has won the most World Championship titles. They have taken home the coveted Swaythling Cup a record 13 times between 1961 and 2001.

**Most women's team World Championships** China has won the most women's team table tennis world titles, with 15 Marcel Corbillon Cup victories. They first won in 1965, then had eight successive biennial wins from 1975 to 1989 and more victories in 1993, 1995, 1997, and 1999–2001.

**Most women's Olympic gold medals** Deng Yaping (China) has won a record four Olympic table tennis titles. She won the women's singles in 1992 and 1996, and the women's doubles (both with Qiao Hang) in 1992 and 1996. A naturally attacking player, Yaping was widely acclaimed as the greatest female player in table tennis history. She was the top-ranked woman in the world for eight consecutive years from 1991.

**Longest table tennis rally** On November 5, 1977, John Duffy and Kevin Schick (both New Zealand) achieved a contrived table tennis rally lasting a record time of 5 hr. 2 min. 18.5 sec. at Whangarei, New Zealand.

**Youngest table tennis international** The youngest age at which any person has won international honors is eight, in the case of Joy Foster, the Jamaican singles and mixed doubles table tennis champion in 1958.

**MOST OLYMPIC MEN'S TABLE TENNIS GOLDS** The most Olympic table tennis gold medals won by a man is two by Liu Guoliang (China). He won in the singles and doubles in 1996.

# SQUASH

**Longest squash match** The longest squash match in competition lasted 2 hr. 45 min., when Jahangir Khan (Pakistan) beat Gamal Awad (Egypt) 9–10, 9–5, 9–7, 9–2 in the final of the Patrick International Festival at Chichester, West Sussex, UK, on March 30, 1983. The first game of the match lasted a record 1 hr. 11 min.

**Most World Championships** Jahangir Khan (Pakistan) has won a record nine squash world championships. He began by winning the International Squash Rackets Federation world title (then amateur) three times, in 1979, 1983, and 1985. When the tournament became professional and renamed the World Open, Khan went on to win six more titles, in 1981–85 and in 1988. He is considered the most successful player in the history of the sport.

Jansher Khan (Pakistan, not related) has won eight squash World Open titles in 1987, 1989, 1990, and from 1992 to 1996.

**Most men's team World Championships** The most World Championship men's squash team titles won is seven by Australia in 1967, 1969, 1971, 1973, 1989, 1991, and 2001.

**Most women's team World Championships** The Australian women's team has won the most squash World Championships, with seven victories in 1981, 1983, 1992, 1994, 1996, 1998, and 2002.

**Fastest squash ball** In tests at Wimbledon Squash and Badminton Club, London, UK, in January 1988, Roy Buckland (UK) hit a squash ball with an overhead serve at a measured speed of 144.6 mph (232.7 km/h) over the distance to the front wall. This is equivalent to an initial speed at the racket of 150.8 mph (242.6 km/h).

# BADMINTON

**Most Olympic medals** Badminton was first contested at the 1992 Barcelona Olympics and no individuals has won more than one gold medal. The most medals won is three by Gil Young Ah (South Korea): gold in the mixed doubles and silver in the women's doubles in 1996, and bronze in the women's doubles in 1992.

**Most World Championship singles titles** Four Chinese players have won two individual world titles. Yang Yang won the men's singles in 1987 and 1989. The women's singles have been won twice by Li Lingwei in 1983 and 1989; Han Aiping in 1985 and 1987, and Ye Zhaoying in 1995 and 1997.

**Most World Championship titles** A record five World Championship badminton titles have been won by Park Joo-bong (South Korea). He won the men's doubles in 1985 and 1991, and the mixed doubles in 1985, 1989, and 1991.

**Most Thomas Cup team wins** The most wins at the men's World Team Championships for the Thomas Cup is 13 by Indonesia between 1958 and 2002.

**Most Uber Cup team wins** The record number of wins at the women's World Team Badminton Championships for the Uber Cup is eight by China between 1984 and 2002.

**Longest badminton match** At the badminton World Championship men's singles final in Glasgow, UK, on June 1, 1997, Peter Rasmussen

**MOST WOMEN'S SQUASH WORLD CHAMPIONSHIPS** The most women's squash World Open titles won is five by Sarah Fitzgerald (Australia, left in the picture shown here) in 1996–98 and 2001–02.

**FASTEST SHUTTLECOCK SPEED** Simon Archer (UK) hit a shuttlecock at a speed of 162 mph (260 km/h) at Warwickshire Racquets and Health Club, Coventry, Warwickshire, UK, on November 5, 1996.

(Denmark) beat Sun Jun (China) 16–17, 18–13, 15–10 in a match that lasted a record 2 hr. 4 min.

**Longest badminton rally** In the men's singles final of the 1987 All-England Championships between Morten Frost (Denmark) and Icuk Sugiarto (Indonesia) there were two rallies of over 90 strokes.

**Shortest badminton match** Ra Kyung-min (South Korea) beat Julia Mann (England) 11–2, 11–1 in 6 minutes at the 1996 Uber Cup in Hong Kong on May 19, 1996.

## RACKETBALL

**Most men's team World Championship wins** The racketball world championships have been held biennially since 1984. The USA has won ten combined team titles between 1981 and 2002.

**Most women's team World Championship wins** The USA has won a record nine women's team titles in 1986, 1988, 1990, 1992, 1994, 1996, 1998, 2000, and 2002.

**Most women's World Championships** Michelle Gould (USA) has won a record three individual women's racketball World Championships in 1992, 1994, and 1996.

# ATHLETICS

**Longest winning sequence in a track event** Ed Moses (USA) achieved 122 wins in the 400-m hurdles between his losses to Harald Schmid (West Germany) in Berlin, Germany, on August 26, 1977, and Danny Lee Harris (USA) in Madrid, Spain on June 4, 1987.

**Longest winning sequence in a field event** Iolanda Balas (Romania) won a record 150 consecutive high jump competitions from 1956 to 1967.

**Oldest athletics Olympic gold medallist** The oldest athlete to win an Olympic title was Irish-born Patrick Joseph "Babe" McDonald (USA, 1878–1954) who was 42 years 26 days old when he won the 56-lb. weight throw at Antwerp, Belgium, on August 21, 1920.

**Youngest athletics Olympic gold medallist** The youngest Olympic athletics gold medallist was Barbara Pearl Jones (USA, b. March 26, 1937) who at 15 years 123 days was a member of the winning 4 × 100-m relay team, at Helsinki, Finland, on July 27, 1952.

**Most Olympics gold medals at one games** Paavo Nurmi (Finland) won five golds at the 1924 games for the 1,500 m, 5,000 m, 10,000-m cross-country, 3,000-m team, and cross-country team.

The most Olympic gold medals at individual events is four by Alvin Kraenzlein (USA) in 1900 for the 60 m, 110-m hurdles, 200-m hurdles, and long jump.

**Most men's Olympic gold medals** The most Olympic gold medals won is ten by athlete Ray Ewry (USA) in the standing high, long, and triple jumps in 1900, 1904, 1906, and 1908.

**Most women's athletics Olympic gold medals** The most gold medals won by a woman is four, shared by: Fanny Blankers-Koen (Netherlands) for the 100 m, 200 m, 80-m hurdles, and 4 × 100-m relay, in 1948; Betty Cuthbert (Australia) for the 100 m, 200 m, 4 × 100-m relay in 1956, and 400 m in 1964; Bärbel Wöckel (née Eckert, GDR) for the 200 m and 4 × 100-m relay in 1976 and 1980; and Evelyn Ashford (USA) for the 100 m in 1984 and 4 × 100-m relay in 1984, 1988, and 1992.

**FASTEST WOMEN'S 2,000 M** Sonia O'Sullivan (Ireland, front) ran the fastest women's 2,000 m on July 8 1994 with a time of 5:25.36. She set the record in Edinburgh, Lothian, UK.

## Most men's athletics Olympic medals

The most medals won is 12 (nine gold and three silver) by Paavo Nurmi (Finland), nicknamed "The Flying Finn," in the Games of 1920, 1924, and 1928.

## Most women's Olympic medals

Three women athletes have each won seven gold medals. Shirley de la Hunty (Australia) won three gold, one silver, and three bronze in the 1948, 1952, and 1956 Games. A re-read of the photo-finish indicates that she finished third, not fourth, in the 1948 200-m event, thus unofficially increasing her medal haul to eight. Irena Szewinska (Poland) won three gold, two silver and two bronze in 1964, 1968, 1972, and 1976, and is the only woman athlete to win a medal in four successive Games. Merlene Ottey (Jamaica) has also won seven medals—two silver and five bronze—in 1980, 1984, 1992, and 1996.

**FASTEST MEN'S 100 M** The men's 100-m record stands at 9.78 seconds and is held by Tim Montgomery (USA, far left of photo). The record was set in Paris, France, on September 14, 2002.

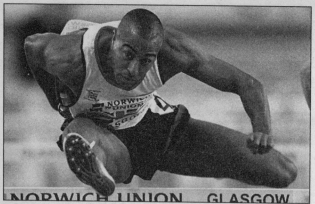

**FASTEST 110-M HURDLES** Colin Jackson (GB) set a new 100-m hurdle record with a time of 12.91 seconds in Stuttgart, Germany, on August 20, 1993. He has competed at this event in four Olympic Games, winning silver in 1988. At the World Championships, Jackson won in 1993 and 1999, came second in 1997, and third in 1987. He was European champion in 1990, 1994, and 1998, and Commonwealth champion in 1990 and 1994.

**Most successful individual in the IAAF Golden League** Hicham El Guerrouj (Morocco) is the only athlete to have twice won a share of the jackpot in the IAAF (International Amateur Athletics Federation) Golden League. For the jackpot, an athlete must win five of the seven IAAF Grand Prix meetings in a season and remain undefeated.

**Fastest men's 100 × 1-mile relay** The record for 100 miles by 100 runners is 7 hr. 35 min. 55.4 sec. by the Canadian Milers Athletic Club set at York University, Toronto, Canada, on December 20, 1998.

The same record for women was set by the Canadian Women's Miler's Club, who ran the 100 × 1-mile relay in a time of 9 hr. 23 min. 39 sec. on December 27, 1999.

**Fastest 100 × 100-m mass relay** The record for a 100 × 100-m relay is 19 min. 14.19 sec. by a team from Antwerp who set the record at Merksem, Belgium, on September 23, 1989.

**Fastest backwards mile** The time for the fastest backwards mile is 6 min. 2.35 sec. and was set by D. Joseph James (India) at Nehru Stadium Athletics Track, Coimbatore, Tamil Nadu, India, on August 10, 2002.

**Fastest 10-km run wearing a pantomime costume** Simon Wiles and Les Morton (both UK) ran the Percy Pud 10-km race in Loxley, Sheffield, South Yorkshire, UK, on December 2, 2001 in a time of 44 min. 2 sec. They wore their pantomime camel costume for the whole race.

| EVENT | RECORD | NAME AND COUNTRY | VENUE | DATE |
|---|---|---|---|---|
| 100 m | 9.78 | Tim Montgomery (USA) | Paris, France | September 14, 2002 |
| 200 m | 19.32 | Michael Johnson (USA) | Atlanta, USA | August 1, 1996 |
| 400 m | 43.18 | Michael Johnson (USA) | Seville, Spain | August 26, 1999 |
| 800 m | 1:41.11 | Wilson Kipketer (Denmark) | Cologne, Germany | August 24, 1997 |
| 1,000 m | 2:11.96 | Noah Ngeny (Kenya) | Rieti, Italy | September 5, 1999 |
| 1,500 m | 3:26.00 | Hicham El Guerrouj (Morocco) | Rome, Italy | July 14, 1998 |
| 1 mile | 3:43.13 | Hicham El Guerrouj (Morocco) | Rome, Italy | July 7, 1999 |
| 2,000 m | 4:44.79 | Hicham El Guerrouj (Morocco) | Berlin, Germany | September 7, 1999 |
| 3,000 m | 7:20.67 | Daniel Komen (Kenya) | Rieti, Italy | September 1, 1996 |
| 5,000 m | 12:39.36 | Haile Gebrselassie (Ethiopia) | Helsinki, Finland | June 13, 1998 |
| 10,000 m | 26:22.75 | Haile Gebrselassie (Ethiopia) | Hengelo, Netherlands | June 1, 1998 |
| 20,000 m | 56:55.60 | Arturo Barrios (Mexico, now USA) | La Flèche, France | March 30, 1991 |
| 25,000 m | 1:13:55.80 | Toshihiko Seko (Japan) | Christchurch, New Zealand | March 22, 1981 |
| 30,000 m | 1:29:18.80 | Toshihiko Seko (Japan) | Christchurch, New Zealand | March 22, 1981 |
| 1 hour distance | 21,101 m | Arturo Barrios (Mexico, now USA) | La Flèche, France | March 30, 1991 |
| 110-m hurdles | 12.91 | Colin Jackson (GB) | Stuttgart, Germany | August 20, 1993 |
| 400-m hurdles | 46.78 | Kevin Young (USA) | Barcelona, Spain | August 6, 1992 |
| 3,000-m steeplechase | 7:53.17 | Brahim Boulami (Morocco) | Zürich, Switzerland | August 16, 2002 |
| 4 × 100-m relay | 37.40 | USA (Michael Marsh, Leroy Burrell, Dennis Mitchell, Carl Lewis) | Barcelona, Spain | August 8, 1992 |
| | | USA (John Drummond Jr., Andre Cason, Dennis Mitchell, Leroy Burrell) | Stuttgart, Germany | August 21, 1993 |
| 4 × 200-m relay | 1:18.68 | Santa Monica Track Club (Michael | Walnut, USA | April 17, 1994 |

| | | | | |
|---|---|---|---|---|
| | | Marsh, Leroy Burrell, Floyd Heard, Carl Lewis, all USA) | | |
| 4 × 400-m relay | 2:54.20 | USA (Jerome Young, Antonio Pettigrew, Tyree Washington, Michael Johnson) | New York City, USA | July 23, 1998 |
| 4 × 800-m relay | 7:03.89 | Great Britain (Peter Elliott, Garry Cook, Steve Cram, Sebastian Coe) | London, UK | August 30, 1982 |
| 4 × 1,500-m relay | 14:38.80 | West Germany (Thomas Wessinghage, Harald Hudak, Michael Lederer, Karl Fleschen) | Cologne, Germany | August 17, 1977 |
| High jump | 8 ft. 0.25 in. (2.45 m) | Javier Sotomayor (Cuba) | Salamanca, Spain | July 27, 1993 |
| Pole vault | 20 ft. 1.75 in. (6.14 m) | Sergei Bubka (Ukraine) | Sestriere, Italy | July 31, 1994 |
| Long jump | 29 ft. 4.5 in. (8.95 m) | Mike Powell (USA) | Tokyo, Japan | August 30, 1991 |
| Triple jump | 60 ft. 0.25 in. (18.29 m) | Jonathan Edwards (GB) | Gothenburg, Sweden | August 7, 1995 |
| Shot | 75 ft. 10.25 in. (23.12 m) | Randy Barnes (USA) | Los Angeles, USA | May 20, 1990 |
| Discus | 243 ft. (74.08 m) | Jürgen Schult (GDR) | Neubrandenburg, Germany | June 6, 1986 |
| Hammer | 284 ft. 7 in. (86.74 m) | Yuriy Sedykh (USSR) | Stuttgart, Germany | August 30, 1986 |
| Javelin | 323 ft. 1 in. (98.48 m) | Jan Zelezny (Czech Republic) | Jena, Germany | May 25, 1996 |
| Decathlon* | 9,026 points | Roman Sebrle (Czech Republic) | Götzis, Austria | May 26–27, 2001 |

*Day 1: 100 m: 10.64; Long jump: 26 ft. 7.25 in. (8.11 m); Shot: 50 ft. 3.5 in. (15.33 m); High jump: 6 ft. 11.5 in. (2.12m)
Day 2: 110-m hurdles: 13.92; Discus: 157 ft. 2.5 in. (47.92 m); Pole vault: 15 ft. 9 in. (4.80 m); Javelin: 230 ft. 2 in. (70.16 m); 1,500 m: 4:21.98

**Highest standing high jump** The best high jump from a standing position is 6 ft. 2.75 in. (1.90 m) by Rune Almen (Sweden) at Karlstad, Sweden, on May 3, 1980.

The women's best is 4 ft. 11.75 in. (1.52 m) by Grete Bjordalsbakka (Norway) in 1984.

**Longest standing long jump** The longest long jump from a standing position is 12 ft. 2 in. (3.71 m) by Arne Tvervaag (Norway) in 1968.

The women's best is 9 ft. 7 in. (2.92 m) by Annelin Mannes (Norway) at Flisa, Norway, on March 7, 1981.

**LONGEST INDOOR TRIPLE JUMP** Ashia Hansen (GB), holds the indoor record for the triple jump with a distance of 49 ft. 8 in. (15.16 m). The record was set in Valencia, Spain, on February 28, 1998.

**Most participants in a relay race** The most participants in a relay race is 7,175, (287 teams of 25), for the Batavieren race, which was run between Nijmegen and Enschede, The Netherlands, on April 24, 1999.

**Fastest 1,000-mile relay by team of ten** The record for the fastest 1,000-mile relay by a team of ten is 99 hr. 3 min. 27 sec. It was run by Willie Mtolo, Graham Meyer, Jan van Rooyen, Dimitri Grishine, Daniel Radebe, Pio Mpolokeng, Oliver Kandiero, Frans Moyo, Simon Mele, and Philip Molefi (all South Africa) who ran from Cape Town to Johannesburg, South Africa, from August 14 to 18, 2002.

## ★ MEN'S TRACK WALKING ★

| EVENT | RECORD | NAME AND COUNTRY | VENUE | DATE |
|-------|--------|------------------|-------|------|
| 20 km | 1:17:25.60 | Bernardo Segura (Mexico) | Fana, Norway | May 7, 1994 |
| 30 km | 2:01:44.10 | Maurizio Damilano (Italy) | Cuneo, Italy | October 4, 1992 |
| 50 km | 3:40:57.90 | Thierry Toutain (France) | Héricourt, France | September 29, 1997 |
| 2 hours | 29,572 m | Maurizio Damilano (Italy) | Cuneo, Italy | October 4, 1992 |

## ★ WOMEN'S TRACK WALKING ★

| EVENT | RECORD | NAME AND COUNTRY | VENUE | DATE |
|-------|--------|------------------|-------|------|
| 5 km | 20:02.60 | Gillian O'Sullivan (Ireland) | Dublin, Ireland | July 13, 2002 |
| 10 km | 41:56.23 | Nadezhda Ryashkina (USSR) | Seattle, USA | July 24, 1990 |
| 20 km | 1:26:52.30 | Olimpiada Ivanova (Russia) | Brisbane, Australia | September 6, 2001 |

**Most athletics world records set on one day** Athlete Jesse Owens (USA) set six world records in 45 minutes at Ann Arbor, Michigan, USA, on May 25 1935 with a 9.4-sec. 100 yd. at 3:15 pm, a 26-ft. 8.25-in.-long 8.13-m) jump at 3:25 pm, a 20.3-sec. 220 yd. (and 200 m) at 3:45 pm, and a 22.6-sec. 220 yd. low hurdles (and 200 m) at 4 pm.

**Most Indoor World Championship medals** First held as the World Indoor Games in 1985, the Indoor World Championships are now staged biennially. The most medals won in an individual event is six by Merlene Ottey (Jamaica) who won three gold (60 m 1995, 200 m 1989, 1991), two silver (60 m 1991, 200 m 1987), and one bronze (60 m 1989).

The men's record is five by Ivan Pedroso (Cuba) in the long jump (gold 1993, 1995, 1997, 1999, 2001) and Javier Sotomayor (Cuba) for the high jump (gold 1989, 1993, 1995, 1999; bronze 1991).

**Most medals won in the World Championships** The athletics World Championships were inaugurated in 1983 in Helsinki, Finland. The most medals won is ten by Carl Lewis (USA) with eight gold medals, (100 m, long jump and 4 × 100-m relay 1983; 100 m, long jump, and 4 × 100-m relay 1987; 100 m and 4 × 100-m relay 1991); silver medals for long jump in 1991, and bronze for 200 m in 1993.

The women's record is 14 medals won by Merlene Ottey (Jamaica), who won three gold, four silver, seven bronze, between 1983 and 1997.

**Most World Championship gold medals** The most golds won to date is nine by Michael Johnson (USA), for the 200 m (1991, 1995), 400 m (1993, 1995, 1997, 1999) and 4 × 400-m relay (1993, 1995, 1999).

The most gold medals won by a woman is five by Gail Devers (USA), for the 100 m (1993), 100-m hurdles (1993, 1995, 1999), and 4 × 100-m relay (1997).

**Most consecutive wins in the World Championships** The most successive wins in the same event at the World Championships is six by Sergey Bubka (Ukraine), who won the pole vault title from 1983 to 1997.

In track events the record is four by Michael Johnson (USA) for 400 m between 1993 and 1999, and Haile Gebrselassie (Ethiopia), who won the 10,000 m between 1993 and 1999.

**Most participants at an Athletics Championships** A record 11,475 participants (9,328 men, 2,147 women) attended the 1993 World Veterans' Athletic Championships in Miyazaki, Japan.

## ★ MEN'S ULTRA LONG DISTANCE WORLD RECORDS ★

| EVENT | RECORD | NAME AND COUNTRY | VENUE | DATE |
|---|---|---|---|---|
| 100 km | 6:10:20 | Don Ritchie (GB) | London, UK | October 28, 1978 |
| 100 miles | 11:30:51 | Don Ritchie (GB) | London, UK | October 15, 1977 |
| 1,000 km | 5 days 16:17:00 | Yiannis Kouros (Greece) | Colac, Australia | November 26– December 1, 1984 |
| 1,000 miles | 11 days 13:54:58 | Piotr Silikin (Lithuania) | Nanango, Australia | March 11–23, 1998 |
| 24 hours | 188 miles 1,038 yards (303.506 km) | Yiannis Kouros (Australia) | Adelaide, Australia | October 4–5, 1997 |
| 6 days | 635 miles 147 yards (1,022.068 km) | Yiannis Kouros (Greece) | New York, USA | July 2–8, 1984 |

## ★ WOMEN'S ULTRA LONG DISTANCE WORLD RECORDS ★

| EVENT | RECORD | NAME AND COUNTRY | VENUE | DATE |
|---|---|---|---|---|
| 100 km | 7:23:28 | Valentina Liakhova (Russia) | Nantes, France | September 28, 1996 |
| 100 miles | 14:29:44 | Ann Trason (USA) | Santa Rosa, USA | March 18–19, 1989 |
| 1,000 km | 8 days 00:27:06 | Eleanor Robinson (GB) | Nanango, Australia | March 11–18, 1998 |
| 1,000 miles | 13 days 01:54:02 | Eleanor Robinson (GB) | Nanango, Australia | March 11–24, 1998 |

| | | | | |
|---|---|---|---|---|
| 24 hours | 149 miles 412 yards (240.169 km) | Eleanor Adams (GB) | Melbourne, Australia | August 19–20, 1989 |
| 6 days | 549 miles 110 yards (883.631 km) | Sandra Barwick (New Zealand) | Campbelltown, Australia | November 18–24, 1990 |

## ★ WOMEN'S OUTDOOR WORLD RECORDS ★

| EVENT | RECORD | NAME AND COUNTRY | VENUE | DATE |
|---|---|---|---|---|
| 100 m | 10.49 | Florence Griffith-Joyner (USA) | Indianapolis, USA | July 16, 1998 |
| 200 m | 21.34 | Florence Griffith-Joyner (USA) | Seoul, South Korea | September 29, 1988 |
| 400 m | 47.60 | Marita Koch (GDR) | Canberra, Australia | October 6, 1985 |
| 800 m | 1:53.28 | Jarmila Kratochvilová (Czechoslovakia) | Munich, Germany | July 26, 1983 |
| 1,000 m | 2:28.98 | Svetlana Masterkova (Russia) | Brussels, Belgium | August 23, 1996 |
| 1,500 m | 3:50.46 | Qu Yunxia (China) | Beijing, China | September 11, 1993 |
| 1 mile | 4:12.56 | Svetlana Masterkova (Russia) | Zürich, Switzerland | August 14, 1996 |
| 2,000 m | 5:25.36 | Sonia O'Sullivan (Ireland) | Edinburgh, UK | July 8, 1994 |
| 3,000 m | 8:06.11 | Wang Junxia (China) | Beijing, China | September 13, 1993 |
| 5,000 m | 14:28.09 | Jiang Bo (China) | Beijing, China | October 23, 1997 |
| 10,000 m | 29:31.78 | Wang Junxia (China) | Beijing, China | September 8, 1993 |
| 20,000 m | 1:05:26.60 | Tegla Loroupe (Kenya) | Borgholzhausen, Germany | September 3, 2000 |
| 25,000 m | 1:27:05.90 | Tegla Loroupe (Kenya) | Megerkirchen, Germany | September 21, 2002 |
| 30,000 m | 1:47:05.60 | Karolina Szabó (Hungary) | Budapest, Hungary | April 22, 1988 |
| 1 hour distance | 18,340 m | Tegla Loroupe (Kenya) | Borgholzhausen, Germany | August 7, 1998 |
| 100-m hurdles | 12.21 | Yordanka Donkova (Bulgaria) | Stara Zagora, Bulgaria | August 20, 1988 |
| 400-m hurdles | 52.61 | Kim Batten (USA) | Gothenburg, Sweden | August 11, 1995 |
| 3,000-m steeplechase | 9:16:51 | Aleysa Turova (Belarus) | Gdansk, Poland | July 27, 2002 |
| 4 × 100-m relay | 41.37 | GDR (Silke Gladisch, Sabine Rieger, Ingrid Auerswald and Marlies Göhr) | Canberra, Australia | October 6, 1985 |
| 4 × 200-m relay | 1:27.46 | United States "Blue" (LaTasha Jenkins, Latasha Colander | Philadelphia, USA | April 29, 2000 |

| | | Richardson, Nanceen Perry and Marion Jones) | | |
|---|---|---|---|---|
| 4 × 400-m relay | 3:15.17 | USSR (Tatyana Ledovskaya, Olga Nazarova, Maria Pinigina and Olga Bryzgina) | Seoul, South Korea | October 1, 1988 |
| 4 × 800-m relay | 7:50.17 | USSR (Nadezhda Olizarenko, Lyubov Gurina, Lyudmila Borisova and Irina Podyalovskaya) | Moscow, Russia | August 5, 1984 |
| High jump | 6 ft. 10.25 in. (2.09 m) | Stefka Kostadinova (Bulgaria) | Rome, Italy | August 30, 1987 |
| Pole vault | 15 ft. 9.25 in. (4.81 m) | Stacy Dragila (USA) | Palo Alto, USA | June 9, 2001 |
| Long jump | 24 ft. 8.25 in. (7.52 m) | Galina Chistyakova (USSR) | St. Petersburg, Russia | June 1, 1988 |
| Triple jump | 50 ft. 10.25 in. (15.50 m) | Inessa Kravets (Ukraine) | Gothenburg, Sweden | August 10, 1995 |
| Shot | 74 ft. 3 in. (22.63 m) | Natalya Lisovskaya (USSR) | Moscow, Russia | June 7, 1987 |
| Javelin | 234 ft. 8 in. (71.54 m) | Osleidys Menéndez (Cuba) | Réthymno, Greece | July 1, 2001 |
| Discus | 252 ft. (76.80 m) | Gabriele Reinsch (GDR) | Neubrandenburg, Germany | July 9, 1988 |
| Hammer | 249 ft. 6 in. (76.07 m) | Mihaela Melinte (Romania) | Rüdlingen, Germany | August 29, 1999 |
| Heptathlon* | 7,291 points | Jacqueline Joyner-Kersee (USA) | Seoul, South Korea | September 23–24, 1988 |

*Day 1: 100-m hurdles: 12.69; High jump: 6 ft. 1.25 in. (1.86 m); Shot: 51 ft. 10 in. (15.80 m); 200 m: 22.56
Day 2: Long jump: 23 ft. 10.25 in. (7.27 m); Javelin: 149 ft. 10 in. (45.66 m); 800 m: 2:08.51

### Longest distance backwards walking in 24 hours

The longest distance recorded for walking backwards in 24 hours is 95.4 miles (153.52 km) by Anthony Thornton (USA) in Minneapolis, Minnesota, USA, from December 31, 1988, to January 1, 1989. His average speed was 3.9 mph (6.4 km/h).

### Fastest marathon

The men's world marathon best is 2 hr. 5 min. 38 sec. set by Khalid Khannouchi (USA) at the London Marathon, London, UK, on April 14, 2002.

The women's world best is 2 hr. 15 min. 25 sec. by Paula Radcliffe (UK), also at the London Marathon, on April 13, 2003.

### Fastest aggregate time to run a marathon on each continent

The fastest aggregate time to complete a marathon on each of the seven continents is 34 hr. 23 min. 8 sec. by Tim Rogers (UK) who ran them all between February 13 and May 23, 1999.

**MOST SIBLINGS TO COMPLETE THE SAME MARATHON** Five sisters—Valerie Lewis, Audrey Kenniford, Frederica Maguire, Sandra Hubbard, and Denise Wilson (all UK, all née Mason, shown)—ran the London Marathon, UK, on April 14, 2002. They all finished within two seconds of each other, in under 6:35.20.

The women's record is 37 hr. 20 sec. by Kimi Puntillo (USA), who ran them all between November 3, 1996 and October 4, 1998.

## ★ MEN'S INDOOR WORLD RECORDS ★

| EVENT | RECORD | NAME AND COUNTRY | VENUE | DATE |
|-------|--------|------------------|-------|------|
| 50 m | 5.56 | Donovan Bailey (Canada) | Reno, USA | February 9, 1996 |
| | | Maurice Greene (USA) | Los Angeles, USA | February 3, 1999 |
| 60 m | 6.39 | Maurice Greene (USA) | Madrid, Spain | February 3, 1998 |
| | | | Atlanta, USA | March 3, 2001 |
| 200 m | 19.92 | Frank Fredericks (Namibia) | Liévin, France | February 18, 1996 |
| 400 m | 44.63 | Michael Johnson (USA) | Atlanta, USA | March 4, 1995 |
| 800 m | 1:42.67 | Wilson Kipketer (Denmark) | Paris, France | March 9, 1997 |
| 1,000 m | 2:14.36 | Wilson Kipketer (Denmark) | Birmingham, UK | February 20, 2000 |
| 1,500 m | 3:31.18 | Hicham El Guerrouj (Morocco) | Stuttgart, Germany | February 2, 1997 |
| 1 mile | 3:48.45 | Hicham El Guerrouj (Morocco) | Ghent, Belgium | February 12, 1997 |

| | | | | |
|---|---|---|---|---|
| 3,000 m | 7:24.90 | Daniel Komen (Kenya) | Budapest, Hungary | February 6, 1998 |
| 5,000 m | 12:50.38 | Haile Gebrselassie (Ethiopia) | Birmingham, UK | February 14, 1999 |
| 50-m hurdles | 6.25 | Mark McCoy (Canada) | Kobe, Japan | March 5, 1986 |
| 60-m hurdles | 7.30 | Colin Jackson (GB) | Sindelfingen, Germany | March 6, 1994 |
| 4 × 200-m relay | 1:22.11 | Great Britain (Linford Christie, Darren Braithwaite, Ade Mafe and John Regis) | Glasgow, UK | March 3, 1991 |
| 4 × 400-m relay | 3:02.83 | USA (Andre Morris, Dameon Johnson, Deon Minor and Milton Campbell) | Maebashi, Japan | March 7, 1999 |
| 5,000-m walk | 18:07.08 | Mikhail Shchennikov (Russia) | Moscow, Russia | February 14, 1995 |
| High jump | 7 ft. 11.5 in. (2.43 m) | Javier Sotomayor (Cuba) | Budapest, Hungary | March 4, 1989 |
| Pole vault | 20 ft. 2 in. (6.15 m) | Sergei Bubka (Ukraine) | Donets'k, Ukraine | February 21, 1993 |
| Long jump | 28 ft. 10.25 in. (8.79 m) | Carl Lewis (USA) | New York City, USA | January 27, 1984 |
| Triple jump | 58 ft. 6 in. (17.83 m) | Aliecer Urrutia (Cuba) | Sindelfingen, Germany | March 1, 1997 |
| Shot | 74 ft. 4.5 in. (22.66 m) | Randy Barnes (USA) | Los Angeles, USA | January 20, 1989 |
| Heptathlon* | 6,476 points | Dan O'Brien (USA) | Toronto, Canada | March 13–14, 1993 |

*Events: 60 m: 6.67; Long jump: 25 ft. 8.75 in. (7.84 m); Shot: 52 ft. 6.75 in. (16.02 m); High jump: 6 ft. 11.75 in. (2.13 m); 60-m hurdles: 7.85; Pole vault: 17 ft. 0.75 in. (5.20 m); 1,000 m: 2:57.96

**Fastest time to complete three marathons in three days** The fastest combined time for three marathons in three days is 8 hr. 22 min. 31 sec. set by Raymond Hubbard (UK). The marathons were run in Belfast (2 hr. 45 min. 55 sec.), London (2 hr. 48 min. 45 sec.), and Boston (2 hr. 47 min. 51 sec.), and all were run between April 16, and 18, 1988.

**Fastest half marathon** The world best time on a properly measured course is 59 min. 5 sec. by Paul Tergat (Kenya) at Lisbon, Portugal, on March 26, 2000. However, the official world best as recognized by the International Amateur Athletics Federation (IAAF) is 59 min. 17 sec., also by Paul Tergat, at Milan, Italy, on April 4, 1998.

The women's official half marathon best is 66 min. 43 sec. by Masako Chiba (Japan) at Tokyo, Japan, on January 19, 1997.

**Most individual wins in the half marathon at the World Championships** Tegla Loroupe (Kenya) has won the IAAF Half Marathon World Championship three times—in 1997, 1998, and 1999.

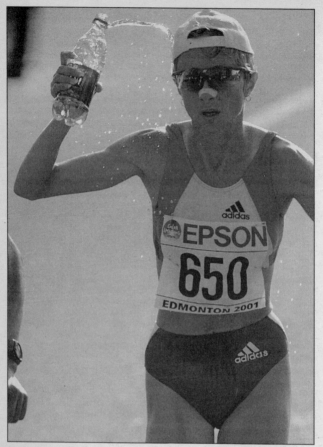

**MOST INDIVIDUAL MEDALS WON AT THE IAAF HALF MARATHON WORLD CHAMPIONSHIPS** The most individual medals won at the IAAF Half Marathon World Championships is eight by Lidia Simon-Slavuteanu (Romania), who won three team gold, one team silver, one individual silver, and three individual bronze medals between 1996 and 2000.

The same record for the men's event is two by Paul Tergat (Kenya) in 1999 and 2000.

**Largest half marathon** The world's largest half marathon is The BUPA Great North Run, which is run between Newcastle upon Tyne and South

Shields, Tyne & Wear, UK. The 2000 event, held on October 22, had 36,822 finishers out of 50,173 entries.

**Fastest marathon speed march team without rifles** The fastest time for a team to complete a marathon while carrying 40-lb. backpacks is 4 hr. 19 min. 7 sec. by eight members of 29 Commando Regiment Royal Artillery at the Luton Marathon, Bedfordshire, UK, on November 29, 1998.

**Greatest average daily mileage run** During the year from August 1, 1996 to July 31, 1997, Tirtha Kumar Phani (India) ran every day, running 14,021.7 miles (22,565.76 km) in total—an average of 38.41 miles (61.824 km) a day.

## ★ WOMEN'S INDOOR WORLD RECORDS ★

| EVENT | RECORD | NAME AND COUNTRY | VENUE | DATE |
|-------|--------|------------------|-------|------|
| 50 m | 5.96 | Irina Privalova (Russia) | Madrid, Spain | February 9, 1995 |
| 60 m | 6.92 | Irina Privalova (Russia) | Madrid, Spain | February 11, 1993 February 9, 1995 |
| 200 m | 21.87 | Merlene Ottey (Jamaica) | Liévin, France | February 13, 1993 |
| 400 m | 49.59 | Jarmila Kratochvilovà (Czechoslovakia) | Milan, Italy | March 7, 1982 |
| 800 m | 1:55.82 | Jolanda Ceplak (Slovenia) | Vienna, Austria | March 3, 2002 |
| 1,000 m | 2:30.94 | Maria Mutola (Mozambique) | Stockholm, Sweden | February 25, 1999 |
| 1,500 m | 4:00.27 | Doina Melinte (Romania) | East Rutherford, USA | February 9, 1990 |
| 1 mile | 4:17.14 | Doina Melinte (Romania) | East Rutherford, USA | February 9, 1990 |
| 3,000 m | 8:29.15 | Berhane Adere (Ethiopia) | Stuttgart, Germany | February 3, 2002 |
| 5,000 m | 14:47.35 | Gabriela Szabo (Romania) | Dortmund, Germany | February 13, 1999 |
| 50-m hurdles | 6.58 | Cornelia Oschkenat (GDR) | Berlin, Germany | February 20, 1988 |
| 60-m hurdles | 7.69 | Lyudmila Engquist (Russia) | Chelyabinsk, Russia | February 4, 1993 |
| 4 × 200-m relay | 1:32.55 | SC Eintracht Hamm (Helga Arendt, Silke-Beate Knoll, Mechthild Kluth and Gisela Kinzel, all West Germany) | Dortmund, Germany | February 19, 1988 |

| | | | | |
|---|---|---|---|---|
| | | LG Olympia Dortmund (Esther Möller, Gabi Rockmeier, Birgit Rockmeier and Andrea Philipp, all Germany) | Karlsruhe, Germany | February 21, 1999 |
| 4 × 400-m relay | 3:24.25 | Russia (Tatyana Chebykina, Svetlana Goncharenko, Olga Kotlyarova and Natalay Nazarova) | Maebashi, Japan | March 7, 1999 |
| 3,000-m walk | 11:40.33 | Claudia Iovan (Romania) | Bucharest, Romania | January 30, 1999 |
| High jump | 6 ft. 9.5 in. (2.07 m) | Heike Henkel (Germany) | Karlsruhe, Germany | February 9, 1992 |
| Pole vault | 15 ft. 9 in. (4.80 m) | Svetlana Feofanova (Russia) | Birmingham, UK | March 16, 2003 |
| Long jump | 24 ft. 2.25 in. (7.37 m) | Heike Drechsler (GDR) | Vienna, Austria | February 13, 1988 |
| Triple jump | 49 ft. 9 in. (15.16 m) | Ashia Hansen (GB) | Valencia, Spain | February 28, 1998 |
| Shot | 73 ft. 10 in. (22.50 m) | Helena Fibingerovà (Czechoslovakia) | Jablonec, Czechoslovakia | February 19, 1977 |
| Pentathlon* | 4,991 points | Irina Belova (Russia) | Berlin, Germany | February 14–15, 1992 |

*Events: 60-m hurdles: 8.22; High jump: 6 ft. 4 in. (1.93 m); Shot: 43 ft. 5.75 in. (13.25 m); Long jump 6.67 m (21 ft. 10.75 in.); 800 m: 2:10.26.

**Longest distance run on a treadmill in 24 hours** Scott Eppelman (USA) ran 116.04 miles (186.74 km) over 24 hours on a treadmill in Addison, Texas, USA, on November 1–2, 2002. He also ran the fastest 100 miles on a treadmill.

**Fastest stroller-pushing marathon** The fastest marathon while pushing a stroller is 4 hr. 6 min. 30 sec. by Patrick Read (UK) at the Abington Marathon, Oxfordshire, UK, on October 20, 2002.

# OLYMPICS

**Greatest attendance at an Olympic Games** The greatest ever total spectator attendance at an Olympic Games was 5,797,923, at the Los Angeles games in California, USA, in 1984.

**Best Olympics attendance by a country** Five countries have been represented at all of the 25 Summer Olympic Games that have been held (1896–2000): Australia, France, Greece, Great Britain, and Switzerland (in

**MOST GOLD MEDALS WON BY A COUNTRY** The USA has won a record 931 gold medals in the history of the Olympic Games, which have been held from 1896 to 2000. Here, the USA's Women's 4 × 200-m freestyle swimming team celebrate with their gold medals after victory at the 2000 Olympic Games in Sydney, Australia.

1956 Switzerland only contested the equestrian events, held in Stockholm, Sweden, and, therefore, did not attend the main Games in Melbourne, Australia). Of these countries, only France, Great Britain, and Switzerland have been present at all the Winter Olympic Games (1924–2002) as well.

**Most countries represented at an Olympics** The most countries ever to be represented at an Olympic Games is 199 at the Sydney games in Australia, between September 15 and October 1, 2000.

**Most participants at an Olympic Games** The Summer Olympic Games held from September 15 to October 1, 2000 in Sydney, Australia, hold the record for the greatest number of participants. In total, 11,084 athletes attended the games, of which a record 4,245 were women.

**Most participants at a Paralympic Games** The most participants in a Paralympic Games is 3,824 for the games held in 2000 in Sydney, Australia. The participants came from 125 different countries, also a Paralympic Games record.

**Longest time as an Olympic competitor** Four Olympic competitors have participated in games over a period of 40 years Ivan Joseph Martin Osiier (Denmark) in fencing (1908–32 and 1948); Magnus Andreas Thulstrup Clasen Konow (Norway) in yachting (1908–20, 1928, and 1936–48); Paul Bystram (Denmark) in yachting (1948–60, 1968–72, and 1984–88), and Durward Randolph Knowles (UK, then Bahamas) in yachting (1948–72 and 1988).

**Most consecutive Olympic gold medals won** The most gold medal wins at successive Olympic games is six by Aladár Gerevich (Hungary), who was a member of the winning sabre team from 1932 to 1960.

**Most consecutive gold medals won in an individual event** The only Olympians to win four consecutive individual titles in the same event are Al Oerter (USA) in the discus (1956–68) and Carl Lewis (USA) in the long jump (1984–96), Paul Elvstrom (Denmark) also won four successive gold medals at monotype yachting events (1948–60), but there was a class change (1948 Firefly class, 1952–60 Finn class).

However, if the Intercalated Games of 1906 (which were staged officially by the International Olympic Committee) are included Raymond Clarence Ewry (USA) won both the standing long jump and the standing high jump in four consecutive games (1900, 1904, 1906, and 1908).

**Most consecutive Olympic gold medals won by a woman** The most consecutive Olympic gold medals won by a woman is four by Birgit Fischer (formerly Birgit Schmidt, Germany) at the Seoul games in 1988 and the Sydney Olympics in 2000. Fischer's medals were all won in canoeing.

**Most consecutive endurance event Olympic gold medals won** The most Olympic gold medals won in an endurance event is five by Steven Redgrave (UK), who won a gold medal for rowing at five consecutive Olympic Games from 1984 to 2000.

**Most medal-winning countries at the Olympic Games** The 2000 Olympic Games in Sydney, Australia, saw the most medal winning countries ever at an Olympics, with 80 countries winning at least one medal.

**MOST PARTICIPANTS AT A WINTER OLYMPIC GAMES** The 2002 Winter Olympic Games, held at Salt Lake City, Utah, USA, were attended by a record 2,550 competitors from 77 different countries.

**MOST MEDAL WINNING COUNTRIES AT A WINTER OLYMPIC GAMES**
The most countries to win medals at a single Winter Olympic Games in
25 in 2002 at Salt Lake City, Utah, USA. Here, the German (silver),
Norwegian (gold), and French (bronze) medal winners celebrate after
the Men's 4 × 7.5-km biathlon relay.

**Most winter Olympic gold medals won by an individual** Bjorn
Dæhlie (Norway) won eight Olympic gold medals in Nordic skiing between
1992 and 1998. The women's record is six by Lidya Skobilkova (USSR) in
speed skating from 1960 to 1964, and Lyubov Yegerova (Russia) in Nordic
skiing from 1992 to 1994.

**Most winter Olympic gold medals won by a country** Norway has
won a record 94 gold medals in the history of the Winter Olympic Games
from 1924–2002.

# COMBAT

## BOXING

**Most fights undefeated** From 1916 to 1923 Edward Henry "Harry"
Greb (USA) was unbeaten in a sequence of 178 bouts including 117 ruled
"no decision," of which five were unofficial losses. Of boxers with complete records, Packey McFarland (USA) had 97 fights from 1905 to 1915
without a defeat, five of which were draws. Pedro Carrasco (Spain) won
83 consecutive fights from April 22, 1964 to September 3, 1970, drew
once and had nine more wins before his loss to Armando Ramos (Mexico)
in a World Boxing Council (WBC) lightweight contest on February 18,
1972.

**MOST HEAVYWEIGHT TITLES BY A FORMER MIDDLEWEIGHT** This remarkable feat has been achieved only twice in 106 years. The first time was by Robert James "Bob" Fitzsimmons (UK) when the former middleweight knocked out James J. Corbett (USA) at Carson City, Nevada, USA, on March 17, 1897. Roy Jones, Jr. (USA, shown) matched this when he beat John Ruiz (USA) for the World Boxing Association heavyweight title by unanimous decision on March 2, 2003 at Las Vegas, Nevada, USA.

**Most world title recaptures** The only boxer to win a world title five times at one weight is "Sugar" Ray Robinson (USA) who beat Carmen Basilio (USA) in Chicago, USA, on March 25, 1958, to regain the world middleweight title for the fourth time.

**Most consecutive knock-outs** The record for most consecutive knock-outs is held by Lamar Clark (USA), who achieved 44 consecutive knock-outs from 1958 to January, 1960. He knocked out six opponents in one night (five in the first round) at Bingham, Utah, USA, on December 1, 1958.

**Longest reigning world heavyweight champion** Joe Louis (USA) was champion for 11 years 252 days, from June 22, 1937, when he knocked out James Joseph Braddock (USA) in the eighth round at Chicago, Illinois, USA, until his retirement on March 1, 1949. During his reign, Louis made a record 25 defenses of his title. This record is also the longest reign of any champion in any weight division.

**Most world titles at different weights** Henry "Homicide Hank" Armstrong (USA) held world titles at three different weights—featherweight, lightweight, and welterweight—simultaneously between August and December, 1938. It is claimed that Barney Ross (USA) held the world lightweight, junior welterweight, and welterweight titles at the same time from May 28 to September 17, 1934, but the date when he relinquished his lightweight title is disputed.

**Most speedball hits in one minute** The greatest number of hits of a speedball in one minute is 366 by Wayne Harbinson (Australia) at the GTV9 Studios, Melbourne, Australia, on October 14, 1996.

## JUDO

**Most men's judo world titles** David Douillet (France) has won five world and Olympic titles: in the Over 95-kg class in 1993, 1995, and 1997; in the Open in 1995; and in the Olympic Over 95-kg class in 1996. Yasuhiro Yamashita (Japan) has also won five world and Olympic titles: three in the Over 95-kg class, and one each in the Open and the Olympic Over 95-kg class.

**Most women's judo world championships** Ingrid Berghmans (Belgium) has won six women's world titles (first held 1980)—in the Open category in 1980, 1982, 1984, and 1986, and in the Under-72 kg class in 1984 and 1989.

**Most judo throws in 10 hours** Patrick Hurley and Tony Cox (both UK) of the Leeds Central Aikido Club completed 46,261 judo and aikido throwing techniques in a ten-hour period at the Aireborough Leisure Centre, Leeds, West Yorkshire, UK, on May 30, 1998.

## FENCING

**Most men's Olympic medals** Edoardo Mangiarotti (Italy) holds the record for the most men's Olympic medals with 13: six gold, five silver, and two bronze. He won them for foil and epée from 1936 to 1960.

**Most men's team World Championships** The greatest number of fencing team World Championships won is 34 by Italy, a record 16 foil, 13 epée, and five sabre titles, between 1929 and 1994. France has won nine foil titles (1924–80) and a record 14 epée titles, (1904–2002). The record number of wins for sabre is 20 by Hungary between 1908 and 1998.

**Most Olympic golds** The most men's individual Olympic fencing gold medals won is three by Nedo Nadi (Italy), who won in 1912 and 1920 (two) and Ramón Fonst (Cuba) who won in 1900 and 1904 (two). Nadi also won three team gold medals in 1920, making five golds at one games—the record for fencing and at the time a record for any sport.

The most fencing gold medals won by a woman at the Olympic Games is four (one individual, three team) by Yelena Dmitryevna Novikova (USSR), who won her titles between 1968 and 1976.

**Most men's world titles** The greatest number of individual fencing world titles won is five by Aleksandr Romankov (USSR) for foil in 1974, 1977, 1979, 1982, and 1983.

**LARGEST YOKOZUNA SUMO WRESTLER** Hawaiian-born Chad Rowan, alias Akebono (USA, facing out), became the first foreign rikishi to be promoted to the top rank of *yokozun* in January, 1993. He is the tallest *yokozuna* in sumo history at 6 ft. 8 in. (2.04 m) high. He is also the heaviest, weighing 501 lb. (227 kg).

# MARTIAL ARTS

**Most concrete blocks broken in a minute** The most concrete blocks smashed by hand in one minute is 55 by Dan Netherland (USA) at Ripley's Aquarium of the Smokies, Gatlinburg, Tennessee, USA, on February 26, 2003. Each block, measuring 30 × 8 × 2.9 in (76.2 × 20.3 × 7.3 cm) was stacked in piles of one, two, three, four, five, six, seven, eight, nine, and finally ten high.

**Most concrete blocks broken using the roundhouse kick method** Mikael Birgersson (Sweden) holds the record for the most concrete blocks broken using the roundhouse kick method. In one minute he smashed 33 blocks at the studios of *Guinness Rekord TV* in Stockholm, Sweden, on November 28, 2001.

**Highest martial arts kick** The highest martial arts kick measured is 9 ft. 8 in. (2.94 m) by Jessie Frankson (USA), who kicked a target with a pin attached, which in turn burst a balloon on the set of *Guinness World Records: Primetime,* Los Angeles, California, USA, on December 21, 2000.

**Most karate kicks in one minute** The most karate kicks in one minute using only one leg is 128 by Fabian Cuenca Pirroti (Spain) on November 11, 2001 on the set of *El Show de los Récords* in Madrid, Spain.

# SUMO

**Most consecutive sumo tournaments won** *Yokozuna* (grand champion) Mitsugu Akimoto (Japan, sumo name Chiyonofuji) won one of the six annual tournaments—the Kyushu Basho—for eight years in a row from 1981 to 1988. He also holds the record for the most career wins, with 1,045, and *Makunouchi* (top division) wins, with 807.

**Most sumo Yokozuna consecutive wins** *Yokozuna* Sadji Akiyoshi (Japan), alias Futabayama, had a record 69 consecutive wins between 1937 and 1939.

**Most rikishi bouts won in a year** Toshimitsu Ogata (Japan), alias Kitanoumi, set a record in 1978 winning 82 of the 90 bouts that top *rikishi* fight annually.

# STAMINA & STRENGTH

## STAMINA EVENTS

**Most skips in 24 hours by a team** The record for the most skips in 24 hours by a team of six is 260,307 and was set by Jim Payne, Neil Gough,

**WOMEN'S 69-KG CLEAN AND JERK** The record for the women's 69-kg clean and jerk is held by Chunhong Liu (China), who lifted 148 kg. at Busan, South Korea, on October 3, 2002.

Larry O'Brien, Christy O'Reilly, Deirdre Hearne, and Martin Murphy (all Ireland) in Waterford, Ireland on May 24–25, 2002. Each skipper skipped for an hour at a time in relay fashion.

**Most push-ups in one hour** Roy Berger (Canada) achieved 3,416 push-ups in one hour at the Central Canada Exhibition, Ottawa, Ontario, Canada, on August 30, 1998.

**Most push-ups in one minute** The record for the most push-ups in one minute is 124, set by Campbell Pentney (New Zealand) at Takapuna Athletic Club, New Zealand, on August 3, 2002.

**Most one-arm push-ups in one minute** Yvan de Weber (Switzerland) completed 120 one-arm push-ups in one minute at the studios of *El Show de los Récords,* Madrid, Spain, on October 23, 2001.

**Most push-ups using back of hands in one hour** The record for the most push-ups using the backs of the hands in one hour is 1,584 and was set by Kevin Jefferson (UK) at Stanley Central Working Men's Club, Stanley, Durham, UK, on October 20, 2002.

**Most parallel bar dips in one hour** Simon Kent (UK) achieved 3,988 parallel bar dips in one hour at Farrah's Health Centre, Lincoln, UK, on September 5, 1998.

Simon Kent also holds the record for the most parallel bar dips in one minute with 140. This was set at Lincoln College, Lincoln, UK, on July 17, 2002.

**Most abdominal frame sit-ups in one hour**  The record for the most sit-ups in one hour using an abdominal frame is 5,633 and was set by Guillermo Subiela (Argentina) at Synergy Fitness Club, Astoria, New York, USA, on October 5, 2002.

**Most squats in one hour**  On January 30, 2002 Attila Horvàth (Hungary) completed 4,656 squats in one hour at the Center of Sports Gym, University of Debrecen, Hungary.

**Most rotations on a pommel horse in one minute**  The record for the most rotations on a pommel horse in one minute is 59 by Andreu Vivo

**FASTEST BACKFLIP OVER 50 M**  On August 31, 1995, at Makuhar Messe Event Hall, Chiba, Japan, Vitaliy Scherbo (Belarus, above) backflipped 164 ft. (50 m) along the ground in 10.22 seconds.

**MOST OLYMPIC WEIGHTLIFTING GOLD MEDALS** The most Olympic weightlifting gold medals won is three by Naim Suleymanoglü (Turkey) in 1988, 1992 and 1996; Pyrros Dimas (Greece) in 1992, 1996, and 2000; and Akakios Kakiasvili (Greece, shown) in 1992, 1996, and 2000. In 1992 Kakiasvili was known as Kakhi Kakhiachbili and he represented EUN/CIS, the Unified team of the former Soviet Republics.

Tomas (Spain). The record was set on *El Show de los Récords* in Madrid, Spain, on October 4, 2001.

## WEIGHTLIFTING

**Most Olympic weightlifting appearances** The most Olympic weightlifting appearances is five by Imre Földi (Hungary) between 1960 and 1976.

**Most Olympic weightlifting medals won** The most Olympic weightlifting medals won is four by Norbert Schemansky (USA) between 1948 and 1964. Schemansky won gold at middle-heavyweight class in 1952; silver at heavyweight class in 1948; and bronze at heavyweight class in 1960 and 1964.

**Most women's weightlifting World Championships** The most gold medals won at the women's weightlifting World Championships is 13 by Chunhong Liu (China) in the 60/64 kg class in 1992–96.

**Most men's world weightlifting titles** The most world weightlifting title wins including Olympic Games, is 10 by Naim Suleymanoglü (Turkey) in 1985–86, 1988–89, and 1991–96.

**Youngest weightlifting world record holder** Naim Suleymanoglü (b. January 23, 1967, Turkey) was 16 years 62 days old when he set world records for clean and jerk at 353 lb. (160 kg) and a combined total of 628 lb. (285 kg) at Allentown, New Jersey, USA, on March 26, 1983.

**Oldest weightlifting world record holder** The oldest weightlifting world record holder is Norbert Schemansky (b. May 30, 1924, USA) who, at age 37 years 333 days, snatched 362 lb. (164.2 kg) in the then unlimited heavyweight class at Detroit, Michigan, USA, on April 28, 1962.

**Most powerlifting world championships** Hideaki Inaba (Japan) holds the most powerlifting world titles with 17, at 52 kg in 1974–83 and 1985–91.

## ★ WEIGHTLIFTING WORLD RECORDS ★

| EVENT | WEIGHT | NAME AND COUNTRY | VENUE | DATE |
|---|---|---|---|---|
| Men's 56-kg clean and jerk | 168.0 kg | Halil Mutlu (Turkey) | Trencin, Slovakia | April 24, 2001 |
| Men's 56-kg snatch | 138.5 kg | Halil Mutlu (Turkey) | Antalya, Turkey | November 4, 2001 |
| Men's 56-kg total | 305.0 kg | Halil Mutlu (Turkey) | Sydney, Australia | September 16, 2000 |
| Men's 62-kg clean and jerk | 182.5 kg. | Maosheng Le (China) | Busan, South Korea | October 2, 2002 |
| Men's 62-kg snatch | 153.0 kg | Shi Zhiyong (China) | Izmir, Turkey | June 28, 2002 |
| Men's 62-kg total | | No record yet set | | |
| Men's 69-kg clean and jerk | 196.5 kg | Galabin Boevski (Bulgaria) | Sydney, Australia | September 20, 2000 |
| Men's 69-kg snatch | 165.0 kg | Georgi Markov (Bulgaria) | Sydney, Australia | September 20, 2000 |
| Men's 69-kg total | 357.5 kg | Galabin Boevski (Bulgaria) | Athens, Greece | November 24, 1999 |
| Men's 77-kg clean and jerk | 210.0 kg | Oleg Perepetchenov (Russia) | Trencin, Slovakia | April 27, 2001 |
| Men's 77-kg snatch | 173.0 kg | Sergey Filimonov (Kazakhstan) | Busan, South Korea | October 4, 2002 |
| Men's 77-kg total | 377.5 kg | Plamen Zhelyazkov (Bulgaria) | Doha, Qatar | March 27, 2002 |
| Men's 85-kg clean and jerk | 218.0 kg | Zhang Yong (China) | Tel Aviv, Israel | April 25, 1998 |
| Men's 85-kg snatch | 182.5 kg | Andrei Ribakov (Bulgaria) | Havirov, Czech Republic | June 2, 2002 |
| Men's 85-kg total | | No record yet set | | |
| Men's 94-kg clean and jerk | 232.5 kg | Szymon Kolecki (Poland) | Sofia, Bulgaria | April 29, 2000 |
| Men's 94-kg snatch | 188.0 kg | Akakios Kakiasvili (Greece) | Athens, Greece | November 27, 1999 |
| Men's 94-kg total | | No record yet set | | |
| Men's 105-kg clean and jerk | | No record yet set | | |
| Men's 105-kg snatch | 198.5 kg | Marcin Dolega (Poland) | Havirov, Czech Republic | June 4, 2002 |
| Men's 105-kg total | | No record yet set | | |
| Men's over-105-kg clean and jerk | 263.0 kg | Hossein Rezazadeh (Iran) | Warsaw, Poland | November 26, 2002 |

| | | | | |
|---|---|---|---|---|
| Men's over-105-kg snatch | 212.5 kg | Hossein Rezazadeh (Iran) | Sydney, Australia | September 26, 2000 |
| Men's over-105-kg total | 472.5 kg | Hossein Rezazadeh (Iran) | Sydney, Australia | September 26, 2000 |
| Women's 48-kg clean and jerk | 115.5 kg | Mingjuan Wang (China) | Warsaw, Poland | November 19, 2002 |
| Women's 48-kg snatch | 92.5 kg | Mingjuan Wang (China) | Warsaw, Poland | November 19, 2002 |
| Women's 48-kg total | 207.5 kg | Mingjuan Wang (China) | Warsaw, Poland | November 19, 2002 |
| Women's 53-kg clean and jerk | 127.5 kg | Xueju Li (China) | Busan, South Korea | November 20, 2002 |
| Women's 53-kg snatch | 102.5 kg | Ri Song-hui (North Korea) | Warsaw, Poland | October 1, 2002 |
| Women's 53-kg total | 225.0 kg | Yang Xia (China) | Sydney, Australia | September 18, 2000 |
| Women's 58-kg clean and jerk | 133.0 kg | Calyan Sun (China) | Izmir, Turkey | June 28, 2002 |
| Women's 58-kg snatch | 106.0 kg | Zhijuan Song (China) | Kazincbarcika, Hungary | October 5, 2002 |
| Women's 58-kg total | 237.5 kg | Calyan Sun (China) | Izmir, Turkey | June 28, 2002 |
| Women's 63-kg clean and jerk | 136.0 kg | Anastasia Tsakiri (Greece) | Warsaw, Poland | November 21, 2002 |
| Women's 63-kg snatch | 112.5 kg | Chen Xiaomin (China) | Sydney, Australia | September 19, 2000 |
| Women's 63-kg total | 242.5 kg | Chen Xiaomin (China) | Sydney, Australia | September 19, 2000 |
| Women's 69-kg clean and jerk | 148.0 kg | Chunhong Liu (China) | Busan, South Korea | October 2, 2002 |
| Women's 69-kg snatch | 115.5 kg | Chunhong Liu (China) | Busan, South Korea | October 6, 2002 |
| Women's 69-kg total | 262.5 kg | Chunhong Liu (China) | Busan, South Korea | October 3, 2002 |
| Women's 75-kg clean and jerk | 152.5 kg | Ruiping Sun (China) | Busan, South Korea | October 7, 2002 |
| Women's 75-kg snatch | 118.5 kg | Ruiping Sun (China) | Busan, South Korea | October 7, 2002 |
| Women's 75-kg total | 270.0 kg | Ruiping Sun (China) | Busan, South Korea | October 7, 2002 |
| Women's over-75-kg clean and jerk | 167.5 kg | Tang Gonghong (China) | Busan, South Korea | October 8, 2002 |
| Women's over-75-kg snatch | 135.0 kg | Ding Meiyuan (China) | Sydney, Australia | September 22, 2000 |
| Women's over 75-kg total | 300.0 kg | Ding Meiyuan (China) | Sydney, Australia | September 22, 2000 |

From January 1, 1998 the International Weightlifting Federation (IWF) introduced modified body-weight categories, thereby making the existing world records redundant. This is the new listing with the world standards for the new bodyweight categories. Results achieved at IWF-approved competitions exceeding the world standards by 0.5 kg for snatch or clean and jerk, or by 2.5 kg for the total, will be recognized as world records.

# WINTER SPORTS

## ALPINE SKIING

**Most World Cup individual race wins**  The most World Cup individual event wins is 86 (46 giant slalom and 40 slalom from a total of 287 races) by Ingemar Stenmark (Sweden) between 1974 and 1989. Stenmark also holds the men's record of 13 wins in one season (1978/79), of which 10 were part of a record 14 successive giant slalom wins from March 18, 1978 (his 22nd birthday) to January 21, 1980. The women's record is held by Annemarie Moser (Austria), who won 62 individual events between 1970 and 1979. She had a record 11 consecutive downhill wins from December 1972 to January 1974. She has also claimed the World Cup Overall Champion (downhill and slalom events combined) title a record six times since the tour began in 1967.

**Highest speed in World Cup skiing**  Armin Assinger (Austria) reached a record speed of 69.8 mph (112.4 km/h) at Sierra Nevada, Spain, on March 15, 1993.

**Most Alpine skiing Olympic gold medals**  The most men's Olympic gold medals won is three. Four skiers share the record: Anton "Toni" Sailer (Austria) won gold in the downhill, slalom, and giant slalom events in 1956; Jean-Claude Killy (France) took home gold in the same events in 1968; Alberto Tomba (Italy) won in the slalom in 1988 and the giant slalom in 1988 and 1992; and Kjetil André Aamodt (Norway) won in the super giant slalom in 1992 and 2002, and in the combined event at the 2002 Games.

The most Olympic gold medals won by a woman is three, a record also shared by four skiers: Vreni Schneider (Switzerland) in the giant slalom in 1988 and the slalom in 1988 and 1994; Janica Kostelic (Croatia) in the combined event, the giant

**HIGHEST SPEED IN AN OLYMPIC DOWNHILL RACE  The highest average speed achieved in an Olympic downhill race was 66.81 mph (107.53 km/h) by Jean-Luc Cretier (France) at Nagano, Japan, on February 13, 1998.**

slalom and slalom in 2002; Katja Seizinger (Germany) for downhill in 1994 and 1998 and combined in 1998; and Deborah Campagnoni (Italy) in the super giant slalom in 1992 and the giant slalom in 1994 and 1998.

**Most Alpine skiing Olympic medals** The most Olympic Games medals won by a male is seven by Kjetil André Aamodt (Norway) who, in addition to his record three gold medals, has won two silver (downhill, combined 1994) and two bronze (giant slalom 1992, super giant slalom 1994).

The most Olympic medals won by a woman is five. Vreni Schneider (Switzerland), in addition to her record three gold medals, won silver in the combined and bronze in the giant slalom in 1994. Katja Seizinger (Germany) also has five Olympic medals. As well as her three golds, she won bronze in 1992 and 1998 in the super giant slalom.

**Most world Alpine skiing championship titles** The greatest number of World Alpine Championship titles won by a man is seven by Anton "Toni" Sailer (Austria), who won all four events (giant slalom, slalom, downhill and the non-Olympic Alpine combination) in 1956 and the downhill, giant slalom, and combined in 1958.

The greatest number of World Alpine Championship titles won by a woman is 12 by Christl Cranz (Germany). She has won seven individual titles (four slalom in 1934, 1937–39, and three downhill in 1935, 1937, and 1939), and five combined in 1934–35 and 1937–39. She also won the gold medal for the combined event in the 1936 Olympics.

**Most World Cup ski wins in a season** Vreni Schneider (Switzerland) won 13 events (and a combined event), including all seven slalom events, in the 1988/89 season.

**MOST BIATHLON OLYMPIC MEDALS** The most Olympic medals won in the men's biathlon is seven by Ricco Gross (Germany, right in this picture). He won three gold for the 4 x 7.5 km in 1992, 1994, and 1998; three silver for the 10 km in 1992 and 1994, and the 4 x 7.5 km in 2002, and a bronze for pursuit in 2002.

**MOST ALPINE NATIONS CUP WINS** The Nations Cup, awarded on the combined results of the men and women in the World Cup, has been won a record 22 times by Austria in 1969, 1973–80, 1982, and 1990–2001. Alexandra Meissnitzer has helped Austria to Nations Cup victory on several occasions.

**Greatest vertical distance skied in one day** On April 29, 1998, Edi Podivinsky, Luke Sauder, Chris Kent (all Canada) and Dominique Perret (Switzerland) skied a record total of 353,600 ft. (107,777 m) in 14 hr. 30 min. on a slope at Blue River, British Columbia, Canada. They made the run 73 times and were helicoptered back to the summit each time.

Jennifer Hughes (USA) holds the women's vertical skiing distance record. On April 20, 1998 she skied 305,525 ft. (93,124 m) at Atlin, British Columbia, Canada. Hughes was accompanied by Tammy McMinn (USA), who broke the snowboarding record for the same feat.

**Greatest vertical distance skied in one day using t-bar lift** Neal Weisenberg skied a total of 153,937 ft. (46,920 m) in one day, from February 27 to 28, 1999 at Kimberley Alpine Resort, Kimberley, British Columbia, Canada. He used a t-bar ski lift to return to the top of the slopes.

**Most extensive skiers** In 1994, Arnie Wilson and Lucy Dicker (both UK) skied every day in a round-the-world expedition. In total they covered 3,678 miles (5,919 km) and 4,146,890 vertical feet (1,263,972 vertical meters) at 237 resorts in 13 countries in five continents.

The first person to ski in all seven continents was Tom Hayes (USA), and the first woman was Norma Rowlerson (UK).

**Most World Cup downhill wins** Franz Klammer (Austria) won a record 25 World Cup downhill races between 1974 and 1984.

**Longest run in downhill skiing** The Weissfluhjoch-Küblis Parsenn course, near Davos, Switzerland is 7.6 miles (12.23 km) long.

**Longest downhill race** The Inferno in Switzerland is 9.8 miles (15.8 km) from the top of the Schilthorn to Lauterbrunnen. The record time for completing the course is 13 min. 53.40 sec. by Urs von Allmen (Switzerland) in 1992. The women's record time for the race is 17 min. 8.42 sec. by Christine Sonderegger (Switzerland) in the same year.

**Highest speed skiing** Harry Egger (Austria) skied at 154.165 mph (248.105 km/h) at Les Arcs, France, on May 2, 1999.

On the same day at Les Arcs, Karine Dubouchet (France) achieved a women's record speed of 145.728 mph (234.528 km/h).

## FREESTYLE SKIING

**Most somersault and twist combinations in a freestyle jump** Matt Chojnacki (USA), completed a quadruple-twisting quadruple back flip at Colorado, USA, on April 4, 2001.

**Most freestyle skiing World Championship titles** The first freestyle World Championships were held at Tignes, France, in 1986. Edgar Grospiron (France) has won a record three titles, for moguls in 1989 and 1991 and aerials in 1995. He also won an Olympic title in 1992.

The most women's skiing freestyle world titles won is also three by Candice Gilg (France) for moguls in 1993, 1995, and 1997.

**Most freestyle World Cup wins** Eric Laboureix (France) achieved five freestyle World Cup wins, winning the overall title in 1986–88 and 1990–91. The same record for women is ten by Connie Kissling (Switzerland) in 1983–92.

## NORDIC SKIING

**Most Nordic skiing world titles** The 1924 Winter Olympics in Chamonix, France, was the first skiing World Nordic Championships. The greatest number of titles (including Olympics) won is 17 by Bjorn Dæhlie (Norway) (12 individual and 5 relay) in 1991–98. Dæhlie has won a record 29 medals in total.

The most women's titles won is 17 by Yelena Välbe (Russia) (10 individual and 7 relay) in 1989–98. She has won a record total of 24 medals.

**Most Nordic skiing Olympic gold medals** The most Nordic skiing Olympic gold medals won by a man is eight by Bjorn Dæhlie (Norway) for

**LONGEST COMPETITIVE MEN'S SKI JUMP** The longest competitive ski jump made by a man is 738 ft. (225 m.) by Andreas Goldberger (Austria) at Plancia, Slovenia, on March 18, 2000.

the 15 km, 50 km, and 4 × 10-km relay in 1992, and the 10 km and 15 km in 1994, the 10 km, 50 km, and 4 × 10-km relay in 1998.

Lyubov Yegorova (Russia) holds the women's record with six wins for the 10 km, 15 km, and 4 × 5-km relay in 1992, and the 5 km, 10 km, and 4 × 5-km relay in 1994.

**Most Nordic combined skiing Olympic gold medals** Ulrich Wehling (Germany) has won three gold medals in the individual event in 1972, 1976, and 1980. Sampaa Lajunen (Finland) shares the record, with golds in the individual, sprint, and relay in 2002. Lajunen also won silver in the individual and relay events in 1998 for a record total of five medals.

**Highest average speed in a Nordic skiing 50-km race** The highest average speed in a major Nordic skiing 50-km race is 16.24 mph (26.14 km/h). The race was completed in a record time of 1 hr. 54 min. 46 sec. by Aleksey Prokurorov (Russia) at Thunder Bay, Canada, on March 19, 1994.

**Greatest distance Nordic skiing in 24 hours** Seppo-Juhani Savolainen (Finland) covered 258.2 miles (415.5 km) in 24 hours at Saariselk, Finland, on April 8–9, 1988.

Kamila Horakova (Czech Republic) is the women's record holder, with 206.91 miles (333 km), achieved on April 12–13, 2000.

**Longest ski jump by a woman**  The longest ski jump performed by a woman is 367 ft. (112 m) by Eva Ganster (Austria), who achieved the distance at Bischofshofen, Austria, on January 7, 1994.

**Longest ski jump on a dry ski slope**  The longest dry ski jump is 302 ft. (92 m) by Hubert Schwarz (Germany) at Berchtesgarten, Germany, on June 30, 1981.

**Most gold Worldloppett Masters titles**  By the end of the 2001 season, the most times an individual had qualified as a Worldloppett Gold Master is nine, by Jan Jasiewicz (Switzerland). To qualify as a Gold Master you must have completed 10 races in the Worldloppett series, all in different countries and at least two different continents.

## SNOWBOARDING

**Most snowboarding World Cup titles**  The most snowboarding World Cup titles won is 16 by Karine Ruby (France). She won overall titles in 1996–98 and 2001–2002; slalom/parallel slalom titles in 1996–98 and 2002; giant slalom titles in 1995–98 and 2001; and snowboard cross titles in 1997 and 2001. The most men's titles won is six, by Mathieu Bozzetto (France). He won the overall title in 1999 and 2000, and the slalom and parallel slalom titles between 1999 and 2002.

**Most men's X-Games snowboarding medals**  Shaun Palmer (USA) has won a record three gold medals at the Winter ESPN X-Games for the

**MOST SNOWBOARDING CHAMPIONSHIP TITLES**  The most snowboarding titles won (including Olympic titles) is three, by Karine Ruby (France). She won the giant slalom in 1996, the Olympic title in 1998, and the snowboard cross in 1997.

**MOST OLYMPIC SNOWBOARDING MEDALS** The most Olympic snowboarding medals won is two. Ross Powers (USA, shown), won bronze in 1998 and gold in 2002 for the halfpipe. Karine Ruby (France) shares the record with a gold in 1998 and a silver in 2002 for the parallel giant slalom.

boarder X discipline (1997–99) since the inaugural X-Games in 1997. Additionally, across all the disciplines, he has won a total of six gold medals at the X-Games. This is as well as a gold in the 1997 X-Games snow mountain biking dual downhill event.

**Most women's X-Games snowboarding medals** The most X-Games snowboarding medals won by a woman is six, by Barrett Christy (USA). Christy took the gold medal in the big air event and the silver medal in the slopestyle discipline at the 1999 Winter X-Games. She also won silver for both events in 1998, and golds at the first X-Games in 1997.

**Fastest snowboard on a bobsled run** In November 1998 at Königssee, Germany, Reto Lamm (Switzerland) managed to surf down a complete bobsled run on his snowboard at a speed of 49.7 mph (80 km/h).

**Greatest vertical distance snowboarded in one day** On April 20, 1998, Tammy McMinn (USA) snowboarded down a slope at Atlin, British Columbia, Canada, 101 times, making a total vertical descent of 305,525 ft. (93,124 m). She was lifted back to the top each time by helicopter. She performed her feat alongside skier Jennifer Hughes (USA). The total duration of the event was 14 hr. 50 min.

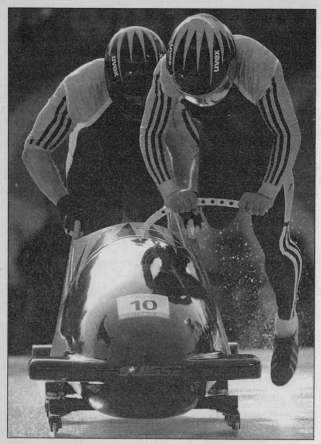

**MOST WORLD CHAMPIONSHIP AND OLYMPIC GAMES TWO-MAN BOBSLED WINS** Switzerland (current team pictured) has won the two-man bobsled title 17 times, in 1935, 1947–50, 1953, 1955, 1977–80, 1982–83, 1987, 1990, 1992, and 1994. They have also had a record four Olympic successes in 1948, 1980, 1992, and 1994.

**Highest speed snowboarding** On May 2, 1999 at Les Arcs, France, Darren Powell (Australia) achieved a record snowboarding speed of 125.459 mph (201.907 km/h).

**Youngest pro snowboarding halfpipe competitor** Born September 3, 1986, Shaun White (USA) began competing as a professional snowboarder in 1999 at 13 years of age.

## BOBSLED AND TOBOGGANING

**Oldest rider of the Cresta Run** The oldest person to have ridden the Cresta Run successfully is Prince Constantin von Liechtenstein at the age of 88 years 54 days, on February 15, 2000. The Cresta Run at St. Moritz, Switzerland, is one of winter sport's legendary challenges. It is an ice run similar to those found in the sport of bobsledding, but with crucial differences. In bobsledding the tracks are man-made, and the corners are banked high, whereas the Cresta is natural ice and uses the contours of the land to form its curves.

**Fastest Cresta Run completion time** The Cresta Run course, which dates from 1884, is 3,977 ft. (1,212 m) long with a drop of 514 ft. (157 m). The record for completing the course is 50.09 seconds by James Sunley (UK) on February 13, 1999. His average speed on the run was 54.13 mph (87.11 km/h).

**Fastest Cresta Run time from Junction** On January 17, 1999 Johannes Badrutt (Switzerland) set a fastest Cresta Run record, beginning at

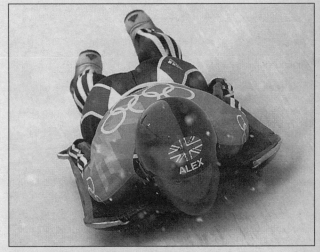

**MOST SKELETON WORLD TITLES** Alex Coomber (UK) has won a record four world skeleton titles. He won the World Cup in 2000, 2001, and 2002, and the World Championships in 2000.

the Junction, the second point of the run from which competitors can officially start. He made a time of 41.02 seconds, covering a total distance of 2,921 ft. (890 m).

**Most Olympic bobsled medals**  The most individual Olympic bobsled medals won is seven (one gold, five silver, and one bronze) by Bogdan Musiol (GDR) between 1980 and 1992.

**Most Olympic gold bobsled medals**  The most Olympic gold bobsled medals won by an individual is three by Meinhard Neher and Bernard Germeshausen (both GDR). They won the two-man event and the four-man event in 1976, and the four-man event in 1980.

**Most world championship and Olympic games four-man bobsled wins**  Switzerland has won the world four-man bob title 20 times, in 1924, 1936, 1939, 1947, 1954–57, 1971–73, 1975, 1982–83, 1986–90, and 1993. They also have a record five Olympic victories, in 1924, 1936, 1956, 1972, and 1988.

**Most world championship bobsled titles**  Eugenio Monti (Italy) won a record 11 world championship bobsled titles between 1957 and 1968. He won three four-man titles and eight two-man titles.

**Oldest Olympic bobsled champion**  Jay O'Brien (USA) was 47 years 357 days old when he won gold with the four-man bobsled team at the 1932 Winter Olympics at Lake Placid, New York, USA.

**Youngest Olympic bobsled champion**  William Guy Fiske (USA) was 16 years 260 days old when he won gold with the five-man team at the Winter Olympic Games in Switzerland in 1928.

**Most men's World Championship and Olympic luge wins**  The most World Championship and Olympic Games luge titles won by a man is six by Georg Hackl (GDR and Germany), who won single-seater titles in 1989, 1990, 1992, 1994, 1997, and 1998.

Stefan Krausse and Jan Behrendt (both GDR and Germany) have won a record six two-seater titles, in 1989, 1991–93, 1995, and 1998.

**Most women's World Luge Championship titles**  The most World Luge Championship titles won by a woman is four by Margit Schumann (GDR), from 1973 to 1975 and in 1977. She also won the gold medal at the 1976 Olympic Games.

**Fastest lugeing speed**  Tony Benshoof (USA) reached a record speed of 86.6 mph (139.39 km/h) on the 2002 Olympic luge track at Park City, Utah, USA, on October 16, 2001. The speed was reached during training for the 2001 Luge World Cup Series.

## SKI-BOB

**Most individual women's combined World Ski-Bob Championship titles** The most individual combined World Ski-Bob Championship titles won by a woman is four by Petra Tschach-Wlezcek (Austria), who won between 1988 and 1991.

**Fastest ski-bob speed** The fastest speed on a ski-bob is 114.89 mph (184.9 km/h) by Romuald Bonvin (Switzerland) on March 21, 2000 at Les Arcs, France.

## CURLING

**Largest curling tournament** The world's largest bonspiel (curling tournament) is the Manitoba Curling Association Bonspiel held annually in Winnipeg, Canada. In 1988 there were 1,424 teams of four men, a total of 5,696 curlers, using 187 sheets of curling ice.

**Fastest eight-ender** Eight curlers from the Burlington Golf and Country Club, Canada, curled the fastest ever eight-end game in a time of 47 min. 24 sec., with time penalties of 5 min. 30 sec., at Burlington, Ontario, Canada, on April 4, 1986, following rules agreed with the Ontario Curling Association. The time is taken from when the first stone crosses the near hogline until the game's last stone comes to a complete stop.

**Most Strathcona Cup wins** The most wins of the Strathcona Cup (instituted in 1903) is seven, by Canada against Scotland in 1903, 1909, 1912, 1923, 1938, 1957, and 1965.

**Most men's World Curling Championship titles** The Canadian men's team has won

**MOST WOMEN'S WORLD CURLING CHAMPIONSHIP TITLES** The Canadian women's team (Kim Kelly, left, and Mary Ann Wayne from the 2002 team pictured here) has won more curling World Championships than any other team, with a record 12 titles, won in 1980, 1984–87, 1989, 1993–94, 1996–97, and 2000–01.

the World Curling Championship 27 times, in 1959–64, 1966, 1968–72, 1980, 1982–83, 1985–87, 1989–90, 1993–96, 1998, 2000, and 2002.

**Longest throw** The longest throw of a curling stone was 576 ft. 4 in. (175.66 m) by Eddie Kulbacki (Canada) at Park Lake, Neepawa, Manitoba, Canada, on January 29 1989. The attempt took place on a specially prepared sheet of curling ice 1,200 ft. (365.76 m) long.

**Largest curling rink** The world's largest ever curling rink was the Big Four Curling Rink in Calgary, Alberta, Canada, which opened in 1959 and closed in 1989. It accommodated 96 teams and 384 players on two floors, each with 24 sheets of ice.

## FIGURE SKATING

**Most women's Olympic gold figure skating medals** The most Olympic gold figure skating medals won by a woman is three by Sonja Henie (Norway) at the Winter Olympic Games of 1928, 1932, and 1936. Henie also holds the record for the most women's individual World Championship figure skating titles, having won 10 times from 1927 to 1936.

**Most men's Olympic gold figure skating medals** Gillis Grafstrom (Sweden) has won three golds, in 1920, 1924, and 1928. He also won silver in 1932.

**Most men's World Championship figure skating titles** Ulrich Salchow (Sweden) won 10 individual world figure skating titles in 1901–05 and 1907–11.

**Most figure skating grand slams won** The most figure skating grand slams, which comprise the European, World and Olympic titles, won by a man is two by Karl Schäfer (Austria) in 1932 and 1936. Two women have won a record two figure skating grand slams: Sonja Henie (Norway) in 1932 and 1936, and Katarina Witt (West Germany) in 1984 and 1988.

**Youngest figure skating world champion** The youngest female winner of a world figure skating title is Tara Lipinski (USA), when she won the individual title at the age of 14 years 286 days on March 22, 1997.

**Longest figure skating jump-flip** The longest figure skating jump-flip was completed by Robin Cousins (UK) with a 19-ft. 1-in. (5.81-m) axel jump and an 18-ft. (5.48-m) back-flip at Richmond Ice Rink, Surrey, UK, on November 16, 1983.

**Most figure skating pairs world championships** Irina Rodnina (USSR) has won 10 pairs titles: four with Aleksey Nikolayevich Ulanov

(USSR) in 1969–72, and six with her husband Aleksandr Gennadyevich Zaitsev (USSR) in 1973–78. The most ice dance titles won is six by Lyudmila Alekseyevna Pakhomova (USSR) and her husband Aleksandr Georgiyevich Gorshkov (USSR), from 1970 to 1974 and in 1976.

## SPEED SKATING

**Most men's Olympic speed skating medals** The most Olympic speed skating medals won by a man is seven. Clas Thunberg (1893–1973, Finland) won five gold, one silver, and one tied bronze. Ivar Ballangrud (Norway) shares the record, with four gold, two silver, and one bronze between 1928 and 1936.

**Most women's Olympic speed skating medals** Karin Kania (born Enke, GDR) has won eight medals. She won three gold, four silver, and one bronze between 1980 and 1988.

**Most men's Olympic gold speed skating medals** Clas Thunberg (Finland) won five golds in 1924 and 1928. Eric Arthur Heiden (USA) shares the record. He won all of his five medals at one Games, at Lake Placid, New York, USA, in 1980.

**Most women's Olympic gold speed skating medals** The most Olympic gold medals won by a woman speed skater is six by Lidiya Pavlovna Skoblikova (USSR). She won two in 1960 and four in 1964.

**FASTEST WOMEN'S 1,500 M SHORT-TRACK SPEED SKATING** The women's short-track speed skating record is held by Choi Eun-kyung (South Korea, far left in picture) with a time of 2:21.069 at Salt Lake City, Utah, USA, on February 13, 2002.

**Most short-track speed skating world championships won** The most successful skater in the World Championships (instituted in 1978) is Marc Gagnon (Canada), who has been the men's overall champion four times in 1993, 1994, 1996, and 1998.

**Most Olympic short-track gold medals** The most gold medals won in men's short-track speed skating at the Olympics Games is three. Kim Ki-hoon (South Korea) won gold medals in the 1,000 m race in 1992 for both the solo and relay events. He also won a 1,000 m gold in 1994. Marc Gagnon (Canada) shares the record. He won gold in the 500-m relay in 1998, as well as the 500-m relay and solo races in 2002.

The most short-track gold medals won by a woman is four by Chun Lee-kyung (South Korea). She won both the solo and relay 1,000 m finals in 1994 and 1998.

## ★ MEN'S SPEED SKATING WORLD RECORDS ★

| EVENT | MIN:SEC | NAME AND COUNTRY | VENUE | DATE |
|---|---|---|---|---|
| 500 m | 34.32 | Hiroyasu Shimizu (Japan) | Salt Lake City, USA | March 10, 2001 |
| 1,000 m | 1:07.18 | Gerard van Velde (Netherlands) | Salt Lake City, USA | February 16, 2002 |
| 1,500 m | 1:43.95 | Derek Parra (USA) | Salt Lake City, USA | February 19, 2002 |
| 3,000 m | 3:42.75 | Gianne Romme (Netherlands) | Calgary, Canada | August 11, 2000 |
| 5,000 m | 6:14.66 | Jochem Uytdehaage (Netherlands) | Salt Lake City, USA | February 9, 2002 |
| 10,000 m | 12:58.92 | Jochem Uytdehaage (Netherlands) | Salt Lake City, USA | February 22, 2002 |
| 500 m short-track | 41.514 | Jeffrey Scholten (Canada) | Calgary, Canada | October 13, 2001 |
| 1,000 m short-track | 1:25.985 | Steve Robillard (Canada) | Calgary, Canada | October 14, 2001 |
| 1,500 m short-track | 2:12.234 | Steve Robillard (Canada) | Calgary, Canada | November 13, 2002 |
| 3,000 m short-track | 4:38.061 | Steve Robillard (Canada) | Calgary, Canada | November 13, 2002 |
| 5,000 m short-track relay | 6:43.73 | Eric Bédard, Marc Gagnon, Jean-Francois Monette, Mathieu Turcotte (Canada) | Calgary, Canada | October 14, 2001 |

# ★ WOMEN'S SPEED SKATING WORLD RECORDS ★

| EVENT | MIN:SEC | NAME AND COUNTRY | VENUE | DATE |
|---|---|---|---|---|
| 500 m | 37.22 | Catriona LeMay Doan (Canada) | Calgary, Canada | December 9, 2001 |
| 1,000 m | 1:13.83 | Christine Witty (USA) | Salt Lake City, USA | February 17, 2002 |
| 1,500 m | 1:54.02 | Anni Friesinger (Germany) | Salt Lake City, USA | February 20, 2002 |
| 3,000 m | 3:57.7 | Claudia Pechstein (Germany) | Salt Lake City, USA | February 10, 2002 |
| 5,000 m | 6:46.91 | Claudia Pechstein (Germany) | Salt Lake City, USA | February 23, 2002 |
| 500 m short-track | 43.671 | Evgenia Radanova (Bulgaria) | Calgary, Canada | October 19, 2001 |
| 1,000 m short-track | 1:30.483 | Byun Chun-sa (South Korea) | Budapest, Hungary | January 12, 2003 |
| 1,500 m short-track | 2:21.069 | Choi Eun-kyung (South Korea) | Salt Lake City, USA | February 13, 2002 |
| 3,000 m short-track | 5:01.976 | Choi Eun-kyung (South Korea) | Calgary, Canada | October 22, 2000 |
| 3,000 m short-track relay | 4:12.793 | Park Hye-won, Joo Min-jin, Choi Min-kyung, Choi Eun-kyung (South Korea) | Salt Lake City, USA | February 20, 2002 |

**Most Olympic short-track medals** The most Olympic medals won by a man in short-track speed skating is five by Marc Gagnon (Canada). He has won three gold, in the 500 m in 2002 and the relay in 1998 and 2002, as well as two bronze, in the 1,000 m in 1994 and the 1,500 m in 2002.

The most Olympic medals won by a woman in short-track speed skating is five. Chun Lee-kyung (South Korea) has won four gold, in the 1,000 m solo and relay in 1994 and 1998, and one bronze in the 500 m in 1998. Yang Yang (China) shares the women's record. She won four silver, in the 500 m, the 1,000 m, and the relay in 1998, and the relay in 2002, and one bronze in the 1,000 m in 2002.

**Longest ice skating race** The *Elfstedentocht* ("Tour of the Eleven Towns"), which originated in the 17th century, was held in The Netherlands in 1909–63, 1985–86, and again in 1997. It covers 124 miles 483 yds. (200 km). As the weather does not always permit an annual race in The Netherlands, alternative Elfstedentocht races take place at other suitable sites throughout the world. These have included Lake Vesijrvi, near Lahti, Finland, and Ottawa River in Canada.

**Most World Championship speed skating titles** The most World Championship speed skating titles won by a man is five by Oscar Mathisen

**FASTEST WOMEN'S 1,500 M SPEED SKATING** The fastest women's 1,500 m in speed skating was achieved by Anni Friesinger (Germany) with a time of 1:54.02 in Salt Lake City, Utah, USA, on February 20, 2002.

(Norway) in 1908–09 and 1912–14. Clas Thunberg (Finland) shares the record with wins in 1923, 1925, 1928–29, and 1931.

The record for the most World Championship speed skating titles won by a woman is eight, by Gunda Niemann-Stirnemann (Germany). She took the title in 1991–93 and 1995–99.

## Most single distance speed skating World Championship titles
The most titles won at the World Single Distance Championships (instituted in 1996) is 11 by Gunda Niemann-Stirnemann (Germany) in the 1,500 m, 3,000 m, and 5,000 m between 1996 and 2001.

The most titles won by a man is seven by Gianni Romme (Netherlands) in the 5,000 m and 10,000 m from 1996 to 2000.

## Best World Championship speed skating score.
The lowest, and therefore best, score in men's World Championship speed skating is 152.651 points, achieved by Rintje Ritsma (Netherlands) in Hamar, Norway, on February 6–7, 1999.

The same record by a woman is 161.479 points by Gunda Niemann-Stirnemann (Germany) at Hamar, Norway on February 6–7, 1999.

# GOLF

**Largest golf tournament** The 1984 Volkswagen Grand Prix Open Amateur Championship, held in the UK, attracted a record 321,778 competitors—206,820 men and 114,958 women.

**Most British Open Titles** Harry Vardon (UK) won six British Open Titles, in 1896, 1898, 1899, 1903, 1911, and 1914.

**Most US Open titles** Willie Anderson (UK), Bobby Jones, Jr., Ben Hogan, and Jack Nicklaus (all USA) have all won the US Open four times. Willie Anderson won in 1901 and 1903–05; Bobby Jones, Jr., in 1923, 1926, 1929, and 1930; Ben Hogan in 1948, 1950–51, and 1953; and Jack Nicklaus in 1962, 1967, 1972, and 1980.

**Most successful Ryder Cup captain** Walter Hagen (USA) captained the US team to victory a record four times—in 1927, 1931, 1935, and 1937. One of the most colorful sports personalities of his time, Hagen is credited with doing more than any other golfer to influence the perception of the game.

**Most individual wins in the Ryder Cup** Nick Faldo (UK) holds the record for match wins, with 23 from 46 played, and points scored with 25, having halved four other matches.

**HIGHEST US LPGA CAREER EARNINGS** The record career earnings for a woman on the US LPGA Tour is by Annika Sorenstam (Sweden), who earned $11,217,687 (£7,124,884) between 1993 and the end of 2002.

**Most Ryder Cup tournament matches played** Nick Faldo (UK) played in a record 11 Ryder Cup contests between 1977 and 1997. The equivalent US record is eight by three players: Billy Casper in 1961–75, Ray Floyd in 1969, 1975–85, 1991–93, and Lanny Wadkins in 1977–79, 1983–93.

**Most Ryder Cup wins** The biennial Ryder Cup professional match between the USA and Europe (British Isles or Great Britain prior to 1979) was instituted in 1927. The USA has won 24 to 8 (with two draws) to 2002.

**Oldest Ryder Cup player** Raymond Floyd (USA) competed in the Ryder Cup in 1993 at the age of 51 years 20 days. Floyd was inducted into the World Golf Hall of Fame in 1989 and still plays on the Senior PGA tour.

**Most team Solheim Cup wins** The female equivalent of the Ryder Cup is contested biennially between the top professional players of Europe and the USA and was first held in 1990. The USA has won five times, 1990, 1994, 1996, 1998, and 2002.

**Most Walker Cup wins** Formerly known as the International Trophy, the Walker Cup has been held biennially since 1922. The USA has won 31, Great Britain & Ireland six (in 1938, 1971, 1989, 1995, 1999, 2001), and the 1965 match was tied.

**Most World Cup successes** The only men to have been on six winning World Cup teams are Arnold Palmer (USA) in 1960, 1962–64, and 1966–67 and Jack Nicklaus (USA) in 1963–64, 1966–67, 1971, and 1973. Nicklaus has taken the individual title a record three times—in 1963–64 and 1971.

**Highest US PGA career earnings** The all-time career earnings record on the US PGA circuit is held by Tiger Woods (USA) who earned $35,944,852 (£22,822,164) between August, 1996, and March, 2003.

**Highest US LPGA season's earnings** The season's record for earnings on the US LPGA Tour is held by Annika Sorenstam (Sweden) who earned $2,863,904 (£1,817,467) in 2002.

**Highest US PGA season's earnings** The season's record earnings for the US PGA Tour is $9,188,321 (£5,720,587) by Tiger Woods (USA) in 2000.

**Fastest round of golf by a team** The Fore Worcester's Children golf team completed 18 holes in 9 min. 28 sec. at the Tatnuck Country Club, Worcester, Massachusetts, USA, on September 9, 1996. They scored 70.

**Lowest score over 18 holes by a woman** The lowest recorded score on an 18-hole course (over 5,600 yd. or 5,120 m) for a woman is 59 by Annika Sorenstam (Sweden) in the 2001 Standard Register PING at Moon Valley Country Club, Phoenix, Arizona, USA, on March 16, 2001.

**NORTHERNMOST GOLF COURSE** The island of Uummannaq, west of Greenland at a longitude of 70°N, hosts the annual World Ice Golf Championship (the 2002 competition shown here). The course varies annually with the variations in ice floes and snow distribution. Frostbite is a constant hazard for competitors.

**Most nations represented in a golf competition** A record 72 nations were involved in the 2000 Junior Open Championships, held at Crail Golf Club, Fife, UK, in July, 2000. The event was organized by the Royal and Ancient Golf Club of St. Andrews, Fife, UK.

**Longest golf ball carry** The greatest recorded carry of a golf ball is 458 yd. (418.78 m) by Jack Hamm (USA) at Highlands Ranch, Colorado, USA, on July 20, 1993.

The longest golf drive at an altitude below 3,281 ft. (1,000 m) is 408 yd. (373 m) by Karl Woodward (UK) at Golf del Sur, Tenerife, Spain, on June 30, 1999.

**Most golf balls hit in 24 hours** The most balls driven in 24 hours over 100 yd. (91.44 m) and into a target area is 10,392 by David Ogron (USA) at Raymore, Missouri, USA, on June 21–22, 2002. Ogron hit a total of 10,887 balls with a strike rate of 95.45%.

**Most golf balls hit in one hour** The most balls driven in one hour over 100 yd. (91.44 m) into a target area is 2,146 by Sean Murphy (Canada) at Swifts Practice Range, Carlisle, Cumbria, UK, on June 30, 1995.

**Most holes played in 12 hours** Brennan F. Robertson (USA) played 476 holes using a cart at Foxfire Golf Club, Sarasota, Florida, USA, on August 19, 2000.

The same record achieved when on foot is held by David Brett (UK), who

**YOUNGEST TO PLAY IN A RYDER CUP** The youngest player to compete in the Ryder Cup is Sergio Garcia (Spain, b. January 9, 1980) who played for Europe in 1999 at the age of 19 years 229 days.

played 218 holes in 12 hours at Didsbury Golf Club, Greater Manchester, UK, on June 22, 1990.

**Longest golf putt** On November 6, 2001, Fergus Muir (UK) successfully sank a putt measuring 125 yd. (114.3 m) on the Eden Course at St. Andrews Links, Scotland, UK. The shot was made directly from the tee on the 5th hole using a hickory-shafted putter.

**Longest golf hole** The longest hole in the world is the 7th hole (par 7) of the Satsuki Golf Club, Sano, Japan, which measures 964 yd. (881 m).

**Greatest distance between two rounds of golf played on the same day** The greatest distance between two rounds of golf played on the same day is 5,954 miles (9,582 km) by Nobby Orens (USA) who played at Stockley Park, Uxbridge, Greater London, UK, and Braemar Country Club, Tarzana, California, USA, on July 20, 1999.

**Youngest hole-in-one golfer** The youngest golfer recorded to have shot a hole-in-one is Christian Carpenter (USA, b. June 6, 1995), who achieved this at the age of 4 years 195 days at the Mountain View Golf Club, Hickory, North Carolina, USA, on December 18, 1999.

**Youngest national champion** Thuashni Selvaratnam (b. June 9, 1976) won the 1989 Sri Lankan Ladies Amateur Open Golf Championship at age 12 years 324 days at Nuwara Eliya Golf Club on April 29, 1989.

# WATER SPORTS

## CANOEING

**Fastest 50-m canoe descent** The fastest time to descend a height of 164 ft. (50 m) on a river by canoe is 4 min. 53 sec. by Shaun Baker (UK) in Snowdonia, Wales, UK, on November 4, 1994.

**Fastest 1000 m in a canoe** The German four-man kayak Olympic team covered 1,093 yards (1,000 m) in 2 min. 51.52 sec. to win gold in Atlanta, USA, on August 3, 1996. Their average speed was 13.04 mph (20.98 km/h).

**Farthest distance in 24 hours on flat water in a canoe** Marinda Hartzenberg (South Africa) paddled 137.13 miles (220.69 km) without the benefit of current in a canoe on Loch Logan, Bloemfontein, South Africa, from December 31, 1990 to January 1, 1991.

**Longest canoe race** The Canadian Government Centennial Voyageur Canoe Pageant and Race from Rocky Mountain House, Alberta, to the Expo '67 site at Montreal, Quebec, was 3,283 miles (5,283 km) long. Ten canoes represented Canadian provinces and territories. The winner of the race, which took place from May 24 to September 4, 1967, was the Province of Manitoba canoe, *Radisson*.

**Most World and Olympic men's canoeing titles** The record for the most World and Olympic men's canoeing titles is 13 and is held by three people: Gert Fredriksson (Sweden) in 1948–1960; Rüdiger Helm (GDR) in 1976–1983; and Ivan Patzaichin (Romania) in 1968–1984.

**Most canoeing gold medals won at a single Olympic Games** The most canoeing gold medals won at one Olympic Games is three, by

**MOST WOMEN'S WAKEBOARDING WORLD TITLES** Two women share the record for the most women's World Championship wakeboarding titles. Tara Hamilton (USA, above) won in 1998 and 2002, and Meghan Major (USA) won in 1999 and 2000.

Vladimir Parfenovich (USSR) in 1980 and Ian Ferguson (New Zealand) in 1984.

**Most women's canoeing World Championship titles** In addition to seven Olympic titles, Birgit Fischer (formerly Birgit Schmidt, GDR/Germany) has won 29 World Canoeing Championships from 1979 to 1998, making a record 34 titles overall.

**Most women's Olympic canoeing gold medals** The most Olympic gold canoeing medals won by a woman is seven by Birgit Fischer (formerly Birgit Schmidt, GDR/Germany) from 1980 to 2000.

**Most Eskimo rolls done consecutively** Randy Fine (USA) completed 1,796 consecutive "Eskimo" canoe rolls at Biscayne Bay, Florida, USA, on June 8, 1991.

## ★ WATER-SKIING WORLD RECORDS ★

| MEN | WOMEN |
|---|---|
| **SLALOM** | |
| 1 buoy on a 9.75-m line by Jeff Rogers (USA) at Charleston, South Carolina, USA, on August 31, 1997 and Andy Mapple (GB) at Miami, Florida, USA, on October 4, 1998. | 1 buoy on a 10.25-m line by Kristi Overton Johnson (USA) at West Palm Beach, Florida, USA, on September 14, 1996. |
| **TRICKS** | |
| 12,120 points by Nicolas Le Forestier (France) at the French Masters, Lancaneau, France, on July 7, 2001. | 8,630 points by Tawn Larsen Hahn (USA) at Wilmington, Illinois, USA, on July 11, 1999. |
| **JUMPING** | |
| 233 ft. (71 m) by Freddy Kreuger (USA) at the Malibu Open, Rio Linda, California, USA, on July 27, 2002. | 186 ft. (56.6 m) by Elena Milakova (Russia) at the Malibu Open, Rio Linda, California, USA, on July 27, 2002. |
| **SKI FLY** | |
| 298 ft. 10 in. (91.1 m) by Jaret Llewellyn (Canada) at the Big Air Challenge event at Orlando, Florida, USA, on May 14, 2000. | 227 ft. 7 in. (69.4 m) by Elena Milakova (Russia) at the Masters event at Pine Mountain, Georgia, USA, on May 26, 2002. |
| **OVERALL** | |
| 2,741.75 points by Patrice Martin (France) at Traver's Sunset Cup, Okahumpka, Florida, USA, on May 20, 2001. | 2,854.01 points by Elena Milakova (Russia) at the Europe, Africa, and Middle East (EAME) Championships, Lincolnshire, UK, on July 29, 2001. |

**Most consecutive kayak cartwheels** The record for the most consecutive cartwheels performed in a kayak is 35 and was set by Koyo Morita (Japan) at Yamanaka Lake, Yamanashi Prefecture, Japan, on August 5, 2002.

## RAFTING

**Most whitewater rafting World Championships won** The World Rafting Challenge Championship has been held since 1995, and the most successful country is Slovenia, with five wins from 1995 to 1999.

## WAKEBOARDING

**Most wakeboarding inverts in a minute** On August 30, 1999 at the John Battleday Waterski Centre, Chertsey, Surrey, UK, Julz Heaney (UK) did 15 inverts (somersaults) in a minute on a wakeboard measuring 49 in. (125 cm) long, 15 in. (39.8 cm) wide and weighing 5 lb. (2.27 kg). The attempt was recorded by the BBC's *Linford's Record Breakers* TV show.

## BAREFOOT WATERSKIING

**World barefoot waterskiing slalom record** The world barefoot waterskiing slalom record is 20.5 crossings of the wake in 15 seconds by Brian Fuchs (USA) in Liverpool, New South Wales, Australia, in April 1994.

**MOST BODYBOARDING WORLD CHAMPIONSHIPS** Mike Stewart (USA) has won every bodyboarding competition he has entered in the last seven years, including nine bodyboarding World Championships, eight national tour titles, and 21 pipeline titles. He has also won every *BodyBoarding Magazine* readers' poll.

**MOST WOMEN'S OLYMPIC WATER POLO TITLES** Women's water polo was introduced at the 2000 Olympic Games in Sydney, Australia. The team from the host nation (shown) won the first and only title to date in a final against the USA on September 23, 2000.

**Women's barefoot waterskiing slalom record** The women's barefoot waterskiing slalom record is 17.0 crossings of the wake in 15 seconds by Nadine de Villiers (South Africa) on January 5, 2001, at the Gauteng Waterski Championships, Wolwekrans, South Africa.

**Highest men's barefoot water-skiing tricks score** The highest men's barefoot waterskiing tricks score is 9,400 points by Keith St. Onge (USA) on August 10, 2002, at Arc sur Tilles, France.

**Highest women's barefoot water-skiing tricks score** The highest barefoot waterskiing tricks score for a woman is 4,400 points by Nadine de Villiers (South Africa) on January 5, 2001 at Gauteng Waterski Championships, Wolwekrans, South Africa.

## WATER POLO

**Most water polo Olympics medals** Five players share the record of three Olympic gold water polo medals: George Wilkinson (UK) in 1900, 1908, and 1912; Paulo "Paul" Radmilovic and Charles Sidney Smith (both UK) in 1908, 1912, and 1920; and Desz Gyarmati and Gyrgy Krpti (both Hungary) in 1952, 1956, and 1964. Paul Radmilovic also won a gold medal for 4,200-m freestyle swimming in 1908.

**Most international water polo goals** The greatest number of goals scored by an individual in an international water polo game is 13 by Debbie Handley for Australia (16) v. Canada (10) at the World Championship in Guayaquil, Ecuador, in 1982.

**Most men's Olympic water polo titles** Hungary has won the men's Olympic water polo title most often with six wins, in 1932, 1936, 1952, 1956, 1964, and 1976.

**Most water polo World Championships** The first water polo World Championships were held at the World Swimming Championships in 1973. The most wins is two, by the USSR (1975 and 1982), Yugoslavia (1986 and 1991), Italy (1978 and 1994), and Spain (1998 and 2001).

## DIVING

**Most diving World Championships** Greg Louganis (USA) won a record five world diving titles. He won the highboard title in 1978, and both the highboard and springboard titles in 1982 and 1986. The most diving titles won in a single event is three by Phil Boggs (USA), who took three gold medals in the springboard, in 1973, 1975, and 1978.

**Most Olympic diving medals** The most medals won by a diver is five. Klaus Dibiasi (Italy) won three gold and two silver between 1964 and 1976, and Greg Louganis (USA) won four golds and one silver won between 1976 and 1988. Dibiasi is the only diver to win the same event (highboard) at three successive Games—in 1968, 1972, and 1976. Two divers have won the highboard and springboard doubles at two Games: Patricia McCormick (USA) in 1952 and 1956, and Louganis in 1984 and 1988.

## ROWING

**Most Olympic and World Championships gold medals** The most gold medals won at the World Championships and Olympic Games is 13 by Steve Redgrave (UK) who, in addition to his five Olympic successes—coxed fours (1984), coxless pairs (1988, 1992, and 1996), and coxless fours (2000)—won World titles at coxed pairs in 1986, coxless pairs in 1987, 1991, and 1993–95, and coxless fours in 1997–99.

Francesco Esposito (Italy) has won nine titles at lightweight events: coxless pairs in 1980–84, 1988 and 1994, and coxless fours in 1990 and 1992.

At women's events Yelena Tereshina (USSR) has won a record seven gold medals, all eights, in 1978–79, 1981–83, and 1985–86. The rowing World Championships, as distinct from the Olympic Games, were first held in 1962, at first four yearly, then from 1974 annually, except in Olympic years.

**Fastest eight over 2,000 m** The men's eights record time for rowing 2,000 m on non-tidal water is 5 min. 22.80 sec. (13.85 mph or 22.30 km/h) by The Netherlands at the World Championships held at St. Catharines, Ontario, Canada, on August 28, 1999. The women's eights record time for

**YOUNGEST DIVING WORLD CHAMPION** Fu Mingxia (China, b. August 16, 1978) won the women's world title for platform diving at Perth, Australia, on January 4, 1991, at the age of 12 years 141 days.

2,000 m on non-tidal water is 5 min. 57.02 sec. (12.53 mph or 20.16 km/h) by Romania at Lucerne, Switzerland, on July 9, 1999.

**Fastest single sculls over 2,000 m** The single sculls men's record is 6 min. 31.67 sec. (11.42 mph or 18.38 km/h) by Leonid Gulov (Estonia) during the Junior World Championships at Plovdiv, Bulgaria, on August 5, 1999.

The women's single sculls rowing record is 7 min. 11.68 sec. (10.36 mph or 16.68 km/h) by Ekaterina Karsten (Belarus) at St. Catharines, Ontario, Canada, on August 28, 1999.

**Most University Boat Race wins** The earliest University Boat Race (won by Oxford) was raced on the River Thames from Hambledon Lock to Henley Bridge, Oxfordshire, UK, on June 10, 1829. In the 149 races to 2003, Cambridge has won 77 times, Oxford 71 times, and there was a dead heat on March 24, 1877.

**Longest annual rowing race** The longest annual rowing race is the annual 100-mile (160-km) *Tour du Lac Leman* in Geneva, Switzerland, for coxed fours (the five-man crew taking turns as cox). The best time is 12 hr. 22 min. 29 sec. by team RG Red Bull (Germany) on October 2, 1994.

**MOST WOMEN'S SURFING PROFESSIONAL WORLD CHAMPIONSHIPS**
The women's professional surfing title (instituted 1979) has been won four times by Frieda Zamba (USA), in 1984–86 and 1988; Wendy Botha (Australia, formerly South Africa) in 1987, 1989, and 1991–92; and Lisa Andersen (USA, above) in 1994–97.

## YACHTING

**Most America's Cup wins** Since its beginnings at Cowes, Hampshire, UK, in 1851 there have been 31 challenges for the America's Cup. The USA has won the Cup every time except in 1983 (when Australia won), in 1995 (when New Zealand won), in 2000 (when New Zealand retained the Cup), and in 2003 (when Switzerland won).

**Most America's Cup individual appearances** Dennis Walter Conner (USA) has been in more cup races as a member of the afterguard than any other sailor. He has taken part six times since 1974, when he was starting helmsman with Ted Hood as skipper. He was winning skipper/helmsman in 1980, 1987, and 1989, and losing skipper in 1983 and 1995.

**Highest yachting speed** The highest speed reached under sail on water by any craft over a 500-m timed run is 46.52 knots (53.56 mph or 86.21 km/h) by trifoiler *Yellow Pages Endeavour,* piloted by Simon McKeon and Tim Daddo (both Australia) at Sandy Point near Melbourne, Victoria, Australia, on October 26, 1993.

The women's record for the highest speed reached under sail on water by any craft over a 500-m timed run is by boardsailer Babethe Coquelle (France), who achieved 40.38 knots (46.5 mph or 74.83 km/h) at Tarifa, Spain, on July 7, 1995.

**FASTEST INTERNATIONAL DRAGON BOAT RACE** The Dragon Boat Race is held annually in Hong Kong, China. The fastest time achieved for the 2,100-ft. (640-m) course is 2 min. 27.45 sec. by the Chinese Shun De team on June 30, 1985.

## SURFING

**Most men's professional World Championships** The men's title has been won six times by Kelly Slater (USA) in 1992 and 1994–98. The World Professional series started in 1975.

**Most amateur World Championships** The most World Amateur Surfing Championships titles won is three, by Michael Novakov (Australia) who won the Kneeboard event in 1982, 1984, and 1986. The World Amateur Surfing Championships were inaugurated in May, 1964, at Sydney, New South Wales, Australia.

**Most consecutive days surfing** Dale Webster (USA) has gone surfing every day since September 2, 1975. He passed his 10,000th consecutive day of surfing on January 1, 2003. Webster set himself the condition that "a surf consists of catching at least three waves to shore each time."

**Largest wave surfed** The largest wave successfully surfed had a face measuring a massive 68 ft. (20.7 m) in height, from crest to trough. The wave was ridden by Carlos Burle (Brazil) at Maverick's, Half Moon Bay, California, USA, on November 22, 2001. Burle was towed into the wave using a 155-hp wave runner.

# SWIMMING

**FASTEST WOMEN'S SHORT-COURSE 200-M FREESTYLE**
Lindsay Benkso (USA) holds the women's short-course 200-m freestyle record, with a swim of 1 min. 54.04 sec. She set the record in Moscow, Russia, on April 7, 2002.

## ★ MEN'S LONG-COURSE SWIMMING WORLD RECORDS ★

| EVENT | TIME | NAME AND COUNTRY | VENUE | DATE |
|---|---|---|---|---|
| 50-m freestyle | 21.64 | Alexander Popov (Russia) | Moscow, Russia | June 16, 2000 |
| 100-m freestyle | 47.84 | Pieter van den Hoogenband (Netherlands) | Sydney, Australia | September 19, 2000 |
| 200-m freestyle | 1:44.06 | Ian Thorpe (Australia) | Fukuoka, Japan | July 25, 2001 |
| 400-m freestyle | 3:40.17 | Ian Thorpe (Australia) | Fukuoka, Japan | July 22, 2001 |
| 800-m freestyle | 7:39.16 | Ian Thorpe (Australia) | Fukuoka, Japan | July 24, 2001 |
| 1,500-m freestyle | 14:34.56 | Grant Hackett (Australia) | Fukuoka, Japan | July 29, 2001 |
| 4 × 100-m freestyle relay | 3:13.67 | Australia (Michael Klim, Chris Fydler, Ashley Callus, Ian Thorpe) | Sydney, Australia | September 16, 2000 |
| 4 × 200-m freestyle relay | 7:04.66 | Australia (Grant Hackett, Michael Klim, William Kirby, Ian Thorpe) | Fukuoka, Japan | July 27, 2001 |
| 50-m butterfly | 23.44 | Geoff Huegill (Australia) | Fukuoka, Japan | July 27, 2001 |
| 100-m butterfly | 51.81 | Michael Klim (Australia) | Canberra, Australia | December 12, 1999 |
| 200-m butterfly | 1:54.58 | Michael Phelps (USA) | Fukuoka, Japan | July 24, 2001 |

| 50-m backstroke | 24.99 | Lenny Krayzelburg (USA) | Sydney, Australia | August 28, 1999 |
|---|---|---|---|---|
| 100-m backstroke | 53.60 | Lenny Krayzelburg (USA) | Sydney, Australia | August 24, 1999 |
| 200-m backstroke | 1:55.15 | Aaron Peirsol (USA) | Minneapolis, USA | March 20, 2002 |
| 50-m breaststroke | 27.18 | Oleg Lisogor (Ukraine) | Berlin, Germany | August 2, 2002 |
| 100-m breaststroke | 59.94 | Roman Sloudnov (Russia) | Fukuoka, Japan | July 23, 2001 |
| 200-m breaststroke | 2:10.16 | Mike Barrowman (USA) | Barcelona, Spain | July 29, 1992 |
| 200-m medley | 1:58.16 | Jani Sievinen (Finland) | Rome, Italy | September 11, 1994 |
| 400-m medley | 4:11.76 | Tom Dolan (USA) | Sydney, Australia | September 17, 2000 |
| 4 × 100-m medley relay | 3:33.48 | USA (Aaron Peirsol, Brendon Hanson, Michael Phelps, Jason Lezak) | Yokohama, Japan | August 29, 2002 |

## ★ WOMEN'S LONG-COURSE SWIMMING WORLD RECORDS ★

| EVENT | TIME | NAME AND COUNTRY | VENUE | DATE |
|---|---|---|---|---|
| 50-m freestyle | 24.13 | Inge de Bruijn (Netherlands) | Sydney, Australia | September 22, 2000 |
| 100-m freestyle | 53.77 | Inge de Bruijn (Netherlands) | Sydney, Australia | September 20, 2000 |
| 200-m freestyle | 1:56.64 | Franziska van Almsick (Germany) | Berlin, Germany | August 3, 2002 |
| 400-m freestyle | 4:03.85 | Janet Evans (USA) | Seoul, South Korea | September 22, 1988 |
| 800-m freestyle | 8:16.22 | Janet Evans (USA) | Tokyo, Japan | August 20, 1989 |
| 1,500-m freestyle | 15:52.10 | Janet Evans (USA) | Orlando, USA | March 26, 1988 |
| 4 × 100-m freestyle relay | 3:36.60 | Germany (Franziska van Almsick, Petra Dallmann, Sandra Volker, Kathrin Meibner) | Berlin, Germany | July 29, 2002 |
| 4 × 200-m freestyle relay | 7:55.47 | GDR (Manuela Stellmach, Astrid Strauss, Anke Möhring, Heike Friedrich) | Strasbourg, France | August 18, 1987 |
| 50-m butterfly | 25.64 | Inge de Bruijn (Netherlands) | Sheffield, UK | May 26, 2000 |
| 100-m butterfly | 56.61 | Inge de Bruijn (Netherlands) | Sydney, Australia | September 17, 2000 |

| 200-m butterfly | 2:05.78 | Otylia Jedrejczak (Poland) | Berlin, Germany | August 2, 2002 |
| 50-m backstroke | 28.25 | Sandra Voelker (Germany) | Berlin, Germany | June 17, 2000 |
| 100-m backstroke | 1:00.16 | He Cihong (China) | Rome, Italy | September 10, 1994 |
| 200-m backstroke | 2:06.62 | Krisztina Egerszegi (Hungary) | Athens, Greece | August 25, 1991 |
| 50-m breaststroke | 30.57 | Zoe Baker (UK) | Manchester, UK | July 30, 2002 |
| 100-m breaststroke | 1:06.52 | Penny Heyns (South Africa) | Sydney, Australia | August 23, 1999 |
| 200-m breaststroke | 2:22.99 | Hui Qi (China) | Hangzhou, China | April 13, 2001 |
| 200-m medley | 2:09.72 | Wu Yanyan (China) | Shanghai, China | October 17, 1997 |
| 400-m medley | 4:33.59 | Yana Klochkova (Ukraine) | Sydney, Australia | September 16, 2000 |
| 4 × 100-m medley relay | 3:58.30 | USA (Megan Quann, Jenny Thompson, B.J. Bedford, Dara Torres) | Sydney, Australia | September 23, 2000 |

**Greatest overall swimming distance** Between June 25 and August 23 2000 (a total of 60 days), marathon swimmer Martin Strel (Slovenia) swam the length of the Danube River, and then three more stages of the river to complete a total distance of 1,866 miles (3,004 km). The Danube River flows from Germany to the Black Sea through eight countries, including Austria and Hungary.

**Fastest underwater 50-m swim** Maarten Sterck (Netherlands) swam 164 ft. (50 m) underwater in a time of 38.98 seconds on March 11, 2001, at Valkenswaard, The Netherlands. No fins or any other swimming aids were worn during the attempt.

**Most continuous rotations under water with one breath** Marta Fernãndez Pèrez (Spain) completed 28 rotations with one breath, in a tank, at the studios of *El Show de los Récords* in Madrid, Spain, on October 18, 2001.

**Most swimming world records** The most swimming world records set by a woman is 42, by Ragnhild Hveger (Denmark) between 1936 and 1942. For currently recognized events (only metric distances in 50-m pools) the most is 23 by Kornelia Ender (GDR) between 1973 and 1976.

The most swimming world records set by a man is 32 by Arne Borg (Sweden) between 1921 and 1929. For currently recognized events the most is 26 by Mark Spitz (USA) between 1967 and 1972.

**Most consecutive swimming Olympic gold medals** Two swimmers have won the same event on three consecutive occasions: Dawn Fraser

**FASTEST WOMEN'S 200-M FREESTYLE** The fastest women's 200-m freestyle is 1 min. 56.64 sec. by Franziska van Almsick (Germany) in Berlin, Germany, on August 3, 2002.

(Australia) in the 100-m freestyle in 1956, 1960, and 1964 and Krisztina Egerszegi (Hungary) in the 200-m backstroke in 1988, 1992, and 1996.

**Most Olympic swimming medals** Mark Spitz (USA) won nine Olympic gold medals at the 1968 and 1972 Games. All but one of his wins were new world records. He also won a silver and a bronze in 1968, for a record overall 11 medals. He holds the record for the most medals won at one Games, with seven in 1972, as does Matt Biondi (USA), for seven medals at the 1998 Games.

The most medals won by a woman is eight by: Dawn Fraser (Australia), with four gold and four silver in 1956–64; Kornelia Ender (GDR) with four gold and four silver in 1972–76; and Shirley Babashoff (USA), with two gold and six silver in 1972–76.

| EVENT | TIME | NAME AND COUNTRY | VENUE | DATE |
|---|---|---|---|---|
| 50-m freestyle | 21.13 | Mark Foster (UK) | Paris, France | January 28, 2001 |
| 100-m freestyle | 46.74 | Alexander Popov (Russia) | Gelsenkirchen, Germany | March 19, 1994 |
| 200-m freestyle | 1:41.10 | Ian Thorpe (Australia) | Berlin, Germany | February 6, 2000 |
| 400-m freestyle | 3:34.58 | Grant Hackett (Australia) | Sydney, Australia | July 18, 2002 |
| 800-m freestyle | 7:25.28 | Grant Hackett (Australia) | Perth, Australia | August 3, 2001 |
| 1,500-m freestyle | 14:10.10 | Grant Hackett (Australia) | Perth, Australia | August 7, 2001 |
| 4 × 50-m freestyle relay | 1:26.78 | USA (Bryan Jones, Matt Ulricksson, Robert Bogart, Leffie Crawford) | Minneapolis, USA | March 23, 2000 |
| 4 × 100-m freestyle relay | 3:09.57 | Sweden (Johan Nystrom, Lars Frolander, Mattias Ohlin, Stefan Nystrand) | Athens, Greece | March 16, 2000 |
| 4 × 200-m freestyle relay | 6:56.41 | Australia (William Kirby, Ian Thorpe, Michael Klim, Grant Hackett) | Perth, Australia | August 7, 2001 |
| 50-m butterfly | 22.74 | Geoff Huegill (Australia) | Berlin, Germany | January 26, 2002 |
| 100-m butterfly | 50.10 | Thomas Rupprath (Germany) | Berlin, Germany | January 27, 2002 |
| 200-m butterfly | 1:50.73 | Frank Esposito (France) | Antibes, France | December 8, 2002 |
| 50-m backstroke | 23.31 | Matthew Welsh (Australia) | Melbourne, Australia | September 2, 2002 |
| 100-m backstroke | 50.58 | Thomas Rupprath (Germany) | Melbourne, Australia | December 8, 2002 |
| 200-m backstroke | 1:51.17 | Aaron Peirsol (USA) | Moscow, Russia | April 7, 2002 |
| 50-m breaststroke | 26.20 | Oleg Lisogor (Ukraine) | Berlin, Germany | January 26, 2002 |
| 100-m breaststroke | 57.47 | Ed Moses (USA) | Stockholm, Sweden | January 23, 2002 |
| 200-m breaststroke | 2:03.17 | Ed Moses (USA) | Berlin, Germany | January 26, 2002 |
| 100-m medley | 52.58 | Thomas Rupprath (Germany) | Berlin, Germany | January 25, 2003 |
| 200-m medley | 1:54.65 | Jani Sievinen (Finland) | Kuopio, Finland | April 21, 1994 |
| | | Atilla Czene (Hungary) | Minneapolis, USA | March 23, 2000 |

| EVENT | TIME | NAME AND COUNTRY | VENUE | DATE |
|---|---|---|---|---|
| 400-m medley | 4:02.72 | Brian Johns (Canada) | Victoria, Canada | February 21, 2003 |
| 4 × 50-m medley relay | 1:35.51 | Germany (Thomas Rupprath, Mark Warnecke, Alexander Luderitz, Stephan Kunzelmann) Sweden (Daniel Carlsson, Patrik Isaksson, Jonas Akesson, Lars Frolander). (Achieved in same race) | Sheffield, UK | December 13, 1998 |
| 4 ×100-m medley relay | 3:29.00 | USA (Aaron Peirsol, David Denniston, Peter Marshall, Jason Lezak) | Moscow, Russia | April 7, 2002 |

## ★ WOMEN'S SHORT-COURSE SWIMMING WORLD RECORDS ★

| EVENT | TIME | NAME AND COUNTRY | VENUE | DATE |
|---|---|---|---|---|
| 50-m freestyle | 23.59 | Therese Alshammar (Sweden) | Athens, Greece | March 18, 2000 |
| 100-m freestyle | 52.17 | Therese Alshammar (Sweden) | Athens, Greece | March 17, 2000 |
| 200-m freestyle | 1:54.04 | Lindsay Benko (USA) | Moscow, Russia | April 7, 2002 |
| 400-m freestyle | 3:59.53 | Lindsay Benko (USA) | Berlin, Germany | January 26, 2003 |
| 800-m freestyle | 8:14.35 | Sachiko Yamada (Japan) | Tokyo, Japan | April 2, 2002 |
| 4 × 50-m freestyle relay | 1:38.21 | Sweden (Annika Lofstedt, Therese Alshammar, Johanna Sjöberg, Anna-Karin Kammerling) | Valencia, Spain | December 15, 2000 |
| 4 × 100-m freestyle relay | 3:34.55 | China (Le Jingyi, Na Chao, Shan Ying, Nian Yin) | Gothenburg, Sweden | April 19, 1997 |
| 4 × 200-m freestyle relay | 7:46.30 | China (Xu Yanvei, Zhu Yingven, Tang Jingzhi, Yang Yu) | Moscow, Russia | April 3, 2002 |
| 50-m butterfly | 25.36 | Anna-Karin Kammerling (Sweden) | Stockholm, Sweden | January 25, 2001 |
| 100-m butterfly | 56.34 | Natalie Coughlin (USA) | New York City, USA | November 23, 2002 |

| | | | | |
|---|---|---|---|---|
| 200-m butterfly | 2:04.16 | Susan O'Neill (Australia) | Sydney, Australia | January 18, 2000 |
| 50-m backstroke | 26.83 | Hui Li (China) | Shanghai, China | December 2, 2001 |
| 100-m backstroke | 56.71 | Natalie Coughlin (USA) | New York City, USA | November 23, 2002 |
| 200-m backstroke | 2:03.62 | Natalie Coughlin (USA) | New York City, USA | November 27, 2001 |
| 50-m breaststroke | 29.96 | Emma Igelström (Sweden) | Moscow, Russia | April 4, 2002 |
| 100-m breaststroke | 1:05.11 | Emma Igelström (Sweden) | Stockholm, Sweden | March 16, 2003 |
| 200-m breaststroke | 2:19.25 | Hiu Qi (China) | Paris, France | January 28, 2001 |
| 100-m medley | 58.80 | Natalie Coughlin (USA) | New York City, USA | November 23, 2003 |
| 200-m medley | 2:07.79 | Allison Wagner (USA) | Palma de Mallorca, Spain | December 5, 1993 |
| 400-m medley | 4:27.83 | Yana Klochkova (Ukraine) | Paris, France | January 19, 2002 |
| 4 × 50-m medley relay | 1:48.31 | Sweden (Therese Alshammar, Emma Igelström, Anna-Karin Kammerling, Johanna Sjöberg) | Valencia, Spain | December 16, 2000 |
| 4 × 100-m medley relay | 3:55.78 | Sweden (Therese Alshammar, Emma Igelström, Anna-Karin Kammerling, Johanna Sjöberg) | Moscow, Russia | April 5, 2002 |

# SADDLE SPORTS

## RODEO

**Highest annual rodeo earnings** The record figure for prize money in a single rodeo season is $377,358 (£240,692) earned by Ty Murray (USA) in 1998.

Murray also holds the record for the most prize money won at a single rodeo with $124,821 (£79,716) won at the National Finals Rodeo in Las Vegas, Nevada, USA, in 1993.

**Largest rodeo attendance** The world's largest rodeo is the National Finals Rodeo organized by the Professional Rodeo Cowboys Association (PRCA) and the Women's Professional Rodeo Association (WPRA). The

**HIGHEST RODEO CAREER EARNINGS  Ty Murray (USA) has record rodeo career earnings of $2,931,227 (£1,870,624) won between 1989 and 2002.**

1991 Finals, held at the Thomas and Mack Center, Las Vegas, Nevada, USA, had a paid attendance of 171,414 for ten performances.

## POLO

**Most polo World Championship goals**  Argentina has scored 35 goals during final matches of the Federation of International Polo (FIP) World Championships. Brazil is second, with 29.

**Most polo World Championships**  Of the five World Championships contested, three have been won by Argentina: in 1987 in Argentina, 1992 in Chile, and 1998 in the USA. The contest is held every three years under the auspices of the FIP.

**Most polo chukkas**  The greatest number of chukkas played on one ground in a day is 43. This was achieved by the Pony Club on the Number 3 Ground at Kirtlington Park, Oxfordshire, UK, on July 31, 1991.

**Highest polo score**  The highest aggregate number of goals scored in an international match is 30, when Argentina beat the USA 21–9 at Meadowbrook, Long Island, New York, USA, in September 1936.

# HORSE RACING

**Greatest total prize money for a day's racing** The richest single day's racing was for a total of $15.25 million (£9.59 million) at the Dubai World Cup at Nad Al Sheba, Dubai, United Arab Emirates, in both 2002 and 2003. The seven races at the meeting are: the Dubai Kahayla Classic for Purebred Arabians, Godolphin Mile, UAE Derby, Dubai Sheema Classic, Dubai Golden Shaheen, Dubai Duty Free, and the world's richest race, the Dubai World Cup.

**Largest prize for a single horse race** The largest prize for a single horse race is for the Dubai World Cup, held in Dubai, United Arab Emirates. The race carries a total purse of $6 million (£4 million), $3.6 million (£2.5 million) of which goes to the winner.

**Most wins by an owner** The most wins in a racehorse owner's career is 4,775 by Marion H. Van Berg (USA). He began his 35-year career in the 1930s and was the leading race-winning owner for 14 years, 11 of them consecutively from 1960 to 1970.

**Oldest race winning horse** Al Jabal, a purebred Arabian ridden by Brian Boulton (UK), is the oldest racehorse to have won on the flat. Al Jabal won the Horseshoes Handicap Stakes (6 furlongs) on June 9, 2002 at Barbury Castle, Wiltshire, UK, aged 19 years.

**Fastest 1,000 Guineas** Las Meninas, ridden to victory by John Reid (UK), achieved the time of 1 min. 36.71 sec. in the 1,000 Guineas horse race in 1994. The race was first held in 1814 at Newmarket, Suffolk, UK.

**Fastest 2,000 Guineas** Mister Baileys, ridden by Jason Weaver (UK), achieved the record time of 1 min. 35.08 sec. in 1994 at Newmarket, Suffolk, UK.

**MOST OLYMPIC DRESSAGE TEAM GOLD MEDALS** Germany (West Germany 1968–90) has won a record ten team gold medals: 1928, 1936, 1964, 1968, 1976, 1984, 1988, 1992, 1996, and 2000. Ulrich Kirchhoff (on left of photo) and Franke Sloothaas are shown celebrating their 1996 gold medals.

**MOST WORLD CUP SHOW JUMPING WINS** The most World Cup show jumping wins is three by Hugo Simon (Austria) in 1979, 1996, and 1997, and Rodrigo Pessoa (Brazil, shown) in 1998, 1999, and 2000.

**Longest odds in the Derby**  Three Derby winners have been returned at odds of 100–1: Jeddah in 1898, Signorinetta in 1908, and Aboyeur in 1913.

**Shortest odds in the Derby**  The shortest-priced Derby winner was Ladas in 1894 at 2–9, and the hottest losing favorite was Surefoot, fourth at 40–95 in 1890.

**Fastest Epsom Derby time**  Lammtarra, ridden by Walter Swinburn (UK), won the Derby at Epsom, Surry, UK, in a time of 2 min. 32.31 sec. in 1995. The Derby Stakes, inaugurated on May 4, 1780 and named after Edward Stanley, 12th Earl of Derby, is the most prestigious of England's five Classics.

**Fastest St. Leger win**  In 1926 Coronach, ridden by Joe Childs (UK), achieved a record St. Leger winning time of 3 min. 1.6 sec. This time was equaled by Windsor Lad, ridden by Charlie Smirke (UK) in 1934. The St. Leger is the oldest Classic race in the world, with its origins in 1776. It is held in September at Doncaster, South Yorkshire, UK.

**Fastest Kentucky Derby**  The fastest winning time for the Kentucky Derby is 1 min. 59.4 sec. by Secretariat, ridden by Ron Turcotte (Canada) on May 5, 1973 at Churchill Downs, Kentucky, USA.

**Most jockey career wins**  The most wins by a jockey in a horse-racing career is 9,531 by Laffit Pincay Jr. (USA), from his first winner on May 16, 1964 to March 1, 2003. He retired in April 2003 after a serious fall.

**Most steeplechase wins in a season by a jockey**  The most steeple-chase wins in a season by a jockey is 289 in 2001/02 by Tony McCoy (UK).

**Most steeplechase wins in a career by a jockey**  The most steeple-chase winners ridden in a career is 1,847 by Tony McCoy (UK) from 1992 to 2003.

**Most jockey wins in a year**  The most races won in a year is 598 from 2,312 rides by Kent Desormeaux (USA) in 1989.

**Most runners in a horse race**  The most horses in a race was 66 in the Grand National at Aintree, Merseyside, UK, on March 22, 1929. The record for a flat race is 58 in the Lincolnshire Handicap at Lincoln, UK, on March 13, 1948.

## DRESSAGE

**Most dressage World Cup wins**  Instituted in 1986, the most World Cup wins in the dressage event is five by Anky van Grunsven (Netherlands) on Bonfire from 1995 to 1997 and 1999 to 2000.

**Most dressage Olympic gold medals**  Dr. Reiner Klimke (West Germany) has won a record six Olympic gold medals in the dressage event, taking five team golds between 1964 and 1988 and an individual gold in 1984. He also won individual bronze in 1976 for a record seven medals overall.

## SHOW JUMPING

**Most Olympic show jumping gold medals**  The most Olympic show jumping gold medals won by a rider is five by Hans Günter Winkler (West Germany). He won four team medals in 1956, 1960, 1964, and 1972 and the individual Grand Prix in 1956. He also won team silver in 1976 and team bronze in 1968 for a record seven medals overall.

# AIR SPORTS

## AEROBATICS

**Most world aerobatic championship team wins**  The men's team aerobatics competition has been won six times by the USA in 1970, 1972, 1980, 1982, 1984, and 1988.

The women's team record is four wins: by the USSR, in 1978, 1982, 1984, and 1986, and Russia in 1996, 1998, 2000, and 2001. The world championships have been held biennially since 1960 (except 1974). Pilots are judged by a panel and scored on their accuracy while performing aerial maneuvers.

**MOST HEIGHT GAINED IN A HANG GLIDER** The greatest height gain in a hang glider is 14,250 ft. (4,343 m) by Larry Tudor (USA) over Owens Valley, California, USA, on August 4, 1985.

The greatest height gain in a hang glider by a woman is 13,025 ft. (3,970 m) by Judy Leden (UK, pictured here being towed to altitude on a later flight) at Kuruman, South Africa, on December 1, 1992.

**Most men's aerobatics world championship wins** Petr Jirmus (Czechoslovakia) is the only man to become world aerobatics champion twice, in 1984 and 1986.

**Most women's aerobatics world championship wins** Svetlana Kapanina (Russia) has won the women's aerobatics World Championships three times, in 1996, 1998, and 2001.

## HANG GLIDING

**Most consecutive hang gliding loops** Chad Elchin (USA) performed 95 consecutive loops with a hang glider at the Highland Aerosports flight park at Ridgely, Maryland, USA, on July 16, 2001. Elchin was towed to 15,900 ft. (4,846 m) and looped his Aeros Stealth Combat non-stop down to 700 ft. (213 m) at speeds of 28 to 18 to 80 mph (128 km/h).

**Longest hang glider flight** The greatest distance flown when setting an official *Fédération Aéronautique International* (FAI) hang gliding record is 435.33 miles (700.6 km) by Manfred Ruhmer (Austria), starting from Zapata, Texas, USA, on July 17, 2001.

The FAI straight line distance record by a woman in a hang glider is 230.44 miles (370.87 km) by Tove Heaney (Australia), from Garnpung Lake, New South Wales, to Bealiba, Victoria, Australia, on December 2, 1998.

**Greatest distance in triangular hang gliding** Tomas Suchanek (Czech Republic) flew the world-record triangular course distance of 221.9 miles (357.12 km) on a hang glider at Riverside, Australia, on December 16, 2000.

The equivalent women's record is 103.9 miles (167.2 km) by Nichola Hamilton (UK) at Croydon Hay, New South Wales, Australia, on January 2, 1997.

## PARAGLIDING

**Longest paraglider flight** The men's paragliding distance record is 263.08 miles (423.4 km) by William Gadd (Canada) who paraglided from Zapata to south of Ozona, Texas, USA, on June 21, 2002.

The women's record is 177.1 miles (285 km) by Kat Thurston (UK) at Kuruman, South Africa, on December 25, 1995.

**Most height gained in a paraglider** The height-gain world record in a paraglider is 14,849 ft. (4,526 m) by Robbie Whittal (UK) at Brandvlei, South Africa, on January 6, 1993. In comparison, Boeing 747s cruise at 35,000 ft. (10,000 m). At his record-breaking altitude, Whittal needed to use bottled oxygen, and ice formed on his clothing and the glider.

The women's record is 14,189 ft. (4,325 m) by Kat Thurston (UK) over Kuruman, South Africa, on January 1, 1996.

## PARACHUTING

**Longest official FAI freefall parachute jump** Eugene Andreev (USSR) holds the official FAI record for the longest freefall parachute jump, after

**LARGEST FAI-APPROVED PARACHUTING FREEFALL FORMATION** A freefall formation consisting of 300 skydivers was held for 7.02 seconds over Eloy, Arizona, USA, on December 12, 2002, at the World Record 300-Way event.

**LARGEST CANOPY FORMATION** In 1996 a record 53 skydivers held the largest canopy formation for six seconds over the skies of Kassel, Germany. A canopy stack formation is when sky divers hook their legs into the parachute directly beneath their feet to form an interlocking human structure.

falling for 80,380 ft. (24,500 m) from an altitude of 83,523 ft. (25,458 m) over Saratov, Russia, on November 1, 1962. He jumped from a balloon, opening his parachute at 3,143 ft. (958 m).

**Longest unofficial free-fall parachute jump** The longest ever non-FAI approved parachute jump was by Captain Joseph W. Kittinger (USA), who dropped 84,700 ft. (25,820 m) from a balloon at 102,800 ft. (31,330 m), at Tularosa, New Mexico, USA, on August 16, 1960. He reached a maximum speed of 625.25 mph (1,006 km/h) in rarified air at 90,000 ft. (27,400 m)—just faster than the speed of sound. He fell for 4 min. 37 sec. before his parachute was deployed automatically.

**Fastest women's speed skydiving** The highest speed ever achieved by a woman in a speed skydiving competition is 268.5 mph (432.12 km/h) by Lucia Bottari (Italy) at Bottens, Switzerland, on September 16, 2002.

**Fastest men's speed skydiving** The highest speed ever reached in a speed skydiving competition is 325.67 mph (524.13 km/h) by Michael Brooke (France) at the Millennium Speed Skydiving Competition over Gap, France, on September 19, 1999. Speed skydiving involves jumping from an aircraft at 13,000 ft. (4,000 m) and accelerating in a near-vertical head-first position into the "measuring zone" that extends from an altitude of 8,850 ft. (2,700 m) to 5,570 ft. (1,700 m). Electronic altimeters are attached to the skydivers to measure their average speed as they cross the measuring zone. Below 5,570 ft. (1,700 m) the jumper must change position to slow down sufficiently to around 120 mph or 200 km/h) to allow the parachute to open safely above 2,620 ft. (800 m).

## MICROLIGHTING

**Highest microlight speed** The highest average speed reached when setting an official FAI world microlight record is 104.73 mph (168.55 km/h) by Serge Ferrari (France) at Belley-Peyrieu, France, on June 29, 1996.

# TARGET SPORTS

## SNOOKER

**Most snooker century breaks in a season** The most century breaks made by an individual player in a snooker season is 53 by Stephen Hendry (UK) in 1994–95.

**Highest snooker break** Wally West (UK) recorded a break of 151 in a match at the Hounslow Lucania, Middlesex, UK, in October 1976. The break involved a free ball, which therefore created an "extra" red, when all 15 reds were still on the table. In these very exceptional circumstances, the maximum break is 155.

**Longest snooker unbeaten run** From March 17, 1990 to his defeat by Jimmy White (UK) on January 13, 1991, Stephen Hendry (UK) won five successive titles and 36 consecutive matches in ranking snooker tournaments.

**HIGHEST MEN'S INDOOR RECURVE ARCHERY SCORE** In November 2001 Michele Frangilli (Italy), scored 598 points from a possible 600 at the 25-m distance in the recurve bow category.

During the summer of 1992, Ronnie O'Sullivan (UK) won 38 consecutive matches but these were in qualifying competitions.

**Fastest snooker 147 break** The fastest ever 147 break (normally the maximum break possible) in a professional snooker tournament was made by Ronnie O'Sullivan (UK) in 5 min. 20 sec. during the World Championships at Sheffield, South Yorkshire, UK, on April 21, 1997.

**Youngest snooker world champion** Stephen Hendry (UK) was the youngest ever snooker world champion when he won the 1990 World Championship aged 21 years 106 days. He was also the youngest ever Scottish amateur champion, at the age of 15.

## POOL

**Most pool balls pocketed in 24 hours** Nick Nikolaidis (Canada) pocketed 16,723 balls in 24 hours at the Unison Bar, Montreal, Canada, on August 13–14, 2001. During the attempt he also broke the record for the fastest pool potting on two tables when he pocketed two consecutive racks in 1 min. 33 sec.

**Fastest pool potting** The record time for potting all 15 pool balls is 26.5 seconds by Dave Pearson (UK) at Pepper's Bar and Grill, Windsor, Ontario, Canada, on April 4, 1997.

**Most pool world championships** Pool, or championship pocket billiards, with numbered balls, began to become standardized around 1890. One of its greatest exponents was Ralph Greenleaf (USA), who won the world professional title 19 times between 1919 and 1937.

## ARCHERY

**Highest FITA 18 archery score in 24 hours** The highest score in 24 hours shooting *Fédération Internationale de Tir à l'Arc* (FITA) 18 rounds is 26,064 by Michael Howson and Stephen Howard (both

**HIGHEST SCORE IN WOMEN'S TRAP-100 SHOOTING Satu Pusila (Finland) and Delphine Racinet (France, shown) have both scored 95 (71+24) in Women's Trap-100 targets clay shooting. Pusila set the record in Nicosia, Cyprus, on June 13, 1998, and Racinet equaled it in Sydney, Australia, on March 26, 2000.**

**MOST DARTS WORLD CHAMPIONSHIP TITLES** Phil Taylor (UK) has won a record 10 darts world championship titles. He won the Embassy World Championship in 1990 and 1992 and the PDC (Professional Darts Corporation) World Championship from 1995 to 2002.

UK) at Oakbank Sports College, Keighley, West Yorkshire, UK, on November 11–12, 2000.

**Most arrows triggered by a crossbow shot** The most arrows triggered by a single crossbow shot, with the final arrows hitting a marked target, is nine. Ross and Elisa Hartzell (both USA) performed the feat on December 18, 1998 on the set of *Guinness World Records: Primetime* in Los Angeles, California, USA.

**Highest horseback kassai-style archery score** Kassai-style archery is inspired by ancient Hungarian and Asian horseback archers. The most points scored in kassai-style archery in 12 hours is 7,126.05 by Kassai Lajos (Hungary) at Kaposmero, Hungary, on May 11, 2002.

## SHOOTING

**Closest grouping at 1,000 yards bench rest shooting** The smallest recorded group of 10 shots fired from a bench rest at 1,000 yards (914 m) is 3.151 in. (8.003 cm) wide. The shots were fired by John Voneida (USA) at Williamsport, Pennsylvania, USA, on July 8, 1995.

**Most consecutive bullseyes in indoor shooting** The most consecutive bullseyes scored in target shooting is 1,530 by Leonard Proteau (Canada) over a period of six months in 1967–68 at the Canadian Forces Station at Mont Apica, Quebec, Canada. He used a Dominion Marksman Model 190 S rifle, with a rear peep sight and hooded front sight, and shot from the prone position over 25 yd. (22.8 m) on an indoor range.

## ★ MEN'S RECURVE ARCHERY WORLD RECORDS ★

| EVENT | SCORE | NAME AND COUNTRY | VENUE | DATE |
|---|---|---|---|---|
| Indoor 18 m | 597 | Michele Frangilli (Italy) | Nimes, France | January 2001 |
| Indoor 25 m | 598 | Michele Frangilli (Italy) | Gallarate, Italy | November 2001 |
| Outdoor 30 m | 360/17 | Kye Dong-hyun (South Korea) | Cheongju, South Korea | September 2002 |
| Outdoor 50 m | 351 | Kim Kyung-ho (South Korea) | Wonju, South Korea | September 1997 |
| Outdoor 60 m | 347 | Choi Young-kwang (South Korea) | Hongseong, South Korea | August 2002 |
| Outdoor 90 m | 334 | Choi Young-kwang (South Korea) | Yecheon, South Korea | March 2002 |
| Outdoor FITA round | 1,379 | Oh Kyo-oon (South Korea) | Wonju, South Korea | November 2000 |
| Outdoor FITA round team | 4,053 | Oh Kyo-oon, Lee Kyung-chul, Kim Jae-pak (South Korea) | Jakarta, Indonesia | August 1995 |

## ★ WOMEN'S RECURVE ARCHERY WORLD RECORDS ★

| EVENT | SCORE | NAME AND COUNTRY | VENUE | DATE |
|---|---|---|---|---|
| Indoor 18 m | 591 | Lena Herasymenko (Ukraine) | Istanbul, Turkey | March 1997 |
| Indoor 25 m | 592 | Petra Ericsson (Sweden) | Oulu, Finland | March 1991 |
| Outdoor 50 m | 345 | Kim Moon-sun (South Korea) | Cheongju, South Korea | November 1996 |
| Outdoor 60 m | 350 | Kim Jo-soon (South Korea) | Ye-chun, South Korea | September 1998 |
| Outdoor 70 m | 348 | Lee Hee-Jeong (South Korea) | Cheongju, South Korea | October 2001 |
| Outdoor FITA round | 1,384 | Chung Chang-sook (South Korea) | Wonju, South Korea | November 2000 |
| Outdoor FITA round team | 4,094 | Cho Youn-jeong, Kim Soo-nyung, Lee Eun-kyung (South Korea) | Barcelona, Spain | August 1992 |

## DARTS

**Largest electronic darts tournament** The largest electronic darts tournament took place in Benalmadena, Malaga, Spain, on March 21–24, 2002. The competition featured 617 teams from all over Spain and 3,622 individual players.

**Youngest darts player in a major tournament** The youngest player in a major competitive darts tournament is Nick Stoekenbroek (b. May 11, 1989, Netherlands), who played in the Dutch Open at Veldhoven, The Netherlands, on February 5–7, 2002 at the age of 12 years 270 days.

# F1

**GREATEST NUMBER OF POLE POSITIONS** Ayrton Senna (Brazil, 1960–1994) achieved 65 pole positions (and 41 wins) from 161 races between 1985 and 1994 for the Toleman, Lotus, McLaren, and Williams teams. He also won the Monaco Grand Prix a record five consecutive times between 1989 and 1993.

**MOST GRAND PRIX WINS BY A DRIVER** Michael Schumacher (Germany, below) won 64 Formula One Grand Prix between 1991 and 2002. He has scored a record 945 points in his career to date (1991–2002).

**MOST FORMULA ONE CONSTRUCTORS' WORLD CHAMPIONSHIP
TITLES** The most Formula One Constructors' World Championship
titles is 12 by Ferrari (Italy, team shown here) in 1961, 1964, 1975–77,
1979, 1982–83, and 1999–2002. In the 2002 season, the Ferrari team
amassed a record 221 World Championship points. The team's drivers
that year were Michael Schumacher (Germany) and Reubens Barichello
(Brazil). The team won 15 races out of 17, wrapping up both the drivers'
and the constructors' titles in record time.

**MOST FORMULA ONE WORLD CHAMPIONSHIPS** The World Drivers'
Championship inaugurated in 1950 has been won a record five times, by
Juan Manuel Fangio (Argentina, shown here driving for Maserati) in 1951
and 1954–57, and Michael Schumacher (Germany) in 1994–95 and 2000–02.

**MOST GRAND PRIX STARTS** The most Grand Prix starts by a driver is 256 by Ricardo Patrese (Italy, shown here driving for Williams-Renault) between 1977 and 1993.

**YOUNGEST FORMULA ONE WORLD CHAMPION** Emerson Fittipaldi (Brazil, b. December 12, 1946) won his first Formula One World Championship on September 10, 1972 at age 25 years 273 days. (He is pictured here at the 1996 Rio 400 IndyCar race.)

**MOST CONSECUTIVE POLE POSITIONS** Alain Prost (France) achieved seven pole positions in the 1993 season, driving for the Williams-Renault team. Prost was also the World Champion that year.

F1

**YOUNGEST DRIVER TO SCORE A WORLD CHAMPIONSHIP POINT**
Jenson Button (UK, b. January 19, 1980) was 20 years 67 days old when
he finished in sixth place in the Brazilian Grand Prix on March 26, 2000,
driving for the BMW Williams F1 team.

**MOST RACES WITHOUT A WIN** Andrea de Cesaris (Italy) competed in
208 Formula One races without a victory between 1980 and 1994. He
drove for Alfa Romeo (1980, 1982–83), McLaren (1981), Ligier (shown
here, 1984–85), Minardi (1986), Brabham (1987), Rial (1988), Dallara
(1989–90), Jordan (1991, 1994), Tyrell (1992–93), and Sauber (1994).

# MOTORBIKE SPORTS

**Most supercross titles won** The most supercross titles won is nine by Jeremy McGrath (USA). McGrath won the AMA (American Motorcycle Association) Supercross 250cc title from 1993 to 1996 and from 1998 to 2000. He also won the World Supercross title (also 250cc) in 1994 and 1995.

**Most 250cc supercross race wins in a career** The most 250cc supercross race wins in a professional career is 74 by Jeremy McGrath (USA) between 1989 and 2002.

**Most 250cc World Motocross Championship wins** Joël Robert (Belgium) won a record six 250cc World Motocross Championships, in 1964 and from 1968 to 1972. Between April 25, 1964 and June 18, 1972 he also won an unequaled fifty 250cc World Motocross races.

**Most 125cc World Motocross Championship wins** The 125cc class of the World Motocross Championship has been won three times by three riders: Gaston Rahier (Belgium) in 1975–77; Harry Everts (Belgium) in 1979–81; and Alessio Chiodi (Italy) in 1997–99.

**Most *Motocross des Nations* wins** The *Motocross des Nations,* also known as the "Olympics of Motocross," has been contested annually in different countries since 1947. The national team with the most wins is Great Britain, with 16 in 1947, 1949–50, 1952–54, 1956–57, 1959–60, 1963–67, and 1994.

**Most 50cc World Championship titles won** The most World Championship 50cc titles won is six by Angel Roldán Nieto (Spain) in 1969–70, 1972, and 1975–77.

**Most 125cc World Championship titles won** The most World Championship 125cc titles won is seven by Angel Roldán Nieto (Spain) in 1971–72, 1979, and 1981–1984.

**MOST WORLD SUPERBIKE CHAMPIONSHIP TITLES** The most World Superbike (WSB) championship titles won is four by Carl "Foggy" Fogarty (UK), in 1994, 1995, 1998, and 1999.

**MOST ISLE OF MAN TT RACE WINS IN A YEAR** The most Isle of Man TT races won in one year is four (Formula One, Senior, Junior, and Production classes) by Phillip McCallen (Ireland) in 1996. McCallen is shown here holding the Senior TT trophy.

**Most World Superbike race wins** The most World Superbike (WSB) Championship race wins is 59 by Carl Fogarty (UK) between 1992 and 1999.

**Most successive Isle of Man TT race wins** James Redman (Rhodesia) won both the 250cc and 350cc events at the Isle of Man TT (Tourist Trophy) races three times in succession, from 1963 to 1965.

**Most Isle of Man TT race wins in a career**  The most Isle of Man TT race wins in a career is 26 by Joey Dunlop (Ireland, 1952–2000) between 1977 and 2000.

**Most Isle of Man TT race wins by a manufacturer**  The most wins by a manufacturer at the Isle of Man TT races is 176 by Yamaha (Japan) from 1965 to 2003.

**Most Suzuka 8 Hours race wins by a manufacturer**  The Japanese manufacturer Honda has provided the winning motorcycle for the Suzuka 8 Hours endurance race (held at Suzuka, Japan) a record 16 times between 1979 and 2002.

**Most Sidecar World Championship titles won**  The most Sidecar World Championship titles won is seven by Rolf Biland (Switzerland), in 1978, 1979, 1981, 1983, and 1992–94.

**Most World Championship titles won**  The most World Championship motorcycling titles won is 15 by Giacomo Agostini (Italy), with seven 350cc titles from 1968 to 1974, and eight 500 cc titles in 1966–1972 and 1975.

**Most World Championship race wins in a career**  The most World Championship motorcycle race wins in a career is 122 by Giacomo Agostini

**MOST INDOOR AND OUTDOOR WORLD TRIALS CHAMPIONSHIP WINS**
Dougie Lampkin (UK) has won 11 Indoor and Outdoor World Trials Championships, claiming both titles every year between 1997 and 2001 and the outdoor title in 2002. Lampkin entered and won his first competition when he was only nine years old, and was awarded the MBE (Member of the British Empire) medal in 2002.

**MOST 250CC WORLD CHAMPIONSHIP TITLES** The most 250cc World Championship titles won is four, by Phil Read (UK) in 1964, 1965, 1968, and 1971, and Max Biaggi (Italy, shown here riding for Aprilia) between 1994 and 1997.

(Italy). He achieved 68 race wins in the 500cc class and 54 race wins in the 350cc class between April 24, 1965 and September 25, 1977.

**Most career wins in a single World Championship class** The most World Championship career wins in a single class is 79 and was achieved by Rolf Biland (Switzerland) in the sidecar class.

**Fastest NHRA Pro Stock bike** The highest terminal velocity for an NHRA (National Hot Rod Association) Pro Stock (gas-powered piston-engine) drag bike is 194.1 mph (312.37 km/h) by Matt Hines (USA) on a Suzuki at Englishtown, New Jersey, USA, in May 2001.

**Fastest 440 yards on an NHRA Pro Stock bike** The lowest elapsed time over 440 yards (402 m) on an NHRA Pro Stock drag bike is 7.049 seconds by Angelle Savoie (USA), riding a Suzuki at Matthews, Louisiana, USA, in May 2002.

**Fastest unimotorcycle drag racer** Unimotorcycles are one-wheeled machines with riders seated on sleds behind the wheel and engine. William Nassau (USA) covered 100 ft. (30.48 m) in 2.88 seconds on his unimotorcycle at the Volusia County Fairgrounds, Daytona Beach, Florida, USA, on March 10, 2000.

**Longest motorcycle race circuit** The 37.73-mile (60.72-km) "Mountain" circuit on the Isle of Man (UK), over which the principal TT (Tourist

Trophy) races have been run since 1911 (with minor amendments in 1920), has 264 curves and corners and is the longest circuit used for any motorcycle race.

**Most Paris-Dakar Rally motorcycle wins** The most wins in the bike category of the Paris-Dakar Rally is six by Stéphane Peterhansel (France) in 1991–93, 1995, and 1997–98.

**Highest motorcycle jump** Tommy Clowers (USA) achieved a motorcycle jump height of 35 ft. (10.67 m) from a steep take-off ramp at the X-Games Moto-X Step Up event in San Francisco, California, USA, on August 18, 2000.

**Highest altitude reached by a motor vehicle** The greatest altitude reached autonomously by a motor vehicle is 20,065 ft. (6,116 m), by two Chinese-produced Jinlong motorcycles on the slopes of Mt. Everest, Tibet, on May 13, 2002.

# MOTORCAR RACING

**Most NASCAR titles won** Since it was first held in 1949, the most titles won in the NASCAR (National Association for Stock Car Auto Racing) Championship is seven, by Richard Petty (USA) in 1964, 1967, 1971–72, 1974–75 and 1979, and Dale Earnhardt (USA) in 1980, 1986–87, 1990–91, and 1993–94.

**Most NASCAR race victories in a career** The most victories in a NASCAR career is 200 by Richard Petty (USA), between 1958 and 1992.

**Most Coca-Cola 600 race wins** The most wins at the Coca-Cola 600, the longest race in the NASCAR series, is five by Darrell Waltrip (USA), in 1979–80, 1985, and 1988–89.

**MOST INDIVIDUAL WINS AT THE LE MANS 24-HOUR RACE** The most wins by an individual at the Le Mans 24-hour race is six by Jacky Ickx (Belgium), in 1969, 1975–77, and 1981–82.

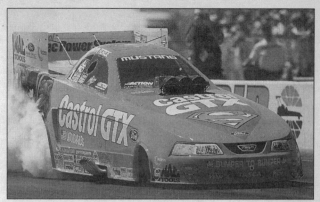

**FASTEST 440 YARDS BY AN NHRA FUNNY CAR** The lowest elapsed time over 440 yards (402 m) in a National Hot Rod Association (NHRA) Funny Car dragster is 4.731 seconds by John Force (USA), driving a Ford Mustang at Reading, Pennsylvania, USA, in October 2001.

**Most Daytona 500 race wins** The most wins of the Daytona 500, the race with the most prize money in the NASCAR series, is seven by Richard Petty (USA), in 1964, 1966, 1971, 1973–74, 1979, and 1981.

**Most Southern 500 race wins** The most wins of the Southern 500, the oldest race in the NASCAR series, is five by Cale Yarborough (USA), in 1968, 1973–74, 1978, and 1982.

**Largest NASCAR speedway track** Talladega Superspeedway in Alabama, USA, is the largest NASCAR speedway. The tri-oval track is 2.66 miles (4.28 km) long with a banking angle of 33 degrees, and has seating for 143,000 spectators and space for thousands more in the 215-acre (87-hectare) infield.

**Highest NASCAR career earnings** The highest earnings in a NASCAR career is $52,800,668 (£33,624,712) by Jeff Gordon (USA), between 1992 and 2003.

**Most wins by a team at the Le Mans 24-hour race** The most wins by a team at the Le Mans 24-hour race is 16 by Porsche (Germany), in 1970–71, 1976–77, 1979, 1981–87, 1993, and 1996–98.

**Fastest lap in the Le Mans 24-hour race** The fastest lap in a Le Mans 24-hour race is 3 min. 21.27 sec. (average speed 150.429 mph or 242.093 km/h) by Alain Ferté (France) in a Jaguar XJR-9LM on June 10, 1989.

**Greatest distance covered in a Le Mans 24-hour race** The greatest distance covered on the current Le Mans 24-hour race circuit is 3,313.15

miles (5,331.998 km)—at an average speed of 138.047 mph (222.166 km/h)—by Jan Lammers (Holland), Johnny Dumfries, and Andy Wallace (both GB) in a Jaguar XJR-9LM from June 11 to 12, 1988.

**Most Formula Nippon Championships won** The Japanese Formula Nippon Championship started in April 1996 as the replacement of the former Japanese Formula 3000 Championship, which had existed for nine years from 1987. The most championships won by a driver is five by Satoru Nakajima (Japan) in 1981–82 and 1984–86. Many drivers have made their way from this championship to Formula One, among them Michael and Ralf Schumacher, Heinz-Harald Frentzen (all Germany), and Jacques Villeneuve (Canada).

**Fastest NHRA Pro Stock dragster** The highest terminal velocity for an NHRA (National Hot Rod Association) Pro Stock (petrol-powered piston-engine) dragster is 204.91 mph (329.77 km/h) by Warren Johnson (USA) in a Pontiac Grand Am in Pomona, California, USA, in February 2003.

**Fastest 440 yards by an NHRA Pro Stock dragster** The lowest elapsed time over 440 yards (402 m) in an NHRA Pro Stock dragster is 6.750 seconds by Jeg Couglin (USA), driving a Chevy Cavalier at Reading, Pennsylvania, USA, in October 2001.

**Fastest NHRA Funny Car** Gary Densham (USA) reached a terminal velocity of 326.87 mph (526.04 km/h) over 440 yards (402 m) from a standing

**MOST CART CHAMPIONSHIP TITLES WON** The most wins in the CART (Championship Auto Racing Teams) Series is seven by A. J. Foyt (USA, shown here racing a Lola T9000 in the 1990 Long Beach Grand Prix). Foyt won the series in 1960–61, 1963–64, 1967, 1975, and 1979. He also holds the record for the most race wins in a CART career, with 67 wins between 1958 and 1993.

**MOST CONSECUTIVE WORLD RALLY CHAMPIONSHIP TITLES WON** The most consecutive World Rally Championship titles won is four by Tommi Mäkinen (Finland) between 1996 and 1999. He won all his titles driving for the Mitsubishi Ralliart team.

start in a Ford Mustang Funny Car at Pomona, California, USA, in February 2002.

**Most Paris-Dakar Rally wins in a car** Ari Vatanen (Finland) has won the Paris-Dakar Rally in a car a record four times—first in 1987 and then three times from 1989 to 1991.

**Most World Rally Championship race wins** The most World Rally Championship race wins is 25 by Colin McRae (UK), in 1993–2002. McRae (b. August 5, 1968) was also the youngest World Rally champion when he won the title in 1995, aged 27 years 89 days.

**Most World Rally Championship race wins in a season** The most World Rally Championship race wins in a season is six by Didier Auriol (France) in 1992, driving for Lancia.

**Most World Rally Championship manufacturer wins** The most World Rally Championship manufacturer titles won is 11 by Lancia (Italy), achieved between 1972 and 1992.

**Most individual Monte Carlo Rally wins** The Monte Carlo Rally, first staged in 1911, is the oldest and best known event in world rally. The most individual Monte Carlo Rally wins is four, by two drivers: Sandro Munari (Italy) in 1972 and 1975–77 driving a Lancia; and Walter Röhrl (with co-driver Christian Geistdorfer; both West Germany) in 1980 and 1982–84, each time in a different car.

**Largest demolition derby** The largest ever demolition derby had 123 participants and took place at Todd Et Pollock Speedway, Mount Maunganui, New Zealand, on March 16, 2002. It took 47 minutes before the winner—the last remaining mobile car—emerged.

**Oldest racing driver** On February 6 and 7, 2000 actor Paul Newman (USA, b. January 26, 1925), aged 75 years 11 days, along with 17-year old co-driver Gunnar Jeannette (USA) and two other members of his racing team, competed in a #75 Champion Racing Porsche 996-GT3 during the Rolex 24 race at the Daytona International Speedway, Florida, USA.

# CYCLING

**Longest platform-to-platform bicycle jump** César Canas and Otilio Pi Isern (both Spain) jumped their mountain bikes between two platforms spaced 9 ft. 8 in. (2.95 m) apart at the studio of *El Show de los Récords*

in Madrid, Spain, on October 23, 2001. No ramps were used, and the 5 ft. 6 in. × 6 ft. 6 in. (1.7-m × 2-m platforms) gave very little run-up before the jumps.

**Most women's downhill mountain biking World Championships** The most mountain biking downhill World Championship wins by a woman is nine, by Anne-Caroline Chausson (France). She won three in the junior championship from 1993 to 1995 and six in the senior class from 1996 to 2001.

**MOST MEN'S DOWNHILL MOUNTAIN BIKING WORLD CHAMPIONSHIPS** Nicolas Vouilloz (France) has won 10 men's mountain biking World Championships—three in the junior championships from 1992 to 1994 and seven in the senior class between 1995 and 2002.

**MOST WOMEN'S CROSS-COUNTRY MOUNTAIN BIKING WORLD CHAMPIONSHIPS** The most mountain biking cross-country World Championships won by a woman is three, by Alison Sydor (Canada) from 1994 to 1996.

**Most men's cross-country mountain biking World Championships** The most cross-country mountain biking World Championships won by a man is three, by Henrik Djernis (Denmark) in 1992–94.

**Longest one-day cycle race** The longest one-day "massed start" road race is the 342–385 mile (551–620 km) Bordeaux-Paris event held in France. Paced over all or part of the route, Herman van Springel (Belgium) is the fastest finisher, covering 363.1 miles (584.5 km) in a record 13 hr. 35 min. 18 sec. in 1981. This gave him a highest average speed of 29.32 mph (47.186 km/h).

**Most Tour de France wins** The greatest number of wins in the Tour de France is five and is shared by five riders: Jacques Anquetil (France), who won in 1957 and 1961–64; Eddy Merckx (Belgium) with triumphs in 1969–72 and 1974; Bernard Hinault (France), who was champion in 1978–79, 1981–82, and 1985; and Miguel Induráin (Spain), the winner in 1991–95.

**Most Tour de France stage wins** The rider with the most Tour de France stage wins is Eddie Merckx (Belgium) with 34.

**Oldest Tour de France winner** The oldest winner of the Tour de France was Firmin Lambot (Belgium), aged 36 years 4 months in 1922.

**Fastest gravity speed bike** On September 26, 1998 Dwight Garland (USA) reached 64.02 mph (103.03 km/h) on a gravity speed bike. These

**CLOSEST TOUR DE FRANCE RACE** The closest Tour de France race (shown here) was in 1989 when, after 23 days (from July 1 to 23) and 2,030 miles (3,267 km), Greg LeMond (USA) crossed the finish line in Paris in 87 hr. 38 min. 35 sec., beating Laurent Fignon (France) by only 8 seconds.

bikes have tubular steel chassis and run on pneumatic racing slicks. They have front and rear brakes and fairings to increase aerodynamic efficiency.

**Fastest single-rider human-powered vehicle speed** Sam Whittingham (Canada) reached 81 mph (130.36 km/h) on a flat road surface on his streamlined recumbent bicycle *Varna Diablo* at the World Human Powered Speed Challenge near Battle Mountain, Nevada, USA, on October 5, 2002.

**Fastest "end-to-end" cycle of the UK** Andy Wilkinson (UK) cycled from Land's End, Cornwall, to John O'Groats, Highland, UK, in 1 day 21 hr. 2 min. 18 sec. from September 29 to October 1, 1990, covering around 1,000 miles (1,600 km).

**Greatest distance cycled in 12 hours** Marko Baloh (Slovenia) cycled a record 280.9 miles (452.196 km), solo and unpaced, in 12 hours at the Novo Mesto Velodrome, Novo Mesto, Slovenia, on August 31, 2002.

**Most steps climbed by bicycle** The most steps ascended on a bicycle is 1,200 by Javier Zapata (Colombia) on June 19, 2001 at the Parque Central Tower in Caracas, Venezuela. The stair climb took Zapata 1 hr. 5 min. to complete.

**Longest static cycling marathon** The record for the longest static cycling marathon belongs to Eddy Kontelj (Australia), who cycled for 72 hours at the Geelong Showgrounds, Geelong, Victoria, Australia, on October 16–19, 2002.

**Greatest distance on a static cycle in 24 hours** The greatest distance achieved on a spinning machine in 24 hours is 466.8 miles (751.4 km) by Ronald Martzloff (Germany) at the Maier Kitchen showroom, Bahlingen, Germany, on June 8–9, 2002.

**Largest static cycle event** The world's largest static cycle event, comprising 300 people cycling simultaneously, took place at the Great Speed Stick Marathon in Bogotá, Colombia, on March 10, 2001.

**Most professional World Championship men's cycling titles** Koichi Nakano (Japan) has won 10 professional World Championship cycling titles in the sprint event between 1977 and 1986.

**Fastest unpaced 200-m cycle from a flying start** The world's fastest unpaced 200-m cycle from a flying start is 9.865 seconds by Curtis Harnett (Canada), in Bogotá, Colombia, on September 28, 1995. The women's record is 10.831 seconds by Olga Slyusareva (Russia), in Moscow, Russia, on April 25, 1993.

**Fastest unpaced 500-m cycle from a flying start** On October 20, 1988 Aleksandr Kiritchenko (USSR) cycled the fastest unpaced 500 m from a flying start in 26.649 seconds in Moscow, Russia. Yong Hua Jiang (China)

**FASTEST UNPACED 1-KM CYCLE FROM A STANDING START** Arnaud
Tournant (France, bottom in this picture) cycled 0.62 mile (1 km),
unpaced and from a standing start, in a record 58.875 seconds at La
Paz, Bolivia, on October 10, 2001.

holds the women's record, with 34 seconds at Kunming, China, on August
10, 2002.

**Fastest women's unpaced 3-km cycle from a standing start** The
fastest women's unpaced 3-km cycle from a standing start, known as the
Women's Individual Cycling Pursuit, is 3 min. 30.816 sec. by Leontien
Zijlaard-Van Moorsel (Netherlands) on September 17, 2000 at the Olympic
Games in Sydney, Australia.

**Fastest men's unpaced 4-km cycle from a standing start** The
fastest unpaced 4 km cycled from a standing start is 4 min. 11.114 sec. by
Chris Boardman (GB), at Manchester, UK, on August 29, 1996.

**Fastest men's 4-km team pursuit** The fastest unpaced team pursuit
over 4 km from a standing start is 3 min. 59.583 sec., by Peter Dawson,
Mark Renshaw, Luke Roberts and Graham Brown (all Australia), at the
Commonwealth Games in Manchester, UK, on August 1, 2002.

# WHEEL SKILLS

**Highest bunny hop on a mountain bike** Daniel Comas Riera (Spain) achieved the highest ever bunny hop on a mountain bike when he cleared a horizontal bar at a height of 45.6 in. (1.16 m) without using a ramp at the studios of *El Show de los Récords* in Madrid, Spain, on November 15, 2001. Although the rules allow the bike to have front suspension, Daniel's bike had no suspension of any sort.

**Highest bunny hop on a micro scooter** Marc Vinco (France) was able to bunny hop on his micro scooter to a 31-in.-high (80-cm) platform, landing with both feet still on the scooter at the studios of *L'Émission des Récords,* Paris, France, on September 14, 2000.

**Highest indoor BMX jump** Timo Pritzel (Germany) and Jesús Fuentes (Spain) cleared a bar at 16 ft. 9.48 in. (5.12 m) above floor level using BMX bikes on the set of *El Show de los Récords* in Madrid, Spain, on September 21, 2001.

**Longest power-assisted bicycle ramp jump** Professional stunt rider Colin Winkelmann (USA) jumped his BMX bike 116 ft. 11 in. (35.63 m) after being towed to approximately 60 mph (100 km/h) behind a motorcycle at Agoura Hills, California, USA on December 20, 2000 on the set of *Guinness World Records: Primetime.*

**Highest vertical drop on a bicycle** Walter Belli (Italy) and David Cachón Labrador (Spain) both rode their BMX bikes off a platform 13 ft. 1.4 in. (4 m) high and continued to cycle upon landing without their feet

**FASTEST CYCLIST ON SNOW** The fastest cycling speed attained down a glacier is 132 mph (212.139 km/h), by downhill mountain bike racer Christian Taillefer (France) on a Peugot Cycle at the Speed Ski Slope in Vars, France, in March 1998.

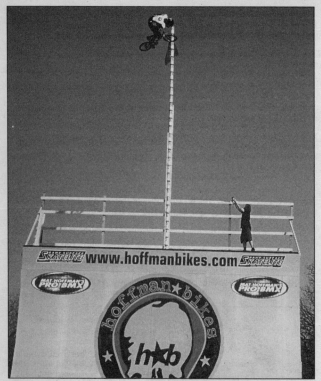

**HIGHEST BMX VERTICAL AIR** The highest air on a BMX is by Mat Hoffman (USA, shown) who achieved a vertical height of 26 ft. 6 in. (8.07 m) jumping from a 24-ft. (7.31-m) quarterpipe on March 20, 2001 in Oklahoma City, Oklahoma, USA. However, Hoffman was towed by a motorcycle in the run-up to the jump. The highest ever unassisted air is 19 ft. (5.8 m) by Dave Mirra (USA) from an 18-ft. (5.4-m) ramp in San Diego, California, USA, in January 2001.

touching the ground on the set of *El Show de los Récords* in Madrid, Spain, on December 5, 2001. In accordance with the rules, they were not allowed a run-up before dropping off the platform.

**Longest duration bicycle wheelie on a front wheel** Martti Kuoppa (Finland) was able to maintain a wheelie on the front wheel of his BMX bike for 23.25 seconds, covering around 328 ft. (100 m) on June 26, 2001 in Helsinki, Finland.

**Most gyrator spins in one minute** The record for the most gyrator spins in one minute is 29 by Sam Foakes (UK) on BBC1's *Blue Peter* TV program in London, UK, on March 11, 2002.

**Most pinky squeaks** Andreas Lindqvist (Sweden) completed 98 continuous 360° rotations of his freestyle BMX bike while balancing on just the front wheel in Stockholm, Sweden, on October 30, 2001.

**Most skips on a unicycle in one minute** The most skips (number of rope revolutions) on a unicycle in one minute is 209 by Amy Shields (USA) in St. Paul, Minnesota, USA, on February 23, 2002.

**Tallest unicycle ride** The tallest unicycle ever mastered is 101 ft. 9 in. (31.01 m) high and was ridden by Steve McPeak (USA) in Las Vegas, USA, in October 1980. He achieved a distance of 376 ft. (114.6 m) using a safety wire suspended from an overhead crane.

**Fastest 100 m on a unicycle** On March 25, 1994 Peter Rosendahl (Sweden) unicycled 100 m from a standing start in 12.11 seconds—a speed of 18.47 mph (29.72 km/h)—at Las Vegas, Nevada, USA.

**Most backflips on a kickscooter from a single jump** Jarret Reid (USA) traveled from a ramp at a height of 18 ft. (5.48 m) and achieved a single scooter back flip, landing with both feet on the scooter, at Van Nuys Airport, California, USA, for the *Guinness World Records: Primetime* TV show on January 21, 2001.

**Skateboarding high jump** The skateboarding high jump record is 5 ft. 5 in. (1.67 m) by Trevor Baxter (UK) at Grenoble, France, on September 14, 1982. This record involves approaching a standard high-jump bar on a skateboard, clearing the bar, and successfully landing on the other side.

**Most continuous skateboard revolutions** Richard Carrasco (USA) completed a record 142 continuous 360° revolutions on a skateboard on August 11, 2000 in Santa Ana, California, USA.

**Highest air on a skateboard** Danny Way (USA) performed a 18-ft. 3-in. (5.56-m) method air off a 20-ft. (6-m) quarterpipe at Point X Camp near Aguanga, California, USA, on April 17, 2002.

**Highest prone skateboard speed** The highest speed recorded on a skateboard, lying face down in a prone position, is 78.37 mph (126.12 km/h) by Roger Hickey (USA) on a course near Los Angeles, California, USA, on March 15, 1990.

**Highest standing skateboard speed** Gary Hardwick (USA) set a speed record, standing on a skateboard, of 62.55 mph (100.66 km/h) at Fountain Hills, Arizona, USA, on September 26, 1998.

**HIGHEST SKATEBOARD DROP INTO A QUARTERPIPE** Adil Dyani
(Norway, above) dropped into a quarterpipe ramp from a height of 29 ft.
7.2 in. (9.03 m) on a skateboard in Oslo, Norway, on August 10, 2002.

**Longest skateboard rail grind** Christian Pujola Herandez (Spain) performed a 21-ft. 4-in. (6.5-m) rail grind on a skateboard on the set of *El Show
de los Récords* in Madrid, Spain, on November 22, 2001.

**Most skateboard rotations in the air off a halfpipe** The most airborne rotations off a skateboard ramp is two and a half, achieved by Tony
Hawk (USA) at the X-Games in San Francisco, California, USA, on June

27, 1999. The so-called "900" (as in 900° spin) is regarded as one of the most difficult skateboarding tricks, with Hawk remaining the first and only person to have achieved it in competition.

**Highest ollie on a skateboard** Danny Wainwright (UK) popped the highest ever ollie at 44.5 in. (1.13 m) off flat ground on February 6, 2000 at the Action Sports Retailers (ASR) Show at Longbeach, California, USA.

**Highest indoor vertical air on inline skates** Taïg Khris (France) achieved an inline skate jump of 10 ft. 2 in. (3.1 m) from a halfpipe on the set of *L'Émission des Records* in Paris, France, on December 6, 2000.

**Farthest inline skates distance in one hour** Mauro Guenci (Italy) covered a distance of 22.88 miles (36.83 km) in one hour on inline skates at Senigallia, Italy, on June 29, 2002. He completed over 34 laps of a 3,487-ft. (1,063-m) street course through the town.

**Fastest downhill inline skating speed** Graham Wilkie and Jeff Hamilton (both USA) set the inline skating speed record of 64.02 mph (103.03 km/h) in Arizona, USA, on September 26, 1998.

**Highest inline skate ramp jump** José Félix Hormaetxe Henry (Spain) cleared a bar set at 14 ft. 8.4 in. (4.5 m) on inline skates on the set of *El Show de los Récords* in Madrid, Spain, on December 14, 2001.

**LONGEST BMX BACKFLIP** Allan Cooke (USA, pictured here performing a tail whip) performed a 54-ft. (16.4-m) backflip on his BMX bike between two specially constructed ramps at Point X Camp near Aguanga, California, USA, on February 9, 2002.

**Farthest distance covered in a 24-hour roller skiing relay** The greatest distance covered by a team of four roller skiers in 24 hours is 303.69 miles (488.74 km) by Simon Tinning, A. Simpson, A. Adamson, and Mark Walker (all UK) at RAF Alconbury, Cambridgeshire, UK, on May 23–24, 1998.

# UNUSUAL SPORTS

**Farthest flying disc run and catch** The men's flying disc throw-run-and-catch record is 304 ft. 11 in. (92.64 m) by Hiroshi Oshima (Japan) at San Francisco, California, USA, on July 20, 1988.

The women's record is 196 ft. 11 in. (60.02 m) by Judy Horowitz (USA) at La Mirada, California, USA, on June 29, 1985.

**Fastest time to make, throw, and catch a boomerang** On August 26, 2001 Lawrence West (UK) cut out a boomerang from a sheet of material (where the shape had already been drawn) and then threw it and caught it in 1 min. 11 sec. at the Boomerang Championships held in Trefriw, Gwynedd, UK. Participants are given the same sized piece of sheet material with the outline of the boomerang drawn on it, and they can use whatever tools they wish to cut it out. They then run 65 ft. (20 m) to a line where they have to throw and catch the boomerang.

**GREATEST FLYING DISC DISTANCE** The record flying disc (formerly Frisbee) distance for men, officiated by the World Flying Disc Federation, is 820 ft. (250 m) by Christian Sandstrom (Sweden, pictured) at El Mirage, California, USA, on April 26, 2002. Jennifer Griffin (USA) holds the women's record, throwing a distance of 454 ft. 6 in. (138.56 m) at Fredericksburg, Virginia, USA, on April 8, 2000.

**FASTEST CROSSING OF THE ENGLISH CHANNEL BY KITE SURFER** Chris Calthrop, Jason Furness, (pictured) and Andy Preston (all UK), from kite manufacturer Flexifoil International (UK), crossed the English Channel using kite surfers—custom-made boards with 52-ft.² (4.9-m²) traction kites. On September 17, 1999 they made the 23.2-nautical mile (42.9-km) Channel crossing from Hythe, Kent, UK, to Wissant, France, in a record time of 2 hr. 30 min. (2 members) and 3 hr. respectively (1 member).

**Farthest Dyno wall climb** The farthest distance achieved in Dyno climbing is 8 ft. 6 in. (2.6 m) by Matt Heason (UK) at the Bendcrete Dyno Competition held at the Edge Climbing Centre, Sheffield, South Yorkshire, UK, on April 20, 2002.

The farthest distance achieved by a woman is 6 ft. 2 in. (1.9 m) by Katherine Schirrmacher (UK) at the same competition. In this event competitors leap from one set of handholds to a higher set (a move known as a dynamic maneuver or dyno) that would otherwise be out of reach.

**Longest four-finger hang** José Antonio Burcio Enrique (Spain) was hoisted up to a bar housing two finger holds, from which he hung with just two fingers of each hand for 2 min. 1 sec. at the studios of *El Show de los Récords* in Madrid, Spain, on December 5, 2001.

**Most footbag kicks in five minutes** The greatest number of kicks of a footbag in five minutes is 1,019 by Andy Linder (USA) at Mount Prospect, Illinois, USA, on June 7, 1996. The doubles record is 132,011 kicks by Gary Lautt and Tricia George (both USA) at Chico, California, USA, on March 21, 1998.

**Most footbag kicks by a woman** The women's world record for keeping a footbag airborne is 24,713 consecutive kicks in a time of 4 hr. 9 min.

27 sec. by Constance Constable (USA) at the California Athletic Club, Monterrey, California, USA, on April 18, 1998.

**Most footbag participants** The greatest number of people playing footbag in a circle at one time is 964. The attempt was organized by Andy Linder (USA) and took place at the Cornerstone Festival, Bushnell, Illinois, USA, on July 6, 2001.

**Highest vertical height climbing stairs** Russell Gill (USA) climbed the 835 steps of the Rhodes State Office Tower in Columbus, Ohio, USA, 53 times (a total of 44,255 steps) in 9 hr. 16 min. 24 sec. on February 20, 1994. This was equivalent to a vertical height of 26,712 ft. (8,141.8 m). He descended by elevator each time.

**Deepest constant-weight freedive** The world record for the deepest AIDA (Association Internationale pour le Développement de l'Apnée) approved constant-weight freedive is 285 ft. (87 m) by Guillaume Néry (France) in Nice, France, on August 31, 2002.

The women's record is 229 ft. (70 m) by Tanya Streeter (USA) in the waters off Guadeloupe on May 11, 2001.

**Deepest variable-weight freedive** The deepest variable-weight freedive is a record 383 ft. (117 m) by Benjamin Franz (Germany) off Safaga, Egypt, on September 1, 2001.

Deborah Andollo (Cuba) is the women's record holder, with a dive of 311 ft. (95 m) off Parghalia, Italy, on July 12, 2000.

**FASTEST BUTT BOARDING** Darren Lott (USA) reached a record speed of 65.24 mph (105 km/h) on a butt board in Fountain Hills, Arizona, USA, on September 26, 1998.

**HIGHEST SPEED ON A SANDBOARD** On April 12, 1999 Erik Johnson (USA) reached a top speed of 51 mph (82 km/h) at the Sand Master Jam at Dumont Dunes, California, USA.

**Deepest no-limits freedive** Using the no-limits freediving method, Tanya Streeter (USA) reached a record depth of 525 ft. (160 m) in the waters off the Turks and Caicos Islands in the Caribbean on August 17, 2002.

The men's record is held by Loic Leferme (France), who reached a depth of 505 ft. (154 m) off Saint-Jean-Cap-Ferrat, France, on August 18, 2001.

**Deepest dynamic apnea freedive without fins** Herbert Nitsch (Austria) made a dynamic apnea freedive without the use of fins to a record depth of 439 ft. (134 m) at Wiesbaden, Germany, on November 24, 2001.

Nathalie Desreac (France) holds the women's record, with a 311-ft. (95-m) dive in the waters off Réunion in the Indian Ocean, on February 7, 1999.

**Fastest female sandboarder** Nancy Sutton (USA) was clocked at 44.7 mph (71.94 km/h) at Sand Mountain, Nevada, USA, on September 19, 1998.

**Longest horseshoe pitching winning streak** The longest winning streak in the horseshoe pitching World Championships is 69 games by Fernando Isais (USA) in 1950–52. This outstanding run was finally broken when Isais was beaten by Jim Johnson (USA).

**Most men's horseshoe pitching World Championships** The most horseshoe pitching World Championships won in the men's category is 10 by Ted Allen (USA) in 1933–35, 1940, 1946, 1953, 1955–1957, and 1959. The championships were not held between 1936 and 1939.

**Most women's horseshoe pitching World Championships** The most horseshoe pitching World Championships won in the women's category is 10 by Vicki Chappelle-Winston (USA). She won in 1956, 1958–59, 1961, 1963, 1966–67, 1969, 1975, and 1981.

**Most ringers in a World Championship horseshoe pitching game** The most ringers scored by an individual in a World Championship game is 175 by Glen Henton (USA) in 1965. A ringer is a shoe that comes to rest encircling the stake.

**Most ewes shorn in eight hours** Hayden Te Huia (New Zealand) sheared 495 ewes in eight hours, under World Shearing Record Committee rules, on December 18, 1999 at Marton, New Zealand.

**Most lambs shorn in eight hours** Justin Bell (New Zealand) sheared a record 731 lambs in eight hours, following World Shearing Record Committee rules, on December 16, 2002 at Opepe Trust Farm, Hawkes Bay, New Zealand.

**Most merino ewes shorn in eight hours** The most merino ewes shorn in eight hours, following World Shearing Record Committee rules, is 466 by Cartwright Terry (Australia) on February 22, 2003 at Westerndale Station, Western Australia, Australia.

**Fastest sheep shearing with a "Mum and Dad" machine** Rod Search and Murray Moser (both Australia) sheared two merino sheep in 5 min. 55.89 sec. using a "Mum and Dad" machine in Euroa, Victoria, Australia, on October 30, 1999.

# BIZARRE SPORTS

**Most consecutive pea shooting World Championships** The most consecutive pea shooting World Championships won is three by Mike Fordham (UK) in 1983–85. He shares the record with David Hollis (UK) who won in 1999–2001. Hollis was also the youngest world champion, at age 13 when he scooped the title in 1999. The Championships are held every year in Witcham, Cambridgeshire, UK. The skill is to shoot a pea at a putty-smeared target the size of a dart-board from a distance of 10 ft. 6 in. (3.2 m). Contestants gain five points for hitting the target in the inner circle, three points for the middle circle, and one point for the outer circle.

**MOST EXTREME IRONING WORLD CHAMPIONSHIPS** Organized by the German Extreme Ironing Section (GEIS) and first held in Munich, Germany, on September 20–21, 2002, the inaugural Extreme Ironing World Championship was won by Inga Kosak (Germany) with a score of 522. Participants (an extreme ironer in action is shown here) are scored on both style and textile, and against the clock, over five disciplines: Forest, Water, Rocky, Urban, and Freestyle.

**Most pea shooting World Championships** The most pea shooting World Championships won by an individual is seven by Mike Fordham (UK) in 1977–78, 1981, 1983–85, and 1992.

**Most toe wrestling World Championships** The most toe wrestling World Championships won in the men's category is five by Alan "Nasty" Nash (UK) in 1994, 1996–97, 2000, and 2002.

**FASTEST INDIVIDUAL COAL CARRYING RACE** David Jones (UK) holds the men's record for the annual coal carrying championship race at Gawthorpe, West Yorkshire, UK. He carried a 110-lb. (50-kg) bag over a 1,107.2-yd. (1,012.5-m) course in 4 min. 6 sec. on April 1, 1991.

Ruth Clegg (UK) holds the women's record, with a time of 5 min. 4 sec. on April 6, 2002.

The women's record is four Championships, won by Karen "Kamikaze" Davies (UK) from 1999 to 2002. The Championships are held annually on the first Saturday in June at Ye Olde Royal Oak, Wetton, Derbyshire, UK. The aim of the contest, the barefoot equivalent of arm wrestling, is to push the opponent's foot to the other side of a specially constructed ring, called a "toerack," using only the toes.

## World Championships with the heaviest participants

Founded in 1982, the World Elephant Polo Association (WEPA) hosts a championship tournament every year. Elephant polo is played by riders on elephants, four to a team. An adult male Asian elephant can weigh over 11,000 lb. (5 tonnes) but the contest has no weight restrictions. Rules state that participants cannot lie down in front of the goal. The invitational tournament is held every December in Megauly, on the edge of Nepal's Royal Chitwan National Park.

## Most men's coal carrying titles

Terry Lyons (UK) holds the record for the most titles at the annual coal carrying championship race. He won eight times between 1977 and 1985 inclusive, with the exception of 1980 when Colin Claypole (UK) was the winner. The contest is held annually at Gawthorpe, West Yorkshire, UK. Contestants carry a 110-lb. (50-kg) bag of coal over a 1,107.2-yd. (1,012.5-m) course.

## Fastest Wife Carrying champion

The fastest ever time to complete the 771-ft. (235-m) course of the World Wife Carrying Championships, held annually in Sonkajärvi, Finland, (first held in 1992) is 55.5 seconds, by Margo Uusorg and Birgit Ulricht (both Estonia) on July 1, 2000. Winners

**LONGEST SUCCESSFULLY ROTATED KIIKING SWING** Kiiking (pictured) is a sport in Baltic and Scandinavian countries where the aim is to complete a 360° revolution on a swing. The platforms of Kiiking swings are suspended on rigid arms, or shafts, and the challenge is to make a full revolution on the longest shaft possible. The longest shafts on a swing to complete a successful rotation were 23 ft. (7.01 m) long. The swinger was Andrus Aasamäe (Estonia) at Rakveres, Estonia, on July 16, 2000. The women's record is 19 ft. 2.7 in. (5.86 m) by Katlin Kink (Estonia) at Parnus, Estonia, on September 2, 2001.

take home liters of beer equivalent to the wife's weight. The contest pits some 30 couples in a challenge to carry a female around the village school playground. She need not actually be a wife, but must be over 17 years of age and wear a crash helmet.

**Farthest grape spitting distance** On May 21, 2000 Robert Bonwell (UK) spat a grape a record distance of 22 ft. 4 in. (6.82 m) at Aston Tirrold Fete in Aston Tirrold, Oxfordshire, UK.

**Highest sheaf toss** Glen Young (Australia) threw a 8-lb. (3.65-kg) sheaf over a 59-ft. 10.5-in. (18.25-m) high crossbar at the Royal Canberra Show, Australian Capital Territory, Australia, on February 22, 1997.

**Most people bungee-jumping in 24 hours** A record 505 people bungee-jumped in 24 hours on October 26, 2000 in Cairns, Queensland, Australia, averaging one bungee jump every 2.85 minutes. The mass bungee was organized by A. J. Hackett Bungy.

**Longest canal jump** In the sport of *Fierljeppen*, or canal jumping, the world record jump is 63 ft. 7.6 in. (19.4 m), using a 40-ft. (12.2-m) aluminum pole, by Aart de Wit (Netherlands) at Winsam, Friesland, The Netherlands, in August 1991.

**Most trampolining hula hoop skips** On May 25, 1999 Ken Kovach (USA) set the world record for the most hula hoop skips while somersaulting and jumping on a trampoline in London, UK. Using a standard 36-in. (91-cm) diameter hula hoop, Kovach passed completely through the hoop 122 times, landing on the trampoline between each jump.

**Greatest gumboot throwing distance** Often called "Wellie Wanging," gumboot throwing is contested by tossing a size 8 Challenger Dunlop boot, and the throwing distance record is 209 ft. 9 in. (63.98 m) by Teppo Luoma (Finland) at Hmeenlinna, Finland, on October 12, 1996.

The women's distance record is 134 ft. 1 in. (40.87 m), thrown by Sari Tirkkonen (Finland) at Turku, Finland, on April 19, 1996.

**Most consecutive World Bog Snorkeling Championships** Steve Griffiths (UK) is the only person to have held the World Bog Snorkeling Championship title three times, winning consecutively from 1985 to 1987. Competitors have to complete two lengths of a 180-ft. (55-m) trench cut through a peat bog in the quickest time possible, wearing snorkels and flippers, but without using any conventional swimming strokes.

**Most entrants at a World Bog Snorkeling Championships** The most entrants for a World Bog Snorkeling Championships is 93 on August 26, 2002 at Waen Rhydd Peat bog, Llanwrtyd Wells, Powys, UK. The title was won by Philip John (UK) in a time of 1 min. 45.22 sec.

**Largest Wellington boot race** Held annually on New Year's Day since 1981, the Castlecomer Wellington Race at Castlecomer, County Kilkenny, Ireland, is run over a 4-mile (6.4-km) circuit and has a turnout of over 400 participants, all wearing standard Wellington boots.

**Longest soccer field** The annual Shrovetide soccer match has been played for more than 300 years in Ashbourne, Derbyshire, UK. It is a game short on rules and long on physical contact contested between the Up'ards (those born north of the River Henmore) and the Down'ards (those born south of the river). The goals are the waterwheels at Clifton (target for the Down'ards) and at Stursdton (target for the Up'ards), 3 miles (4.8 km) apart. The playing field is all the water and land in between, excluding the churchyard, where ball games are forbidden. Players must be in the river to score a goal, which they do by banging the ball three times against the waterwheel.

# Index

This index concentrates on the subjects of the records (e.g., weddings, jellyfish, teddy bears) rather than the type of record (e.g., highest, widest, longest). Personal names of record holders are not included. Page numbers in bold type indicate the main entry on a topic.

attendances *see* audiences; gatherings; mass participation events
auctions, 174–8
audiences
American football, 364–8
Australian football, 403–4
baseball, 368–73
building capacities, 204–8
concerts & tours, 165–7
dance festivals, 358
football (soccer), 165, 206
Gaelic football, 405
Olympic Games, 428–31
rugby union, 391
*see also* gatherings; mass participation events
auditory ossicles, 7
aurorae, 115
Australian football, 404
authors
best selling books, 318–20
scriptwriters, 307, 322
autobiographies & biographies, 43, 300, 318, 320
autographs, 183
automobiles *see* cars
automotive (motor) shows, 217
avalanches, 119–20
awards *see* prizes & awards

# B

babies & births, 12–15, 251–2
backflips
BMX, 509
freestyle skiing, 444
gymnastics, 437
jump-flips (figure skating), 452
kickscooters, 507
backwards driving, 219
backwards motorcycling, 227
backwards running, 416
backwards walking, 423
bacteria, 8, 245–8
badminton, 16, 411–21
baggage labels, 183
bagpipes & drums bands, 357
bags, airline sickness, 182
baiji (Yangtze River dolphin), 103
baked beans eaten with a cocktail stick, 21
balancing
spoons on face, 25
weights on body, 35
weights on head, 35, 37

*see also* specific activities requiring balance (e.g., unicycling)
ball boys, tennis, 17
ball sports *see* specific sports (e.g., baseball)
ballet, 358–9
ballistic weapons, 279
balloons (aircraft) & balloon flights, 33, 55, 231–2, 265
balloons (toys)
balloon pops, 32
balloon sculptures, 27, 291
balls
baseball, 174
basketballs spinning, 25
bowling balls stacking, 26
football (soccer), 388
speed of delivery, 384, 395, 405–6, 411
bamboos, 66
bananas, 69
banana splits, 194–5
bandages, first-aid, 183
bandwidth, 256–7
banknotes & coins, 148, 151, 174
coin murals, 289
bankruptcies, 149
banks, 150, 152
bareback bronc riding, 19
barefoot water skiing, 464–5
BASE jumping, 17, 34, 314
baseball, 368–73
fan mail, 165
memorabilia, 174
basketball, 373–6
basketball spinning, 25
baskets, hand-woven, 181
batik, 289
bats (mammals), 77
bats (sports equipment), baseball, 373
batting averages
baseball, 368
cricket, 394, 397
battlefield simulators, 272
battles *see* wars, battles & peacekeeping
battleships, 282
baubles, Christmas, 178
bays, 62
beach volleyball & volleyball, 399, 402
beaks, birds, 88
beans
baked beans eaten with a cocktail stick, 21
castor bean, 69
Mary's bean, 67
runner beans, 71

viruses (life form), 8, 249
vocabulary, birds, 81, 86
voice-overs, 324
volcanoes & eruptions, 58, 60–1,
118–19
volleyball & beach volleyball, 399
volunteer ambulance services, 44
vomit, 107
voting & elections
internet jokes, 254
politics, 136–7
telephone votes, 257
*Voyager* spacecraft, 267
vultures, 90
VX gas, 281–2

# W

Waco siege, 159
waist measurement, 2
wakeboarding, 464
Walker Cup (golf), 458
walking
athletics, 420, 425, 428
dog walking, 28
extra-vehicular activity (spacewalks),
266, 269
stilt-walking, 24–5
tightrope walking, 19
*Wall, The* (album/rock concert), 345,
349
walls, 212
dyno wall climbing, 511
Walt Disney movies & theatrical
productions, 46, 165, 297, 300,
307, 360
wars, battles & peacekeeping, 140–2,
159, 282–6
battlefield simulators, 272
*see also* specific aspects (e.g.
weapons)
warships, 282–5
Washington Monument, 204
waste generation, 122
water
aquatic life, 67, 90–4, 103
bores, 129
bottled water labels, 184
droplets, 242
geological features, 62–5
pollution, 122–3, 124
sports *see* specific types (e.g.
windsurfing)
transport *see* specific types (e.g. ships
& boats)

*see also* oceans & seas; underwater
events; water speed
water polo, 465
water skiing, 42, 463, 464
water speed
mammals, 94
reptiles, 98
ships & boats, 229, 230–1, 468
swimming, 470–3
waves
gravitational waves, 245
Mexican waves, 28
sea waves, 62, 469
*see also* microwaves
weapons, 278–82
nuclear devices & tests, 104–5,
124–5, 126, 279
revolvers, 181
weather & climate, 114–18, 119
Webb Ellis Trophy (rugby), 392
weddings, 160–4, 329
weight (living things)
birds, 86–90
elephants, 516
marine life, 91, 92
men & women, 2
plants, 66, 70, 71
quadruplets at birth, 15
reptiles, 98–101
sportsmen, 434
weightlifting, 35, 38, 438–40
Wellington boots
racing, 519
wellie wanging (gumboot throwing),
518
Westerns (movies), 298
wet & dry places, 115, 116
whale sharks, 90
whales, 94
wheel, earliest use, 273
wheelchair events, 48
wheelies
bicycles, 51, 506
motorcycle, 227
trucks, 238
wheelchairs, 48
whiskers, cat's, 82
white blood cells, 7
whitewater rafting, 464
whoopee cushion sitting, 31
wickets & wicketkeeping, cricket, 394,
397
wife carrying, 516
wild boar, 77
Wimbledon tennis, 406, 409

# Picture Credits

# Acknowledgments

Special thanks go to the following people for their work during the production of this year's edition:

Kat Aalam
James Bradley
Sally Brown
Caroline Butler
Scott Christie
Ann Collins
Sam Fay
Simon Gold
Richard Gue
Mary Hill
Laura Hughes
Peter Laker
Helen Laughton
Joyce Lee
Anthony Liu
Andi Mercer
Shazia Mirza
David Roberts
Alistair Richards
Malcolm Smith
Amanda Sprague
Jamie Thackwell
Ryan Tunstall
Kate White
Sophie Whiting

The team also wishes to thank the following individuals and organizations:

A. C. Nielsen
ACI (Airports Council International)
Ernest Adams
Dr. Leslie Aiello
American Birding Association
American Museum of Natural History, New York
Amnesty International
Dr. Martyn Amos
Jorgen Vaaben Andersen
Anritsu
Argentinian Embassy
Arran Frood
Aviation Security International
Ron Baalke
Dr. Peter Barham
BBC's *Life of Mammals*
Guenter Bechly
Roy B. Behrens
Clive Bevan
Richard Boatfield
Dr. Richard Bourgerie
BP
Dr. John Brackenbury, University of Cambridge, UK
Sean Breazeal
Dr. Elliott Brent, Lindley Library
Britannica *Book of the Year*
British Antarctic Survey
British Museum
British National Space Centre
Professor John Brown
Oliver Brown
BT
Dr. Robert Angus Buchanan
Caida
Caltech
Cambridge University
Dr. Robert Carney
CERN
Dr. Franklin Chang-Diaz
Dr. Hubert Chanson
Professor Phil Charles
Christie's
*CIA Factbook*
Admiral Roy Clare
Isabelle Clark
Richard Clark
CNN.com
Competitive Media Reporting/TNS Media Intelligence
ConocoPhillips

Dr. Mike Coughlan
Dr. Paul Craddock
CRM Team
Crufts
Professor A. M. Cruise
Professor Mike Cruise
Margaret Cudlipp
Peter D'Amato
*Daily Mail*
Dr. Pam Dalton
Professor Kris Davidson
Dr. Ashley Davies
Department of Conservation, New
    Zealand
Dr. David Dilcher
*Discovery News*
Martin Dodge
eBay
*The Economist*
Economist Intelligence Unit
*EETimes*
Chris Ecroyd, Forest Research,
    New Zealand
Dr. Farouk El-Baz
Dr. Cynan Ellis-Evans
Elysium
Dr. John Emsley
ESA
Euromonitor
Everesthistory.com
Everestnews.com
Exeter University
FAI—Fédération Aéronautique
    Internationale
FIA—Fédération Internationale de
    l'Automobile
Dr. Xiaohui Fan
Anton Fatti
Sarah Finney
Peter et Angela Folkard
Brian Ford
*Forbes*
*Fortune*
Mike Foster, Jane's
FTSE Group
Tim Furniss
Lorenzo Gallai
Martin Gedny

Genealogische Handbuch des
    Adels
Geological Society of London
Dr. Richard Ghail
Andy Gillard, *Scootering* Magazine
Tim Goodyear (IATA press office)
Stephanie Gordon
Professor John Guest
Dr. Jim Gunson
David Hancock, Screen Digest
Mary Hanson
Harvard-Smithsonian Center for
    Astrophysics
D & L Hegarty
*Hello!* Magazine
Ron Hildebrant
Dr. Paul Hillyard
History of Advertising Trust
    Archive, UK
Hoover's
Dr. David Horne
Graham Hudson
IATA—International Air Transport
    Association
Imperial College London
*Independent*
Institute of Nanotechnology
Intel
International Boundaries Research
    Unit, UK
International Energy Agency
International Union for the
    Conservation of Nature
Intersec Security Exhibition, UK
IUCN Red List
Professor Steve Jones
Emily Kao
Abigail Keeny
Dr. Nichol Keith
Sophie Kemp, Mycological
    Herbarium, Royal Botanical
    Gardens, Kew, UK
Keo Films
Professor Joseph Kirschvink
Sir John Kreb
Lancaster University
Dr. Rolf Landua
Dr. Roger Launius

Alain Leger
Daniel Lemin, Google
Lockheed Martin
M & J Long
Los Alamos National Laboratories
Dr. Robert Loss
Louisiana State University
Neil Lucas, Knoll Gardens
Simone Mangaroo
Professor Giles Marion
Brian Marsden
Jenny Marshall
Dr. Jim Marshall
MastroNet Inc.
Dave McAleer
Dr. Alan McNaught
Met Office
Mi2g
Lucy Millington
*Mirror*
Dr. Edgar Mitchell
Monell Chemical Senses Center
Moody's
Bill Moore, EV World
Dr. Sir Patrick Moore
Professor Jon Morse
Munich Re
Martin Munt
NASA
National Academy of Sciences
National Amateur Gardening Show, UK
National Birds of Prey Centre, UK
National Geographic
National Maritime Museum
National Physical Laboratory
National Science Foundation
Natural History Museum
*Nature* Magazine
Dr. Ted Nield
NetNames
*Newsweek*
Night Vision & Electronic Sensors Directorate (NVESD)
NOAA
Barry Norman, WKVL Amusement Research Library
Andrew Nottage

Nua.com
OANDA
Oracle
Oxford University
Peak Beam Systems Inc., USA
Hilary Pearce
William Pirowski
PPARC
Sean Price
Prison Activist Resource Center
Productschap voor Gedistilleerde Dranken
Qinetiq
Dr. Paul A. Racey
John Reed, WSSRC
Professor Sir Martin Rees
W., B. & J. Rees
Regional Planetary Image Facility, University College London
Reuters
Ian Ridpath
Scott Robb
Eileen Rodriguez, Google
Dr. Mervyn Rose
Royal Astronomical Society
Royal Horticultural Society, UK
Royal Institution
Royal Philips Electronics
Royal Ontario Museum
Royal Society of Chemistry
Rutherford Appleton Laboratory
Ryan Sampson
John Satterfield, Boeing
Science Museum, London
*Scottish Daily Record*
Search Engine Watch
Istvan Sebestyen
Dr. Paul Selden
Prof. Dick Selley
SETI Institute
Dr. Seth Shostak
Dr. Martin Siegert
Siemens
Sotheby's
Lara Speicher
Standard & Poors
State Bank of India, New York
Danny Sullivan

Greg Swift
Charlie Taylor
Telegeography
*Time* Magazine
Tim Tindall
Tinsley
UK National Giant Vegetable
    Championship
Professor Martin Uman
UK Planetary Forum
*UN Fact Book*
United Nations
United Nations High Commission
    for Refugees
University of Aberdeen
University of Bath
University of Birmingham
University of Boston
University of Colorado
University of Dundee
University of Florida
University of Greenwich

University of Hertfordshire
University of Oklahoma
University of Southampton
University of Toronto
US State Department
Juhani Virola
Dr. David Wark
Professor Kevin Warwick
Richard Winter
Dr. Rick Winterbottom
Dr. Richard Wiseman
Greg Wood
World Bank
World Federation of Exchanges
World Meterological Organization
World Roads Federation
WTO (World Tourism
    Organization)
Dr. David Wynn-Williams
Professor Joshua Wurman
Paul Zajac, Wards
    Communications

# BE A RECORD BREAKER

### IF YOU THINK YOU'VE GOT WHAT IT TAKES TO BE A WORLD RECORD HOLDER WE WANT TO HEAR FROM YOU!

# COULD YOU BE A RECORD BREAKER?

## *DECIDE WHICH RECORD YOU WANT TO BREAK*

Guinness World Records features many people who have accomplished extraordinary feats. If you think you have what it takes to join this exclusive record-breaking club then read on. There are thousands of records to choose from. You could gather a large group of people to break a mass participation record, or perhaps you have an unusual collection that we would be interested in. You might even suggest something new, as we are always on the lookout for innovative and exciting categories.

What we are looking for in a new category is a challenge that is inspiring, interesting, requires skill and is likely to attract subsequent challenges from people all around the world.

## *MAKE AN APPLICATION*

You need to contact us BEFORE you make your attempt. Every Guinness World Record is governed by a unique set of rules that MUST be followed. You need to apply for these rules before you can make an attempt. If you have a new record idea, you need to find out if we have accepted your proposal before you attempt the record. If we like your idea, we will draw up rules specifically for your attempt in order to set a standard for all subsequent challenges.

The easiest and fastest way to make an application is via our website. Click on the link that says "Make a Record Attempt"; this will take you to an online application form. You'll be asked to choose a password which we will send you with a membership number to allow you access to our new tracking feature. Through this you can monitor the progress of your claim and ask any questions that you have about your record attempt.

If you don't have Internet access, you can contact us by post. Ensure that you have provided adequate contact details. Please be advised that proposals received this way take much longer to process than those received via the website.

**Our website:**
www.guinnessworldrecords.com